London
for Children

timeout.com

Time Out Guides Limited
Universal House
251 Tottenham Court Road
London W1T 7AB
Tel + 44 (0)20 7813 3000
Fax + 44 (0)20 7813 6001
Email guides@timeout.com
www.timeout.com

Editorial

Editor Ronnie Haydon
Deputy Editor Jan Fuscoe
Copy Editor Simon Cropper
Listings Editor Cathy Limb
Researchers Alex Brown, Meryl O'Rourke, Gemma Pritchard
Proofreader Cathy Limb
Indexer Ismay Atkins

Managing Director Peter Fiennes
Financial Director Gareth Garner
Editorial Director Sarah Guy
Series Editor Cath Phillips
Editorial Manager Holly Pick
Accountant Ija Krasnikova

Design

Art Director Scott Moore
Art Editor Pinelope Kourmouzoglou
Senior Designer Henry Elphick
Graphic Designers Gemma Doyle, Kei Ishimaru
Digital Imaging Simon Foster
Advertising Designer Jodi Sher

Picture Desk

Picture Editor Jael Marschner
Deputy Picture Editor Katie Morris
Picture Researcher Gemma Walters
Picture Desk Assistant Marzena Zoladz

Advertising

Commercial Director Mark Phillips
Sales Manager Alison Wallen
Advertising Sales Ben Holt, Alex Matthews, Jason Trotman
Advertising Assistant Kate Staddon
Copy Controller Annabel Bates

Marketing

Marketing Manager Yvonne Poon
Sales & Marketing Director, North America Lisa Levinson

Production

Group Production Director Mark Lamond
Production Manager Brendan McKeown
Production Controller Caroline Bradford
Production Coordinator Julie Pallot

Time Out Group

Chairman Tony Elliott
Financial Director Richard Waterlow
Group General Manager/Director Nichola Coulthard
Time Out Magazine Ltd MD Richard Waterlow
Time Out Communications Ltd MD David Pepper
Time Out International MD Cathy Runciman
Group IT Director Simon Chappell
Head of Marketing Catherine Demajo

Contributors

Introduction Ronnie Haydon. **Trips & Tours** Ronnie Haydon. **My London** Ronnie Haydon. **Old Father Thames** Paul Edwards, Ronnie Haydon, Rick Jones (*Pottering in Putney* Martin Horsfield). **Festivals & Events** Cathy Limb. **Attractions** Simon Cropper, Ronnie Haydon, Martin Horsfield (*Great Days Out: Westminster, South Bank, Covent Garden* Jan Fuscoe; *Life in the past lane* Cathy Limb). **Museum & Galleries** Joe Bindloss, Simon Cropper, Tom Davies, Paul Edwards, Ronnie Haydon (*Great Days Out: Bloomsbury, South Kensington, Docklands, Chelsea* Jan Fuscoe; *Hot for tots?* Meryl O'Rourke; *London uncovered, The yuck factor* Joe Bindloss). **Parks & Gardens** Simon Cropper, Ronnie Haydon, Lisa Mullen (*Great Days Out: Camden* Lisa Mullen; *Great Days Out: Greenwich* Ronnie Haydon; *Space to grow* Cathy Limb). **Meet the Animals** Ronnie Haydon, Martin Horsfield. **Parties** Chloë Lola Riess. **Arts & Entertainment** Ronnie Haydon (*Musical youth, Artfully messy, Telling tales* Nana Ocran; *Play's been framed* Meryl O'Rourke; *And now read on* Paul Edwards). **Sport** Tom Davies, Kathryn Miller, Andrew Shields (*Tiger feat* Rick Jones). **Eating** contributors to Time Out Eating & Drinking guide (*Winning ways, Eating lessons, Pizza chains* Ronnie Haydon; *Playing with their food* Jan Fuscoe). **Shopping** Ronnie Haydon. **Directory** Ronnie Haydon, Gemma Pritchard.

The Editor would like to thank John, Bruce and Jane Jones, Finn Jordan, Teresa, Tony and Mary Trafford and all the contributors to previous editions of *London for Children*, whose work forms the basis for parts of this book.

Maps john@jsgraphics.co.uk
Cover art direction/artwork by Gemma Doyle
Cover photography by Rob Greig
Illustrations by Mary Kilvert
Photography by pages 3, 31, 131 (bottom), 182, 260, 263 Andrew Brackenbury; pages 5, 7, 52, 53, 71, 91, 104, 105, 132, 116, 117, 119, 123, 126, 181, 185, 186, 193, 200, 209, 219, 223, 228, 249, 250, 254, 255, 257, 259, 264, 270, 271, 275, 279, 280, 282, 283, 287 Heloise Bergman; page 9 (left) Christina Theisen; pages 9 (right),18, 161, 237 Jonathan Perugia; page 10 Laurence Cendrovicz; page 15 Simon Leigh; pages 20, 111, 133 Nick Ballon; page 23 Kit Houghton; pages 26, 134, 135, 140, 144 (left), 240, 266, 276 Tricia de Courcy Ling; pages 29, 36, 37, 51, 59, 67, 74, 90, 93, 100, 108, 113, 141, 164, 165, 168, 169, 177, 188 (left), 194, 195, 212, 213, 234 Tove K Breitstein; page 32 The Royal Collection © reproduced by kind permission of the Cuneo Estate; page 33 The Royal Collection © Her Majesty Queen Elizabeth II; pages 42, 63, 68, 78, 81, 82, 85, 112, 196, 197, 172 Susannah Stone; page 96 Robert Paterson; page 120 Cathy Limb; pages 131 (top), 156 Rob Greig; page 138 ZSL; page 144 (right) Scott Wishart; pages 147, 188 (right), 231 (top), 247 Alys Tomlinson; page 148 JWK Photography; page 154 Eamonn McGoldrick; page 204 Andrew Shields; page 224 Britta Jaschinski; page 231 (bottom) Kate Peters; page 242 Maya Smend.

The following images were provided by the featured establishment/artist: pages 27, 149, 152, 159, 217, 269.

Printer St Ives (Web) Ltd, Storeys Bar Road, Eastern Industrial Estate, Peterborough, PE1 5YS
Time Out Group uses paper products that are environmentally friendly, from well managed forests and mills that use certified (PEFC) Chain of Custody pulp in their production.

ISBN 978-1-905042-25-8
ISSN 1753-7916

The best guides to enjoying London life

(but don't just take our word for it)

'More than 700 places where you can eat out for less than £20 a head... a mass of useful information in a genuinely pocket–sized guide'

Mail on Sunday

'Armed with a tube map and this guide there is no excuse to find yourself in a duff bar again'

Evening Standard

'I'm always asked how I keep up to date with shopping and services in a city as big as London. This guide is the answer'

Red Magazine

'Get the inside track on the capital's neighbourhoods'

Independent on Sunday

'You will never again be stuck for interesting things to do and places to visit in the capital'

Independent on Sunday

Rated
'Best Restaurant Guide'

Sunday Times

Contents

Introduction

'What shall we do today?' That most frequent of questions, followed by the classic 'I'm bored!' lament, are well-known parent-baiters. In London, however, neither gambit need cause alarm. There are hundred of choices with which to spoil your children, all listed in this book. What do you fancy doing? Visiting a museum? We've listed our favourites according to category in the **Museums & Galleries** chapter. How about storming a fortress, a stately home, a historic monument? They'll be in **Attractions**. A breath of fresh air, a picnic, a spot of duck feeding? No problem: just look in **Parks & Gardens**. A trip to a zoo, or a free city farm? Try **Meet the Animals**. We've covered entertainment too, in the **Activities** section, from puppet-making in Islington to dragonboat racing in Millwall Dock. After that, there's the tasty selection of restaurants and shops – in **Consumer**. With so much scope for having fun in this city we've designed a series of **Great Days Out**, with suggestions of where to walk, what to visit and where to eat.

There's always something new to do every day in London. Some valuable lessons to be learned too; not least, that the best things in life are free. Here, the best museums, the best parks, even the best buses in the world cost nothing for under-18s (let them remain so, Mayor Boris!). So what do you mean, you're bored? Go explore!

TIME OUT LONDON FOR CHILDREN GUIDE

This is the eighth edition of the Time Out *London for Children* Guide, produced by the people behind the successful listings magazines and travel guide series. It is written by resident experts to provide you with all the information you'll need to explore the city, whether you're a local or a first-time visitor.

THE LOWDOWN ON THE LISTINGS

Addresses, phone numbers, websites, transport information, opening times, admission prices and credit card details are included in the listings.

Details of facilities, services and events were all checked and correct as we went to press. Before you go out of your way, however, we'd advise you to phone and check opening times, ticket prices and other particulars. While every effort has been made to ensure the accuracy of the information contained in this guide, the publishers cannot accept any responsibility for any errors it may contain.

FAMILY-FRIENDLY INFORMATION

Having visited all the places with our children, we've added essential information for families. Where we think it's important, we've stated whether a building can accommodate buggies, or if there's a place to change a nappy. We've also listed the nearest picnic place.

Attractions are required to provide reasonable facilities for disabled visitors, although it's always best to check accessibility before setting out. Disabled visitors requiring information about getting around the city should contact GLAD (Greater London Action on Disability, www.glad.org.uk)

PRICES AND PAYMENT

We have noted where venues accept the following credit cards: American Express (AmEx), Diners Club (DC), MasterCard (MC) and Visa (V).

THE LIE OF THE LAND

Map references are included for each venue that falls on our street maps (starting on page 310), but we recommend that you also use a standard A-Z map of the city.

PHONE NUMBERS

The area code for London is 020. All phone numbers given in this guide take this code unless otherwise stated, so add 020 if calling from outside London; otherwise, simply dial the number as written. The international dialling code for the UK is 44.

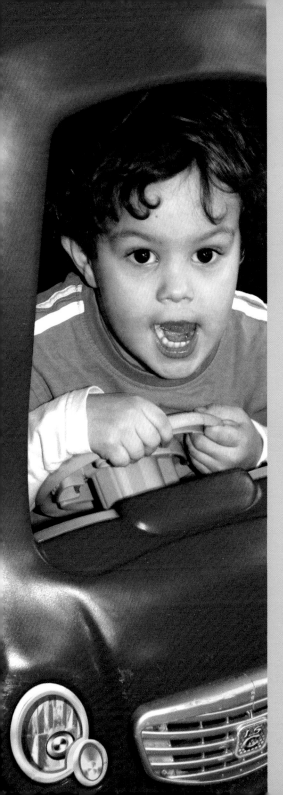

Out & About

Trips & Tours

The way you see it.

Getting around

The tube (*see p287*) is the quickest way to get around, but the bus is more scenic. Good routes for sightseeing are the 7, 8, 11 and 12 (all double-deckers) and, on the river, the RV1. A couple of old-style Routemaster buses – numbers 9 and 15 – run as Heritage Routes; the 9 runs from the Aldwych via the Strand, Trafalgar Square and Piccadilly Circus to the Royal Albert Hall, and the 15 from Trafalgar Square to Tower Hill and allows passengers to get a glimpse of the Strand, Fleet Street and St Paul's Cathedral. Normal fares apply; see www.routemaster.org.uk.

Tourist information

Whatever form of transport you take, a useful first stop in your trip around the city is a tourist information office. **Visit London** (7234 5800, www.visit london.com) is the city's official tourist information service, with its main office in Lower Regent Street. There are also offices in Greenwich, Leicester Square and next to St Paul's Cathedral.

If your sightseeing programme includes pricey places, a **London Pass** (01664 485020, www.londonpass.com) gives you pre-paid access to more than 50 attractions. Check the website for prices.

In our listings, the initials 'EH' means English Heritage members, and their kids, get in free. 'NT' means National Trust family members get free admission.

Britain & London Visitor Centre *1 Lower Regent Street, SW1Y 4XT (8846 9000/ www.visitbritain.com). Piccadilly Circus tube.* **Open** *Oct-May* 9.30am-6.30pm Mon; 9am-6.30pm Tue-Fri; 10am-4pm Sat, Sun. *June-Sept* 9.30am-6.30pm Mon; 9am-6.30pm Tue-Fri; 9am-5pm Sat; 10am-4pm Sun.
London Information Centre *Leicester Square, WC2H 7BP (7292 2333/www. londontown.com). Leicester Square tube.* **Open** *Phone enquiries* 8am-midnight Mon-Fri; 9am-10pm Sat, Sun. *In person* 8am-6pm Mon-Fri; 10am-6pm Sat, Sun.

London Visitor Centre *Arrivals Hall, Waterloo International Terminal, SE1 7LT.* **Open** *In person* 8.30am-10.30pm Mon-Sat; 9.30am-10.30pm Sun.

Moving experiences

See also p12 **Old Father Thames**.

On the river

City Cruises *7740 0400/www.citycruises.com.* **Credit** AmEx (over £50), MC, V.
City Cruises' Rail River Rover ticket (£12; £6 5-16s, reductions; free under-5s) usefully combines hop-on, hop-off travel on any of its regular cruises (pick-up points: Westminster, Waterloo, Tower and Greenwich piers) with unlimited travel on the DLR.
London Duck Tours *7928 3132/www.london ducktours.co.uk.* **Tours** phone for details. *Pick-up* Chicheley Street, behind the London Eye. **Fares** £19; £15 reductions; £13 1-12s; £57.50 family (2+2). **Credit** AmEx, MC, V.
City of Westminster tours in a bright yellow amphibious vehicle. The road and river trip, lasting 75 minutes, starts at the London Eye and enters the Thames at Vauxhall.
London RIB Voyages *7928 2350/ www.londonribvoyages.com.* **Tickets** £29-£43. **Credit** AmEx, MC, V.
Part speedboat ride, part sightseeing tour, the RIB powers up to 12 passengers from the London Eye to either Canary Wharf (£29; £18 under-16s, 50mins) or the Thames Barrier (£43; £27 under-16s, 80mins). It's popular, so you'll need to book in advance.
London Waterbus Company *7482 2660/ www.londonwaterbus.com.* **Tours** check website for departure details. **Fares** *Single* £6.50; £5 3-15s. *Return* £9; £6 3-15s. Free under-3s. **No credit cards**.
Thames Clippers *0870 781 5049/ www.thamesclippers.com.* **Departures** 10am-5pm Mon-Fri; 9am-midnight Sat, Sun. **Credit** MC, V.
With a River Roamer ticket (£8; £4 5-15s; free under-5s) you can hop-on and hop-off along the banks of the Thames between Millbank Pier and Royal Arsenal Woolwich pier, with intervening stops at Waterloo, Embankment, Tower, Canary Wharf, Greenwich and the O2. The Family Roamer costs £18 (2+2).

On the buses

Big Bus Company *0800 169 1365/7233 9533/www.bigbustours.com.* **Departures** every 10-20mins. *Summer* 8.30am-6pm daily. *Winter* 8.30am-4.30pm daily. *Pick-up* Green Park (near the Ritz); Marble Arch (Speakers' Corner); Victoria (outside Thistle Victoria Hotel, 48 Buckingham Palace Road, SW1W 0RN). **Fares** £22; £10 5-15s; free under-5s. Tickets valid for 24hrs, interchangeable between routes. **Credit** AmEx, DC, MC, V. Open-top buses, with commentary, stop at the major tourist sights, where customers can hop on and off at will. Big Bus also runs cruises and walking tours.

Original London Sightseeing Tour *8877 1722/www.theoriginaltour.com.* **Departures** *Summer* every 5-10mins, 9am-10pm daily. *Winter* every 10-25mins, 9am-5pm daily. *Pick-up* Grosvenor Gardens; Marble Arch (Speakers' Corner); Baker Street tube (forecourt); Haymarket (Piccadilly Circus); Embankment tube; Trafalgar Square. **Fares** £22; £12 5-15s; free under-5s. **Credit** AmEx, MC, V.
A similar operation to the Big Bus tours, also with open-top buses. Kids' Club tours include a special activity pack.

Pedal power

London Bicycle Tour Company *1A Gabriel's Wharf, 56 Upper Ground, SE1 9PP (7928 6838/www.londonbicycle.com). Blackfriars or Waterloo tube/rail.* **Open** 10am-6pm daily. **Hire** £3/hr; £18/1st day, £9/day thereafter. **Credit** AmEx, DC, MC, V.
Bike and tandem hire; children's bike seats are free with an adult bike. Guided tours covering major sights in central London start at 10.30am.

London Pedicabs *7093 3155/www.london pedicabs.com.* **Fares** from £3 per person per mile. **No credit cards.**
Rickshaws based in Covent Garden and Soho.

Take a walk

Guided walking tours are also offered by **And Did Those Feet** (8806 4325, www.chr.org.uk), **Performing London** (01234 404774, www.performinglondon. co.uk) and **Silver Cane Tours** (07720 715295, www.silvercanetours.com).

Original London Walks *7624 3978/ www.walks.com.* **Tours** £7; £5 reductions; 1 free under-15 per adult. **No credit cards.**
Around 140 different walks on numerous different themes, all over London. Plenty are suitable for kids, especially the Harry Potter walk (5pm Sunday) and Ghosts of the Old City walk (7.30pm, Tuesday and Saturday).

'Taxi!'

Black Taxi Tours of London *7935 9363/ www.blacktaxitours.co.uk.* **Cost** £90-£100. **No credit cards.**
A tailored two-hour tour for up to five people.

My London

Children's Laureate **Michael Rosen** loves living in Dalston, but is less happy with the capital's obsession with regeneration.

Once every two years an eminent writer or illustrator of children's books is chosen to be the Children's Laureate. The current incumbent, until June 2009, is Michael Rosen. His books, which include bestsellers *We're Going on a Bear Hunt* and *Little Rabbit Foo Foo*, are renowned for their quirkiness and originality, much like the man himself. Rosen, who's also a poet, journalist, broadcaster, former teacher and father of five (ranging impressively in age from three to 32), is a hero among children.

His latest book, *Dear Mother Goose*, published in May 2008, has a typically eccentric theme, as he explains: 'It's nursery rhyme characters writing to an agony aunt. For example, Humpty Dumpty has a problem with walls – he keeps falling off them. It's illustrated by Nick Sharratt.'

As well as dealing with his collection of troubled personalities in the world of children's fiction, Rosen, applying his customary boundless enthusiasm and imagination to the Laureate job, has been busy in the slightly less whimsical environs of classrooms and libraries.

'I'm rushing around the country a lot more as Children's Laureate. For example, I'm doing an exhibition on the history of children's poetry – with live performances – at the British Library from March to August in 2009. Then there's my website about how to establish book clubs in schools, and making classrooms poetry-friendly. I'm also instigating an annual Funny Prize for the funniest children's book of the year, and an A to Z of Children's Poetry Tour, which kicked off at the Royal Festival Hall in February 2008.'

The main point of his two-year tenure, of course, is to promote reading among children. Rosen says: 'We just have to keep reminding ourselves that books need as much of a buzz around them as other media. New films attract a vast amount of coverage, but new books struggle to get themselves noticed. So you need people like me, creating shows, festivals, treading the boards to spread the world about books. Books are amazing. They need no batteries, you stuff one in your backpack and read it on the bus or in the park.'

When he's not touring the country promoting books, Rosen the writer is at home in Dalston, in east London, where he has lived since 1978: 'I live 200 yards from where my grandparents lived. I can remember coming to this part of London whenever I visited my mother's parents, maybe once a month. It was quite a schlep from where I grew up, in Pinner. We would take the train to Baker Street, then the number 30 bus to Dalston. My grandfather used to take me for walks on Hackney Downs. He pronounced it 'Acknee Dans' and that's what I thought the great green field was called until I was about 15.'

Hackney then seemed to young Michael to be '100 per cent Jewish.' But it's more diverse now, he says: 'The Jews moved from Whitechapel up to Dalston, then Stamford Hill, then Golders Green and

More than 30 years of carting small children around the city has made Michael Rosen an expert on London for children. Here are his suggestions for great family outings.

Sightseeing

'Starting local, we're fond of **Clissold Park** (*see p112*) and London Fields. They're our favourite venues in Hackney – although I must confess I haven't swum in **London Fields Lido** (*see p214*) yet. If I was showing guests around, I might take them to the **Tower of London** (*see p41*) – I'm rather keen on that. Another favourite is **Hampton Court Palace** (*see p36*). And a **river trip** (*see p8*) is a fine way of seeing the city. I think the bridges are great; Tower Bridge is beautiful, and the one that was known as wobbly – the Millennium Bridge – is marvellous. My favourite bridge? It has to be Albert. It's prettier than all the others.

'We love going up west on the 73 or 38 bus, or perhaps on the tube. I don't mind bendy buses, neither do my children. We all like to stand on the twirly bit in the middle.'

Theatre

'We enjoy going to the theatre. I'm a patron of **Polka Theatre** (*see p190*), and I've written a Christmas show there: *Pinocchio* (running 14 November 2008 to 7 February 2009). We also have a strong connection with the **Little Angel Theatre** (*see p183*); my daughter goes to puppet-making workshops there on Saturdays.'

Eating out

'If we're heading further west, we usually start off in Islington; we're great fans of **Carluccio's Caffè** (*see p243*). It has the edge because everyone in the family is happy with it – from the ice-creams and little gingerbread men to all that lovely stuff in the deli that you can bring back for the in-laws. Or you may find us in **Giraffe** (*see p222*) or one of those smart burger places, such as **Fine Burger Company** (*see p246*). **Gallipoli Café Bistro** (*see p251*) is another eating-out treat. It's like a little museum of the Ottoman Empire in there; there are hundreds of lamps and photographs and it's a really great place to take kids.

'I've noticed a change for the better in taking children out to eat. London – certainly places like Islington – has adopted a continental attitude to eating. You don't get restaurant managers scowling at kids now; you can expect a warm welcome. Eating out more means children are more experimental in their tastes too. I wasn't fussy as a kid. I had Jewish food from the age of five, so was passionate about pickled herring, pickled cucumbers and latkes. My parents weren't religious, so I had bacon and ham too.'

Stanmore. Today residents come from all over. I just wish that Hackney could find more ways to celebrate such cultural richness. The authorities seem to have a terribly formal approach – they want to 'do' diversity. Some initiatives work, however, like the way Hackney and other councils celebrate Black History Month.'

If there's one thing that gets his goat, however, it's the city's endless 'regeneration'. 'I call it *de*generation,' he says.

'All around me they're mowing down buildings that could have been refurbished, then developing blocks that don't benefit most of those living in the borough, who can't afford them. There's a terrible attitude towards 'cleaning up' the area, but they're not creating streets that people can call community. People want to be able to walk to coffeeshops, launderettes, parks, just as they did in the old Jewish communities my grandparents knew. Instead, developers create arid, soulless, childless, old people-less loft-style apartments, replacing the old quarters that took hundreds of years to establish, where all levels of humanity lived close to one another, looked after each other. These glassy blocks create a false demography of people who don't need hospitals or schools.'

So does he want to move away from the bulldozers, rubbish and lofty aspirations of the recipients of his Council Tax?

'No. The country is very pleasant, but it's just not lively enough. I love it in London. I don't even mind the rubbish.'

Old Father Thames

Stuck for inspiration? Take them to the river.

A large statue of a bearded geriatric – Old Father Thames – marks the river's source in St John's Lock, near the town of Lechlade, Gloucestershire. From here the Thames flows east for 210 miles (338 kilometres), making it the longest river in Great Britain. For its last 30 miles (48 kilometres), from Teddington on the outskirts of London all the way to the sea, the river is tidal; London is a seaside town, where seagulls wheel and cry and sandy beaches are revealed at low tide around the Millennium Bridge.

For 2,000 years, from the time the Romans expanded the settlement that became Londinium, the Thames has been a working river; now its primary function is leisure and pleasure. Attractions, swanky residential developments and hotels all benefit from being within sight of it, strollers, runners and cyclists congregate on its banks, boats ply its waters.

All Londoners treasure the Thames. They love to take their visitors to the South Bank for cultural powerhouses such as **Tate Modern** (*see p69*) and grand attractions such as the **London Eye** (*p30*). They go west to Richmond and Putney for tranquil, tree-lined walks. For man-made wonders, **Docklands** (*see p86*), with its shimmering towers of glass, evokes a different kind of city pride. Then there's beautiful, royal **Greenwich** (*see p124*), with its maritime history and undulating parkland, from where the views of this great European river and the city that burgeons on its north bank, sum up the role of the Thames past and present. Further east, even once-charmless areas such as Silvertown are in line for a makeover. This part of the river's north bank, which now boasts the unexpectedly glorious **Thames Barrier Park** (*see p119*), a lovely green haven overlooking the silver cocoons of the Thames Barrier (*see below*), has some big fish to fry (or exhibit in large tanks). The Zoological Society of London is overseeing the building of Europe's largest aquarium in Silvertown Quays – Biota! (7449 6363, www.zsl.org/biota) – set to open in 2011.

A dam good time

The small Learning Centre attached to the **Thames Barrier** (1 Unity Way, SE18 5NJ, 8305 4188, www.environment-agency.gov.uk) has a working model that explains how the barrier works and a map showing which parts of London would be submerged if it stopped doing so (watch out, Deptford). If you want to time your visit to see the barrier in action, contact the centre: every September there's a full-scale testing, with a partial test closure once a month.

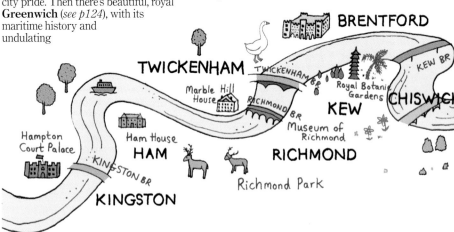

Environmental activities and workshops for school groups take place in the wildlife garden, created on disused land using £50,000 of Environment Agency and Heritage Lottery Fund money. It's intended to become an urban oasis filled with flowers, trees and creatures. Occasional activities led by teaching assistants involve such delights as scrabbling about for mini beasts under old logs and stones, and learning to love the wormery (some children draw the line at this). Intrepid entomologists can have a go at 'pooting' – sucking a bug up a tube in order to get a closer look. Young visitors can also create 'bug art' out of recycled materials, and make bird treats using lard and bird seed.

It's a fine destination to take inquisitive youngsters, if only to develop awareness of London as a river town. It's also the end-point of the riverside path, so the centre's café (baked potatoes, sandwiches, drinks), overlooking the big silver fins, is a good way to finish off a walk or a cycle ride.

Messing about in boats

For visitors to London, travel on the Thames is not only more pleasurable than squeezing on to overcrowded buses and trains, but it also offers access to dozens of London's key attractions – and traffic-free connections between them.

Although the Thames has always been central to London's development, it's been a long time since it was used properly as a transport link. In the 18th century, the Pool of London was so crammed with vessels it was said you could cross the river just by

Glorious mudlarking

In the 19th century, barefoot children could often be seen scavenging in the mud and rubble on the shores of the Thames. They'd be looking for stuff to use or sell, anything from lumps of coal to coins, jewellery and clothing. It was a dangerous business – tides and heavy pollution meant that many children drowned, or contracted some lethal disease. It certainly was not a leisure activity.

These days, there's not much to stop curious Thameside beachcombers on the South Bank from descending down damp steps to the sandy beach that's revealed at low tide. Apparently, though, in order to do any serious digging, you have to obtain a special licence from the elusive Society of Thames Mudlarks. The Port of London Authority is the official body that owns most of the mud along the river so perhaps the best, and safest, way to be a modern mudlark is to contact the **Museum in Docklands** (see p85) or the **Museum of London** (see p89) to find out when the education officers are organising the next Thames foreshore dig. This happens relatively often in the holidays and it's all above board and highly regulated – the original mudlarks could have done with a few education officers in their day.

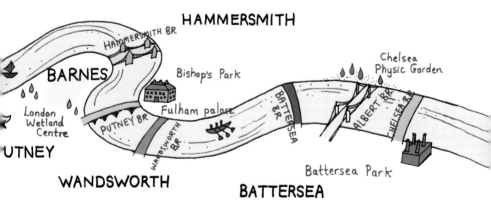

HAMMERSMITH
HAMMERSMITH BR
BARNES
Bishop's Park
Chelsea Physic Garden
London Wetland Centre
Fulham palace
PUTNEY BR
WANDSWORTH BR
BATTERSEA BR
ALBERT BR
CHELSEA BR
UTNEY
WANDSWORTH
Battersea Park
BATTERSEA

stepping from one boat to the next. Of course, it's unlikely the river will ever be so busy again, but there are moves to win back the Thames for ordinary travellers. **Thames Clippers** (*see p8*), whose fast, reliable boat service between Embankment and Tower Bridge is a top commute for workers, transports a million passengers every year and has doubled its fleet in recent years. Its River Roamer ticket for families (*see p8*) is an excellent way to stay close to Old Father Thames for a day.

Tourists already get a pretty good deal out of the Thames. You can feel the wind in your hair courtesy of **London RIB Voyages** (*see p8*). The rigid inflatable boat ambles from Waterloo to Tower Bridge before cranking things up to zoom downriver to the Thames Barrier at an exhilarating 30 knots. More sedately, and infinitely more eccentrically, **London Duck Tours** (*see p8*) trundles a decommissioned DUKW amphibious truck, built for use in World War II, around the major sights of the West End before ducking into the river. Then there's Thames Clippers' tourist boats, notably the Tate to Tate Damien Hirst dotty number (*see p8*).

Park. This is the best way to get to the zoo, as boats tie up right inside their premises.

Wildlife superhighway

It's true, the Thames is cleaner than it has ever been. Dolphins and seals are frequent commuters into town (there's a seal that hangs around Billingsgate fish market in Poplar for obvious reasons) and there was much excitement recently when seahorses were found to be favouring the river's comforts. This is quite incredible when you consider how filthy the river became as the city grew. The Romans weren't above throwing their detritus in the Thames, but as the population of the city exploded, so the river went into terminal decline. By the Victorian era, large-scale polluters such as gasworks and water closets put paid to all but the toughest river wildlife. The fishing industry was eliminated in the decades that followed, and by the 1950s the river was more or less dead. Improved sewage systems in the '60s gave the Thames a bit of a spring clean and ongoing work to improve the river – masterminded by organisations such as the Environment

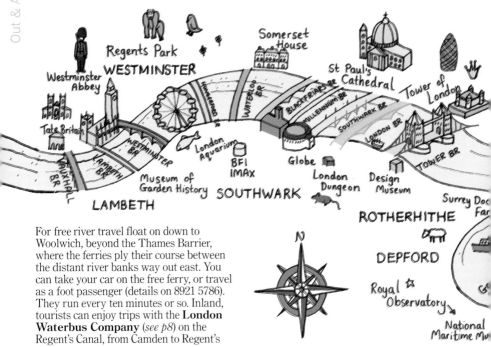

For free river travel float on down to Woolwich, beyond the Thames Barrier, where the ferries ply their course between the distant river banks way out east. You can take your car on the free ferry, or travel as a foot passenger (details on 8921 5786). They run every ten minutes or so. Inland, tourists can enjoy trips with the **London Waterbus Company** (*see p8*) on the Regent's Canal, from Camden to Regent's

View of Tower Bridge from **More London**. *See p49.*

Agency (www.environment-agency.gov.uk) and the London Wildlife Trust (www.wild london.org.uk), a charity that does untold good work throughout the city – has paid dividends. The river is now known as a wildlife superhighway, used by birds and fish from the continent or the Atlantic as a migration pit stop. Nowhere is this more evident – in terms of birdlife – than at the **WWT Wetland Centre** (*see p139*).

Underneath the surface, there are more than 100 types of fish. You're hardly likely to see them on a river walk, but flounders, dover sole, smelts, sea lampreys, even salmon down Teddington way, have all reconciled themselves to the river's waters.

Such is the variety of wildlife around London's river that its ecological importance goes beyond giving Londoners something to brag about when provincial visitors try to play the 'dirty old town' card. The Thames is a major player in the lifespan of migrating wildlife as well as the ecology of the North Sea. Groups such as the Tidal Thames Habitat Action Plan (www.thamesweb.com) are making sure

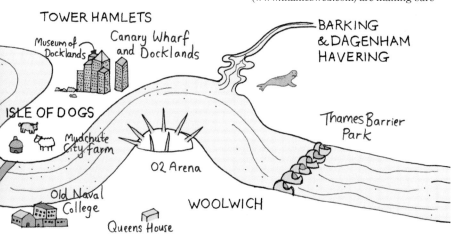

THE CITY

TOWER HAMLETS

Museum of Docklands

Canary Wharf and Docklands

BARKING & DAGENHAM HAVERING

ISLE OF DOGS

Mudchute City farm

Thames Barrier Park

O2 Arena

Old Naval College

WOOLWICH

Queens House

Walk
New Greenwich

After the damp squib that was the Millennium Dome, the reborn O2 and the regenerated peninsula it squats on are an exciting work in progress, and an exhilarating riverside walk for the family. This much-maligned spit of land now sees visitors flocking to high-profile exhibitions and entertainments at the O2, and the Thames Path has specially commissioned artworks and panels telling the site's history.

Emerge from North Greenwich tube and you'll see the O2 across Peninsula Square, with its towering steel spire and Meridian Line and pavement plaques of poetic (Shakespeare, Larkin) reflections on time. With the building on your right, head west. Look over the desolate pyramids of waste to the Manhattan-like cityscape of Docklands. Past a jetty-cum-nature reserve (the pier providing a home for teasels and sea buckthorn) is Richard Wilson's *A Slice of Reality*. It's the middle section of a ship, cut out, given glass sides so that you can peer inside. Old-style mileposts remind you that historic London is less than seven miles away. An information panel promises teal, shore crabs and sea asters on the terraced banks below.

As you walk, notice four stout pillars supporting Antony Gormley's *Quantum Cloud*. This candy-floss of wires forms within it the figure of a man shaping up for a free-kick. Did it inspire Beckham's Football Academy (*see p199*) nearby?

Cut right on to the unpromising-looking road heading inland, then left down East Parkside to a little row of houses, one of which is the Pilot Inn (68 River Way, 8858 5910), a friendly Fuller's pub. At the space-friendly Millennium Village, turn left to rejoin the Thames Path, and south to enter **Greenwich Peninsula Ecology Park** (*see p127*).

When you've done with nature, head north along the Thames Path. An elongated 'History in Motion' panel cross-refers the depth of the Thames at different periods with significant events. Back at the junction with Edmund Halley Way, turn left, then first right to reach the tube.

the good news keeps coming as they protect and preserve these historic waters. We'll look forward to the day when salmon leap around Westminster Bridge.

Holding back the tide

Lives depend on the Thames, but sometimes Londoners need protecting from its surging enthusiasm. The Thames Barrier does this. It spans the river at Woolwich (where it is 520 metres/568 yards wide) to protect the city from flooding and is the result of one of the biggest engineering projects in UK history. Completed in 1982, it took ten years to build and cost more than £500 million. Ten circular steel gates, held in place by massive concrete piers, are raised whenever a surge in the North Sea threatens Gordon Brown's carpets. It was built to prevent another catastrophe like the 1953 flood, which killed more than 2,000 people around the North Sea coastline. The alternative to the Barrier would have been to raise the embankments in central London to such a height that the river would be virtually cut off from the city (and its annual three million tourists).

In 2007 London was spared the general flood misery only because the rains didn't fall when the river was high: because the Thames is tidal. Understandably, not wanting to cause a panic (and a rush to B&Q for sandbags), the Environment Agency are cagey about admitting how much more often the dam is raised in these times of global warming and summer deluges. They assure us it's not up-and-down like the proverbial yo-yo, but its operation is certainly more frequent. The Barrier was planned to last only until 2030 and was built before global warming had been thought of; beyond 2030, something else is clearly going to be needed. Present thinking is that in future we will need to allow some of the estuary downstream to be flooded. Ironically, this is going back to nature's original solution. All our rivers have floodplains. The problem is that we've built Barratt homes on them.

The strange silver shapes – designed to resemble the hulls of ships – are just the housing for the dam's machinery; Red Ken of GLC vintage wanted something that looked nice. The working bit of the dam is mostly invisible, being underwater.

Walk
Pottering around Putney

Though the South Bank certainly has its attractions, and there are some fascinating post-industrial nooks and piratical crannies around Rotherhithe and Limehouse, undoubtedly the best stretch of the River Thames to take the young ones for a toddle lies between Putney and Barnes.

Start on the opposite side of the river in Fulham to give them a chance to run around beautiful, bijou Bishop's Park which neighbours **Fulham Palace** (*see p37*) before crossing the bridge to make your first coffee and nappy-change pit stop in Putney. The Exchange Shopping Centre might be typically soulless, but it does boast some excellent facilities – and the Gymboree activity room (www.gymboreeplayuk.com), if it looks like the weather's on the turn. The muffins are baked on the premises and staff will warm up baby food.

Head out from here along the Thames path (turn left at the bridge). This first stretch of Putney Embankment will take you past the boathouses made famous

once a year by Oxford and Cambridge. Everyone enjoys watching the rowers glide by (there's usually some action along here, especially on a Saturday), and if your posse are themselves sporty, you can earn extra points by showing them Craven Cottage, home of Fuham FC, across the river.

After the footbridge over Beverley Brook, the path becomes tree-lined and muddy (over-eager cyclists are also an occasional hazard). In late summer, come armed with Tupperware as this is an excellent blackberry picking spot; look out too for herons, cormorants and, occasionally, kingfishers buzzing around the riverbank. There's more birdlife at Britain's biggest wetlands conservation reserve, the **WWT Wetland Centre** (take a left down Queen Elizabeth Walk after Barn Elms School sports fields; *see p139*). The admission price is almost worth it for the playground alone.

If you're carrying on along the river, go under Hammersmith Bridge, past St Paul's Boys' School's playing fields and you'll end up at another nature reserve – free, this time – Leg O'Mutton, named after the reservoir's unusual shape. Lush with cow parsley and pussy willow in the spring, it attracts nowhere near as many human visitors as the Wetland Centre, but the birds frequent it just the same: keep an eye out for the colourful parakeets. Alternatively, push on to Barnes and feed the ducks at the village pond before treating your brood to fish and chips at the Tanya Fish Bar (39A High Street, SW13, 8878 4750).

On a summer's evening, parents might want to go their separate ways at this point: those with tired legs can get the train home from Barnes Bridge and put the kids to bed, while the more robust could make this a circular walk by crossing the bridge and ambling back via the charming riverside pubs of Chiswick and Hammersmith.

For more on the Thames Path, which follows the river for 184 miles (296 kilometres) as it meanders from its source through several counties to the city, log on to www.nationaltrail.co.uk/thamespath.

WWT Wetland Centre.
See p139.

Festivals & Events

You'll never be short of something to do in London – and to prove it we've included the main events and festivals taking place throughout the city. The past few years have seen an increase in outdoor festivals, usually held during the summer, as well as some imaginative sponsored seasons and one-off events. Check *Time Out* magazine every week for the news, and for details of fairs and circuses coming to a park near you. Zippo's, London's largest traditional touring circus, has a new show every year; see www.zipposcircus.co.uk for details of new acts, plus venues and dates for 2008. We've given exact dates for events where possible; phone or check websites nearer the time for unconfirmed timings.

SUMMER

Coin Street Festival

Bernie Spain Gardens, next to Oxo Tower Wharf, SE1 9PH (7021 1686/www.coinstreet festival.org). Southwark tube/Waterloo tube/rail. **Date** June-Aug 2008. **Map** p318 N7.

The Coin Street Community Builders saved this part of the South Bank from demolition in the 1970s. Every year they organise a series of culturally themed weekday and weekend events that celebrates different communities in the capital (a South American shindig is planned for 2008). Festivities take place on the South Bank and include music, dance and performances for all ages, as well as craft and refreshment stalls and workshops for families. Check the website for more information nearer the time.

Beating Retreat

Horse Guards Parade, Whitehall, SW1A 2AX (booking 7414 2271). Westminster tube/Charing Cross tube/rail. **Date** 4-5 June 2008. **Map** p317 K8.

This patriotic ceremony begins at 7pm, with the 'Retreat' beaten on drums by the Mounted Bands of the Household Cavalry and the Massed Bands of the Guards Division.

Trooping the Colour

Horse Guards Parade, Whitehall, SW1A 2AX (7414 2271). Westminster tube/Charing Cross tube/rail. **Date** 14 June 2008; 20 June 2009. **Map** p317 K8.

Though the Queen was born on 21 April, this is her official birthday celebration for practical reasons. At 10.45am she makes the journey from Buckingham Palace to Horse Guards Parade, then scoots home to watch a Royal Air Force flypast and receive a formal gun salute from Green Park.

Open Garden Squares Weekend

Various venues (www.opensquares.org). **Date** 7-8 June 2008.

For one weekend a year the London Parks & Gardens Trust opens to one and all. Tickets (£7.50, £6 in advance, free under-12s) allow entry to all participating gardens, from usually locked exclusive-looking squares to delightful, secret 'children-only' play areas and jolly green potagers. Many are wheelchair-accessible and host activities and plant sales.

Greenwich & Docklands International Festival

Various venues (8305 1818/www.festival.org). **Date** 19-22 June 2008; 25-28 June 2009.

This free, family-friendly festival, with its mixture of theatrical, musical and site-specific events, celebrated its tenth anniversary in 2007. Look out for aerialists at the O2, choreographed runners at the National Maritime Museum and pyrotechnic displays at the Royal Arsenal and in Bow. In Woolwich, beware the 60-foot long musical caterpillar. He's very hungry and has been known to gobble up unsuspecting members of the audience.

City of London Festival

Venues across the City, EC2-EC4 (7796 4949/www.colf.org). St Paul's tube/Bank tube/DLR/Blackfriars, Cannon Street, Farringdon or Moorgate tube/rail. **Date** 20 June-10 July 2008.

Now in its 46th year, this festival celebrating London's global trading links takes place in some of the Square Mile's finest historic buildings. The Romanticism theme for 2008 is inspired by Indian and Swiss landscapes and journeys; the wide-ranging events include classical, jazz and world music concerts, a special film programme at the Barbican, and architecture walks, visual arts and talks.

Outdoor events run until 24 August; watch the London Youth Circus performing on the steps of St Paul's Cathedral or try a spot of Bollywood dancing at the family fun day on Hampstead Heath (22 June).

Wimbledon Lawn Tennis Championships

All England Lawn Tennis Club, PO Box 98, Church Road, SW19 5AE (8944 1066/info 8946 2244/www.wimbledon.org). Southfields tube/Wimbledon tube/rail. **Date** 23 June-6 July 2008.

Netting tickets for this prestigious tennis tournament takes some advance planning. For Centre Court and Court Number One seats, request an application form from the All England Lawn Tennis Club between August and mid December the year before; this form gives you access to the public ticket ballot. Queueing on the day should gain you entry to the outside courts. In the afternoon, returned show-court tickets are available from the booth opposite Court One so it may be worth hanging about to see stars in action on one of the most famous courts in the world.

Henley Royal Regatta

Henley Reach, Henley-on-Thames, Oxon RG9 2LY (01491 572153/www.hrr.co.uk). Henley-on-Thames rail. **Date** 2-6 July 2008; 1-5 July 2009.

First held in 1839, and under royal patronage since 1851, Henley is still going strong; it's now a five-day affair. Boat races range from open events for men and women through club and student crews to the Princess Elizabeth race for juniors (boys under the age of 19).

Watch This Space

Theatre Square, outside the National Theatre, South Bank, SE1 9PX (7452 3400/www. nationaltheatre.org.uk). Waterloo tube/rail. **Date** 4 July-14 Sept 2008. **Map** p318 M7.

This free outdoor festival on the South Bank is one of our favourite annual arts events in London. It showcases the best street theatre, circus, cinema, music, art and dance from all over the world. Phone or check the website for details nearer the time.

London Youth Games

Various venues (8778 0131/www.londonyouth games.org). **Date** 5-6 July 2008.

This mini-Olympics, now in its 32nd year, attracts 12,000 sporting hopefuls, all of them under 17, representing the 33 London boroughs in 28 different sports. The teams are selected

Notting Hill Carnival. *See p22.*

locally, and activities include archery, fencing, canoeing, cycling, rugby and athletics. Note that due to a major refurb, only outdoor events will be held at Crystal Palace Sports Ground this year. Various entertainments including DJs, dance demonstration, street sports and graffiti art complement the main event.

Streatham Festival

Various venues (www.streathamfestival.com). **Date** 5-13 July 2008.
Now in its seventh year, this local fest celebrates this south London neighbourhood and its diverse community with more than 50 events in a variety of locations, from churches and youth centres to parks and bars. Around 3,000 people attended in 2007. There are family heritage walks and talks, garden parties, parades, plus poetry workshops, theatre, dance, comedy and film. Check the online programme for details.

Big Dance

Various venues (www.london.gov.uk/bigdance). **Date** 5-13 July 2008.
A week-long celebration of all styles of dance, with hundreds of free events and performances taking place in parks, museums, theatres and streets throughout London. Try a lindy hop or salsa class or just cheer on the attempts to break the Big Dance world record in Trafalgar Square – currently 752 dancers performing 44 different dance styles simultaneously to one music track. Check the website for events near you.

Chap & Hendrick's Olympiad

Bedford Square Gardens, WC1 (www.hendricks gin.com). Tottenham Court Road tube. **Date** mid July 2008. **Map** p315 K5.
Terribly silly and terribly English, this is a jolly afternoon out for children to watch adults engage in a spot of splendid tomfoolery. Events kick off with the lighting of the Olympic Pipe, with 'sports' including umbrella hockey, the three-trousered limbo, and curling (yep, with curling tongs). And there's free G&Ts for the grown-ups – hurrah!

BBC Sir Henry Wood Promenade Concerts

Royal Albert Hall, Kensington Gore, SW7 2AP (box office 7589 8212/www.bbc.co.uk/proms). Knightsbridge or South Kensington tube/9, 10, 52 bus. **Date** 18 July-13 Sept 2008. **Map** p313 D9.
This annual event brings together an eclectic range of mainly classical concerts over the course of two months. Most are broadcast on radio or TV, but there's nothing like seeing them

in person. Choose carefully and you should find something in the grown-up Proms programme that will appeal to children too. On 27 July, the Doctor Who prom (yes, really) costs £5-£10. Under-16s get half-price tickets to every Prom (apart from the Last Night).

Lambeth Country Show

Brockwell Park, SE24 0NG (7926 9000/ www.ubiqueleisure.co.uk). Brixton tube/rail, then 2, 3, 68, 196 bus/Herne Hill rail. **Date** 19-20 July 2008.
This free annual urban country show fills the rolling hills of Brockwell Park with a mix of farmyard and domestic animal attractions (horse show, dog show, farm animals and birds of prey). Aside from meeting and greeting the beasts, children can have fun on numerous bouncy castles and fairground rides, and there are also international food and craft stalls, and a whole lot of music and dancing.

Sundae on the Common

Clapham Common, SW4 (www.benjerry. co.uk/sundae). Clapham Common tube. **Date** 26-27 July 2008.
Ben & Jerry's are 30 in 2008, so this year's bash promises a few birthday surprises alongside the usual mix of family-friendly activities and live music. Oh, and free ice-cream all day. Check the website for the latest updates and line-ups; previous acts have included Echo & the Bunnymen, Badly Drawn Boy and José González. You can pet farm animals, scoot down the helter skelter, burn off all that ice-cream on bouncy castles (there's also a quieter tent and outdoor play area for the tinies) and have your fortune told by Mystic Moo.

Time Out's 40th Birthday

Various venues (www.timeout.com). **Date** Aug 2008.
A month of superb cultural events, focused around the 40th birthday of London's best listings mag (if we say so ourselves).

Summer in the Square

Trafalgar Square, WC2 (7983 4100/www. london.gov.uk/trafalgarsquare). Embankment tube/Charing Cross tube/rail. **Date** Aug 2008. **Map** p317 K7.
An annual programme of free (and usually fun) live cultural performances – music, dance and street theatre – for all ages, Summer in the Square is keenly supported by the Mayor of London. As we went to press the programme had not yet been confirmed. Check the website for details nearer the time.

Out & About

Innocent Village Fete

Gloucester Green, north-east corner of Regent's Park, NW1 (8600 3939/www. innocentdrinks.co.uk). Baker Street or Regent's Park tube. **Date** 2-3 Aug 2008. **Map** p314 G3.

This weekender is about summer's gentler pastimes: picnics, own-made cakes, the tombola, lying around in the grass. Music and comedy acts do feature, but you'll also find arts and crafts and fancy dress games for children, massage and yoga lessons and, possibly, snail racing and duck herding. Tickets go on sale a few weeks before the event; check the website for details.

Carnaval del Pueblo

Burgess Park, SE5 (7686 1633/www.noticias. co.uk). Elephant & Castle tube/12, 25, 36, 68, 68A, 100, 172 bus. **Date** 3 Aug 2008.

The UK's largest Latin American celebration pulled in over 130,000 people in 2007 and is growing more popular with every year. It kicks off at noon with a colourful parade from Tower Bridge, arriving at Burgess Park around 3pm. The entertainment runs until 9.30pm and includes exotic food and crafts stalls, a children's zone with bouncy castles and funfair activities, and four stages of live Brazilian samba, Latin hip hop, Mexican mariachi and Colombian salsa.

Underage

Victoria Park, Old Ford Road, E3 5DS (8985 1957/www.myspace.com/underage_club). Mile End tube/Cambridge Heath or Hackney Wick rail/8, 26, 30, 55, 253, 277, S2 bus. **Date** 8 Aug 2008. **Tickets** £23.

Underage, the world's first strictly under-17s music festival, returns with more alternative/ rock/electronic bands for young fans. With an anticipated attendance of 7,000, this is a more accessible affair than the summer's big-name festivals. Confirmed bands include the Horrors, Foals and indie faves the Maccabees. No beer tents: soft drinks only are served.

Free Time Festival

Somerset House, Strand, WC2R ORN (7845 4600/www.somerset-house.org.uk). Covent Garden or Temple tube (closed Sun)/Charing Cross tube/rail. **Date** 15-18 Aug 2008. **Map** p317 M7.

Somerset House's courtyard provides a handsome stage for events during the summer holidays, and the four-day Family Free Time Festival promises a host of entertaining games, art, dance, music and storytelling events. Last year saw Maori music and Professor Jake and the Whacky Windbags. Phone for a programme.

A Country Affair

The Green, Hampton Court Palace, Surrey KT8 9AU (8977 0705/www.hamptoncourt show.com). Hampton Court rail/boat from Westminster or Richmond to Hampton Court Pier. **Date** 23-25 Aug 2008.

This family-friendly show has a host of hands-on activities for children: traditional fairground rides, morris dancers, falconry displays, animal shows plus bands and a farmers' market.

Notting Hill Carnival

Notting Hill, W10 & W11 (0870 059 1111/ www.lnhc.org.uk). Ladbroke Grove, Notting Hill Gate & Westbourne Park tube. **Date** 24-25 Aug 2008.

The August Bank Holiday Sunday is traditionally children's day at this annual shindig, second in the world only to Rio in terms of sheer scale. It livens up the posh neighbourhood with masquerades, steel bands, decorative floats and more ground-shaking sound systems than you could shake a paper plate of curried goat at. Its reputation for bringing short, sharp spikes to the annual crime charts continues to court controversy, but increasing commercialism and a strong police presence have made the carnival safer than ever.

Kempton Park Family Fun Day

Kempton Park, Sunbury-on-Thames, Middx TW16 5AQ (01372 470047/www.kempton. co.uk). Kempton Park rail. **Date** 25 Aug, 6 Sept 2008.

Hop on the train from Waterloo to enjoy a family-friendly day out at the races. Entertainment for kids (simulator rides, crafts and soft play area, face-painting, balloon-modelling) is free.

AUTUMN

Young Pavement Artists Competition

www.muscular-dystrophy.org/pavementart.

The Young Pavement Artists Competition (YPAC) is a national competition to raise awareness of muscular dystrophy. Over 5,000 schools and community and youth groups take part by holding their own creative pavement event to help raise funds. The 2008 theme is Endangered Species of the World; children aged four to 19 compete, with pitches costing around £1 per entrant. Photos of the day's winners are then entered into the national competition, judged by members of Tate Britain and the Royal Academy of Arts. Winners are displayed at an autumn exhibition (dates to be confirmed).

Out & About

Regent Street Festival

Regent Street, W1 (7287 9601/www.regent streetonline.com). Oxford Circus or Piccadilly Circus tube. **Date** 7 Sept 2008. **Map** p316 J7.
Running from noon to 8pm, this festival sees one of the capital's smartest streets close to traffic to make room for fairground rides, theatre, storytelling, street entertainers, a variety of live music and, of course, shopping. There's usually plenty of input from Regent Street's busy toy emporium Hamley's.

Great River Race

River Thames, from Ham House, Richmond, Surrey, to Island Gardens, Greenwich, E14 (8398 9057/www.greatriverrace.co.uk). **Date** 13 Sept 2008.
Attracting everyone from professional racers to enthusiastic Sea Scouts, more than 260 boats – you'll find Cornish pilot gigs alongside Hawaiian war canoes – compete over a 22-mile (35km) course in the UK's traditional boat championships. The race begins at 12.55am and reaches the finish at around 4.30pm. The best viewing points are at Richmond Bridge, along the South Bank or on the Millennium and Hungerford Bridges.

Mayor's Thames Festival

Between Westminster & Blackfriars Bridges (7983 4100/www.thamesfestival.org). Blackfriars or Waterloo tube/rail. **Date** 13-14 Sept 2008.

Always fun and occasionally spectacular, this waterfest celebrating the Thames runs from noon to 10pm all weekend, finishing with an atmospheric lantern procession and dramatic fireworks on Sunday evening. Expect riverside market stalls, an alfresco ballroom, performers, foreshore sand sculptures, environmental activities, creative workshops, and a lively assortment of dance and music performances. And it's all free.

Spitalfields Show & Green Fair

Allen Gardens & Spitalfields City Farm, Buxton Street, E1 (7375 0441/www. alternativearts.co.uk). Whitechapel tube. **Date** 14 Sept 2008.
This east London horticultural show (noon-6pm) offers oodles of own-made produce, handicrafts, Fairtrade goods, healthy food and healing therapies, plus activities for children. There are also stalls promoting projects raising environmental awareness.

City Harvest Festival

Capel Manor Gardens, Bullsmoor Lane, Enfield, Middx EN1 4RQ (08456 122122/ www.capel.ac.uk). Turkey Street rail (closed Sun)/217, 310 bus. **Date** 20 Sept 2008.
This agricultural extravaganza makes for a pleasant family day out. Events and activities include a farm animal show, milking and shearing demonstrations, vegetable and plant sales, crafts displays and food stalls.

And they're off! To the **London International Horse Show**. *See p26.*

Horseman's Sunday

Church of St John's Hyde Park, Hyde Park Crescent, W2 2QD (7262 1732/www.stjohns-hydepark.com/horsemans). Edgware Road or Lancaster Gate tube/Paddington tube/rail. **Date** 21 Sept 2008. **Map** p313 E6.

This ceremony dates back to 1967, when local stables, threatened with closure, held an outdoor service to protest. At noon, after morning service, the vicar of St John's rides out to bless and present rosettes to a procession of horses and riders, and delivers a short service with hymns and occasional guest speakers. There are children's activities, games and face-painting in the church grounds.

Punch & Judy Festival

Covent Garden Piazza, WC2 (0870 780 5001/www.coventgardenmarket.co.uk). Covent Garden tube. **Date** early Oct 2008. **Map** p315 L6.

More domestic incidents involving a crocodile, a policeman and Mr Punch giving Judy a few slaps (and vice versa). Performances take place around the market building. Puppetry means prizes, and there's also puppet-related merchandise for sale. Call nearer the time to confirm this year's date as it hadn't been finalised as we went to press.

Children's Book Week

8516 2977/www.booktrust.org.uk. **Date** 6-12 Oct 2008.

Children's Book Week celebrates and encourages reading for pleasure for children of primary school age. The theme for 2008 is Rhythm and Rhyme; countrywide events include hands-on activities and author visits. Details will be available from libraries and schools, otherwise visit the Booktrust website. National Poetry Day (www.nationalpoetryday.co.uk) is on 9 October.

Pearly Kings & Queens Harvest Festival

St Paul's Church, Bedford Street, WC2E 9ED (8778 8670/www.pearlysociety.co.uk). Covent Garden tube. **Date** 12 Oct 2008. **Map** p317 L7.

Pearly kings and queens – so named because of the shiny white pearl buttons sewn in elaborate designs on their dark suits – have their origins in the 'aristocracy' of London's early Victorian costermongers, who elected their own royalty to look after their interests. Now charity representatives, today's pearly monarchs gather in their traditional 'flash boy' outfits an hour before the 11am thanksgiving service.

The Baby Show

Earl's Court Exhibition Centre, SW5 9TA (booking 0870 122 1313/www.thebabyshow.co.uk). Earl's Court tube. **Date** Earl's Court 17-19 Oct 2008; ExCel 27 Feb-1 Mar 2009.

Want to enjoy a healthy pregnancy and raise splendid, cherubic babies and toddlers? Find out how here – and check out an obscene amount of nursery equipment, stimulating toys and other paraphernalia into the bargain. Consult the website to search for your area of interest.

Trafalgar Day Parade

Trafalgar Square, WC2 (7928 8978/www.ms-sc.org). Charing Cross tube/rail. **Date** 26 Oct 2008. **Map** p401 K7.

More than 500 sea cadets parade with marching bands and musical performances. Events culminate in a wreath-laying at the foot of Nelson's Column.

London to Brighton Veteran Car Run

Start at Serpentine Road, Hyde Park, W2 (01327 856024/www.lbvcr.com). Hyde Park Corner tube. **Date** 1-2 Nov 2008. **Map** p311 F8.

Get up bright and early to catch this parade of 500 vintage motors leaving London, or join the crowds lining the route. The shiny fleet sets off from Hyde Park at 7am; the first cars reach Brighton around 10am, with the rest arriving by 4pm. Average speed is a whopping 32kmph (20mph). The handsome vehicles are on display in Regent Street the day before (11am-3pm, Saturday 1 November).

Bonfire Night

Date 5 Nov.

Numerous public pyrotechnics to commemorate Guy Fawkes and the Gunpowder Plot are held on the weekend nearest 5 November. Among the best in London are the displays at Battersea Park, Alexandra Palace and Crystal Palace. Alternatively, try to book a late ride on the relevant nights on the London Eye.

Lord Mayor's Show

The City (7332 3456/www.lordmayorsshow.org). **Date** 8 Nov 2008.

This is the day when, under the conditions of the Magna Carta, the newly elected Lord Mayor is presented to the monarch, or his or her justices. Amid a procession of around 140 floats, the Lord Mayor leaves the Mansion House at 11am and travels through the City to the Royal Courts of Justice on the Strand, then receives a blessing at St Paul's Cathedral before returning to Mansion House. The procession takes around

Pooch paradise at **Discover Dogs**.

75 minutes to pass by. The event is rounded off by a fireworks display at around 5pm from a barge moored on the Thames between Waterloo and Blackfriars Bridges... anywhere along the Embankment is a good vantage point.

Discover Dogs

Earl's Court 2 Exhibition Centre, entrance on Lillie Road, SW5 9TA (7518 1012/www.the-kennel-club.org.uk). West Brompton tube/rail. **Date** 8-9 Nov 2008. **Map** p312 A11.
This canine extravaganza is far less formal than Crufts and is a great place to gather information on all matters of the mutt. You can meet around 190 pedigree pooches and their breeders, watch Heelwork to Music displays and husky teams and police-dog agility demonstrations. There are also competitions in categories as wide-ranging as 'dog that looks most like a celebrity' to Scruffts (family crossbreed dog of the year). The Good Citizen Dog Scheme offers discipline and agility courses.

State Opening of Parliament

House of Lords, Palace of Westminster, SW1A 0PW (7219 4272/www.parliament.uk). Westminster tube. **Date** Nov 2008 (exact date to be confirmed). **Map** p317 L9.
In a ceremony that has changed little since the 16th century, the Queen officially reopens Parliament after its summer recess. Watch Her Maj arrive and depart in her Irish or Australian State Coach, attended by the Household Cavalry.

Children's Film Festival

Main venue: Barbican Centre, Silk Street, EC2Y 8DS (Barbican box office 7638 8891/ www.londonchildrenfilm.org.uk). Barbican tube. **Date** 22-30 Nov 2008 (phone to check).
Map p318 P5.
Few of the films screened at the Children's Film Festival would find a multiplex slot, but if the encouraging outcome of past festivals is anything to go by, children appreciate more than just blockbusters. The First Light Young Juries scheme, in which children aged between seven and 16 are invited to be film critics and vote for their favourites, came up with two winners, both from the world-cinema category with subtitles. The popular costume and make-up workshops, many of which are free, plus a range of activities to complement the screenings, are again planned for 2008. Organisers aim to keep ticket prices low (with further reductions for advance bookings).

Christmas Lights & Tree

Covent Garden (0870 780 5001/www.covent gardenmarket.co.uk); Oxford Street (7462 0680); Regent Street (7152 5853/www.regent-street.co.uk); Bond Street (www.bondstreet association.com); Trafalgar Square (7983 4234/www.london.gov.uk). **Date** Nov-Dec 2008.
Much of the childhood wonder of Xmas still remains in the glittering lights on St Christopher's Place, Marylebone High Street, Bond Street and Kensington High Street. The giant fir tree in Trafalgar Square each year is a gift from the Norwegian people, in gratitude for Britain's role in liberating their country from the Nazis during World War II.

WINTER

London International Horse Show

Olympia Exhibition Centre, Hammersmith Road, W14 8UX (01753 847900/ www.olympiahorseshow.com). Kensington (Olympia) tube/rail. **Date** 16-22 Dec 2008.
This annual extravaganza for enthusiasts of all things equestrian offers dressage, show-jumping, mounted military displays, dog agility contests and a Shetland Pony Grand National. The grand finale features Father Christmas (with sledge pulled by horses) and there are over 200 trade stands, so you can also do some seasonal shopping.

Bankside Frost Fair

Bankside Riverwalk, next to Shakespeare's Globe, SE1 9DT (details from Tourism Unit, Southwark Council, 7525 1139/www.visit southwark.com). London Bridge tube/rail. **Date** Dec 2008.

Frost fairs took place in the winter of 1564, when the Thames froze over and Londoners set up stalls of mulled wine and roast meats on the ice. Sadly, the future of this wonderfully festive fair, with cosy food and crafts stalls, ice sculptors, children's shows and a lantern parade, looks uncertain; phone or check the website for updates.

Peter Pan Swimming Race

The Serpentine, Hyde Park, W2 2UH (7298 2100/www.royalparks.gov.uk). Hyde Park Corner tube. **Date** 25 Dec.

Established in 1864 by *Peter Pan* author JM Barrie, this chilly 100-yard race draws swimmers (Serpentine Swimming Club members only) and spectators every Christmas morning, competing for the Peter Pan cup. However mild the weather is, the Serpentine always looks less than inviting.

New Years' Eve Celebrations

Date 31 Dec.

Traditionally, London's New Year celebrations have been concentrated around Trafalgar Square; the spectacular fireworks on the South Bank are a more recent draw. Both, however, attract daunting numbers of revellers, so young children should stay away.

London International Mime Festival

Various venues (7637 5661/www.mimefest. co.uk). **Date** 10-25 Jan 2009.

This must surely be London's quietest festival. LIMF invites companies from around the UK and abroad to perform circus skills, mask, mime, clown and visual theatre shows for audiences of all ages. A brochure is available by phone or via the website.

Chinese New Year Festival

Around Gerrard Street, Chinatown, W1, Leicester Square, WC2 & Trafalgar Square, WC2 (7851 6686/www.chinatownchinese. co.uk). Leicester Square or Piccadilly Circus tube. **Date** 26 Jan 2009 (to be confirmed). **Map** p317 K7.

Kung hei fat choi! ('congratulations and be prosperous') is the traditional greeting for Chinese New Year. This is the most important of the Chinese festivals, so expect quite a

Lord Mayor's Show, in November. *See p24.*

bunfight around Chinatown. Celebrations for the Year of the Cow begin at 11am with a children's parade going from Leicester Square Gardens to Trafalgar Square, where lion and dragon dance teams perform traditional dances. And there are, of course, firework displays (at lunchtime and 5pm).

National Storytelling Week

Various theatres, museums, bookshops, libraries, arts centres, schools & pubs (Del Reid 8866 4232/www.sfs.org.uk). **Date** 31 Jan-7 Feb 2009.

This annual storytelling week sees venues across the country hosting events for tellers and listeners. It's organised by the Society for Storytelling, an outfit that aims to increase public awareness of the art, practice and value of oral storytelling and the narrative traditions of world cultures and peoples. In 2008 over 1,000 storytelling events and performances were organised; expect more of the same for 2009. Note: stories cater to all ages.

Great Spitalfields Pancake Day Race

Dray Walk, Old Truman Brewery, 91 Brick Lane, E1 6QL (7375 0441/www.alternative arts.co.uk). Aldgate East tube/Liverpool Street tube/rail. **Date** 24 Feb 2009. **Map** p319 S5.

Flipping good fun, this. Kick-off is at 12.30pm, with teams of four tossing pancakes as they run (it's all done for the charity London Air Ambulance). Phone in advance if you want to take part (everyone races together, so it isn't suitable for younger children) and bring your own frying pan (pancakes provided) or just show up if all you're after is seeing silly costumes and pancakes hit the pavement.

SPRING

St Patrick's Day Parade & Festival

Trafalgar Square, Leicester Square & Covent Garden (7983 4100/www.london.gov.uk). **Date** around 17 Mar 2009. **Map** p317 K7.
This fun, colourful and noisy parade departs from Hyde Park Corner at noon and continues to romp through the streets until 6pm. Expect Irish music in Trafalgar Square, a Covent Garden food market, ceilidh dancers in Leicester Square, and lots of other activities for all ages.

National Science & Engineering Week

Various venues (www.the-ba.net).
Date 6-15 Mar 2009.
A week of scientific shenanigans across the capital hosted by the British Association for the Advancement of Science. From hands-on shows for youngsters to in-depth discussions for adults, each event celebrates different aspects of science, engineering and technology. Heaven for science geeks – and not as boring as some might think!

Streatham Kite Day

Streatham Common (Bob Colover 8764 9655/ www.streathamkiteday.org.uk). Streatham rail.
Date Apr 2009.
Central London's splendid parks don't see a lot of kite-flying action, but not to worry, the 12th annual Streatham Kite Day has demonstrations galore and experts on hand with pointers (and stalls selling kites) if you fancy taking to the skies yourself. The teddy bear parachute drops are always popular, so do bring Paddington or Rupert along.

London Marathon

Greenwich Park to the Mall via the Isle of Dogs, Victoria Embankment & St James's Park (7902 0200/www.london-marathon. co.uk). **Date** 26 Apr 2009.
One of the world's biggest metropolitan marathons, the London Marathon started back

in 1981. The 2008 race attracted over 34,000 participants, many in outrageous costumes. Spectators are advised to arrive early; the front runners reach the 13-mile mark near the Tower of London at around 10am. If you think you're fit enough, you must apply by the October before the race. The 2009 entry system is via a form in a free magazine called *Marathon News*, which is available from major sports stores.

Shakespeare's Birthday

Various venues around South Bank & Bankside. **Date** 23 Apr 2009.
The days leading up to and after the Bard's birth date are busy ones at Shakespeare's Globe and Southwark Cathedral, when performances, music, readings and walks mark the great man's contribution to literature.

Canalway Cavalcade

Little Venice, W9 (01923 711114/www. waterways.org.uk). Warwick Avenue tube/ Paddington tube/rail. **Date** 2-4 May 2009.
This three-day Bank Holiday boat bash transforms the pool of Little Venice with an assembly of more than 130 colourful narrowboats, all decked out in bunting and flowers. Events include craft, trade and food stalls; a teddy bears' picnic, Punch and Judy shows, music and boat trips. The beautiful lantern-lit boat procession on Sunday evening is a must-see.

May Fayre & Puppet Festival

St Paul's Church Garden, Bedford Street, WC2E 9ED (7375 0441/www.alternative arts.co.uk). Covent Garden tube. **Date** 10 May 2009. **Map** p317 L7.
Celebrating the first recorded sighting of Mr Punch in England (by Pepys, in 1662), this free event offers puppetry galore from 10.30am to 5.30pm. A grand brass band procession around Covent Garden is followed by a service at 11.30am in St Paul's Church, with Mr Punch in the pulpit. Then there are puppet shows, booths and stalls, as well as workshops for puppet-making and dressing-up. Folk music and maypole dancing, clowns and jugglers are added bonuses.

Kew Summer Festival

Royal Botanic Gardens, Kew, Richmond, Surrey TW9 3AB (8332 5655/www.kew. org.uk). Kew Gardens tube/rail/Kew Bridge rail. **Date** May-Sept 2009.
Each season at Kew Gardens brings its own programme of events and family activities. Phone or check the website for details.

Out & About

Sightseeing

Attractions

With so much to see, the school hols just aren't long enough.

All of London's most attractive bits – the postcard-perfect historic monuments and grand designs – are listed in this chapter. Some are educational, some quirky (but cool), some scary – perhaps too much so for the youngest kids. But unlike the city's grand museums and galleries, these places are more likely to charge for the fun they supply, so it's doubly important to check they're appropriate to your child's age and stage of development. We've marked the recommended age range in green at the end of the listings to help parents out. Don't be beguiled by every 'free under-fives' offer you read in listings; it's generous in the case of the pricey London Eye, but less appealing at the London Dungeon, from whose horrors all children under eight should be steered well clear.

ASTRONOMY

Royal Observatory & Planetarium
Greenwich Park, SE10 9NF (8312 6565/ www.rognmm.ac.uk). Cutty Sark DLR/ Greenwich DLR/rail. **Open** 10am-5pm daily (last entry 4.30pm). *Tours* phone for details. **Admission** free. *Starlife* £6; £4 1-16s, reductions; free under-1s. *Tours* free. **Credit** MC, V. 3+ (7+ for shows)
The Observatory, originally built for Charles II by Wren in 1675 benefitted from a £15m

refurbishment in 2007. The Peter Harrison Planetarium is the impressive result. Neighbouring galleries chart timekeeping since the 14th century. The Observatory's dome houses the largest refracting telescope in the country. In the courtyard the Prime Meridian Line is the star of a billion snaps of tourists with a foot in each hemisphere.

The planetarium shows a 30-minute Starlife show several times a day. It uses a digital laser projector to enact the birth and death of stars; there are more stars in the galaxy than the total number of heartbeats in the history of human existence. Starlife is presented by a Royal Observatory astronomer, who enjoys fielding knotty nipper questions. Shows take place for children (over six) daily (shows for younger kids are at weekends and school holidays).
Buggy access (courtyard only). Café. Nappy-changing facilities. Nearest picnic place: Greenwich Park. Shop.

BIRD'S EYE VIEWS

London Eye
Riverside Building (next to County Hall), Westminster Bridge Road, SE1 7PB 0870 990 8883/www.londoneye.com). Westminster tube/Waterloo tube/rail. **Open** *Oct-May* 10am-8pm daily. *June-Sept* 10am-9pm daily. **Admission** £15.50; £12 reductions (not applicable weekends, or July and Aug); £7.75 5-15s; free under-5s. Fastrack tickets £25. **Credit** AmEx, MC, V. **Map** p317 M8. All ages

---

The best

For thrill-seekers
Thorpe Park (*see p54*).

For gore blimey
London Bridge Experience (*see p53*),
London Dungeon (*see p54*).

For posh frocks
Kensington Palace (*see p37*).

For treasure-hunters
Buckingham Palace (*see p34*),
Ranger's House (*see p47*),
Tower of London (*see p41*).

For views
London Eye (*see p30*),
St Paul's Cathedral (*see p42*).

It's hard to believe that this giant wheel was, at first, intended to spin by the river for only five years. It has proved so popular that no one wants to see it come down, and it's very near the top of every child's must-do list. Some kids, expecting a more white-knuckle affair, express disappointment that it turns so slowly, but it's still pretty exciting. Each ride – one complete revolution – takes half an hour, long enough to have a good look at the Queen's back garden and trace the silvery snaking of the Thames. You can queue for tickets on the day, but if you pre-book online (and take a gamble with the weather) you get a 10% discount. Night flights provide a twinkly experience, and the Eye gets festive with fairy lights at Christmas; other holiday specials include Hallowe'en and Easter. A guide to the landmarks, and photos of you, are on sale (£7.50); visit the website for special Eye and river cruise packages.

Buggy access. Café. Disabled access: toilet. Nappy-changing facilities. Nearest picnic place: Jubilee Gardens. Shop.

Monument

Monument Street, EC3R 8AH (7626 2717/ www.cityoflondon.gov.uk). Monument tube. **Open** 9.30am-5pm daily. **Admission** £2; £1 5-15s; free under-5s. **No credit cards**. **Map** p319 Q7. 6+

From a **London Eye** pod the city looks a treat.

Sightseeing

A glass pavilion and a new square now surround this monument to the Great Fire of London of 1666, all refurbished in 2006. The 61-metre (202ft) column is 61 metres (202ft) west of the exact location of the bakery in Pudding Lane where the fire broke out. It was designed by Sir Christopher Wren, and, for all the skyscrapers being built nearby, still stands out – thanks to the golden urn of flames on top. The internal spiral staircase reopens in December 2008; children who make it up the 311 steps can expect two treats: the view from the top, and a commemorative certificate. At ground level, you can admire the hundreds of pieces of mirrored glass on the new pavilion's roof: these reflect a golden orb at the top of the Monument. *Nearest picnic place: riverside by London Bridge.*

Tower Bridge Exhibition

Tower Bridge, SE1 2UP (7403 3761/www. towerbridge.org.uk). Tower Hill tube/Tower Gateway DLR. **Open** *Apr-Sept* 10am-6.30pm daily (last entry 5.30pm). *Oct-Mar* 9.30am-6pm daily (last entry 5pm). **Admission** £6; £4.50 reductions; £3 5-15s; free under-5s; £14 family (2+2). **Credit** AmEx, MC, V. **Map** p319 R8. 6+

For stupendous views and a lesson in Victorian engineering, step this way – but be warned, they take your picture when you enter, and try to sell you the resultant two snaps for £15. A lift transports you to the walkway foyer, where you watch a short film on the history of Tower Bridge, then pass through both walkways to catch the east and west views. Large aerial photographs pinpoint famous landmarks, and there are photo points where you can slide open the windows to get an unimpeded shot. Ring for details of occasional school-holiday storytelling events. From the walkways it's a short walk to the south tower and the Victorian engine rooms for a more thorough explanation of hydraulics. To find out when the the bridge is next going to open, phone 7940 3984.

Buggy access. Disabled access: lift, toilet. Nappy-changing facilities. Nearest picnic place: Potters Field, Tower of London Gardens. Shop.

LIVING HISTORY

Age Exchange Reminiscence Centre

11 Blackheath Village, SE3 9LA (8318 9105/ www.age-exchange.org.uk). Blackheath rail. **Open** 10am-5pm Mon-Fri; 10am-4pm Sat. **Admission** free. Groups must book in advance; charges vary. **Credit** MC, V. 8+

You're treated to a low-key, cosy, living-history experience here. Run by the charity Age Exchange, it has several different areas: a mock-up of a grocer's shop from about 60 years ago

features drawers of comestibles; an old-fashioned sweetie shop that stocks classics like rosy apples; and a sitting room circa 1940 full of vintage toys, a stove, old-style furnishings and crockery. There's also a small café and theatre space at the back. The Centre's programme of exhibitions is based on older people's memories, and recent events have included recreations of a VE Day street party and a wartime London Docks soundscape. Check the website for dates of future attractions.
Buggy access. Café. Disabled access: toilet. Nearest picnic place: centre gardens. Shop.

Dennis Severs' House

18 Folgate Street, E1 6BX (7247 4013/www. dennissevershouse.co.uk). Liverpool Street tube/rail. **Open** noon-4pm 1st & 3rd Sun of mth; noon-2pm Mon (following 1st & 3rd Sun of mth); Mon evenings (times vary; booking required). **Admission** £8 Sun; £5 noon-2pm Mon; £12 Mon evenings. No under-10s. **Credit** MC, V. **Map** p319 R5. 10+
This restored Huguenot house is the work of Dennis Severs (1948-1999), an American who fell in love with the 18th century. He lived in this restored Huguenot house *sans* bathroom, modern cooking facilities or electricity, and narrated tours in which each room was the scene of a drama, set between 1724 and 1914.

Today, as you make your way around the place, you chance on the everyday activities and belongings of a fictitious family of Huguenot silk-weavers. You may hear their voices; you certainly feel the warmth of their log fires, the scent of their pomanders, the gorgeous sheen of their heavy silk drapes. It's as if the inhabitants deserted these rooms just moments before. The house is still lived in, and no museum can provide an experience quite like it.
Nearest picnic place: Broadgate Circus (Liverpool Street Station), Elder Street Gardens. Shop.

Golden Hinde

Pickfords Wharf, Clink Street, SE1 9DG (0870 011 8700/www.goldenhinde.org). Monument tube/London Bridge tube/rail. **Open** daily; times vary. Phone for details. *Tours* phone for times. **Admission** £6; £4.50 reductions; £4.50 4-13s; free under-4s; £18 family (2+3). **Credit** MC, V. **Map** p319 P8. 5+
Children love this thoroughly seaworthy replica of Sir Francis Drake's 16th-century flagship, the first ship to circumnavigate the globe (in 1577 and 1580). The replica was built in 1973 to mark the admiral-pirate's 400th birthday, after which it sailed to San Francisco. 'Living History' overnighters, in which participants dress in period clothes, eat Tudor food and learn ancient seafaring skills, are a hit with families and kids; these take place on Saturdays and cost £39.95 per person (minimum age is six), costumes and entertainment provided; book ahead and bring a sleeping bag. The regular daytime Pirate Fun Days provide more dressing-up fun. During the school holidays there are storytelling sessions, craft activities and special workshops every weekend; details are on the website. You can also have a party here; ring or check online.
Nearest picnic place: Southwark Cathedral Gardens, riverside benches. Shop.

Houses of Parliament

Parliament Square, SW1A 0AA (Commons info 7219 3000/Lords info 7219 3107/tours 7219 4206/www.parliament.uk). Westminster tube. **Open** (when in session) *House of Commons Visitors' Gallery* 2.30-10.30pm Mon, Tue; 11.30am-7.30pm Wed; 10.30am-6.30pm Thur; 9.30am-3pm Fri. Closed bank hols. *House of Lords Visitors' Gallery* 2.30-10pm Mon, Tue; 3-10pm Wed; 11am-7.30pm Thur; 10am until close of business Fri. Check website for debate times. *Tours* summer recess only; phone for details for other times. **Admission** *Visitors' Gallery* free. *Tours* £12; £8 reductions; £5 5-15s; free under-5s; £30 family (2+2). **Credit** MC, V. **Map** p317 L9. 10+

Sightseeing

Buckingham Palace. *See p34.*

When Henry VIII relocated to Whitehall in 1532, his Palace of Westminster became Parliament's permanent home. These days, the only parts of the original palace still standing are Westminster Hall and the Jewel Tower; the rest was destroyed by fire in 1834. The building we see today was rebuilt by Charles Barry and Augustus Pugin. Children are usually satisfied by the mere proximity of the big old bell known as Big Ben, but only UK residents over 11 can climb the Clock Tower to take a closer look; tickets must be booked through your MP. *Buggy access. Disabled access: lift, toilet. Nappy-changing facilities. Nearest picnic place: Victoria Tower Gardens. Shop.*

Linley Sambourne House

18 Stafford Terrace, W8 7BH (Mon-Fri 7602 3316/Sat, Sun 7938 1295/www.rbkc. gov.uk/linleysambournehouse). High Street Kensington tube. Tours (groups only; maximum 12 people. Pre-booking essential) 11.15am, 1pm, 2.15pm, 3.30pm Sat, Sun; also by appointment. **Admission** £6; £4 reductions; £1 under-18s. **Credit** MC, V. **Map** p314 A9. 5+
Edward Linley Sambourne was a Victorian cartoonist, famous for his work in *Punch*. His house, which has almost all its original fittings and furniture, can be visited only on one of the terrific (if eccentric) tours. These are guided by costumed actors; especially popular with children is gossipy housekeeper Mrs Reffle, who shines a cheeky light into Victorian family life and tells jokes along the way. There's a visitors' centre where children can take part in craftwork sessions relating to objects in the house. *Shop.*

Shakespeare's Globe

21 New Globe Walk, Bankside, SE1 9DT (7401 9919/tours 7902 1500/www. shakespeares-globe.org). Mansion House tube/London Bridge tube/rail. **Open** *Box office theatre bookings* Apr-Oct 2008 10am-6pm daily. *Tours* 9am-5pm daily. May-Sept afternoon tours only visit the Rose Theatre, not the Globe. **Tickets** £5-£33. *Tours* £9; £7.50 reductions; £6.50 5-15s; free under-5s; £20 family (2+3). **Credit** AmEx, MC, V. **Map** p318 P7. 8+
This reconstruction of the Bard's own theatre, built less than 100 metres from where the original stood, was the brainchild of actor Sam Wanamaker (who, sadly, died before it was finished). Tours of the 'wooden O' take place all year, and include the UnderGlobe exhibition on the reconstruction, Elizabethan theatres and

Shakespeare's London; but the annual theatre season – this is an unroofed venue, after all – runs from late April to early October. Historically authentic performances of Shakespeare's plays make the bulk of the programme, but new theatre also gets a showing. Events for students of all ages include half-term activities for children, with costume dressings and sword-fighting displays. There's also fun for all around the time of Shakespeare's birthday (23 April). In summer, drama sessions for eight- to 11-year-olds accompany the theatre season; see the website or ring 7902 1433 for details. The remains of the Rose Theatre (www.rosetheatre.org.uk), where many of Shakespeare's works were staged, are around the corner in the basement of an office block. *Café. Disabled access: lift, toilet. Nappy-changing facilities. Nearest picnic place: South Bank benches. Restaurant. Shop.*

PALACES & STRONGHOLDS

Buckingham Palace & Royal Mews

SW1A 1AA (7766 7300/www.royal collection.org.uk). Green Park or St James's Park tube/Victoria tube/rail. **Open** *State Rooms* 1 August-28 Sept 2008 9.45am-3.45pm daily. *Royal Mews* Mar-Oct 11am-3.15pm Mon-Thur, Sat, Sun (last entry 4.15pm when palace is open); 29 July-29 Sept 10am-5pm daily (last entry 4.15pm). *Queen's Gallery* 10am-4.30pm (closes 5.30pm) daily. Closed during Ascot & state occasions. **Admission** *State Rooms* £15.50; £8.75 5-17s; £14 reductions; free under-5s; £39.75 family (2+3). *Royal Mews* £7.50; £4.80 5-17s; £6.75 reductions; free under-5s; £19.80 family (2+3). *Queen's Gallery* £8.50; £4.25 5-17s; £7.50 reductions; free under-5s; £21.50 family (2+3). *Joint ticket* (Royal Mews and Queen's Gallery) £14.50; £8 5-17s; £12.50 reductions; £37 family (2+3). **Credit** AmEx, MC, V. **Map** p316 H9. All ages (Royal Mews). 5+ (Queen's Gallery).
This, the world's most famous palace, is the seat of the British monarchy and one of the showpieces of the London tourism industry, drawing millions of visitors a year. Buckingham Palace has belonged to the royal family since 1762, but it became the official royal residence in 1837. It used to be smaller, but Queen Victoria moved the Marble Arch to the end of Park Lane to make way for extensions. The royal stables

and the ostentatious State Apartments, used for banquets and investitures, are opened up in January, March, April and during the summer (check the website for dates), when the Queen is off on her hols. The Queen's Gallery, open all year round, has paintings by Dürer, Rembrandt, Canaletto, Rubens and Van Dyck, as well as some exquisite Fabergé eggs.

There's a nature trail for children in the gardens and a family activity room, open throughout August. At the Royal Mews, children can watch horses being groomed, fed and exercised, and examine the royal Rolls-Royces and the Gold State Coach, last used for the 2002 Golden Jubilee.

Buggy access. Disabled access: lift, toilet (Buckingham Palace). Nappy-changing facilities (Buckingham Palace). Nearest picnic place: Green Park. Shop.

Hampton Court Palace

East Molesey, Surrey KT8 9AU (0870 751 5175/www.hrp.org.uk). Hampton Court rail/riverboat from Westminster or Richmond to Hampton Court Pier (Apr-Oct). **Open** *Palace* Mar-Oct 10am-6pm daily. Nov-Feb 10am-4.30pm daily. Last entry 1hr before closing. *Park* dawn-dusk daily. **Admission** *Palace, courtyard, cloister & maze* £13.30; £11.30 reductions; £6.65 5-15s; free under-5s; £37 family (2+3). *Gardens only* £4.60; £4 reductions; free under-16s. *Maze only* £3.50; £2.50 5-15s; free under-5s; £10 family. **Credit** AmEx, MC, V. 6+

It may be a half-hour train ride from central London, but this spectacular palace is worth the trek. The 1514 monument is a reminder of the majesty of Henry VIII, and a vital site in English history: Elizabeth I was imprisoned in its tower by her elder sister Mary; Shakespeare performed here. After the Civil War, Cromwell made his home here (against the puritanical grain). There's much to see. The imposing buildings sprawl over six acres, with costumed guides adding a lively dimension to the state apartments, courtyards and cloisters. Ghosts and gardens are the other bewitching attractions: the ghost of Catherine Howard, fifth wife of King Henry VIII, who had her executed for adultery at the Tower of London, is said to shriek around in the Haunted Gallery; and the gardens are astounding. The famous maze is the oldest in the country, having been planted between 1689 and 1694 – but in which, as it happens, it's virtually impossible to get lost.

Tower of London. *See p41.*

Themed activities during the school holidays include outdoor fun that delighted Henry VIII, such as jousting, archery, hunting, shooting and jesters. On some bank holidays and weekends, Tudor cookery demonstrations take place in the kitchens, where children love the bubbling cauldrons and game bird carcasses. For about six weeks from the beginning of December to mid January (call or check the website for dates), the west front of the palace is iced over for a scenic skate rink.
Buggy access. Café. Disabled access: lift, toilets. Nappy-changing facilities. Nearest picnic place: palace gardens/picnic area. Restaurant. Shops.

Fulham Palace & Museum

Bishop's Avenue, off Fulham Palace Road, SW6 6EA (7736 3233/www.fulhampalace .org). Hammersmith or Putney Bridge tube/220, 414, 430 bus. **Open** times vary; phone to check. *Tours* phone for details. **Admission** *Museum* free; under-16s must be accompanied by an adult. *Tours* £5; free under-16s. **No credit cards.** 3+
The recent restoration of Fulham Palace revealed traces of human habitation going back to the Iron Age, but it was as the official residence of the Bishops of London (from 704 until 1973) that the site is best known. The main house – more manor than palace – is Tudor (try out the echo in the courtyard), with significant Georgian and Victorian additions. Refurbishment has left the East Quadrangle looking beautiful, and the café is a particularly pleasant place to sit in. The museum has plenty of new interactive features, lots more room to display treasures dug up in the grounds, and a brand new programme of theatre, exhibitions and activities for families: music workshops for nippers between two and five, for example, or craft sessions where the over-fives turn out Roman armour and jewellery. All must be pre-booked; most cost £5-£10 a head. Leave time to admire the lovely grounds.
Buggy access. Café. Disabled access: toilet (in palace). Nearest picnic place: grounds. Shop.

Kensington Palace

Kensington Gardens, W8 4PX (0870 751 5170/www.hrp.org.uk). Bayswater or High Street Kensington tube/9, 10, 49, 52, 70 bus. **Open** *Mar-Oct* 10am-6pm daily. *Nov-Feb* 10am-5pm daily. Last entry 1hr before closing.

Sightseeing

Great Days Out

Great Days Out
Westminster

There's plenty to keep you occupied around Westminster, an area of London that has been the centre of power for nearly 1,000 years. Back in the 11th century Edward the Confessor built his church, West Minster, on marshy Thorney Island, to the west of the established city, and so the foundations of power were laid. The minster stood on the site now occupied by **Westminster Abbey** (*see p43*), where the remains of Edward are entombed, no-one knows where.

The Abbey competes with the neo-Gothic **Palace of Westminster** (*see p33*) for prominence on Parliament Square, the central garden of which was laid out in 1868. There are statues of great British prime ministers Benjamin Disraeli and Winston Churchill, and of Nelson Mandela. Another permanent fixture, it would seem, is Brian Haw, the peace protester who has been campaigning for freedom of speech and against the Iraq War, since 2001.

Clockwatching

The only surviving fragments of the original medieval Palace of Westminster are the Jewel Tower, which has a permanent exhibition dedicated to the development of Parliament, and Westminster Hall, where the Queen Mother's body lay in state before her funeral in 2002. The rest of the palace was destroyed by fire in 1834. The grand old building we see today was rebuilt by Charles Barry and Augustus Pugin.

UK residents can visit Parliament to watch laws being made, attend debates, committees or judicial hearings, use the Archives, tour the estate and climb the Clock Tower, which is the world's largest four-faced, chiming clock. Public committee sessions – meetings are held from Monday to Thursday most weeks when Parliament is sitting – are open to everyone. Visitors queue on the day, as places cannot be booked in advance.

38 Time Out London for Children

Tickets from your MP or a peer are necessary to secure entrance to Question Time and Prime Minister's Question Time in the House of Commons.

Children are usually satisfied by the mere proximity of the big old bell known as Big Ben (the tower is St Stephen's). The bell weighs 13.5 tonnes and is named after Sir Benjamin Hall, the man who was Commissioner of Works when it was installed in 1859. It is the clock's 150th anniversary in 2009. Everyone aged 11 and over can climb the Clock Tower to have a closer look at Big Ben, but the free hour-long tour is only available for UK residents, who need to put in a request to their local MP.

Town square

Admiral Nelson stands proud atop a tall column at the other end of Whitehall in London's centrepiece, **Trafalgar Square** (www.london.gov.uk/trafalgarsquare), which commemorates the Battle of Trafalgar (1805), and Nelson's naval victory during the Napoleonic Wars. The Square takes its name from Cape Trafalgar, a headland in Cadiz Province in the south-west of Spain, where the battle took place. The four great lions at the column's base beg to be clambered over and captured on film. The square has long been a site for political demonstrations

As well as Nelson's Column, the Square is renowned for its four plinths – three of them are taken up with King George IV (north-east), and Henry Havelock (south-east) and Sir Charles James Napier (south-west) – the latter two British generals associated with India. But take a look at the fourth plinth in the north-west corner of the square – this is the one that hosts a temporary work. The latest, rather unusual sculpture is Thomas Schütte's *Model for a Hotel 2007*. The modernist sculpture is a fusion

LUNCH BOX

Also in the area: Pizza Express.
Bank Westminster *45 Buckingham Gate, SW1E 6BS (7379 9797/www. bankrestaurants.com).* Upmarket Modern European with kids' menu.
Café in the Crypt *St Martin-in-the-Fields, Duncannon Street, WC2N 4JJ (7839 4342/www.smitf.org).* Nourishing grub in Trafalgar Square.
Inn The Park *St James's Park, SW1A 2BJ (7451 9999/www.innthepark. com).* Smart park café with kids' menu. *See p228.*
Laughing Halibut *38 Strutton Ground, SW1P 2HR (7799 2844).* No-nonsense fish and chips.
Texas Embassy Cantina *1 Cockspur Street, SW1Y 5DL (7925 0077/www. texasembassy.com).* Tex-Mex cantina.

of jewel-coloured sheets of glass; it was previously known as *Hotel for Birds 2007*, but once Schütte realised what a controversial subject the pigeons were, (efforts to rid the square of the birds are ongoing) he claimed he didn't want to get into the 'pigeon war' and changed its name.

Class art

Head into the **National Gallery** (*see p62*) at the top of Trafalgar Square to see one of the greatest art collections in the world. The Gallery runs a host of events such as storytelling sessions (aimed at under-fives), workshops (material provided) and exhibition-related activities. The education centre employs professional sculptors, printmakers and other artists who teach children the different techniques based on the paintings in the galleries. Lunch choices here include the Espresso Bar (cakes and coffees) or the National Dining Rooms (*see p229*) on the first floor.

More art can be absorbed at the **National Portrait Gallery** (*see p62*), whose Young People's Programme encourages 14- to 21-year-olds to get involved. The Portrait Restaurant here affords wonderful views – you practically eyeball Nelson.

Great Days Out

WWT

LONDON Wetland CENTRE

DISCOVER THE WILDER SIDE OF LONDON

Explore the London Wetland Centre and discover the beautiful wildlife that lives in this 100 acre wetland haven. Visit the Bird Airport observatory, discover rare and endangered birds in World Wetlands or just relax in the Water's Edge café. Let your children run wild in the Explore adventure area and Discovery Centre.

Open 7 days a week from 9.30am to 5pm
T: 020 8409 4400   Visit wwt.org.uk/london

WWT London Wetland Centre, Queen Elizabeth's Walk, Barnes, SW13 9WT
Alight at Barnes Station or take the no. 283 Duck Bus from Hammersmith Tube

Admission (incl audio guide) £12.30; £10.75 reductions; £6.15 5-15s; free under-5s; £34 family (2+3). **Credit** MC, V. **Map** p310 B8. 7+

William III and his wife Mary came to live in this Jacobean mansion in 1689, when Kensington was still a country village. They moved from Whitehall Palace to escape the smoggy air, which played havoc with William's asthma, having commissioned Sir Christopher Wren to turn the existing house into a palace. Since then, many royals have called it home: Queen Victoria, born and baptised here, liked living in Kensington so much that she gave the borough its 'Royal' status; the Duke and Duchess of Kent have apartments here. The palace is open for tours of the State Apartments (which you enter via Wren's lofty King's Staircase), the King's Gallery and the Queen's Apartments, where William and Mary lived quite simply. The most popular part is the Royal Ceremonial Dress Collection; 'Diana, Fashion and Style', a special exhibition of outfits worn by Diana, Princess of Wales, the most famous resident, runs until January 2009. 'The Last Debutantes', which runs until June 2009, marks the 50th anniversary of the last ever formal presentation of well bred young ladies at court.
Buggy access. Disabled access: toilet. Nappy-changing facilities. Nearest picnic place: grounds. Restaurant. Shop.

Tower of London

Tower Hill, EC3N 4AB (information 0870 756 6060/bookings 0870 756 7070/www.hrp.org.uk). Tower Hill tube/Tower Gateway DLR/Fenchurch Street rail. **Open** 10am-6pm Mon, Sun; 9am-6pm Tue-Sat (last entry 5pm). *Tours* Beefeater tours (outside only, weather permitting) every 30mins until 3.30pm. **Admission** £16.50; £9.50 5-15s; £14 reductions; free under-5s; £46 family (2+3). Audio guide £3. *Tours* free. **Credit** AmEx, MC, V. **Map** p319 R7. 5+

This centuries-old fortress, palace, prison and execution ground (two of Henry VIII's wives got the chop here) is one of Britain's finest historic towers to explore, you can easily spend a whole day here. The crown jewels are the Tower's biggest draw, and the permanent exhibition, Crowns and Diamonds, is a must for lovers of sparkle. It includes a model of the uncut, fist-sized Cullinan I, the world's largest diamond, and a display showing how it was cut into nine stunning diamonds – the two largest are now part of the crown jewels. You can't miss the 2m-wide Grand Punch Bowl – it gives a whole new meaning to the phrase family silver.

The Medieval Palace, where kings and queens stayed until the reign of Elizabeth I, has been recently restored, and uses smells and sound effects to whisk you back in time. Interactive displays spill the beans about the ordeals of life as a prisoner, and an exhibition about the palace, which includes stories about 13th-century royal life, runs until January 2009. Outside, on Tower Green, stands the place where felons of the stamp of Anne Boleyn and Lady Jane Grey were beheaded; a glass pillow sculpted by artist Brian Catling marks the spot. Battle fans love the armoury in the White Tower (there's usually a half-term event centred on the collection).

The beautiful vaulted chamber of the Bowyer Tower has been open to visitors since Easter 2007. Legend has it the Duke of Clarence met a grisly fate here in 1478, drowning in a barrel of malmsey. The most entertaining way to hear such stories is to join one of the highly entertaining free tours let by a Yeoman Warder (Beefeater). The Warders, photogenic in their black and red finery, are genial hosts and a mine of information. Check the website for details of family trails and daily special events.
Buggy access (Jewel House). Café. Nappy-changing facilities. Nearest picnic place: riverside benches, Trinity Square Memorial Gardens. Shops.

PLACES OF WORSHIP

London Central Mosque

146 Park Road, NW8 7RG (7724 3363/www.iccuk.org). Baker Street tube/13, 82, 133 bus. **Open** 9.30am-6pm daily. **Admission** free. All ages

Offices around a large courtyard accommodate the Islamic Cultural Centre, bookshop and information booth. Visitors must remove their shoes; women should wear a headscarf.
Buggy access. Café. Disabled access: ramp, toilet. Nappy-changing facilities. Nearest picnic place: Regent's Park. Shop.

Southwark Cathedral

London Bridge, SE1 9DA (7367 6700/tours 7367 6734/www.dswark.org/cathedral). London Bridge tube/rail. **Open** from 8am daily (closing times vary). *Restaurant* 8.30am-6pm Mon-Fri; 10am-6pm Sat, Sun. Closed 25 Dec, Good Friday, Easter Sunday. *Services* 8am, 8.15am, 12.30pm, 12.45pm, 5.30pm Mon-Fri; 9am, 9.15am, 4pm Sat; 8.45am, 9am, 11am, 3pm, 6.30pm Sun. **Admission** *Audio tour* £2.50; £2 reductions; £1.25 under-16s, students. Donations appreciated. **Credit** MC, V. **Map** p319 P8. 5+

The oldest bits of this building, one of the few places south of the river that Dickens had a good word for, were built more than eight centuries ago. The part dating from those medieval days is the retro-choir and lady chapel and the north transept. The church fell into disrepair after the Reformation (one part was used as a bakery, another as a pigsty), but in 1905 it became a cathedral; it now has an Education Centre, a shop and a refectory. Memorials include one to the 51 people who drowned in the 1989 *Marchioness* accident, as well as others to Shakespeare (whose brother Edmund is buried here), John Gower and John Harvard. The windows show images of Chaucer, who set off on pilgrimage to Canterbury from a pub in Borough High Street, and John Bunyan, who preached locally. In the churchyard there's a flattish, ribbed stone monument to Mahomet Weyomon, a Mohegan chief buried in the churchyard in 1735. He died of disease after travelling here to state his case in the Mohegan Land Dispute.

The cathedral choir is one of the UK's best. Hear them sing evensong on Mondays and Thursdays (girls) and Tuesdays, Fridays and Sundays (boys). An all-male choir usually sings morning Eucharist, except on high days and holidays. Joining the choir gives kids a fantastic musical education; phone for audition dates. *Buggy access. Disabled access: lift, ramp, toilet. Nappy-changing facilities. Nearest picnic place: gardens. Restaurant. Shop.*

St Paul's Cathedral

Ludgate Hill, EC4M 8AD (7236 4128/ www.stpauls.co.uk). St Paul's tube. **Open** 8.30am-4pm Mon-Sat. *Galleries, crypt & ambulatory* 9.30am-3.45pm Mon-Sat. Closed for special services, sometimes at short notice. *Tours* 11am, 11.30am, 1.30pm, 2pm Mon-Sat. **Admission** *Cathedral, crypt & gallery* £10; £3.50 7-16s; £8.50-£9 reductions; free under-7s; £23.50 family (2+2). *Tours* £3; £1 7-16s; £2.50 reductions; free under-7s. Audio guide £4; £3.50 reductions. **Credit** MC, V. **Map** p318 O6. 5+

The world-famous cathedral celebrates the 300th anniversary of its topping out in 2008, and the ongoing £40 million restoration project has scrubbed the main façade back to its 1708 cleanliness; other commemorative efforts include a complete rebuild of the organ, and the creation of a new set of ecclesiastical robes by Royal College of Art designer Marie Brisou. The building is one of London's most recognisable monuments, but it very nearly didn't happen: were it not for Sir Christopher Wren's dogged persistence, the authorities would have vetoed his project as too ambitious and expensive.

The audio guide has quirky facts about everything from the organ pipes (some big enough to crawl through) to Nelson's corpse (they had a hell of a time getting it back to England for the funeral) to enliven the tour. During Christmas and Easter holidays, there are trails that are rewarded at the end with a small

Children are bowled over by **St Paul's Cathedral**. *See p42.*

prize; parents who need help for a self-guided tour can download the activity sheets for schools. The most fun of all is the Whispering Gallery, whose acoustics simply have to be heard to be believed. From there, it's a few more steps up to the Stone Gallery for an amazing 360-degree view of London. If you think you're likely to have the energy to ascend still further to the Golden Gallery, go early, or you may find yourself jostled by boisterous teens on the cramped balcony.

Down in the airy crypt are tombs of historical figures such as Nelson, Wellington and Wren; Lawrence of Arabia and Florence Nightingale are honoured with memorials. At the back is the shop and Crypt Café. And if you want to experience the true spirit of St Paul's, come for evensong, held every day at 5pm.
Buggy access. Café. Disabled access: lift, ramp, toilet. Nappy-changing facilities. Nearest picnic space: garden. Restaurant. Shops.

Shri Swaminarayan Mandir Temple

105-119 Brentfield Road, NW10 8LD (8965 2651/www.swaminarayan.org). Wembley Park tube, then BR2 bus/Neasden tube, then 15min walk. **Open** 9am-6.30pm daily. **Admission** free. Exhibition £2; £1.50 6-15s; free under-6s. **Credit** AmEx, MC, V. 5+
Built in 1995, this beautiful Hindu temple in Neasden is an extraordinary structure. Much of its stone was sent to India to be intricately carved by master sculptors, then brought back to London: this cost over £10 million. The temple has a permanent exhibition (with video) called 'Understanding Hinduism', which is especially useful for children in Years 6 and 7 studying world religion.
Buggy access. Café. Disabled access: lift, toilet. Nappy-changing facilities. Shop.

Westminster Abbey

20 Dean's Yard, SW1P 3PA (7222 5152/tours 7654 4900/www.westminster-abbey.org). St James's Park or Westminster tube/11, 12, 24, 88, 159, 211 bus. **Open** *Nave & Royal Chapels* 9.30am-3.45pm Mon, Tue, Thur, Fri; 9.30am-6pm Wed; 9.30am-1.45pm Sat. *Abbey Museum & Chapter House* 10.30am-4pm daily. *Cloisters* 8am-6pm daily. *College Garden* Apr-Sept 10am-6pm Tue-Thur. Oct-Mar 10am-4pm Tue-Thur (last entry 1hr before closing). *Tours* phone for details. **Admission** £10; £7 11-15s, reductions; free under-11s with adult; £24 family (2+2). *Chapter House* free. *Abbey Museum* free (audio guide £4). *Tours* £5. **Credit** AmEx, MC, V. **Map** p317 K9. 5+

Edward the Confessor's church was completed in perfect time for his funeral: it was consecrated eight days before he died. His body is entombed in the abbey, though no one knows exactly where: it was removed from its elaborate shrine and reburied in an unmarked spot during the Reformation. With just two exceptions, every coronation since 1066 has taken place in Westminster Abbey, and many royal bodies are interred here, including Elizabeth I and Mary Queen of Scots. Poets' Corner is the final resting place of Geoffrey Chaucer; you can also see the graves of Dickens, Dryden, Johnson, Browning and Tennyson. Statues of several 20th-century martyrs (including Martin Luther King) occupy 15th-century niches above the west door.

You can escape the crowds in the 900-year-old College Garden, one of the oldest cultivated gardens in Britain. The Abbey Museum (Broad Sanctuary; free if you have a ticket to the Abbey, £1 otherwise) is in the vaulted area under the former monks' dormitory, in one of the oldest parts of the Abbey. Here you'll find a collection of effigies and waxworks of British monarchs, such as Edward II and Henry VII, wearing the robes they donned in life; the Queen's Coronation

Sightseeing

Top five Tot attractions

Places to take the under-fives, who have no say in the matter.

Fulham Palace & Museum
Where there's a lovely garden to play in after the museum. *See p37.*

Legoland
Where gentle rides and brick-built magic make a grand day out. *See p53.*

London Eye
Where they're a captive audience, and they ride free anyway. *See p30.*

Syon House
Where there's indoor play at Snakes & Ladders and real snakes to discover in a Tropical Forest. *See p50.*

Tower of London
Where the Beefeaters are jolly, the venues are varied and hands-on games keep them amused. *See p41.*

robes are also on show. The Choir School is the only school in Britain exclusively for the education of boy choristers from eight to 13; voice trials are held twice a year. Its Christmas services are magnificent. Next door is St Margaret's Church (free to visit), where the weddings of Samuel Pepys and Winston Churchill (in 1655 and 1908 respectively) took place; Sir Walter Raleigh is buried here. *Buggy access. Café. Disabled access: toilet. Nearest picnic place: college gardens (10am-6pm Tue-Thur), St James's Park. Shop.*

SCIENCE

Centre of the Cell
64 Turner Street, E1 2AB (7882 2562/ www.centreofthecell.org). Whitechapel tube. **Open** *Sessions* 10-11.30am, noon-1.30pm, 2-3.30pm, 4-5.30pm, 6.30-8pm daily. Session times may vary; phone to check. **Admission** free. 9+
This multimedia jamboree in the heart of an active, cutting-edge medical research centre is set to open in autumn 2008. A glass-walled walkway takes visitors over the labs and their white-coated occupants to a large 'pod' (designed to take 40 people), which is where the fun takes place. A film introduces children to the amazing work going on around them, then a huge silver tube opens up to reveal more audio-visual magic and interactive jollies illustrating different aspects of biomedical science. One game compares the size of a cell to a five-pence piece (a quarter of the size of one of the little dots around the coin edge), another charts the growth of an embryo. Other features show how to repair a damaged spinal cord, or grow real skin for grafts; there are even (oo-er!) real body organs. Even better, the pod is intended to be regularly updated in line with the discoveries of the boffins in the labs.
The whole experience lasts around 90 minutes, but what with the cosy space, the setting and the theatricality of the presentation, young 'uns will be entertained throughout, and hardly aware that they're learning things. *Buggy access. Disabled access: lift; toilet. Café. Nearest picnic place: Whitechapel hospital grounds. Shop.*

Eltham Palace
Court Yard, SE9 5QE (8294 2548/www. elthampalace.org.uk). Eltham rail. **Open** *Apr-Oct* 10am-5pm Mon-Wed, Sun. *Nov, Dec, Feb, Mar* 11am-4pm Mon-Wed, Sun. Closed week before Christmas-31 Jan. **Admission**

House & grounds (incl audio tour) £8.20; £6.60 reductions; £4.10 5-15s; £20.50 family (2+3); free under-5s. *Gardens only* £5.10; £4.10 reductions; £2.60 5-15s; free under-5s. **Credit** MC, V. 5+
The palace was acquired by Edward II in 1305; it was a royal home until Henry VIII's heyday, then fell out of favour. Its Great Hall, the largest surviving medieval hall outside the Palace of Westminster, was used as a barn for many years, and it was only in 1931 that the wealthy Stephen Courtauld, patron of the arts, commissioned a new house to stand beside the relics of the old palace. The Great Hall, with its stained glass and hammer beam roof, was used for glamorous society parties, concerts and banquets; as for the house, all polished veneer and chunky marble, it was kitted out with such mod cons as hidden lighting, underfloor heating and a room-to-room vacuuming system. Even the Courtaulds' pet ring-tailed lemur, Mah-Jongg, had specially designed quarters. The grounds are beautifully restored – check the website for details of concerts, costumed events, falconry and children's trails. The tearoom and shop have a distinctly 1930s flavour. *Café. Disabled access: lift. Shop.*

Top five
Teen attractions

They might not approve of our choices.

Dennis Severs House
Where there's no phone, no screens and no bathroom to barricade yourself into for hours. *See p33.*

Madame Tussaud's
Where they can get their mates to snap them planting a smacker on Johnny Depp, Kate Moss et al. *See p54.*

Shakespeare's Globe
Where GCSE English Shakespeare papers might seem relevant. *See p34.*

Thorpe Park
Where a good scream will help them lose their inhibitions. *See p54.*

Trocadero
Where they know their parents will never want to follow them. *See p54.*

STATELY HOMES

Chiswick House

Burlington Lane, W4 2RP (8995 0508/ www.chgt.org.uk). Turnham Green tube, then E3 bus/Hammersmith tube, then 190 bus/ Chiswick rail. **Open** *Easter-Oct* 10am-5pm Mon-Wed, Sun. Last entry 30mins before closing. Closed Nov-Mar. *Tours* by arrangement; phone for details. **Admission** (EH) incl audio guide £4.20; £3.40 reductions; £2.10 5-16s; free under-5s; £10.50 family (2+3). **Credit** MC, V. 5+

Walk through the gardens of this lovely Palladian villa, and you feel as if you've stepped into a classical landscape painting: there are obelisks among the trees, an exquisitely domed temple, a lake and a cascading waterfall. Families come here on warm summer days for picnics, and you can take a leisurely jaunt along the river, which is just a stone's throw away. A multi-million-pound restoration of the grounds began in the spring of 2008; for news of it, see the website. English Heritage organises a variety of activity days and historical re-enactments here; check www.english-heritage. org.uk for details.

Buggy access. Disabled access: stairlift, toilet. Nearest picnic place: Chiswick Park. Shop.

Fenton House

3 Hampstead Grove, NW3 6RT (7435 3471/ information 01494 755563/box office 01494 755572/www.nationaltrust.org.uk). Hampstead tube/Hampstead Heath rail. **Open** *Mar* 2-5pm Sat, Sun. *Apr-Oct* 2-5pm Wed-Fri; 11am-4.30pm Sat, Sun, bank hols. *Tours* phone for times. **Admission** (NT) £5.20; £2.70 5-15s; free under-5s; £13 family (2+2). **No credit cards.** 5+

This late 17th-century house has a beautiful garden, and houses the impressive Benton Fletcher collection of early keyboard instruments, as well as Peter Barkworth's 19th- and early 20th-century English paintings. Children enjoy the orchard, carefully tended vegetable garden and lawns, and are fascinated by the harpsichords, clavichords, virginals and spinets indoors; the Benton Fletcher bequest was made on condition that professional musicians be allowed to play them, so phone for details of lunchtime and evening concerts in the summer. The house has a porcelain collection that includes a 'curious grotesque teapot' and several poodles; Apple Day is celebrated in the orchard in October.

Buggy access. Disabled access: ramp. Nappy-changing facilities.

19 Princelet Street

19 Princelet Street, E1 6QH (7247 5352/ www.19princeletstreet.org.uk). Aldgate East tube/Liverpool Street tube/rail. **Open** check website or phone for occasional open days. *Tours* groups by appointment. **Admission** free; donations appreciated. **Map** p319 S5. 3+

No.19 was home to Huguenot silk weavers (you can still see a big bobbin hanging above the door), then to Irish dockers. In 1869 the house was a synagogue, and, in the 20th century, it hosted English lessons for Bangladeshi women. Now the Grade II-listed building makes a highly unusual museum. First, it's the only one in Europe dedicated to immigration and cultural diversity; and second, the opening hours are infrequent, to say the least (just a few days in 2008, including every day in Refugee Week, 15-22 June), to preserve the worryingly fragile building until trustees raise the £3 million needed to mend it. Still, it's worth making an effort to join in on one of its open days, as they give you a rare opportunity to see what is a truly fascinating building.

Buggy access. Nearest picnic place: Christ Church grounds.

Ham House

Ham Street, Ham, Richmond, Surrey TW10 7RS (8940 1950/www.nationaltrust.org.uk). Richmond tube/rail, then 371 bus. **Open** *House* mid Mar-Oct noon-4pm Mon-Wed, Sat, Sun. *Gardens* 11am-6pm or dusk Mon-Wed, Sat, Sun. Closed 1 Jan, 25, 26 Dec. *Tours* Wed (pre-booking essential); phone for details. **Admission** (NT) *House & gardens* £9; £5 5-15s; free under-5s; £23 family (2+2). *Gardens only* £3.30; £2 5-15s; free under-5s; £8 family (2+2). **Credit** AmEx, MC, V. 5+ (house). All ages (gardens)

Built in 1610 for one of James I's courtiers, this riverside mansion was lavishly restored, and its interiors boast exemplary original furniture, paintings and textiles; television drama *Elizabeth* was filmed here. Of greatest interest to children, though, is Ham House's reputation as one of the most haunted buildings in Britain: ghostly visitors include William's daughter, the Duchess of Lauderdale, and her pet dog. Regular family events include entertaining Ghost Tours (suitable for over-fives; a torch-lit adult version is also available).

The landscaped grounds include the Cherry Garden with its central statue of Bacchus, the South Garden, and the maze-like Wilderness, as well as the oldest thorn bush and orangery in the country. Open-air theatre takes place in the

Sightseeing

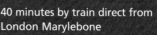

garden in the summer, and there are egg trails for Easter, art and craft days for the August bank holiday weekend, more spooky tours for Hallowe'en, and all manner of carols, feasts and craft events for Christmas. A ferry crosses the river to Marble Hill House (*see below*).
Café. Disabled access: lift, toilet. Nappy-changing facilities. Shop.

Marble Hill House

Richmond Road, Middx TW1 2NL (8892 5115/www.english-heritage.org.uk). Richmond tube/rail/33, 90, 290, H22, R70 bus. **Open** Apr-Oct 10am-2pm Sat; 10am-5pm Sun. **Closed** Nov-Mar. **Admission** (EH) £4.20; £3.40 reductions; £2.10 5-15s; free under-5s; £10.50 family (2+2). Price includes tour.
Credit MC, V. 5+
This stunning riverside villa was built in the 1720s for Henrietta Howard, mistress of King George II when he was Prince of Wales. The property is packed to the brim with Georgian objects and paintings, but the star of the decorative show is the Honduran mahogany staircase, whose construction nearly sparked a war with Spain. Marble Hill House hosts events throughout the year, including Easter trails and open-air concerts; guided tours can be taken of the house and its surrounding parkland, and there's a ferry to Ham House across the river. In 2008, a special trail commemorating the 500th anniversary of the birth of influential Renaissance architect Andrea Palladio explains the property's Palladian features and takes in the beautiful first-floor gallery, recently been returned to its original colour scheme.
Café. Nearest picnic place: Marble Hill Park. Shop.

Osterley House

Osterley Park, off Jersey Road, Isleworth, Middx TW7 4RB (8232 5050/www.national trust.org.uk). Osterley tube. **Open** 12 Mar-2 Nov 2008 *House* 1-4.30pm Wed-Sun, bank hol Mon. Gardens 11am-5pm Wed-Sun. *Park 30 Mar-25 Oct 2008* 8am-7.30pm daily. 26 Oct 2008-31 Jan 2009 8am-6pm daily. *Tours* by arrangement; minimum 15 people. **Admission** (NT) *House & garden* £8; £3.50 5-18s; free under-5s; £20 family (2+3). *Garden only* £3.50; £1.75 5-18s; free under-5s. *Park* free. **Credit** MC, V. 3+
Once a fine manor in the heart of the countryside, Osterley is now a National Trust retreat in the heart of the western suburbs. It was built for Sir Thomas Gresham (founder of the Royal Exchange) in 1576, but came into the hands of Sir Francis Child, the head of Child's

Bank, as a result of a mortgage default. Child had it altered by fashionable architect Robert Adam in the 18th century; Mrs Child's flower garden, set out at that time, is still delightful. The splendour of the state rooms alone makes the house worth a visit, but the still-used Tudor stables, the vast park (the subject of an ongoing restoration) and the resident ghost – said to lurk in the basement – add to Osterley's allure. Visitors can buy produce in a farm shop; regular events include tours of the house, bluebell walks, bay walks, outdoor performances and the annual, free Osterley Day (29 June 2008), full of arts and fun.
Buggy access (not when busy). Café. Disabled access: stair climber, toilet. Nappy-changing facilities. Nearest picnic place: front lawn, picnic benches in grounds. Shop.

PM Gallery & House

Walpole Park, Mattock Lane, W5 5EQ (8567 1227/www.ealing.gov.uk). Ealing Broadway tube/rail/65 bus. **Open** *May-Sept* 1-5pm Tue-Fri, Sun; 11am-5pm Sat. *Oct-Apr* 1-5pm Tue-Fri; 11am-5pm Sat. Closed bank hols. *Tours* by arrangement; phone for details. **Admission** free. Audio guide £1. **Credit** AmEx, MC, V. 5+
Ealing's flagship cultural centre is Pitzhanger Manor, a beautiful Regency villa rebuilt at the start of the 19th century by Sir John Soane. Among the exhibits is the Hull Grundy Martinware pottery collection, and there's an art gallery and workshop programme for all ages; special events for kids include half-term craft sessions and 'clay play'. Outside is Walpole Park, the borough's rose-scented pride and joy, which hosts jazz and comedy in summer.
Buggy access. Disabled access: lift, ramp, toilet. Nappy-changing facilities. Nearest picnic place: Walpole Park.

Ranger's House

Chesterfield Walk, SE10 8QX (8853 0035/ www.english-heritage.org.uk). Blackheath rail/Greenwich DLR/rail/53 bus. **Open** *Apr-Sept* 10am-5pm Wed-Sun, bank hol Mon. *Oct-Dec* group bookings only Thur. Closed Jan-Mar. **Admission** (EH) £5.50; £4.40 reductions; £2.80 5-16s; free under-5s.
Credit MC, V. 5+
This Georgian villa dates from 1723, and was from 1815 the residence of the Greenwich Park Ranger, a post held by George III's niece Princess Sophia Matilda. It now contains the collection of treasure amassed by millionaire diamond-trader Julius Wernher, who died in 1912. His bejewelled and unusual collection of

Sightseeing

Great Days Out
South Bank & Bankside

A stroll along the South Bank is one of London's most popular Sunday walks – and in recognition of that fact, the Cross River Partnership (CRP), the body responsible for the area's regeneration, has produced a series of walking guides entitled 'Walk This Way'. The guides cover Riverside London, the South Bank, Bermondsey and nearby areas easily accessed via the footbridges (log on to www.southbanklondon.com for details).

It works on two levels: 'Above the Thames' takes you on the walks, across bridges and to tourist attractions; 'Below the Thames' is more of a factfile. It touches on (but doesn't lead you down) the sewers, London's lost rivers and the river's extensive wildlife.

Above the Thames three walking routes are suggested. There's a short stroll from the **Houses of Parliament** (see p33) across Westminster Bridge then eastward to the **National Theatre** (see p189). The second walk takes you from **Somerset House** (see p68) across Waterloo Bridge to **Tate Modern** (see p69) and walk number three starts at **Shakespeare's Globe** (see p34).

Our walk is a combination of all three (though you could leave out the start and the end (as these are the most expensive bits of the walk) if you're looking for a cheap day out. The full walk starts at the **London Aquarium** (see p129) with its impressive million-litre Pacific shark tank. Next up is the **London Eye** (see p30) – the world's largest big wheel – which is a must for a bird's eye view of the city. Book in advance. If you want to miss the expense of those two, start from the Golden Jubilee Bridge (connecting Embankment station to the **Southbank Centre** (see p164).

Arts and crafts

Wander into the **Royal Festival Hall** (see p164) where there are often free performances and workshops, including mask-making, dancing, singing, making music and poetry-reading. Next along this strip is the **BFI Southbank National Film Theatre** (see p165) where you can book a viewing station in the Mediathèque and choose from the 1,000-plus clips and films from the BFI archive. The lawn outside the National Theatre is utilised for the 'Watch this Space' free summer festival (see p20).

Strolling further along you'll arrive at **Gabriel's Wharf** – a riverside conglomeration of arts and crafts shops interspersed with places to eat and drink. This area is busy at the best of times, but when the **Coin Street Festival** (7021 1686, www.coinstreet.org, see p19) takes place, it's overrun, with musicians, poets, dancers and families. All events are free and take place in and around the green spaces of **Bernie Spain Gardens** – which is always a good place to stop for a picnic. The riverside gardens were named after Bernadette Spain, one of the original Coin Street Action Group campaigners.

You can see Tate Modern from here – a magnificent symbol of the success of the South

LUNCH BOX

Also in the area: Nando's, Pizza Express (four branches), Strada, Wagamama.

Amano *Victor Wharf, Clink Street, SE1 9DG (7234 0000).* Lunch and coffee.

Café Rouge *Hay's Galleria, SE1 2HD (7378 0097/www.caferouge.co.uk).* French café with £4.95 'enfants menu'.

EAT *Oxo Tower Wharf, Bargehouse Street, SE1 9PH (7636 8309/ www.eat.co.uk).* Inexpensive 'real food'.

House of Crêpes *56 Upper Ground, SE1 9PP (7401 9816).* Flippin' lovely pancakes in sweet and savoury forms.

Riverside Terrace Café *Royal Festival Hall, Southbank Centre, SE1 8XX (0871 663 2501).* Arts centre café.

Tate Modern Café 2 *2nd Floor, Tate Modern, SE1 9TG (7401 5014/ www.tate.org.uk).* Highly recomended for children. *See p222.*

Bank's regeneration. Entrance is free and there are plenty of resources for kids, from the Family Zone on Level 3 to the Bloomberg Learning Zone on Level 5.

You could peel off here and cross the Millennium Bridge to **St Paul's** (*see p42*) or carry on towards the striking Shakespeare's Globe. It's worth checking to see if there are any special live events on, such as performances by the Globe musicians, sword-fighting demonstrations and costume dressings.

Crime and punishment

Stroll under the foot of Southwark Bridge, where one wall is covered with an etching depicting the frost fairs in the days when the Thames was 'frozen o'er'. Walk as far as you can beside the river until you are diverted past Vinopolis the wine museum, down Clink Street, listening to the strains of monkish chanting emanating from the **Clink Prison Museum** (*see p100*) on your right.

Ahead you'll see the **Golden Hinde** (*see p33*) – a replica of Sir Francis Drake's 16th century flagship. Check the website for Pirate Fun Days. Further on you'll see the gardens of **Southwark Cathedral** (*see p41*). Turn left at the cathedral, taking the pavement studded with winking green and blue lights that goes under London Bridge (this is Montague Close). Keep walking until you emerge on Tooley Street, not far from the **London Dungeon** (*see p53*). From here follow the signs into **Hay's Galleria**. This is a touristy enclave, where there's a sparkly Christmas shop, stalls selling London souvenirs, jewellery and accessories and a few restaurants. There's also a ship-like sculpture by David Kemp, called 'The Navigators'.

A rather more substantial vessel looms outside on the river. Regain the Thames footpath to admire this floating wing of the Imperial War Museum, **HMS Belfast** (*see p104*). Carry on eastwards until you reach City Hall, the odd-shaped, glass-sided headquarters of Mayor Boris Johnson, the London Assembly and the Greater London Authority. This is part of a 13-acre riverside development known as **More London**, which includes **Potters Fields** – another fine place for a picnic and within view of **Tower Bridge** (*see p32*). From the riverside walkway you can mount steps up to the bridge, then stroll across, pausing in the middle to admire the river views, before setting off for the **Tower of London** (*see p41*), a very grand day out in itself.

19th-century art, including bronzes, tapestries, furniture, unusual porcelain and paintings is displayed in 12 elegant rooms. Look out for the enamelled skulls and miniature coffins. *Buggy access. Disabled access: lift, toilet. Nearest picnic place: Greenwich Park. Shop.*

Syon House

Syon Park, Brentford, Middx TW8 8JF (8560 0881/Tropical Forest 8847 4730/Snakes & Ladders 8847 0946/www.syonpark.co.uk). Gunnersbury tube/rail, then 237, 267 bus/ Kew Bridge rail. **Open** *House* mid Mar-late Oct 11am-5pm Wed, Thur, Sun, bank hol Mon (last entry 4pm). *Gardens* Mar-Oct 10.30am-5pm daily. Nov-Feb 10.30am-4pm Sat, Sun. *Tours* by arrangement; phone for details. *Snakes & Ladders* 10am-6pm daily (last entry 5.15pm). **Admission** *House & gardens* £8; £7 reductions; £4 5-16s; free under-5s; £18 family (2+2). *Gardens only* £4; £2.50 reductions, 5-16s; free under-4s; £9 family (2+2). *Tropical Forest* £5; £4 3-15s; free under-3s; £16 family (2+3). *Snakes & Ladders* £3.70 under-2s; £4.75 under-5s; £5.75 over-5s; free over-16s. Reduced rate after 4pm. **Credit** MC, V. 5+
Overlooking Kew on the left bank is the turreted Tudor mansion Syon House, built on the site of a medieval abbey that was brutally dissolved by Henry VIII. His coffin was later brought here in transit to Windsor Castle, and as if by divine retribution, it mysteriously burst open during the night: the king's corpse was found being licked by dogs. It was also here that the doomed Lady Jane Grey reluctantly accepted the crown and became queen for nine days.

Each room seems more impressive than the last, from the grand Roman hallway to the Red Drawing Room, with its crimson silk walls and Roman statues, and the outside is as grand as the interior. The restored 19th-century Great Conservatory, with its huge iron and glass dome, is a wonder, and the park is famed for its rare trees; *The Madness of George III* was filmed here. A miniature steam train chuffs around the trees and flowers on Sundays in spring and summer, but most children find their thrills in the park's other attractions. Snakes & Ladders is an indoor adventure playground designed like a castle, with three tiers of play areas, slides, hanging ropes and enormous ball pools; then there's the Aquatic Experience enclosure, full of endangered animals that live in or near water, such as piranhas, snakes, crocs and poison tree frogs. A programme of family-friendly events includes demonstrations and re-enactments. In summer the best eating locations are outside. *Café. Nappy-changing facilities. Nearest picnic place: Syon House Gardens, Syon Park. Shop.*

Guildhall

corner of Gresham Street and Aldermanbury, EC2P 2UJ (7606 3030/tours 7606 3030 ext 1463/www.corpoflondon.gov.uk). St Paul's tube/Bank tube/DLR/Moorgate tube/rail. **Open** *May-Sept* 9.30am-5pm daily. *Oct-Apr* 9.30am-5pm Mon-Sat. Last entry 4.30pm. Closes for functions; phone ahead to check. *Tours* by arrangement; groups of 10 or more only. **Admission** free. **Map** p318 P6. 8+
The Guildhall survived the Great Fire of London and the Blitz, making it one of the few structures in the City built before 1666. Now it's the seat of local government: the Court of Common Council meets at 1pm on various Thursdays each month, in the vast 15th-century Great Hall (visitors are welcome; phone for dates). The Hall is also open when not being used for official business. The impressive space has a vaulted ceiling, marble monuments, and banners and shields of 100 livery companies on the walls; every Lord Mayor since 1189 is named on the windows. Two large wooden statues of Gog and Magog, carved in 1953 to replace the pair destroyed in the Blitz, stand in the West Gallery. They represent the mythical conflict between Britons and Trojan invaders; the result of this struggle was the founding of Albion's capital city, New Troy, on whose site London is said to stand. On the north wall hangs a fascinating list of trials and grisly executions.

Visits to the Guildhall's enormous medieval crypt are allowed only in the context of group tours. In the absence of a café, packed lunches can be scoffed in the cloakroom area, which has a water cooler. *Buggy access. Disabled access: lift, ramp, toilet. Nappy-changing facilities. Nearest picnic place: grassy area by London Wall. Shop.*

THRILLS & CHILLS

Chessington World of Adventures

Leatherhead Road, Chessington, Surrey KT9 2NE (0870 444 7777/www.chessington.com). **Getting there** *By rail* Chessington South rail, then 71 bus or 10-min walk. *By car* J9 off M25. **Open** 10 Feb-2 Jan 2008. Check website for timetables. **Admission** (online advance price) £31; £23 3-15s; annual pass £49; £36 3-15s. Free under-3s. Check website for on-the-day prices and other annual passes. **Credit** AmEx, MC, V. All ages
Where Thorpe Park (*see p54*) is good for older children, Chessington is the softer option for younger families. It has two things to offer: animals and rides. The zoo part of the 76-year-

Sightseeing

Life in the past lane

Most museums and historic sites understand that engaging kids with a spot of dressing up and hands-on participation is far more productive than simply having them file past display cases; many have come up with wonderful ways for children to eat, breathe and sleep the antique experience. Call the venue before you visit to find out what's on offer; a few of our favourites are listed below.

Many places have dressing-up boxes and out-of-work actors at their disposal, who can help kids to get into character. They can try on replica Georgian costumes in **Dr Johnson's House** (*see p80*) and at the **Handel House Museum** (*see p91*). Wannabe Fireman Sams, after admiring the engines at the **London Fire Brigade Museum** (*see p75*) can try on old uniforms and experience how much weight fire-fighters had to carry. At the **Old Operating Theatre, Museum & Herb Garret** (*pictured, see p94*), Victorian surgery events let you take a turn on the operating theatre while everyone gawps at you having a leg cut off. Historical Experience shows run five times a day (Wed-Sun) at the **Benjamin Franklin House** (*see p78*); the 'in period' actress-guided tours bring visitors right into life in Franklin's day.

Little Jack Sparrows and Elizabeth Swanns can become crew members on a Living History overnighter to be a Tudor on board the **Golden Hinde** (*see p33*).

History buffs can doze among the treasures in the **British Museum** (*see p74*) – a rare treat for Young Friends of the BM (and guests of existing members). Kids these days, they simply don't appreciate how good they've got it. Sampling life as a student of the **Ragged School** (*see p73*) will soon open their eyes to the grimy realities of the lives of impoverished Victorian schoolchildren as they dress up and take a 45-minute 'class' at a well-used desk with inkwell.

Gore fans over the age of ten love the **London Dungeon** (*see p53*); the interactive experience throws the lot at visitors and somewhere among the screams, looming costumed actors and dry ice, there's information to be gleaned about London's more horrible history.

Every first weekend of the month, in the bowels of **Hampton Court Palace** (*see p36*), visitors are immersed in the sights and smells of the working 16th century kitchen and watch cooks prepare recipes that would have rumbled Henry VIII's tummy. The 'food archaeologists' use authentic ingredients and traditional cooking methods and utensils.

A few decades down the timeline **Shakespeare's Globe** (*see p34*) offers gainful summer employment to actors and education officers, who enliven Bard studies with storytelling, raiding the dressing-up box, even a spot of sword-fighting in school holiday workshops.

Sightseeing

old theme park is home to gorillas, tigers, sea lions and otters, and two recently launched attractions – a cheerful walk-through squirrel monkey enclosure and a Monkey and Bird Garden. The brand new Sea Life Centre gives visitors a good look at shrimps, sharks and stingrays. Events and feeding sessions includes a 'Zoo Keeper for a Day' package (over-sevens only) that takes visitors behind the scenes to help with some of the animals.

The generally gentle funfair part is equipped to supply entertainment to children of all ages: there's the lovable Beanoland with Dennis the Menace and Bash Street shenanigans, and Mystic East, which concludes a leisurely boat ride with a surprise plunge (height restrictions apply); older children will enjoy the thrilling Dragon's Fury rollercoaster and Tomb Blaster shoot 'em up game.
Buggy access. Café. Car park (free). Disabled access: toilets. Nappy-changing facilities. Restaurant. Shops.

Chislehurst Caves
Old Hill, Chislehurst, Kent BR7 5NB (8467 3264/www.chislehurstcaves.co.uk). Chislehurst rail. **Open** 9am-5pm Wed-Sun. *Tours* phone for details. **Admission** £5; £3 5-15s, reductions; free under-5s. **Credit** MC, V. 8+
Carved out of the hillside by Druids digging for chalk and flint, these caves were later used by Romans, then as a World War I ammunition dump, then a mushroom farm, and finally as Britain's largest bomb shelter during World War II. The 45min tour covers about a mile (1.5km).
Restaurant. Shop.

Legoland
Winkfield Road, Windsor, Berks SL4 4AY (0870 504 0404/www.legoland.co.uk). **Getting there** *By rail* Windsor & Eton Riverside or Windsor Central rail, then shuttlebus. *By car* J3 off M3 or J6 off M4. **Open** *Mid Mar-late Oct* times may vary, check website for timetables. **Admission** *One-day ticket* £31; £24 reductions, 3-15s. *Two-day ticket* £61; £47 3-15s; free under-3s. Shuttlebus £3.50; £2 reductions, 3-15s. Free under-3s. **Credit** AmEx, MC, V. All ages
Lovable Legoland is a top family day out (it won the 2007 Tommy's Parent Friendly award), and fab for all ages – even teens. With its witty, plastic brick surprises around every corner, and its beautifully landscaped features, it's a treat, astronomical entry fee notwithstanding. The new Longboat Invader ride is a prelude to the park's biggest and wettest ride, Vikings' River Splash. There's a new maze, Loki's Labyrinth,

and a Mole in One mini golf course; existing rides include Dragon Coaster and Pirate Falls.

The London skyline in Miniland features striking replicas of Canary Wharf, the Gherkin, City Hall and the Millennium Bridge; we also love the live action shows and the Lego driving school. Tots can get a groove on at the Legoland Live! music festival – a sort of junior Glastonbury, with the live acts like Pingu, Bob the Builder and Barney the purple dinosaur. Amazing Machines is a weekend of monster trucks and vintage cars; and the end of season fireworks are truly spectacular.

When you go to Legoland, pack a picnic, because the food is a let-down. Check the day before you set off that the attractions your children are interested in are running. And if your children are young enough to be unconstrained by term dates, seize to opportunity to visit outside school hols.
Buggy access. Cafés. Disabled access: toilet. Nappy-changing facilities. Nearest picnic place: grounds. Restaurants. Shops.

London Bridge Experience
2-4 Tooley Street, SE1 2SY (0800 043 4666/ www.londonbridgeexperience.com). London Bridge tube/rail. **Open** 10am-6pm daily. **Admission** £19.95; £15.95 reductions; £14.95 under-16s; free under-5s; £59.95 family (2+2). **Credit** MC, V. All ages (Bridge Experience). 11+ (London Tombs)

The experience is a split-level one. The first part is a fun-for-all-the-family history lesson that serves the choicest cuts from the crossing's 2,000-year history. The second takes you underground to 'the London Tombs', and frightens the pants off you. We like the first bit best, where actors appear at every turn: in a cobwebbed replica of a Victorian study, we meet the ghostly portrait of Sir John Rennie, who designed the 1831 bridge, and whose ravings are translated by a dusty butler; through heavy doors and along dank passages, we're shown Boudicca's sacking of London, narrated by a bloodied Roman soldier amid disembowelled corpses; and then there's the Russell Crowe-like viking, who asks his guests to help pull down the bridge's wooden piers. After that, we're introduced to William Wallace's ghost, and taken into a chamber of gore run by the chap in charge of heads on sticks – for display purposes on London Bridge. Each period involves interaction with the key players, which also include a garrulous lighterman's widow, the American who bought the bridge in 1970, (it's a myth that he thought he was buying Tower Bridge, he insists), and a disconcertingly unplummy Queen. It's all quite kitsch and entertaining; the shocks and horrors come downstairs in the dark and threatening Tombs, where zombie actors show little mercy.
Buggy access. Café. Disabled: lift; toilets. Nearest picnic place: South Bank. Shop.

London Dungeon

28-34 Tooley Street, SE1 2SZ (7403 7221/ www.thedungeons.com). London Bridge tube/ rail. **Open** times vary, phone or check website for details. **Admission** £19.95; £17.95 reductions; £14.95 5-14s; £2 reduction for registered disabled; free carers, under-5s. **Credit** AmEx, MC, V. **Map** p319 Q8. 8+
The London Dungeon leads its visitors through the gruesome bits of London history: the Great Plague; the Great Fire; a gruesome section devoted to Jack the Ripper; and another for demonic 18th-century barber Sweeney Todd. Costumed actors are constantly on the prowl, springing from drifts of dry-ice fog to let out blood-curdling screams; guaranteed to provoke more high-pitched exclamation is 'Labyrinth of the Lost', the largest horror mirror maze in the world. If that's not enough depravity for you, there's the Traitor Boat Ride to Hell (visitors play the part of condemned prisoners, death sentence guaranteed), and Extremis: Drop Ride to Doom, which aims, charmingly, to recreate at least part of the experience of being hanged.

All in all, the Dungeon is clearly on to a winner, judging from the length of the weekend queues outside the Victorian railway arches that are its home. There are always plenty of small children standing in line, where gorily made-up Dungeon staff work the crowds, but we'd advise against taking anyone younger than ten – our

Madame Tussaud's. *See p50.*

Sightseeing

eleven-year-old tester came out rather whey-faced but said he loved it. Tours last around 90 minutes; you can purchase fast-track tickets on the website to beat the queues.
Buggy access. Disabled access: toilet. Nappy-changing facilities. Nearest picnic place: Hay's Galleria. Shop.

Madame Tussauds

Marylebone Road, NW1 5LR (0870 400 3000/www.madame-tussauds.co.uk). Baker Street tube/13, 27, 74, 113, 159 bus. **Open** 9am-6pm daily (last entry 5.30pm). Times vary during holiday periods. **Admission** 9.30am-5pm Mon-Fri, 9.30am-6pm Sat, Sun £22.50; £18.50 reductions; £19.99 5-15s; free under-5s. 5-5.30pm daily £12.50; £10 reductions; £10 5-15s; free under-5s. Internet booking only for family tickets. **Credit** AmEx, MC, V. **Map** p314 G4. 3+

This celebrated (and sometimes maligned) tourist magnet compensates for the inherently static quality of its attractions with a flurry of attendant activity. As you enter the first room, you're dazzled by paparazzi flashbulbs. Starry-eyed kids can then take part in a 'Divas' routine with Britney and Beyoncé; Robbie Williams has a kiss sensor that activates a twinkle in his eye. New figures are constantly added and old ones updated: Kylie Minogue and the Queen have been recast four times (the current Kylie wears her new scent). There's a *Pirates of the Caribbean* diorama in the hull of the *Black Pearl*, staffed by Keira, Orlando and Johnny; the World Stage hall is an interactive room split into zones for sports, culture, politics, popular music, royals and history. Holographs and touch screens add pizzazz. Nobody prevents visitors hugging the stars (or pinching their bottoms).

Elsewhere, the kitsch Spirit of London ride takes you through 400 years of London life in a taxi pod. Children love this, and always want to ride again to spot the historic figures depicted around them. Below stairs, the Chamber of Horrors is really not child-friendly. It surrounds you with hanged corpses and eviscerated victims of torture, with a terrifying 'live' experience (actors dressed up as psycho killers jump out and stalk you – for an extra £2 – over-12s only). Such morbid thrills chime with the work of Marie Tussaud (1761-1850), who made death masks out of wax in the French Revolution. Her cast of the mask of Marie-Jeanne du Barry, Louis XV's mistress, is the oldest work on display: it's the peaceful face of the reclining, animatronic *Sleeping Beauty*.
Café. Disabled access: lift, toilet. Nappy-changing facilities. Nearest picnic place: Regent's Park. Shop.

Thorpe Park

Staines Road, Chertsey, Surrey KT16 8PN (0870 444 4466/www.thorpepark.com). **Getting there** *By rail* Staines rail, then 950 shuttlebus. *By car* J11 or J13 off M25. **Open** times vary, check website for timetables. Height restrictions vary, depending on rides. **Admission** £32; £21 under-12s; free under-1m tall. £88-£105 family (2+2 or 2+3). Check the website or phone for advance bookings; allow 24hrs for processing. **Credit** MC, V. 5+

Thorpe Park is the destination of choice for older children and hardened thrill-seekers. It has Europe's fastest rollercoaster, Stealth, a gut-wrenching machine that propels riders from a standstill to 80mph in under two seconds. In the extreme ride stakes, there's also Colossus, the world's first ten-loop rollercoaster; Nemesis Inferno, where the train mounts a volcano and subjects the body to 4.5g; Tidal Wave (tagline 'You'll wet yourself'); and the Vortex, which whirls at great heights above the lake. Slammer – one of only two 'sky-swat' rides in the world (don't ask) – could reduce parents to tears; and Rush, the world's largest speed swing, is no walk in the park either. Although Thorpe's more extreme rides aren't suitable for small children, there are tamer attractions: swinging seashells, happy halibuts, the Banana Boat ride, and the popular Flying Fish. In a bid to unite the family over foot-tapping tunes, there's the Top Rockers Show, performed by Billy, Bo and Benny in the Sing Zone. But that's not one for the Goths Rude Boys in the family, we suspect.
Buggy access. Café. Disabled access: toilets. Nappy-changing facilities. Restaurants. Shops.

Trocadero

Coventry Street, W1D 7DH (7439 1791/ www.londontrocadero.com). Piccadilly Circus tube. **Open** 10am-midnight Mon-Thur, Sun; 10am-1am Fri, Sat. **Admission** free; individual attractions vary. **Credit** varies. **Map** p317 K7. 5+

In this pulsating indoor complex there's a vast arcade of coin-in-the-slot video games, simulator rides and dance machines. The noise and disorientating lights are a fast track to tantrums and headaches – and still they come to spend all their pocket money. There's a seven-screen cinema, a dodgem track, a ten-lane bowling alley (the only one in central London) and various fast-food outlets. The sports bar is grown-ups only.
Buggy access. Cafés. Disabled access: lift, toilet. Nappy-changing facilities. Nearest picnic place: Leicester Square, Trafalgar Square. Restaurants. Shops.

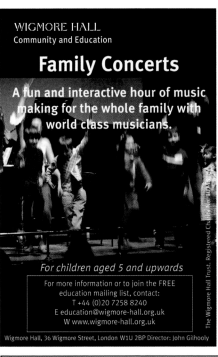

Great Days Out
Covent Garden

While it's no mean feat avoiding the melée of tourists that descend upon London's shopping mecca, there is plenty to make it worth the struggle. The name Covent Garden is most likely drawn from the 'convent garden' surrounding the historic abbey on the original site. The land that belonged to the Convent of St Peter at West Minster was handed over by the Crown to John Russell, the first Earl of Bedford following the dissolution of the monasteries.

In the 1630s, the Earl commissioned master architect Inigo Jones to design a series of Palladian arcades. These tall terraces, opening on to a central courtyard, constituted the first public square in the country and proved popular with wealthy tenants, until the fruit and vegetable market expanded on to their patch. There are few signs left of the original market where fruit and veg were sold for three centuries (and, thankfully, the gambling dens and brothels that followed are long gone too), but Inigo Jones's Piazza remains an attractive space – albeit where living statues and jugglers keep the crowds entertained – and Charles Fowler's market hall gets lovelier with age.

Be transported

As with most of our days out, weekdays are best for exploring this area. Head straight down James Street, cut through the market, and start off at one of London's most joyful museums: the **London Transport Museum** (*see p83*), where you can trace the city's transport systems from the horse age to the present day, and younger children will love the opportunity to drive a bus or tube train. Older children will enjoy the online games and the latest gadgets available in the shop. It's worth checking the website to see what's on as there is always a full programme of events and exhibitions, such as Poetry Slams. During the holidays the museum has drama characters from London Transport's past who retell their stories throughout the day, as well as workshops (make a London bus and handle a working ticket machine).

If all that travelling has made you peckish, nip upstairs to the Upper Deck café that overlooks the Piazza. In addition to the Upper Deck, the Museum also has a small picnic area where visitors can eat their packed lunches. Refuelled, head out again and have a mooch around the **old covered market** (7836 9136, www.covent garden market. co.uk) where cool and quirky

LUNCH BOX

Also in the area: Pizza Express, Strada, Wagamama.

Bagel Factory *18 Endell Street, WC2H 9BD (7497 1115/www.bagelfactory. co.uk)*. Great for grabbing healthy nosh on the go.

Café Pasta *2-4 Garrick Street, WC2E 9BH (7497 2779/www.cafepasta. co.uk)*. Plus pizza and grills from this Italian mini-chain.

Christopher's *18 Wellington Street, WC2E 7DD (7240 4222/www. christophersgrill.com)*. Attractive restaurant with excellent US cuisine.

Spaghetti House *24 Cranbourn Street, WC2H 7AB (7836 8168/www.spaghetti-house.co.uk)*. Children's menu is £5.

Upper Deck Café *London Transport Museum, WC2E 7BB (7595 1355/ www.ltmuseum.co.uk)*. Museum café.

shops are mixed up with upmarket chain stores (Hobbs, Whistles). The Apple Market in the North Hall is where you find the arts and crafts stalls (Tuesday to Sunday, antiques on Monday). Jubilee Market is a bit tackier: novelty T-shirts and other tat.

Piazza the action

When the traders moved out of the market, property developers loomed large, but the area was saved from office-block ignominy through demonstrations. Now its residential community thrives alongside shops, bars and street artists – comedians, musicians – who perform in front of the portico of St Paul's Church or in the square. It was under the portico that Samuel Pepys observed what is thought to have been Britain's first Punch and Judy show ('an Italian puppet play', as he described it) on 9 May 1662, and it

is probably for this reason that the **Punch & Judy Festival** (*see p24,*) is held here on the first Sunday in October. Every summer there are open-air operatics courtesy of the **Royal Opera House** (*see p173*). The ROH itself is a beautiful space and has an upstairs café with wonderful views over the Piazza.

There are guided tours giving the curious a glimpse into working dressing rooms and rehearsal rooms. If you have time to take in a performance, forthcoming shows include Chen Shi-Zheng's *Monkey: Journey to the West* (in collaboration with Damon Albarn and artist Jamie Hewlett).

Out of the market, head towards the river and down to the Strand. In the 14th century, the Strand was a residential street with desirable waterside homes. All this changed when the overflow from Covent Garden threatened to overwhelm this hitherto narrow strip. By 1600 the wealthy folk had run away, and the Strand held a reputation for poverty and bawdiness. Sir Christopher Wren suggested the creation of a reclaimed embankment to ease congestion and house the main sewer. At the eastern end is the Aldwych, a grand crescent that dates to 1905, although name 'ald wic' (old settlement) has its origins in the 14th century. On its south side is the splendid **Somerset House** (*see p22 and p68*).

Museums & Galleries

This way for fabulous treasure.

London being the vast and ancient city that it is, it's no surprise that you're spoilt for choice when it comes to museums and galleries. This year we've arranged the capital's monumental banquet of artistic and historic delights by theme, so if your kids are particularly keen on a particular subject – medicine, say – you can easily compare the major venues and pick the one (or two, or three) that best fits the bill.

What is most gratifying is that practically all the venues make a special effort to engage children. Some, like the **Science Museum** (*see p94*) and the **Natural History Museum** (*see p92*), are famous for their family-friendliness (although our researcher would beg to differ on her toddler's account; *see p90* **Hot for tots?**), but others come as a big surprise. Who would have thought that the **Bank of England Museum** (*see p97*) could be such fun? To find out about the children's activities going on in particular places, make their websites your first stop and (if they do one) sign up for an e-newsletter.

Make sure you have ample time to look around, and avoid the crowds by turning up bright and early. We've given opening times and admission prices, but it's always a good idea to phone ahead to check them before setting out.

ART & DESIGN

Camden Arts Centre
Corner of Arkwright Road & Finchley Road, NW3 6DG (7472 5500/www.camdenarts centre.org). Finchley Road tube/Finchley Road & Frognal rail. **Open** 10am-6pm Tue, Thur-Sun; 10am-9pm Wed. **Admission** free. **Credit** MC, V. 7+ (parental advisory)
The three new galleries host exhibitions, a state-of-the-art ceramics studio and a busy programme of courses and talks for adults and children. Typically, half-terms bring two-day courses in, say, clay and mixed media for £46 (£28 reductions). Four term-time courses (Saturdays) cater for young people of various age groups. *Bookshop. Buggy access. Café. Disabled access: lift, toilet. Nappy-changing facilities. Shop.*

Design Museum
Shad Thames, SE1 2YD (7403 6933/ www.designmuseum.org). Tower Hill tube/ London Bridge tube/rail/47, 100, 188 bus. **Open** 10am-5.45pm 7 days. **Admission** £8.50; £6.50 reductions; free under-12s. **Credit** AmEx, MC, V. **Map** p319 S9. 5+
Design of all kinds is celebrated in this white ex-warehouse, and the place is surprisingly child-friendly: every child gets a 'Design Action

Pack' to spice up the visit, and the museum runs an acclaimed Sunday afternoon programme of design-and-make sessions for five- to 11-year olds. The themes, anything from modern millinery to furniture and architecture, change monthly; the cost is just £4 per child, though participants must be accompanied by a paying adult (£8.50). Booking is essential.
Buggy access. Café. Disabled access: lift, toilet. Nappy-changing facilities. Nearest picnic place: Butler's Wharf riverside benches. Shop.

Dulwich Picture Gallery
Gallery Road, SE21 7AD (8693 5254/www. dulwichpicturegallery.org.uk). North Dulwich or West Dulwich rail. **Open** 10am-5pm Tue-Fri; 11am-5pm Sat, Sun, bank hol Mon. **Admission** £5; £4 reductions; free under-18s, students, unemployed, disabled. **Credit** MC, V. 6+
The first purpose-built art gallery in the country gives weight to the argument that the best things come in small packages. Its gallery houses an outstanding collection of work by the Old Masters, and offers a fine introduction to the baroque era via pieces by Rembrandt, Rubens, Poussin and – batting for the home team – Thomas Gainsborough. The programme of children's activities is consistently praised. Seven-to ten-year olds learn a range of techniques on

Design Museum

Sightseeing

Saturdays (10.30am-1pm); the after-school art club for ages 11 to 14 is held on Thursdays (4.30-6pm); and students aged between 15 and 18 can attend Tuesday art clubs (4.30-6pm). These four-week courses cost between £40 and £60, but there are shorter holiday courses and workshops on themes such as Fairytale Landscapes; Art in the Garden takes place on Wednesdays in the summer hols and costs £2 per child; and free Art Play afternoons (2-3.30pm, first Sunday of each month) let parents and children over four partake of artist-led activities in various media. There's a lively programme of readings by children's authors, and art lectures for older kids. Check the website for details and fees of all courses and classes; booking is essential for most of them.
Buggy access. Café. Disabled access: ramp, toilet. Nappy-changing facilities. Nearest picnic place: gallery gardens. Shop.

Fashion & Textile Museum

83 Bermondsey Street, SE1 3XF (7407 8664/ www.ftmlondon.org). London Bridge tube/rail. **Open** 11am-5pm Wed-Sun (last entry 4.15pm). **Admission** £5-£7; £3-£4 reductions; free under-12s. **Credit** MC, V. **8+**
Nippers with a passion for fashion will be in seventh heaven at this cutting-edge centre for contemporary textiles and jewellery, founded by

famous British designer Zandra Rhodes and relaunched in November 2007 after an extensive redesign. Now run by Newham College, the FTM occupies a building by Mexican architect Ricardo Legorreta in modish Bermondsey Village, and aims not only to display items relating to fashion, jewellery and textile design, but also to offer inspiration to a new generation of talent. Recent temporary exhibitions have focused on the little black dress and masculine style; the events programme is mainly talks. The FTM Café was about to open as we went to press.
Buggy access. Café. Disabled access: lift, toilet. Nearest picnic place: Bermondsey Square.

Geffrye Museum

136 Kingsland Road, E2 8EA (7739 9893/ www.geffrye-museum.org.uk). Liverpool Street tube/rail, then 149, 242 bus/Old Street tube/ rail, then 243 bus. **Open** 10am-5pm Tue-Sat; noon-5pm Sun, bank hol Mon. **Admission** free; donations appreciated. *Almshouse* £2; £1 reductions; free under-16s. **Credit** MC, V. **5+**
The Geffrye Museum is a simply marvellous physical history of the English interior, housed in attractive former almshouses (1715) around a deep, lawned courtyard. The rooms represent various periods in history, from the Elizabethan era to the present day, and visitors walk past in

a roped-off corridor, admiring the changing tastes and styles of succeeding generations. The second, newer, half of the museum has space for changing exhibitions. In winter, the Christmas Past exhibition is always a hit, with each room decorated for the festive season according to its period, and the museum also holds a Twelfth Night ritual (6 January), when a Christmas tree is burned to the accompaniment of cheers and mulled wine. What keeps the children occupied is the packed programme of activities: cookery and craft workshops for kids young and older on weekdays, two-hour Saturday Specials on the first Saturday of each month (for ages five to 16; on a first-come basis), and a variety of outdoor fun in the garden in spring and summer. Summer Sundays (once a month in June, July and August) typically involve the making of lavender cookies and so on, with live music and plant sales. The airy restaurant is a pleasure all year round. *Buggy access. Disabled access: lift, toilet. Nappy-changing facilities. Nearest picnic place: museum grounds. Restaurant. Shop.*

Guildhall Art Gallery

Guildhall Yard, off Gresham Street, EC2V 5AE (7332 3700/www.guildhall-art-gallery. orguk). Mansion House or St Paul's tube/Bank tube/DLR/Moorgate tube/rail/8, 25, 242 bus. **Open** 10am-5pm Mon-Sat; noon-4pm Sun. **Admission** £2.50; £1 reductions; free under-16s. Free to all after 3.30pm daily, all day Fri. **Credit** (over £5) MC, V. **Map** p318 P6. 6+
The City of London's gallery contains numerous portraits of stuffy politicians and a few surprises, including works by Constable, Reynolds and the Pre-Raphaelites, and an absorbing display of topographical works showing London down the ages. Upstairs in the Main Gallery is the vast *Siege of Gibraltar* by John Copley, the largest painting in Britain; down in the basement lie the scant remains of London's sole amphitheatre. Although only the foundations of the walls and entrance survive, the slick presentation of the site does an excellent job of suggesting how the amphitheatre would have looked, with the staggered seats printed on a screen, dynamic illustrations of gladiators, and sound effects. The Victorian Galleries hold more dramatic and recognisable art to interest the kids, and there are art materials and tables dotted around for children's use. In October the gallery takes part in the annual nationwide Big Draw, and there are workshops during half-terms; every Friday, four free tours (hourly from 12.15pm, no booking needed) take in the highlights of the collection. *Buggy access. Disabled access: toilet. Nappy-changing facilities. Nearest picnic place: Finsbury Circus.*

Hayward Gallery

Belvedere Road, SE1 8XX (information 7921 0813/08703 800400/www.hayward.orguk). *Embankment tube/Waterloo tube/rail.* **Open** 10am-6pm Mon-Thur, Sat, Sun; 10am-10pm Fri. **Admission** £9; £5.50-£8 reductions; £4.50 12-16s; free under-12s. Prices vary; phone for details. **Credit** AmEx, MC, V. **Map** p318 M8. 8+ (parental advisory)
Inside the light, bright pavilion by Daniel Graham, casual visitors can watch cartoons on touch screens or just wander around the visually confusing space created by curved, two-way mirrors. The neon tower on the gallery roof was commissioned by the Arts Council in 1970. Its yellow, red, green and blue tubes are controlled by changes in the direction and strength of the wind. 2008 is the Hayward's 40th anniversary, and the big exhibition (until late August) is Psycho Buildings, which looks at architecture as 'mental space'. Family activities linked to the current exhibitions might include mask-making sessions or music and dance workshops; consult the website for details. *Buggy access. Café. Disabled access: lift. Nappy-changing facilities. Nearest picnic place: Jubilee Gardens/riverside benches. Shop.*

Museum of Brands, Packaging & Advertising

2 Colville Mews, Lonsdale Road, W11 2AR (7908 0880/www.museumofbrands.com). Ladbroke Grove or Notting Hill Gate tube/ 23 bus. **Open** 10am-6pm Tue-Sat; 11am-5pm Sun. Last entry 1hr before closing. **Admission** £5.80; £2 7-16s; £3.50 reductions; free under-7s; £14 family (2+2). **Credit** MC, V. **Map** p310 A6. 6+
If you go weak at the knees when you see original boxes of Bassett's Liquorice Allsorts or Rowntree's Black Magic, this is the museum for you. It began when consumer historian Robert Opie filed a Munchies wrapper when he was 16. His collection grew, and this museum – opened in 2005 – charts the evolution of consumer society over 200 years. It covers Victorian leisure pursuits, the advent of the radio, the chirpy thrift of wartime Britain and the liberal revolution of the swinging '60s. The displays are geared towards nostalgic adults, but historically-minded children may be amused by the antiquated toys, magazines and comics on show – not to mention old versions of all their favourite chocolate wrappers. Maltesers looked quite different, you know. *Buggy access. Café. Disabled access: toilet. Nappy-changing facilities. Nearest picnic place: Kensington Gardens. Shop.*

Sightseeing

LET THE KIDS CREATE

FOUNTAINS, RIVER VIEWS, WORKSHOPS
AND PLAY FOR FREE

Open daily. Admission to Somerset House is free.
Entry fees apply to the Embankment Galleries and events.
Tel: 020 7845 4600 Strand, London WC2 www.somersethouse.org.uk
⊖ Temple, Charing Cross, Embankment, Covent Garden

The best
Museums

For trains and boats and planes

HMS Belfast (see p104), **Kew Bridge Steam Museum** (see p83), **London Transport Museum** (see p83), **Royal Air Force Museum Hendon** (see p106).

For dressing up

Fashion and Textile Museum (see p59), **Guards Museum** (see p104), **Victoria & Albert Museum** (see p70).

For time travel

Geffrye Museum (see p59), **Museum of Brands, Packaging & Advertising** (see p60), **Ragged School Museum** (see p73).

For wartime wonders

Churchill Museum & Cabinet War Rooms (see p103), **Imperial War Museum** (see p104).

For famous faces

Charles Dickens Museum (see p80), **National Portrait Gallery** (see right).

For gold and silver

Bank of England (see p97), **Somerset House** (see p68).

For old bones

British Museum (see p74), **Petrie Museum** (see p75).

For hands-on activities

Horniman Museum (see p75), **Science Museum** (see p94).

For great grub

National Gallery (see below), **Tate Britain** (see p69), **Tate Modern** (see p69).

National Gallery

Trafalgar Square, WC2N 5DN (information 7747 2885/www.nationalgallery.org.uk). Charing Cross tube/rail/24, 29, 176 bus. **Open** 10am-6pm Mon, Tue, Thur-Sun; 10am-9pm Wed. *Tours* 11.30am, 2.30pm daily. **Admission** free. *Temporary exhibitions* prices vary. *Tours* free. **Credit** MC, V. **Map** p317 K7. 5+

It started with just 38 paintings, but now our national collection has more than 2,000 items of Western European art. If you have a buggy to push, enter via the impressive Getty Entrance for step-free access from Trafalgar Square. Pick up a plan at the info desk opposite the door and make for the Impressionists room (45), with its wall of Van Goghs and an atmospheric Monet – *London at Westminster*, painted in 1871. The unmissable *Bathers at Asnières* by Seurat is in the next room. The famed *Execution of Lady Jane Grey* is in room 41 – children are fascinated by Lady Jane, who was queen for nine days in 1553 and beheaded aged just 17 at the Tower of London. The long gallery (room 34) has many famous works, including Constable's *Hay Wain* and Turner's *The Fighting Temeraire*. Blood-and-guts fans will like room 24, which has Cornelis van Haarlem's *Two Followers of Cadmus Devoured by a Dragon*. In the Sainsbury Wing, look for *David holding the head of Goliath* and Paolo Uccello's *Saint George and the Dragon*. When it's time to eat, Oliver Peyton's National Dining Rooms restaurant is fabulous.

ArtStart computer terminals in the Espresso Bar on Level 0 let visitors customise their own tour. Listening posts offering commentary on more than 1,000 works, and there are audio tours and paper trails. Laid-back children's events include Magic Carpet storytelling for under-fives (Tuesday to Saturday during school holidays), and the two-hour Holiday Workshops (same days, at 11am and 2pm), led by a contemporary artist. Kids aged 12 to 17 can Get Into Art at five-hour workshops led by a painter and a sculptor. Each of these events provides the necessary materials and is free.

Buggy access. Café. Disabled access: lift, toilet. Nappy-changing facilities. Nearest picnic place: Trafalgar Square. Restaurant. Shop.

National Portrait Gallery

2 St Martin's Place, WC2H 0HE (7306 0055/ tours 7312 2483/www.npg.org.uk). Leicester Square tube/Charing Cross tube/rail/24, 29, 176 bus. **Open** 10am-6pm Mon-Wed, Sat, Sun; 10am-9pm Thur, Fri. *Tours* times vary, phone for details. **Admission** free. *Temporary exhibitions* prices vary. *Audio guide* £2. *Tours* free. **Credit** MC, V. **Map** p317 K7. 5+

The National Portrait Gallery presents a pantheon of people who have made a mark on British society, taking in faces as varied as William Shakespeare (the only known contemporary portrait of the Bard) and Benny Hill. Portraits are all done in a variety of media (painting, photography, sculpture) by artists ranging from

Sightseeing

medieval illuminators to celebrity snappers like Mario Testino. The permanent collection is organised by period. Temporary exhibitions are held here all year round, including the highlights of the annual BP Portrait Award from June to September. Free trails are available from the information desk, and sometimes activity packs too: ask on arrival. There are regular holiday workshops, Are You Sitting Comfortably storytelling sessions every month for under-fives, and Small Faces art activities for over-fives.
Buggy access. Café. Disabled access (Orange Street entrance): lift, ramp, toilet. *Nappy-changing facilities. Nearest picnic place: Leicester Square, Trafalgar Square. Restaurant. Shops.*

Orleans House Gallery
Riverside, Twickenham, Middx TW1 3DJ (8831 6000/www.richmond.gov.uk/orleans_house_gallery). St Margaret's, Richmond or Twickenham rail/33, 490, H22, R68, R70 bus. **Open** *Apr-Sept* 1-5.30pm Tue-Sat; 2-5.30pm Sun, bank hols. *Oct-Mar* 1-4.30pm Tue-Sat; 2-4.30pm Sun, bank hol Mon. **Admission** free; donations appreciated. **Credit** MC, V. 5+

Sightseeing

Foundling Museum – where children discover they never had it so good. *See p73.*

Great Days Out
Bloomsbury

This part of London has a rich bohemian past, being a cauldron of literary and artistic creativity in the 1930s and '40s. But as far as most visitors are concerned, the central beacon of the area is the gargantuan **British Museum** (*see p74*), an embodiment of the Enlightenment concept of all of the arts and sciences being interconnected.

Yummy mummies

Youngsters are captivated by the Egyptian mummies, so start in the Great Court, London's largest covered public square, where you can begin by exploring the Egyptian antiquities (the Rosetta Stone, imposing statues, mummies) as well as ancient Greek treasures, including the Elgin Marbles. During half-terms and holidays, Egyptology-related activities are often organised, both here and at the **Petrie Museum of Egyptian Archaeology** (*see p75*).

It's worth trying to appreciate the museum in bite-sized chunks, so make a decision to return to explore the less famous prehistoric, ethnographic, Asian and European collections. Sampler tours of the museum's top treasures and EyeOpener tours, which concentrate on specific aspects of the collection, such as Africa, the Americas or the classical world, are run by volunteer guides. Check the website for details of free special family EyeOpeners, run twice daily during half-terms and irregularly through the school holidays (book at the information desk), or pick up a family backpack (deposit required) from the Paul Hamlyn Library on the ground floor to navigate the galleries independently. The Roman Britain, Mexico, Africa, Greece and Egypt trails contain hands-on activities. Young Friends of the British Museum (£20 per year for children aged eight to 15) receive a welcome pack, ten per cent discount in the shop and magazines three times a year.

Young Friends can also book a museum sleepover. *See p50* **Life in the past lane**.

On the Lower Ground Floor, the Clore Educational Centre and the Ford Centre for Young Visitors are dedicated family areas… there's space for picnics, nappy-changing, rest and recuperation. Alternatively, you could pick up a lunch pack from the café in the Great Court and head for **Coram's Fields** (*see p113*).

Fields of dreams

Famous long before it became one of young Londoners' favourite parks, this site dates back to 1747, the year Thomas Coram established the Foundling Hospital for abandoned children (site of the Foundling Museum). Following the demolition of the orphanage in the 1920s, a campaign to turn the site into a children's play area kept the developers at bay; the park finally opened in 1936.

There are spacious lawns, sandpits and slides, a paddling pool, an AstroTurf football pitch, a basketball court, a wooden climbing tower, swings, a helter-skelter chute and an assault-course pulley. There's also an animal enclosure, with goats, geese, a duck pond, rabbits, guinea pigs and an aviary. Occasionally during the summer, bands and circus performers entertain picnicking families. Activities for the holidays include sports and arts workshops; ring for details. A small veggie café (closed Mon in winter) provides healthy fuel.

Parents love the park because it's safe. It's permanently staffed, and adults are admitted only if accompanied by children. Sports such as football, basketball, aerobics and trampolining are all available free. In the Band Room and play centre, a range of classes are offered; and there are IT courses for 13- to 19-year-olds. There are toilets and shower rooms in the sports area (including facilities for wheelchair-users). The nursery, after-school and holiday play centres are run by Camden Council (7837 0255). All activities are dependent on funding, so donations are appreciated.

Foundlings' father

From here it's a short walk to the appealing **Foundling Museum** (*see p73*), a memorial to London's abandoned children. During the life of the hospital more than 27,000 abandoned infants were taken in and cared for until they were of apprentice age. The museum tells the story of those children – and the adults who campaigned for them, such as William Hogarth, whose support and gifts of paintings caused the hospital to become established as Britain's first public art gallery; and George Frederic Handel, whose manuscripts are on display on the top floor. Handel was a governor and benefactor of the hospital, and annual performances of his *Messiah* provided it with income.

Most poignant is the array of humble items left by mothers for their children – a key, buttons, a piece of shell engraved with the child's name and date of birth, a scrap of poetry. Sadly, the foundlings were never given these tokens and the mother's identity was kept anonymous; it was felt that the children should be starting with a fresh slate.

Children and families can explore the museum through activity packs, audio games, story books and special events throughout the year. These include workshops, drop-in family fun days, concerts and author visits.

Great Days Out

Set in pretty woodland gardens on a secluded riverside path, the 18th-century Orleans House contains the Richmond-upon-Thames art collection. The refurbished Stables Gallery, venue for exhibitions of contemporary art, reopened in 2008. Orleans House runs an upbeat series of year-round workshops for kids: the after-school Art Club caters for five- to ten-year olds; 10:15 entertains the tens to 15s; and the Star Club (fives to tens) focuses on arts of the performing variety. All need to be booked via the website. The Coach House education centre hosts holiday art workshops using the gallery's exhibitions as a starting point. Events for 2008 include Heritage Day (September), Family Learning Week and the Big Draw.
Buggy access. Café. Disabled access: ramp, toilet. Nappy-changing facilities. Nearest picnic place: Orleans House Gallery grounds, Marble Hill Park or riverside benches. Shop.

Queen's House
Romney Road, SE10 9NF (8312 6565/www. nmm.ac.uk). Cutty Sark DLR/Greenwich DLR/ rail. **Open** 10am-5pm daily (last entry 4.30pm). *Tours* noon, 2.30pm daily. **Admission** free; occasional charge for temporary exhibitions. *Tours* free. **Credit** (over £5) MC, V. **4+**
Designed in 1616 by Inigo Jones, Queen's House is now home to the National Maritime Museum's art collection. It's also reputedly home to a ghost, captured on film by a couple of Canadian visitors in 1966, and spotted as recently as 2002 by a gallery assistant. An exhibition on the ground floor charts the house's former life as a boarding school for the sons of sailors, and Turmoil and Tranquillity (until January 2009) brings together depictions of ships and the sea by Dutch and Flemish masters of the 16th and 17th centuries. On the Trail of the Stuarts is a 'detective notebook' that leads children around the building, and a trail for young children works on their spotting skills; download them from the website before you go. A colonnade connects the building to the National Maritime Museum (*see p105*).
Buggy access. Cafés. Disabled access: lift, ramp, toilet. Nappy-changing facilities. Nearest picnic place: picnic area on grounds, Greenwich Park. Shop.

Royal Academy of Arts
Burlington House, Piccadilly, W1J 0BD (7300 8000/www.royalacademy.org.uk). Green Park or Piccadilly Circus tube. **Open** *Temporary exhibitions* 10am-6pm Mon-Thur, Sat, Sun; 10am-10pm Fri. *John Madejski Fine Rooms* 1-4.30pm Tue-Fri; 10am-6pm Sat, Sun.

London Transport Museum. *See p83.*

Sightseeing

Admission *Fine Rooms* free. *Exhibitions* prices vary; free under-7s. **Credit** AmEx, DC, MC, V. **Map** p316 J7. 7+
Britain's first art school was founded in 1768, and moved to Burlington House a century later. Works by Constable, Reynolds, Degas and others from its holdings are on permanent, free display in the John Madejski Fine Rooms – but the main focus is on the major temporary exhibitions. Most popular of these is the annual Summer Exhibition (until 17 August), which, for more than two centuries, has shown work submitted by the general public. Interactive family workshops and gallery talks are part of the Summer Exhibition; at other times, there are talks and activities for school groups, and activity sheets for 'art detectives' available at reception.
Buggy access. Café. Disabled: lift, ramp, toilet. Nappy-changing facilities. Nearest picnic place: Green Park, St James's Square. Restaurant. Shop.

Serpentine Gallery

Kensington Gardens (near Albert Memorial), W2 3XA (7402 6075/www.serpentine gallery.org). Lancaster Gate or South Kensington tube. **Open** 10am-6pm daily. **Admission** free; donations appreciated. **Credit** AmEx, MC, V. **Map** p311 D8. 7+ (parental advisory)

Housed in a 1930s tearoom, this lovely, airy gallery is a cutting-edge space for contemporary art. Its high profile in the art world is maintained by a rolling two-monthly line-up of exhibitions, and the annual Serpentine Pavilion commission, which enlists an internationally famed architect to design and build a new pavilion, visible until November: this year it's megastar Frank Gehry. The events programme includes family days, artist-led drawing and painting courses, and trails relating to the current exhibitions; check the website for dates.
Buggy access. Disabled access: toilet. Nappy-changing facilities. Nearest picnic place: Hyde Park. Shop.

Somerset House & Galleries

Strand, WC2R ORN (7845 4600/www.somerset house.org.uk). Embankment or Temple tube/ Charing Cross tube/rail. **Open** 10am-6pm daily. *Courtyard* 7.30am-11pm daily. *River Terrace* 8am-6pm daily (extended hours apply for restaurant). *Embankment Galleries* 10am-6pm Mon-Wed, Fri-Sun; 10am-9pm Thur. *Courtauld Gallery* 10am-6pm daily. *Tours* 1.30pm, 2.30pm, 3.45pm 1st Sat of mth; free. **Admission** *Parts of South Building, Courtyard & River Terrace* free. *Exhibitions* prices vary; phone for details. **Credit** MC, V. **Map** p317 M7. 8+ (galleries), 5+ (courtyard)

Oh, I do like to be beside the quayside, at the **Museum in Docklands**. *See p85.*

Built where a Tudor palace used to stand, this grand exercise in neoclassical design – formerly home to public bodies (all gone except for the Inland Revenue) – houses some of the UK's finest galleries. The Courtauld Gallery has a huge collection of Impressionist and post-Impressionist paintings and stages themed exhibitions throughout the year.

The Gilbert Collection of silver, gold and gemstones is closed but will reopen at the V&A in 2009 (*see p70*). The Hermitage Rooms have also closed and the 750 square metre space now houses the Embankment Galleries, which opened in April 2008. Exhibitions will focus on photography, design, fashion and architecture.

Somerset House is a great family attraction at any time of the year, but it really comes into its own in December and January, when the courtyard becomes an ice rink. Vast crowds notwithstanding, it's truly enchanting. Just as lovely, in the temperate months, is the big square fountain in the centre, with its waterjets that dance in formation. On hot days, children love running down the brief corridors of water. The courtyard also provides a stage for events during the summer holidays, and the annual four-day Free Time family festival – a jamboree of art, dance, music and storytelling – in mid August. *Buggy access. Cafés. Disabled access: lift, toilet. Nappy-changing facilities. Restaurant. Shops.*

South London Gallery

65 Peckham Road, SE5 8UH (7703 6120/ www.southlondongallery.org). Peckham Rye rail/ 12, 36, 171, 345 bus. **Open** noon-6pm Tue-Sun. Closed bank hols. **Admission** free. donation appreciated. 5+ (parental advisory) This gallery was one of the main showcases for Young British Artists in the 1990s, giving shows to Tracey Emin, Marc Quinn and Gavin Turk. Remaining one of the capital's foremost contemporary art galleries, it has a forward-thinking approach and futuristic atmosphere. Family workshops tie in with the current exhibitions, and there are film courses aimed at older children: for details, check the website. *Buggy access. Disabled access: lift, ramp, toilet. Nappy-changing facilities. Nearest picnic place: gallery garden.*

Tate Britain

Millbank, SW1P 4RG (7887 8888/www.tate. org.uk). Pimlico tube/77A, 88, C10, bus. **Open** 10am-5.50pm daily; late opening 6-10pm first Fri of mth. *Tours* 11am, noon, 2pm, 3pm Mon-Fri; noon, 3pm Sat, Sun. **Admission** free. *Temporary exhibitions* prices vary. *Tours* free. **Credit** MC, V. **Map** p317 L7. 5+

Elder sister to the Modern one, this Tate collection of British fine art from 1500 to the 20th century includes all the big names from Blake to Bacon. As well as the permanent exhibition, regular temporary shows are staged in its several large halls. Best of all is the Tate's ongoing effort to help younger audiences enjoy the art on display. The time-honoured Art Trolley is wheeled out every Saturday and Sunday (11am-5pm) and is laden with a wide range of make-and-do activities; other youthful entertainments include the new Tate Tales trail, a treasure hunt. Check the website for more family and kids' goings-on. And then, of course, there's the annual, headline-grabbing Turner Prize exhibition for contemporary art, from October to January. When you've finished here, you can cruise swiftly to Tate Modern for another art fix, on the Damien Hirst-decorated Tate to Tate boat. It sails every 40 minutes and takes about 20 minutes to get from Millbank to Bankside, stopping off at the London Eye in between (£4, £2 under-16s, £10 family, discounts for Travelcard holders). *Buggy access. Café. Disabled access: lift, ramp, toilet. Nappy-changing facilities. Nearest picnic place: lawns, Riverside Gardens. Restaurant. Shop.*

Tate Modern

Bankside, SE1 9TG (7887 8000/www.tate. org.uk). St Paul's tube/Blackfriars tube/rail. **Open** 10am-6pm Mon-Thur, Sun; 10am-10pm Fri, Sat. Last entry 45mins before closing. **Admission** free. *Temporary exhibitions* prices vary. **Credit** AmEx, MC, V. **Map** p318 O7. 5+ Just ambling around this awesome space is an experience in itself. Relics of the building's industrial days remain – the original gantries and lifting gear in the vast Turbine Hall, where the annual Unilever commision is displayed. Each year's large-scale, specially commissioned work is installed in the autumn, and stays there until April: Doris Salcedo's crack in 2007-2008, was amusing, and hardly any toddlers got stuck in it. The permanent collections are shown in four wings on Levels 3 and 5, guided by themes such as Cubism, Futurism and Vorticism, Surrealism, Abstract Expressionism and European Informal Art, and Minimalism.

Family activities are mostly available from Level 3: a pack called Start, which contains puzzles, art materials and an architectural trail, is available every Sunday (11am-5pm) and in school holidays; there's a children's audio tour too. Also on Level 3 is the Family Zone, where you can pick up a Tate Teaser paper trail and play art-related games. On Level 5, the Bloomberg Learning Zone has a variety of interactive

Sightseeing

activities. Plans for a colossal expansion are underway, with the current proposal – an extension resembling a stack of glass boxes – looking bold and not a little crackers.
Buggy access. Café. Disabled access: lift, toilet. Nappy-changing facilities. Nearest picnic place: grounds. Restaurant. Shops.

Vestry House Museum
Vestry Road, E17 6HZ (8509 1917/ www.walthamforest.gov.uk). Walthamstow Central tube/rail. **Open** noon-4pm Thur, Fri; 10am-5pm Sat, Sun; noon-4pm Wed (during school hols). *Tours* groups only, by prior arrangement. **Admission** free; donations appreciated. **No credit cards**. 6+
At various times a private home, a police station and a workhouse, this lovely little museum has displays that are engaging even for children. One room is devoted to attractive vintage toys and games; another is done up as a Victorian parlour. On the ground floor you can see a reconstructed police cell, complete with amusing wax figures dressed as village bobby and drunkard. Other displays are cosily domestic: carpet beaters, meat mincers and knife sharpeners survive as relics of the housewife's former lot. An airy space has been created to house a reconstructed Bremer Car, London's first petrol-driven vehicle.
Buggy access (ground floor). Disabled access: toilet (ground floor). Nappy-changing facilities. Nearest picnic place: museum garden. Shop.

Victoria & Albert Museum
Cromwell Road, SW7 2RL (7942 2000/www. vam.ac.uk). South Kensington tube. **Open** 10am-5.45pm Mon-Thur, Sat, Sun; 10am-10pm Fri. *Tours* daily; phone for details. **Admission** free; charges apply for special exhibitions. **Credit** AmEx, MC, V. **Map** p313 E10. 5+
The V&A enchants visitors, young or old, with its massive collection of sumptuous sculpture, textiles, and household treasures. On Saturdays and school hols, kids over five can borrow backpacks from the children's desk, then delve in to find puzzles, costumes and scenes to act out. Sundays and holidays bring out the Activity Cart for the over-threes, with the materials for samurai helmets, elephant masks or whatever the weekend's hot topic is. Hands-on fun is available at all times – children can try on replica Victorian underwear and build the Crystal Palace.
Summer 2008 sees the opening of the ambitious Sackler Centre, with its art studios, media labs, auditorium and new activities; and in February 2009, the long-awaited Theatre and Performance galleries open to display the best

bits of the dear, departed Theatre Museum. Until November 2008, a giant pink sheep and giggling Granny welcome you to the colourful Collaborators: UK Design For Performance, a free exhibition of theatre costume on the 3rd floor; teens may enjoy Fashion V Sport (also until November), a look at the crossover between sport brands and high fashion. Kids over 12 are also catered for at the Create! workshops (£9.50), in which they spend a day learning interior design or digital arts. The Gilbert Collection, moving from Somerset House (*see p68*), opens here in autumn 2009. The V&A's café is an absolute treat offering hot dishes and snacks.
Buggy access. Café. Disabled access: toilet. Nappy-changing facilities. Nearest picnic place: basement picnic room (weekends & school holidays), museum garden, Pirelli Gardens. Restaurant. Shop.

Wallace Collection
Hertford House, Manchester Square, W1U 3BN (7935 0687/www.wallacecollection.org). Bond Street tube/2, 10, 12, 30, 74, 113 bus. **Open** 10am-5pm daily. **Admission** free. **Credit** MC, V. **Map** p314 G5. 6+
The beautiful Wallace Collection is chock-full of priceless paintings, furniture, and, of greatest interest to children, the largest collection of armour (including swords and daggers in Britain). Prize paintings in the main collections include Frans Hals's *Laughing Cavalier* (neither laughing, nor a Cavalier) and Fragonard's *The Swing*; the Study and Oval Drawing Rooms are recreated in the style of Marie Antoinette's Versailles boudoir and include objects once held in her royal palaces. The splendid restaurant in the central courtyard is a new Oliver Peyton outfit, and has a children's menu. The armour workshops in the Conservation Gallery are hugely popular; *see also p6* **Great Days Out**.
Buggy access. Disabled access: lift, toilet. Nappy-changing facilities. Nearest picnic place: courtyard benches. Restaurant. Shop.

William Morris Gallery
Lloyd Park, Forest Road, E17 4PP (8527 3782/www.walthamforest.gov.uk/wmg). Blackhorse Road tube, then 123 bus. **Open** noon-4pm Thur, Fri; 10am-5pm Sat, Sun; noon-4pm Wed (during school hols). *Tours* phone for details. **Admission** free; donations appreciated. **Credit** MC, V. 5+
Artist, socialist and creator of all that flowery wallpaper, William Morris lived as a child (between 1848 and 1856) in this handsome, moated building. Its rooms are now kept as galleries, showing as many works by Morris's

Sightseeing

London uncovered

Dig down below London and you might find some surprising bits of history. Archaeologists uncovered the remains of a prehistoric lion at Bexley Heath and the skull of a woolly rhino on Fleet Street. Mammoths once rumbled through Ilford, and polar bears roamed over the ice sheets that formerly covered Kew Bridge. Two hundred thousand years later, Julius Caesar set up camp at Heathrow Airport, and the Saxons built a village on the site of the Savoy Hotel. You don't have to go to a museum to witness ancient history in the capital: fragments of the old Roman walls poke up all over the City, particularly along the appropriately-named London Wall.

The Romans deserve most of the credit for transforming London from a patch of marshy ground into an economic powerhouse. The Roman town of Londinium was founded in around 50 AD as a bridging point across the Thames, and was burned to the ground by Boudicca's armies a few years later. For the first of many times in its history, London bounced back. By the year 200,

Londinium, renamed Augusta, had grown into a mighty walled city, with the largest Roman basilica west of the Alps. The official extents of the City of London are still marked out by the line of the old Roman walls, which families can follow on a self-guided walk, starting on London Wall and finishing at the Tower of London. En route, you can see intriguing traces of Roman civic life at the Temple of Mithras on (Queen Victoria Street; see map p318 P6), and the atmospheric amphitheatre in the basement of the **Guildhall** (see p60).

To really get a feel for Roman London, the **Museum of London** (see p89), set amongst crumbling sections of the Roman wall, is your goal. As well as statues, coins and mosaics, the museum includes a walk-through recreation of a Roman villa, and reproductions of objects from ancient London that kids can pick up and play with. After the fall of the Roman Empire, London was abandoned for 400 years before the Anglo-Saxons moved in and took the city to the next stage of history. The rise of London from ghost town to teeming metropolis is covered in vivid detail in the remaining galleries of the museum, though the displays currently stop, as London almost did, with the Great Fire of London in 1666. Until the rest of the museum reopens in 2009, you can pick up the story of London at the **Museum in Docklands** (see p85). This child-friendly museum covers the history of trade along the River Thames, which provided most of London's wealth right up until the 20th century.

The museum has an excellent section on Docklands at War but to really get a feel for wartime London, go to the small community museums in the suburbs. Northeast London was ravaged by the firestorms of the Blitz, and you can read the personal stories of many ordinary Londoners at the **Bruce Castle Museum** (see p81) in Haringey. Not for the first time, London picked itself up from the ashes.

London's post-war history is the focus at the **Hackney Museum** (see p82) and **Islington Museum** (see p83), with particular emphasis on the immigration that began in the 1960s and made London the cosmopolitan city it is today.

Sightseeing

friends and collaborators as by the man himself. Kids may enjoy the trails, which encourage them to examine ceramic tile illustrations of stories like *Beauty and the Beast*. To the rear of the house, invisible from the road, is Lloyd Park, with its aviary, hillock and moat.
Buggy access. Nearest picnic place: Lloyd Park. Shop.

CHILDHOOD

Foundling Museum

40 Brunswick Square, WC1N 1AZ (7841 3600/www.foundlingmuseum.org.uk). Russell Square tube. **Open** 10am-5pm Tue-Sat; 11am-5pm Sun. *Tours* by arrangement. **Admission** £5; £4 reductions; free under-16s. **Credit** MC, V. **Map** p317 L4. 3+
This museum honours the Hospital for the Maintenance and Education of Exposed and Deserted Children, or 'Foundling Hospital', founded in 1739 by retired sea captain Thomas Coram, and funded by donations from the painter William Hogarth and the composer George Frederic Handel. For the next 250 years, the hospital provided education for babies who had been abandoned by their mothers. The charity founded by Coram still provides support for young people and parents today.

As well as paintings by William Hogarth and other artists, the museum has a room dedicated to Handel. Kids love the 'musical chairs', with hidden speakers playing excerpts from the composer's works. The best time to visit the museum is on the first Saturday of every month, when activities are laid on for children. Kids can dress up in costumes, listen to stories and design cards. Extra family fun-days take place on Tuesdays and Thursdays in the school holidays. In 2008, inaugural Coram, Hogarth and Handel Fellowships were bestowed on writer Jacqueline Wilson, sculptor Richard Wentworth and musician Damon Albarn: the dynamic trio will work with the museum to develop exciting new activities for kids.
Buggy access. Café. Disabled access: lift. Nappy-changing facilities. Nearest picnic place: Brunswick Square, Coram's Fields. Shop.

London International Gallery of Children's Art

O2 Centre, 255 Finchley Road, NW3 6LU (7435 0903/www.ligca.org). Finchley Road tube. **Open** 4-6pm Tue-Thur; noon-6pm Fri-Sun. **Admission** free; donations requested. 5+
LIGCA celebrates the creativity of children all over the world. There are free Sunday afternoon workshops for five- to 12-year olds, and birthday parties can be held here too. The gallery is run by volunteers, so phone before setting out.
Buggy access. Disabled access: lift, toilet. Nappy-changing facilities (O2 Centre).

Pollock's Toy Museum

1 Scala Street (entrance on Whitfield Street), W1T 2HL (7636 3452/www.pollocks toymuseum.com). Goodge Street tube. **Open** 10am-5pm Mon-Sat. **Admission** £4; £3 reductions; £2 3-16s; free under-3s. **Credit** MC, V. 5+
Named after Benjamin Pollock, the last of the Victorian toy theatre printers, this museum is a warren of atmospheric rooms containing treasures gathered from nurseries across the world: the oldest item is a 4,000-year-old Egyptian clay toy mouse. Adults are more likely to appreciate the nostalgia value of the old board games and playthings, but the museum shop has child appeal, with its reproduction cardboard theatres, wind-up music boxes, animal masks and tin robots.
Nearest picnic place: Crabtree Fields, Colville Place. Shop.

Ragged School Museum

46-50 Copperfield Road, E3 4RR (8980 6405/ www.raggedschoolmuseum.org.uk). Mile End tube. **Open** 10am-5pm Wed, Thur; 2-5pm 1st Sun of mth. *Tours* by arrangement; phone for details. **Admission** free; donations welcome. **No credit cards** 6+ (term time), 2+ (school holidays)
Ragged schools, providing tuition, food and clothing for destitute children, were an early experiment in public education, and this one was London's largest; Dr Barnardo taught here. The place is now a fascinating museum that has a mock-up of a classroom, where formal lessons – complete with slates – are staged for kids. There's also an Edwardian kitchen and displays on local history and industry. Holiday activities are always popular (*see p50* **Life in the past lane**).
Buggy access. Café. Disabled access: toilet. Nappy-changing facilities. Nearest picnic place: Mile End Park. Shop.

V&A Museum of Childhood

Cambridge Heath Road, E2 9PA (8983 5200/ recorded information 8980 2415/www.vam. ac.uk/moc). Bethnal Green tube/rail/8 bus. **Open** 10am-5.45pm daily. **Admission** free. Under-12s must be accompanied by an adult. **Credit** MC, V. 1+
This museum is full of fun. The basement complex of activity rooms, as well as loads of

Sightseeing

foyer space, mean that children can run around without fear of knocking anything over. There's plenty of hands-on and interactive exhibits, such as the rocking horses, but some things remain safely behind glass, like the detailed dolls houses, ancient teddy bears and children's clothes from various periods in history. The Benugo café is tasteful and cheerful, and the pleasant basement picnic space is next to a workshop area. The mezzanine is configured to house temporary and touring exhibitions: Top to Toe (October 2008-April 2009) lines up garments from the museum's own collection to examine the way children are sometimes dressed as miniature adults; and Snozzcumbers and Frobscuttle (May-September 2009) is a celebration of the combined creative forces of Roald Dahl and Quentin Blake. *Buggy access. Café. Disabled access: lift, ramp, toilet. Nappy-changing facilities. Nearest picnic place: basement, museum grounds. Shop.*

ETHNOGRAPHY

British Museum

Great Russell Street, WC1B 3DG (7323 8000/ 7323 8299/www.britishmuseum.org). Holborn, Russell Square or Tottenham Court Road tube. **Open** *Galleries* 10am-5.30pm Mon-Wed, Sat, Sun; 10am-8.30pm Thur, Fri. *Great Court* 9am-6pm Mon-Wed, Sun; 9am-11pm Thur-Sat. *Tours* Highlights 10.30am, 1pm, 3pm daily; phone for details. Eye Opener phone for details. **Admission** free; donations appreciated. *Temporary exhibitions* prices vary; phone for details. *Highlights tours* £8; £5 under-11s, reductions. *Eye Opener tours* free. **Credit** AmEx, DC, MC, V. **Map** p317 K5. 5+

There are four or five truly great museums in the world and the British Museum is up there with the best of them. Hidden behind the vast, Parthenon-like Portland-stone façade is an incredible array of treasures from across the globe, amassed over 255 years of collecting. Many of the displays here are so famous and significant that they have achieved an almost mystical quality – the Rosetta Stone, the Lewis Chessmen, the Anglo-Saxon helmet from Sutton Hoo, the Elgin Marbles. There is more here than you could see in a week, so take your time.

A good place to start is the permanent Enlightenment exhibition in the restored King's Library. Other must-see exhibits include the Egyptian mummies and funerary objects in the Roxie Walker Galleries (it's still a bone of contention that so many of Egypt's treasures are displayed here rather than in the Cairo museum). The Africa galleries, full of vivid colours and spooky masks, and Living & Dying – a surreal collection of tribal objects relating

Plenty to get your teeth into at the **Natural History Museum**. *See p92.*

to death and mortality from the collection of the Wellcome Trust, are also atmospheric. For more information on the British Museum, *see also p64* **Great Days Out**.
Buggy access. Cafés. Disabled access: lift, toilet. Nappy-changing facilities. Nearest picnic place: Russell Square. Restaurant. Shops.

Horniman Museum

100 London Road, SE23 3PQ (8699 1872/ www.horniman.ac.uk). Forest Hill rail/122, 176, 185, 312, 356, 363, P4, P13 bus. **Open** 10.30am-5.30pm daily. **Admission** free; donations appreciated. **Credit** MC, V. 3+
This museum's fascinating collection of curiosities and family activity programme is one of the wonders of south-east London. Its café becomes quite the toddler group with mums and babies who lunch. The museum is named after Frederick Horniman, a tea trader and inveterate collector who assembled a curious museum at his home in Forest Hill, then later in this art nouveau pile. The Natural History gallery has skeletons, pickled animals, stuffed birds and insect models in glass cases, all presided over by an overstuffed walrus; the atmospheric World Cultures section has an astonishing 80,000 objects from pretty much everywhere; and the Music Room has hundreds of instruments and touch screens that unleash their sounds. A 'Hands-On' room gives young visitors carte blanche to bash away at world instruments. There are also cases of exotic reptiles and a living beehive in the Environment Room. Outside, the delightful gardens have an animal enclosure, an elegant conservatory and a picnic spot with superb views. For the Horniman's **Aquarium**, *see p129.*
Buggy access. Café. Disabled access: lift, toilet. Nappy-changing facilities. Nearest picnic place: museum gardens. Shop.

Petrie Museum of Egyptian Archaeology

University College London, entrance through DMS Watson Library, Malet Place, WC1E 6BT (7679 2884/www.petrie.ucl.ac.uk). Goodge Street or Warren Street tube/29, 73, 134 bus. **Open** 1-5pm Tue-Fri; 10am-1pm Sat. Closed Easter hols; 24 Dec-2 Jan. **Admission** free; donations appreciated. **Map** p317 K4. 7+
Named after Flinders Petrie, excavator of ancient Egyptian treasures, this museum was set up in 1892 by traveller and diarist Amelia Edwards. It contains ancient Egyptian items that were used in everyday life. Items to rouse interest include ancient toys, jewellery, painted coffin cases, a rat trap, the world's oldest piece of clothing (a dress worn by a teenager in 2800 BC) and a mummy head, with eyelashes and eyebrows still intact. There are plans to rehouse the collections in purpose-built galleries in 2009, but until then its gloomy surroundings give the place a spooky, Indiana Jones-like atmosphere. Children can work through the Rock Trail, a themed journey around the collection; there's also a Petrie Family Pack archaeology kit. For activities and events, contact the Education Officer on 7679 2151.
Buggy access. Disabled access: lift, toilet. Nearest picnic place: Gordon Square. Shop.

EMERGENCY SERVICES

London Fire Brigade Museum

Winchester House, 94A Southwark Bridge Road, SE1 0EG (7587 2894/www.london-fire.gov.uk). Borough tube/Southwark tube/rail/ 344 bus. Tours by appointment 10.30am, 2pm Mon-Fri. **Admission** £3; £2 7-14s, reductions; £1 under-7s. **Credit** MC, V. **Map** p318 O9. 5+
Any child who wants to be a firefighter should be taken on one of the hour-long tours of this friendly museum, which is housed in eight small rooms at the London Fire Brigade Training Centre. As well as memorabilia, photos, uniforms, paintings and equipment, the tours take in a potted history of firefighting since the Great Fire of 1666, and the appliance bay, where pumps dating back to 1708 stand in tribute to blazes past. Small children are most smitten with, but may not touch, the 20 shiny fire engines from a 1830s model to red and brass motors. Kids are given fireman uniforms to try on, as well as colouring materials. Booking is essential.
Buggy access. Disabled access: toilet. Nearest picnic place: Mint Street Park. Shop.

Museum & Library of the Order of St John

St John's Gate, St John's Lane, EC1M 4DA (7324 4005/www.sja.org.uk/museum). Farringdon tube/rail/55, 63, 243 bus. **Open** 10am-5pm Mon-Fri; 10am-4pm Sat. *Tours* 11am, 2.30pm Tue, Fri, Sat. **Admission** free; suggested donations for tours £5; £4 reductions. **Credit** MC, V. **Map** p318 O4. 5+
St John Ambulance, always in demand at pop concerts, has its own museum. The order began with the crusaders in 11th-century Jerusalem, and this long history is told in exhibits divided between a static collection of antiques and a brighter, more interactive room that showcases the order's medical history. The museum is set

Great Days Out
South Kensington

South Kensington is the busiest end of the Royal Borough of Kensington & Chelsea, as far as cultural and academic institutions are concerned. With three of London's most heavyweight museums, a royal palace and swathes of lovely parkland, there's plenty to keep a family occupied. Tops on the 'grand day out' itinerary is the world-renowned Natural History Museum, for dinosaurs and other animals. The Science Museum shows how science touches all aspects of life and the Victoria & Albert Museum is a stunner. (If you have a toddler, you might be interested in the experience of our reviewer; *see p90*). These three museums form an oasis of learning envisaged by Prince Albert, who bought the land on which they stand with the profits from the 1851 Great Exhibition, to

'extend the influence of Science and Art upon Productive Industry'. They've proved their might as far as the tourist industry is concerned.

Taking on all three in one day would likely to make your head spin. Pick one, and combine it with a pootle up to Hyde Park or Kensington Gardens.

Walking with dinosaurs

At the **Natural History Museum** (*see p92*) grab a free map from one of the information desks at the entrances and, with the help of an army of staff, you'll soon be navigating with ease.

To get the most out of your visit, take advantage of the children's packs, available at the entrance. If you're

entertaining under-sevens, then pick up a free (£25 deposit needed) Explorer Backpack; or for under a quid you can buy a themed Discovery Guide for children up to the age of 16. Ring nearer the time to check whether the ice rink and fair will take place again this winter.

Space base

The **Science Museum** (*see p94*) is a thrilling day out. The vast collection includes landmark inventions such as Stephenson's *Rocket*, Arkwright's spinning machine, Whittle's turbo-jet engine and the Apollo 10 command module. The collections are enlivened through imaginative interactive displays. Children can spend hours learning through play at one of the museum's six play zones. Under-sixes dig the Garden area in the basement. On the ground floor, in the Wellcome Wing, the Pattern Pod introduces under-eights to patterns and repetition in the natural world.

In school holidays, look out for the museum's free educational events and workshops – they can't be booked in advance so turn up early on the day and check out their website for advanced details. Science Night sleepovers are held once a month (£30 per person, eight- to 11-year-olds, in groups of five or more), with an evening of activities that might include creating slime or making balloon-powered buggies. You have to book as much as two months ahead (24hr information line 7942 4747).

The **Victoria & Albert Museum** (*see p70*) is a delightful place to wander, crammed as it is with beautiful displays of ceramics, fashion, paintings, sculpture and textiles. Its halls are tailor-made for whiling away the hours. To amuse potentially restless children, however, try one of the many laid-on free activities. There are also many interactive exhibits dotted around the museum; most of them can be found in the British Galleries and they're available at all times. A great way for families to explore the museum is to follow one of the trails devised by the education officers; for instance the Picnic Trail invites you to plan the perfect picnic as you journey through South Asia, the Middle East and East Asia Galleries. There's also a family-friendly café.

LUNCH BOX

Also in the area: Carluccio's Caffè, Giraffe, Wagamama.

Café Crêperie *2 Exhibition Road, SW7 2HF (7589 8947/www.kensington creperie.com).* Made to order.

Green Fields Café *13 Exhibition Road, SW7 2HE (7584 1396).* Takeaway sandwiches, salads and mini pizzas.

Orangery *Kensington Palace, Kensington Gardens, W8 2UH (7376 0239/www.digbytrout.co.uk).* Light lunches and traditional afternoon teas.

Pâtisserie Valerie *215 Brompton Road, SW3 2EJ (7823 9971); 27 Kensington Church Street, W8 4LL (7937 9574); www.patisserie-valerie.co.uk.* Breakfast, lunches, coffee, posh French gateaux.

Pizza Organic *20 Old Brompton Road, SW7 3DL (7589 9613/www.pizza piazza.co.uk).* Pizzas, burgers, pasta.

Park life

Whichever of the 'big three' you choose, once you've seen all you can manage, head for some green and take a walk to Hyde Park and Kensington Gardens.

Hyde Park (*see p123*) is the largest of London's Royal Parks and was the first to be opened to the public. Year-round, the park's perimeter is popular with skaters, cyclists and horse-riders (there are riding schools near Rotten Row, part of the wide riding track around Hyde Park). At the west side of the park is the Serpentine, London's oldest boating lake, with its complement of wildfowl. You can rent rowing boats and pedalos from March to October.

Across the road from the Serpentine Gallery is the Diana, Princess of Wales Memorial Fountain, designed by Kathryn Gustafson as a Cornish granite channel filled with running water (amid a welter of controversy). It's a great place to cool your toes on hot days.

Kensington Gardens covers 260 acres and meets Hyde Park at the Serpentine. It is home to the **Diana, Princess of Wales Memorial Playground** (*see p112*), as well as the Albert Memorial, with its huge statue of Prince Albert, all blinged out in gold and seated under a 180-foot (55-metre) spire and canopy (for guided tours, ring 7495 0916).

Bank of England Museum. *See p97.*

beside St John's Gate, a Tudor stone edifice, part of the original priory. If you take the tour, you'll see the extant 12th-century crypt. Kids wanting to get some hands-on experience can sign up for first-aid training as a member of the Badgers (fives to tens) or Cadets (tens to 18s). In the next couple of years, the museum will undergo a major, Lottery-funded redevelopment; keep an eye on the website for news.
Buggy access (not tours). Nearest picnic place: Clerkenwell Close. Shop.

GREAT LIVES

Apsley House: The Wellington Museum

149 Piccadilly, W1J 7NT (7499 5676/www. english-heritage.org.uk). Hyde Park Corner tube. **Open** *Apr-Oct* 11am-5pm Wed-Sun. *Nov-Mar* 11am-4pm Wed-Sun. Also open Mon bank hols. *Tours* by arrangement. **Admission** £5.50 (includes audio guide if available); £2.80 5-16s; £4.40 reductions; free under-5s. *Joint ticket with admission to Wellington Arch* £6.90; £3.50 5-16s; £5.50 reductions; free under-5s; £17.30 family (2+3). *Tours* phone for details. **Credit** MC, V. **Map** p316 G8. 5+
This stately Portland stone mansion (former address, No. 1 London) was the family home of Arthur Wellesley, the first Duke of Wellington,

and scourge of Napoleon at Waterloo. His descendants still live in the building, but some of it has been given over to a museum about the duke, his campaigns and his extravagant taste in tableware. A basement room contains the man's medals, death mask and boots; families can pick up a 'Wellington Boot' pack with activities for children aged five to 11. Special talks and storytelling sessions for children take place throughout the year.
Buggy access. Nearest picnic place: Hyde Park. Shop.

Benjamin Franklin House

36 Craven Street, WC2N 5NF (information 7930 9121/bookings 7930 6601/www.benjamin franklinhouse.org). Embankment tube/ Charing Cross tube/rail. **Open** 10.30am-5pm daily. **Admission** £7; £5 reductions; free under-16s. *Tours* noon, 1pm, 2pm, 3.15pm, 4.15pm Wed-Sun. Booking advisable. **Credit** MC, V. **Map** p317 L7. 6+
Franklin, a scientist, inventor, philosopher, diplomat and all-round founding father lived in this house from 1757 to 1775. It's not a museum exactly, but visitors can take part in the Historical Experience, during which Franklin's landlady speaks to her guests using sound and projected imagery to conjure up the period in which the great man lived.
Buggy access (ground floor). Nearest picnic place: Victoria Gardens, Embankment. Shop.

Glamour Grandeur
Sleaze Disease

Discover a great city in the making

FREE ENTRY

150 London Wall, EC2Y 5HN
⊖ St Paul's, Barbican
www.museumoflondon.org.uk

MUSEUM OF LONDON

BLOOD BLITZ
BANANAS

MUSEUM IN DOCKLANDS
How the world came to the East End

West India Quay, London E14 4AL
⊖ Canary Wharf ⊖ West India Quay
www.museumindocklands.org.uk

Registered charity number: 1060415

Charles Dickens Museum

48 Doughty Street, WC1N 2LX (7405 2127/ www.dickensmuseum.com). Russell Square tube. **Open** 10am-5pm Mon-Sat; 11am-5pm Sun. **Admission** £5; £4 reductions; £3 5-15s; free under-5s; £14 family (2+4). **Credit** AmEx, DC, MC, V. **Map** p317 M4. 8+

After the success of *The Pickwick Papers* in 1836, Dickens left his cramped chambers in Holborn and moved to Doughty Street for three years, at that time a private street sealed at each end with gates and porters; *Oliver Twist* and *A Christmas Carol* were written here. The building is the author's only surviving London residence, now crammed with memorabilia and artefacts. In the basement, visitors can see a 25-minute film on Dickens's life in London; children's 'handling sessions' let kids get to grips with real Dickens possessions. These take place most Wednesdays, but call ahead as they are run by volunteers. There are two mini-trails for children, based on Dickens stories.
Buggy access (ground floor). Nearest picnic place: Coram's Fields/Russell Square. Shop.

Dr Johnson's House

17 Gough Square, off Fleet Street, EC4A 3DE (7353 3745/www.drjohnsonshouse.org). Chancery Lane or Temple tube/Blackfriars tube/rail. **Open** *May-Sept* 11am-5.30pm Mon-Sat. *Oct-Apr* 11am-5pm Mon-Sat. *Tours* by arrangement (groups of 10 or more). **Admission** £4.50; £1.50 under-18s; £3.50 reductionss; £10 family (2+unlimited children). *Tours* free. *Evening tours* by arrangement; phone for details. **No credit cards**. **Map** p318 N6. 6+

This Georgian house was home to the author of the *Dictionary of the English Language*, where he lived with his cat, Hodge. Hodge is honoured by a statue outside the house, one of the few items that will really interest children, though they might enjoy trying on replica Georgian costumes in the garret.
Buggy access. Nearest picnic place: Lincoln's Inn Fields. Shop.

Florence Nightingale Museum

St Thomas's Hospital, 2 Lambeth Palace Road, SE1 7EW (7620 0374/www.florence-nightingale.co.uk). Westminster tube/Waterloo tube/rail. **Open** 10am-5pm Mon-Fri; 10am-4.30pm Sat, Sun. Last entry 1hr before closing. **Admission** £5.80; £4.80 5-18s, reductions; free under-5s; £16 family (2+2). **Credit** AmEx, MC, V. **Map** p317 M9. 5+

Flo's important status in Key Stage One and Two of the National Curriculum means school holidays are always busy at the museum dedicated to her life (1820-1910). Mementoes and tableaux evoke the field hospitals of Scutari, where Nurse Nightingale first came to public attention, and details of her privileged life before then, and her studious life thereafter, are told in a 20-minute film. Other displays include clothing, furniture, books, letters, and Athena, Florence's pet owl (stuffed). Trails for children are available, and other art and history activities are put on during school holidays.
Buggy access. Disabled access: toilet. Nappy-changing facilities. Nearest picnic place: benches by hospital entrance, Archbishop's Park. Shop.

Sherlock Holmes Museum

221B Baker Street, NW1 6XE (7935 8866/ www.sherlock-holmes.co.uk). Baker Street tube/74, 139, 189 bus. **Open** 9.30am-6pm daily (last entry 5.30pm). **Admission** £6; £4 6-16s; free under-6s. **Credit** AmEx, MC, V. **Map** p311 F4. 6+

The house is set up as if the fictional master detective and associate are in situ – ditto affable housekeeper Mrs Hudson, who can tell you all you need to know about the great man, whose chair you can keep warm in his study. Upstairs is the room belonging to his sidekick Watson; the third-floor exhibit rooms contains wax models of scenes from the stories. Sherlock Holmes and Moriary can be seen in the same room.
Nearest picnic place: Regent's Park. Shop.

Sir John Soane's Museum

13 Lincoln's Inn Fields, WC2A 3BP (7405 2107/education officer 7440 4247/www.soane. org). Holborn tube. **Open** 10am-5pm Tue-Sat; 10am-5pm, 6-9pm 1st Tue of mth. *Tours* 2.30pm Sat. **Admission** free; donations appreciated. *Tours* £5; free reductions, under-16s. **Credit** AmEx, MC, V. **Map** p315 M5. 7+

Illustrious architect John Soane (1753-1837) collected stuff with a passion, filling his home with everything from an ancient Egyptian sarcophagus to paintings by satirist William Hogarth. The museum has a floor devoted to holiday workshops for families and children (£10 a head, book in advance): learn how mirrors increase light in a room and produce optical illusions, or get stuck into plaster moulding. There are also free drop-in family sessions on the third Saturday of the month. Children aged seven to 13 can sign up to the Young Architects Club, which meets for three hours on the first Saturday of the month. Note that buggies cannot be accommodated.
Nearest picnic place: Lincoln's Inn Fields. Shop.

Sightseeing

LONDON & LOCAL

Bruce Castle Museum

Lordship Lane, N17 8NU (8808 8772/ www.haringey.gov.uk). Wood Green tube then 123 or 243 bus/Seven Sisters tube/rail then 123 or 243 bus/Bruce Grove rail. **Open** 1-5pm Wed-Sun. **Admission** free; donations welcome. **No credit cards.** 4+

Housed in a gorgeous 16th-century mansion that pops up unexpectedly on a suburban street, this local museum is devoted to the history and achievements of Haringey and its residents. The borough was the home of madcap illustrator William Heath Robinson and Rowland Hill, the inventor of the Penny Post, who coincidentally worked as a school master on this site. The museum's 'Inventor Centre' has numerous buttons to press and levers to pull. There are black-and-white photos dating back to the days when the borough was open countryside and White Hart Lane was a sleepy country track. Football fans should keep an eye out for the displays on Tottenham Hotspur and read the surprising history of Walter Tull, one of the first black football players in Britain. There are free activity sheets for kids, including a nature trail that explores the pleasant 20 acre park around the museum. Free art and craft sessions for families take place from 2pm to 4pm on Sundays year-round, and on Wednesdays, Thursdays and Fridays in the school holidays. In the absence of a museum café, Bruce Castle buggy pushers make straight for the Marmalade café on Lordship Lane (8808 9111) for scrummy coffee and pastries. *Buggy access. Disabled access: lift, toilet. Nappy-changing facilities. Nearest picnic place: museum grounds. Shop.*

Brunel Engine House & Tunnel Exhibition

Brunel Engine House, Railway Avenue, SE16 4LF (7231 3840/www.brunelenginehouse.org. uk). Rotherhithe tube. **Open** 10am-5pm daily. **Admission** £2; free-£1 reductions; free under-16s; £5 family (2+2). **No credit cards.** 5+

The Brunels, father and son (Sir Marc and Isambard Kingdom), worked together from 1825 until 1843 to create the world's first underwater tunnel, with Isambard nearly drowning in the process. The story of what the Victorians hailed as 'the Eighth Wonder of the World' is told in this museum in the original engine house. The tunnel is now used by the East London tube line. There's plenty for children, not least the popular summer play-scheme in the sculpture garden. The giant figure of Brunel that is owned by the museum is always (and literally) a big player in the Bermondsey and Rotherhithe carnivals. Excitingly, the temporary closure of the East London Line in 2008 has given the museum the chance to expand: by the time work has finished, it will have a splendid new café overlooking the river, a new schools and activity room, and new visitor centre above an operating railway.

Wimbledon Lawn Tennis Museum. *See p101.*

Sightseeing

Buggy access. Café. Disabled access: toilet. Nearest picnic place: museum gardens & riverbank. Shop.

Crystal Palace Museum

Anerley Hill, SE19 2BA (8676 0700/ www.crystalpalacemuseum.org.uk) Crystal Palace rail. **Open** 11am-4.30pm Sat, Sun, bank hol Mon. *Tours* noon 1st Sun of mth. **Admission** free. 7+

To learn about the majestic exhibition hall that gave this area its name, visit this friendly museum, housed in the old engineering school where John Logie Baird invented television. Opening hours are limited, as the museum is run by volunteers. The 'exhibition of an exhibition' includes Victorian artefacts from the original Hyde Park edifice, as well as video and audio presentations about the great glass building. A small Logie Baird display marks the birth of home entertainment; from June 1934 the Baird Television Company had four studios at Crystal Palace. *Buggy access. Nearest picnic place: Crystal Palace Park. Shop.*

Hackney Museum

Technology & Learning Centre, 1 Reading Lane, off Mare Street, E8 1GQ (8356 3500/ www.hackney.gov.uk). Hackney Central rail. **Open** 9.30am-5.30pm Tue, Wed, Fri; 9.30am-8pm Thur; 10am-5pm Sat. **Admission** free. 3+

A £400,000 grant from the Heritage Lottery Fund provided the money to develop this community-focused museum beside Hackney Town Hall. Kids will enjoy the way the museum is rooted in the local community – displays include a recreation of Cooke's pie and eel shop

'Eyes *always* right' at the **Firepower Royal Artillery Museum**. *See p103.*

and the activity stations which tie into the history of the borough. Highlights include a recreated Saxon boat that kids can pile up with goods (the original is displayed under glass in the floor) and the section on the Matchbox car factory, founded in Hackney in 1952 to help kids get around a ban on taking large toys to school. Toddlers can take advantage of the comfy reading corner while older kids can dress up in Victorian clothes and try their hand at making matchboxes, an industry that employed countless children in Victorian times. Interactive art and role-playing workshops take place on Wednesday and Thursday afternoons. The temporary exhibition changes every four months; the theme for summer 2008 is 'Sporting Heroes of Hackney'.

Buggy access. Disabled access: toilet. Nappy-changing facilities. Nearest picnic place: benches in square, London Fields. Shop.

Islington Museum

Finsbury Library, 245 St John Street, EC1V 4NB (7527 3235/www.islington.gov.uk). Angel or Farringdon tube/153 bus. **Open** 10am-5pm Mon, Tue, Thur-Sat. **Admission** free. 5+
Following a big injection of cash from the Heritage Lottery Fund, Islington Museum, reopened in a new, purpose-built facility at Finsbury Library in April 2008. Its collection spans centuries of local history, from the days when Islington dairies provided the milk for medieval London to the contribution of migrant communities since WWII. Children will enjoy the sections on Edwardian school life and the special activity desks and quiz screens.

Buggy access. Disabled access: lift, toilet. Nearest picnic place: Northhampton Square. Shop.

Kew Bridge Steam Museum

Green Dragon Lane, Brentford, Middx TW8 0EN (8568 4757/www.kbsm.org). Gunnersbury tube, then 237 or 267 bus/ Kew Bridge rail/65, 391 bus. **Open** 11am-4pm Tue-Sun, bank hol Mon. *Tours* times vary; phone for details, book in advance. **Admission** *Mon-Fri* £5; £4 reductions; free under-16s. *Sat, Sun* £8.50; £7.50 reductions; free under-16s. Under-16s must be accompanied by an adult. **Credit** MC, V. 5+
This Victorian riverside pumping station is 'all systems go' every weekend, when steam engines – the pumping variety, as well as the locomotive sort – burst into life. *Cloister*, the narrow-gauge locomotive (the only steam train in London) gives rides on Sundays between March and November; various family activities

are held during the school and bank holidays. The fascinating Water for Life gallery saturates you with facts about the history of water supply and usage in London, including cholera, toshers (sewer scavengers) and domestic water usage. Down Below takes you down the sewers to learn about the work of Bazalgette and modern-day underground heroes.

Buggy access. Café (Sat, Sun). Disabled access: lift, ramp, toilet. Nappy-changing facilities. Nearest picnic place: Kew Green. Shop.

London Canal Museum

12-13 New Wharf Road, N1 9RT (7713 0836/www.canalmuseum.org.uk). King's Cross tube/rail. **Open** 10am-4.30pm Tue-Sun, bank hol Mon. Last entry 3.45pm. **Admission** £3; £2 reductions; £1.50 8-15s; free under-8s. **Credit** MC, V. **Map** p315 M2. 5+
This small shrine to life on Britain's canals is a real charmer. Apart from panels of text relating the historic importance of the waterways, there's a real narrowboat to explore, complete with domestic chit-chat on speakers; a children's corner with canal-themed books and lots of pictures of Rosie and Jim to colour in; a life-size 'horse' in its stable; and videos showing life afloat in all its grim griminess. A touch screen introduces visitors to the life and times of one Carlo Gatti, sometime owner of the warehouse at 12 New Wharf Road. He was an Italian-Swiss immigrant who rose from humble chestnut seller to wealthy ice-cream manufacturer, simply by importing ice blocks from the frozen lakes of Norway. There are regular craft sessions in the school holidays.

Buggy access. Disabled access: lift, toilet. Nappy-changing facilities. Nearest picnic place: museum terrace, canal towpath. Shop.

London Transport Museum

The Piazza, WC2E 7BB (7379 6344/ www.ltmuseum.co.uk). Covent Garden tube. **Open** 10am-6pm Mon-Thur, Sat, Sun; 11am-9pm Fri. **Admission** £10; £6-£8 reductions; free under-16s. **Credit** AmEx, MC, V. **Map** p317 L7. 2+
This jolly green tribute to the city's prime movers – on road, rail and river – made a welcome return to Covent Garden in 2007. Two years of thorough refurbishment have given the old flower market building, which houses the displays, a sleek and colourful look. On the ground floor, an art installation called 'World Cities' puts the city's transport in a global context, but children are inclined to steam past this to reach the hands-on stuff. Train carriages and buses (from the horse-drawn Shillibeer's model to a sliced-through

Sightseeing

modern bus, whose driver's seat children love to sit in) are open for exploration, and there are computerised driving games all over the place; one of the favourites is the tube driver's simulator. Children are given a stamper guide, and use a museum plan to find the 13 stamper stations, insert their cards in each one and collect the set. There's also an under-sixes play area, with climb-on vehicles and soft play, a family picnic room and education rooms, a great little restaurant and a well stocked shop (Thomas has pride of place). Of such distractions are great family outings made, but beware of the queues in school holidays.

Buggy access. Disabled access: lift, toilet. Nappy-changing facilities. Nearest picnic place: musuem picnic room, piazza. Restaurant. Shop.

Museum in Docklands

No.1 Warehouse, West India Quay, Hertsmere Road, E14 4AL (0870 444 3857/recorded information 0870 444 3856/www.museumin docklands.org.uk). Canary Wharf tube/West India Quay DLR. **Open** 10am-6pm daily. **Admission** (annual ticket, allows for multiple visits) £5; free-£3 reductions; free under-16s. **Credit** MC, V. 4+

This thought-provoking museum explores the history of how 'the world came to the East End'.

Displays of nautical relics and atmospheric recreations tell the complex story of shipping on the Thames. There's a section on whaling and gibbets and cutlasses from the days of piracy. The galleries on the modern history of the docks are more interesting for adults than children, but everyone can learn something from the 'London, Sugar & Slavery' and 'Docklands at War' exhibits. Many of the displays come with an entertaining audio commentary, voiced by *Time Team*'s Tony Robinson.

Highlights include Sailortown, a moody recreation of 18th-century Wapping, the Mudlarks Gallery, a large interactive playground with a soft-play area and the Foreshore Discovery Box. Costumed storytelling sessions and craft workshops take place on Saturday afternoons, there are extra sessions during the school holidays. Look out for the workshops based on the life of Joseph Johnson, a real-life 19th-century story-teller. Special sessions for under-fives take place on Mondays and Thursdays (phone for details). There's a refectory, but the best place to enjoy your sandwiches is out on the quayside, beneath the giant loading cranes. *See also p86* **Great Days Out**.

Buggy access. Café. Disabled access: lift, toilet. Nappy-changing facilities. Nearest picnic place: quayside benches, refectory. Restaurant. Shop.

Sightseeing

Experience life on the ocean wave on the **HMS Belfast**. *See p104.*

Great Days Out
Docklands

The docks, which up until the 19th century were fundamental to the prosperity of the British Empire, were redundant for a while. Over the last three decades, however, since £790m of public money was pumped into redeveloping the area, Docklands has become a rather chipper destination, with plenty of entertainment options.

The best way to get around Docklands is on the **Docklands Light Railway** (DLR; 7363 9700, www.tfl.gov.uk/dlr). With various extensions over the years, the DLR now reaches from Bank in the City to Beckton in the east, and from Lewisham south of the Thames (it will be all the way to Woolwich by the beginning of 2009) to Stratford to the north. Much of the network runs on raised tracks, making the journey a sightseeing pleasure. Pick quiet times (weekdays after 10am and before 5pm) and the kids can sit in the front of the train and pretend to drive.

Snap up a **Rail & River Rover** ticket (£10.50, £5.25 children, free under-5s, £26 family), which combines travel on the DLR with trips on City Cruises sightseeing boats. Disembark at Tower Pier to check out the marina of St Katharine Docks, with its flashy yachts. Then stroll the ten minutes past Tower Bridge and the Tower of London to the DLR station at Tower Gateway. If you stay on board and enjoy the views you can enjoy **Greenwich**'s numerous attractions (*see p124*), then take the DLR back under the river to the Isle of Dogs.

Dogs day afternoon

One of the most spectacular aspects of the relandscaping of the area is the contrast between the skyscraping glass and steel buildings and the water flowing between them, channelled beautifully between the walkways. The kids might enjoy finding artworks along

LUNCH BOX

Also in the area: Carluccio's Caffè, Pizza Express, Wagamama.

Gun *27 Coldharbour, E14 9NS (7515 5222/www.thegundocklands.com).* Smart gastropub that does great chips and welcomes nippers.

Itsu Level *2 Cabot Place East, E14 4QT (7512 5790/www.itsu.com).* A hugely entertaining sushi restaurant.

Mudchute Kitchen *Mudchute Farm, Pier Street, E14 3HP (7515 5901/www.mud chutekitchen.org).* Farm grub. *See p229.*

Nando's *Unit 25-26, Jubilee Place, E14 4QT (7513 2864/www.nandos.co.uk).* Ubiquitous chicken merchant.

Royal China *30 Westferry Circus, E14 8RR (7719 0888).* Chinese. *See p233.*

Smollensky's *1 Nash Court, E14 5AG (7719 0101/www.smollenskys.com).* Great steaks, great with kids. *See p248.*

Canary Wharf's sculpture trail (click the 'Lifestyle' link at www.canarywharf.com or phone 7418 2000 for a map). The fountain in Cabot Square is lovely, and there are benches, but the Japanese Garden beside the Jubilee line tube station is the best place to picnic. There are chain shops in the pristine mall.

The Isle of Dogs is the pre-eminent destination for visitors. You can explore all the area's history, as well as such arcane areas of debate as to whether the Isle of Dogs is an island and what dogs have to do with it (answers: not really, not much), at the excellent **Museum in Docklands** (*see p85*). It stands in a row of converted Grade I-listed warehouses, most of them cafés of one sort or another, on a cobbled quayside overlooking the water. The museum is across the bouncing bridge (it's supported on floats) from Cabot Square, which looks up at Canary Wharf.

This three-floor museum tells the story of the Thames, the port of London and its people, from Roman times to the Docklands redevelopment. The Docklands at War gallery is as moving as it is vivid – much helped by period black and white footage. The reward for taking in so much information is surely the Mudlarks Gallery, with all its hands-on discovery games, which is so popular that (free) entry is by timed ticket.

A south-bound DLR ride from Canary Wharf takes you to Mudchute, which offers what is surely East London's most surreal experience: standing in a vast meadow full of cattle, while taking in the New York-style skyscrapers of Canary Wharf. Approaching **Mudchute City Farm** (*see p132*), from Mudchute station, you are obliged to walk on a raised path past parkland and allotments, spying the llamas only sporadically through the trees as you trudge. The closer you get, the more audible the sounds of farm animals such as ducks, chickens, pigs, goats, donkeys and horses. You can walk to Island Gardens (cross the main road from the eponymous station) with its view of Greenwich over the Thames.

There's also the spookily drippy Victorian foot tunnel under the river; the attendant-operated lifts (7am-7pm Mon-Sat, 10am-5.30pm Sun) are large enough for a fleet of buggies. Note that you're not allowed to cycle through the tunnel.

Museum of London

150 London Wall, EC2Y 5HN (0870 444 3852/www.museumoflondon.org.uk). Barbican or St Paul's tube/Moorgate tube/rail. **Open** 10am-5.50pm Mon-Sat; noon-5.50pm Sun. Last entry 5.30pm. **Admission** free; charges apply for special exhibitions. **Credit** MC, V. **Map** p318 P5. 6+

This excellent museum tells the life story of London, Dick Whittington and all. The museum is currently in the throes of a massive redevelopment, which will inject £20.5 million worth of new ideas into the galleries covering the 17th century to the modern day. If all goes according to plan, the new exhibits will open in Autumn 2010. For now, you can follow London's history from the last Ice Age, when mammoths roamed through Ilford and hippos grazed where Regent Street now lies, to 1666, when London burned like dry sticks. London's most famous disaster, the Great Fire, is bought vividly to life in a temporary exhibition.

The 'London Before London' gallery is full of stone tools and primitive weapons, with modern recreations that kids can safely handle, and there are more objects to touch and costumes to play with in the Roman and Medieval London galleries. Computer stations throughout the museum offer activities based on the displays, and activity sheets for families are available at the information desk.

Storytelling sessions and hands-on craft workshops take place on Sunday afternoons, and there are special activities for all the school holidays. At least once a month, the museum runs a themed walk through the City, visiting sections of the Roman Wall and other relics of London's ancient history. Free tours of the collection inside the museum take place at 3pm on Thursdays and 1.45pm on Saturdays. *Buggy access. Café. Disabled access: lift, toilet. Nappy-changing facilities. Nearest picnic place: Barber Surgeon's Garden. Shop.*

North Woolwich
Old Station Museum

Pier Road, E16 2JJ (7474 7244/www.newham. gov.uk). North Woolwich rail/101, 473, 474 bus. **Open** *Jan-Nov* 1-5pm Sat, Sun. *Newham school holidays* 1-5pm daily. **Admission** free. **No credit cards**. 4+

Carefully preserved old engines, timetables, signs and other relics from the age of steam travel are arranged in this little place. There's an old ticket office, models and information, but the children will clamour to go round to the back and explore *Coffee Pot* (a Victorian commuter train from the 1890s) and *Pickett*

(from the 1940s); they can also climb all over *Dudley* the diesel, which will sometimes even take them for a gentle spin. There's outside play equipment and, indoors, a Brio layout, a computer running a Thomas the Tank Engine game, and the Hornby Virtual Railway. During school holidays, jolly drop-in Wednesday afternoon arts and crafts sessions keep fledgling railway buffs amused. *Buggy access. Disabled access: ramp, toilet. Nappy-changing facilities. Shop.*

Old Royal Naval College

King William Walk, SE10 9LW (8269 4747/ tours 8269 4799/www.greenwichfoundation. org.uk). Cutty Sark DLR/Greenwich DLR/rail. **Open** 10am-5pm daily. *Tours* by arrangement. **Admission** free. *Tours* £4; free under-16s. **Credit** MC, V. 5+

Built by Wren in 1696, these buildings were originally a hospital, then a naval college, and they're now part of the University of Greenwich. Visitors can admire the rococo chapel and Painted Hall, a tribute to William and Mary by artist Sir James Thornhill. In 1806 the Upper Hall was draped in black for three days while the body of Lord Nelson lay in state. In the chapel, free organ recitals take place on the first Sunday of each month. The Greenwich Gateway Visitor Centre (0870 608 2000) is in the Pepys Building, where there's an exhibition on 2,000 years of Greenwich history, the story of the Royal Hospital for Seamen, and information on other Greenwich attractions; school holiday activities take place here. Make a date to skate: the courtyard will be iced over as usual to form a seasonal rink from December 2008. *Buggy access. Café. Disabled access: toilet. Nappy-changing facilities. Nearest picnic place: Naval College grounds. Restaurant. Shop.*

Museum of Richmond

Old Town Hall, Whittaker Avenue, Richmond, Surrey TW9 1TP (8332 1141/www.museum ofrichmond.com). Richmond tube/rail. **Open** 11am-5pm Tue-Sat. **Admission** free. **No credit cards** . 4+

Richmond's museum flaunts its regal history, portraying the lives of former silver-spoon residents from the 12th-century Henry I to Elizabeth I, 400 years later. There are permanent and temporary displays, including local art, and the broad programme of children's activities includes workshops for pre-schoolers. Harry the Herald's Saturday Club for six- to 11-year olds is held on the third Saturday of each month (10-11.15am, £2 per child); an

Sightseeing

Hot for tots?

Just how child-friendly are the Big Three of Albertopolis? **Meryl O'Rourke** *and Lily (18 months) put them to the test.*

Studies show that children learn more in their first three years than any other time – so what are those behemoths of factual knowledge, the Victoria & Albert, Natural History and Science Museums, doing to encourage the very young? All provide the basics (pram access, changing tables and high chairs) – but when it comes to letting tinies interact, the attitude varies wildly.

First stop, the **Science Museum** (*see p94*), which proudly claims to cater for any age. The garden is perfect for littlies, with soft play and a spellbinding water feature; babes-in-arms can lie in a skip of cuddly animals (if they only had seating, it would be nearly as much fun for parents). Launchpad, the main children's gallery, is officially for the over-eights, and activities are a little high and heavy; but it's still worth a potter. In the holidays and at weekends, it gets too crowded to let a baby roam free, and you have to queue. Most refreshingly, the staff here have the unusual attitude that if you, the parent, think a gallery is OK for your toddler, that's fine with them. I wasn't given a second glance as I took

my 18-month-old into a talk about 'Force and Structure' (billed for the over-eights); she really enjoyed it, and babbled about the squashed eggs all afternoon.

This contrasts with the attitude at **Natural History Museum** (*see p92*). 'There's nothing for her here,' I was told when we went in. Worse, I felt like an idiot for bringing her: 'Don't let her put animals in her mouth.' NHM advertises a soft play area, but this is removed most weekends and in school holidays – just when it's needed. At half terms, the museum was unbearably crowded, and I found nowhere to let a mobile baby out of the pram. Even if your kid is happy to be buggy-bound, there are problems: when we stopped to look at the bird display, I was told to remove the pushchair. Such a shame – my toddler loved the insects in the Creepy Crawlies gallery, and in the Investigate children's lab there were books and pond life to enthral her. The NHM has a baby-feeding room, so they clearly once had a vague idea to make the place infant friendly; it's disappointing they didn't extend that welcome to the galleries. To be fair, they told me exhibitions are for over-fours, but this is not publicised.

At the **V&A** (*see p70*), staff regard marauding tots with bemusement. The exhibitions rarely get crowded, even at weekends, and the long galleries are good places to let kiddies off the leash. Mine liked the sculpture rooms with its family scenes. There's a baby-feeding room at this museum too. Craft activities are laid on for the over-threes, and although these are tricky for tinies, staff are happy to let junior run about while older siblings work. The backpacks they hand out to families have puzzles, and stickers keep baby amused. Funnily enough, this museum of textiles and furnishings is the only one of the three not to have a soft-play area.

You get tired shepherding toddlers about these huge museums, so find an area they like and stay put. Try to go midweek, though school trips mean they're never totally free of excitable big kids.

So who wins? It's no contest. In the words of the information desk at NHM: 'Take your baby to the Science Museum.'

Sightseeing

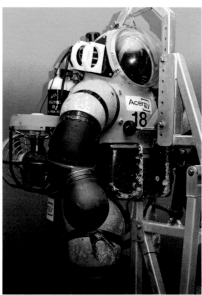

Seafaring fun – and the Observatory – at the **National Maritime Museum**. *See p105*.

under-fives club, Mini Heralds, takes place on the third Wednesday of every month (2-2.40pm, £1 per child). Free trails and drop-in activities change with the museum's various exhibitions. *Buggy access. Disabled access: lift, toilet. Nearest picnic place: Richmond Green, riverside. Shop.*

Wimbledon Windmill Museum

Windmill Road, Wimbledon Common, SW19 5NR (8947 2825/www.wimbledonwindmill museum.org.uk). Wimbledon tube/rail. **Open** *Apr-Oct* 2-5pm Sat; 11am-5pm Sun, bank hols. School groups by appointment only. **Admission** £1; 50p under-16s, reductions. **No credit cards**. 5+

Run by volunteers, this weekend-opening museum – believed to be the only remaining example of a hollow-post flour mill in the country – has a long history. It was built in 1817 by carpenter Charles March, at the request of the locals who wanted to grind their own wheat. The two-storey brick base has a room that's been re-designed to give an idea of 1870s living conditions; exhibits include an entrance display showing how the windmill was built, and the woodworking tools used in its restoration. There's milling machinery on the first floor, and the chance for children to have a go at grinding wheat with a saddle-stone. There are commentaries at the push of a button, more farm machinery on display

outside, and a small Robert Baden-Powell exhibition (the founder of the Scout movement wrote *Scouting For Boys* here in 1908). *Buggy access (ground floor). Café. Shop.*

MUSIC

Handel House Museum

25 Brook Street (entrance at rear), W1K 4HB (7495 1685/www.handelhouse.org). Bond Street tube. **Open** 10am-6pm Tue, Wed, Fri, Sat; 10am-8pm Thur; noon-6pm Sun. **Admission** £5; £2 6-16s; £4.50 reductions; free under-6s. **Credit** MC, V. **Map** p316 H6. 5+

The great composer lived in this Georgian townhouse from 1723 until his death in 1759 (and Jimi Hendrix lived at no.23 from 1968 to 1969). It now contains a modern museum whose agenda is to sow enjoyment of classical music in the young. As well as recitals of baroque music every Thursday, the museum runs weekend concerts and Talking Music events; Saturdays are best for families, when there's storytelling, live music, dressing up, art and music activities. The main exhibition celebrates Handel's life and music, and includes letters, scores and a reproduction of his harpsichord. The child-friendly ethos extends to trails, quizzes and activities to go with the displays.

Sightseeing

Buggy access. Disabled access: lift, toilet. Nappy-changing facilities. Nearest picnic place: Hanover Square. Shop.

Musical Museum

399 High Street, Brentford, Middx TW8 0DU (8560 8108/www.musicalmuseum.co.uk). Kew Bridge rail. **Open** 11am-5.30pm Tue-Sun, bank hol Mon. Last entry 4.30pm. **Admission** £7; £5.50 reductions; free under-16s. **Credit** MC, V. 5+

After a hiatus while this antique automatic musical instrument collection was between homes, the musem reopened in these new premises in late 2007. Exhibits in the four ground-floor galleries include clockwork musical boxes, reproducing pianos, orchestrions (a mechanical instrument that sounds like a large ensemble), residence organs and violin players. Most are in working order and are demonstrated by the staff, with their functions fully explained. There's also a street diorama with shop windows full of musical toys and street instruments. Upstairs is a concert hall with an orchestra pit from which a Wurlitzer console rises, as it did in cinemas in the 1930s. A programme of changing exhibitions and family events is planned.

Buggy access. Café. Disabled access: lift, toilet. Nappy-changing facilities. Nearest picnic place: riverside. Shop.

NATURAL WORLD

Museum of Garden History

Church of St Mary-at-Lambeth, Lambeth Palace Road, SE1 7LB (7401 8865/ www.museumgardenhistory.org). Lambeth North tube/Waterloo tube/rail, then 507 bus/C10, 3, 77 bus. **Open** 10.30am-5pm Tue-Sun. **Admission** free; suggested donation £3 (£2.50 reductions). **Credit** *Shop* (over £10) AmEx, MC, V. **Map** p317 L10. 6+

The first museum in the world dedicated to gardening is housed in a deconsecrated church in Lambeth; the Tradescants (a pioneering family of gardeners and botanists), Captain William Bligh (of *Bounty* fame) and half a dozen Archbishops of Canterbury are buried in the graveyard. Look out for the Pedlar's Window, a stained-glass window illustrating a man and his dog. History has it that an 16th-century pedlar acquired an acre of land (now the site of County Hall) and donated it to the church on condition that an image of him be preserved in glass. The current window is the fourth, made in 1956 after its predecessor was

destroyed in 1941. Exhibitions include a display about the borough of Lambeth over the past 1,000 years, horticultural practices through the ages, plant hunting, and garden designer Gertrude Jekyll. It's quite a child-friendly place, with hands-on gardening workshops and garden-related activities for children.

Buggy access. Café. Disabled access: ramp, toilet. Nappy-changing facilities. Nearest picnic place: Archbishop's Park. Shop.

Natural History Museum

Cromwell Road, SW7 5BD (information 7942 5725/switchboard 7942 5000/www.nhm. ac.uk). South Kensington tube. **Open** 10am-5.50pm daily. **Admission** free; charges apply for special exhibitions. **Credit** AmEx, MC, V. **Map** p313 D10. 4+

From the minute children goggle at the 150-million-year-old diplodocus in the Cromwell Road entrance hall, the wow factor stays high as they work their way round the 70 million exhibits at this museum. There is something for all tastes: if they don't think much of the bones, they'll enjoy leaf-cutter ants at work, or recognise themselves in the face of Neanderthals. There's another spectacular welcome at the Exhibition Road entrance: an escalator that carries you to Power Within. This gallery houses an earthquake simulation, always a reliable source of youthful giggles.

NHM is split into zones: Blue has the huge blue whale and scary animatronic T-Rex; Green includes the interactive Creepy Crawlies gallery; and Red is geology, with Earth Lab. The Darwin Centre runs behind-the-scenes tours for the over-12s, but at the time of going to press was closed for renovations, so phone first. Another reason to ring is to see if the Dippy Puzzle is in operation, as this soft-play area for the under-fours is closed when the museum gets busy. Explorer backpacks are available for the four- to seven-year olds (£25 refundable deposit), but apart from an adorable pith helmet, there's not much more to them than pad and pen. For real involvement, visit Investigate (sevens and over). This laboratory makes kids feel like proper scientists, as they scrutinise specimens (some living) through a microscope – the star being undoubtedly the stuffed baby alligator. The restaurant is somewhat limited and pricey, so it's a good idea to pack a picnic. Call the museum in autumn for details of the yearly winter ice rink. *See p90* **Hot for tots?**

Buggy Access. Cafés. Disabled access: lift, toilet. Nappy-changing facilities. Nearest picnic place: basement picnic room, museum grounds. Restaurant.

RELIGION

For an update on Camden's **Jewish Museum** – currently under development and scheduled to reopen in summer 2009, visit www.jewishmuseum.org.uk.

Museum of Methodism & John Wesley's House

Wesley's Chapel, 49 City Road, EC1Y 1AU (7253 2262/www.wesleyschapel.org.uk). Moorgate or Old Street tube/rail. **Open** 10am-4pm Mon-Sat. *Tours* ad hoc arrangements on arrival; groups of 10 or more must phone ahead. **Admission** £4 donation requested. *Tours* free. **Credit** MC, V. **Map** p319 Q4. 8+
This lovely chapel, with its gated courtyard ringed by Georgian buildings, is a welcome refuge from the thunderous traffic of City Road. Known as the cathedral of world Methodism, it was built by John Wesley in 1778. Museum displays in the crypt allude to Methodism's beginnings, and Hogarthian prints depict poverty, alcoholism and moral degradation in 18th-century England. The house has been restored; much of the furniture is of the period, although the tiny four-poster in the bedroom is reproduction, as is the curious 'chamber horse' in the study, an early form of home-gym equipment. *Buggy access. Disabled access: lift, toilet. Nappy-changing facilities. Nearest picnic places: enclosed courtyard at entrance, Bunhill Fields. Shop.*

SCIENCE & MEDICINE

Alexander Fleming Laboratory Museum

St Mary's Hospital, Praed Street, W2 1NY (7886 6528/www.st-marys.nhs.uk). Paddington tube/rail/7, 15, 27, 36 bus. **Open** 10am-1pm Mon-Thur; also by appointment. Closed bank hols. **Admission** £2; £1 reductions, 5-16s; free under-5s. **No credit cards. Map** p313 D5. 8+
In the era of the superbug, this shrine to antibiotics is both increasingly relevant and a relic from a simpler time. The museum recreates the lab where Alexander Fleming discovered penicillin back on 3 September 1928, and displays and a video celebrate his life and the role of penicillin in fighting disease. Staff run tours for family and school groups. Note that the museum is not accessible to the disabled. *Nearest picnic place: canalside, Hyde Park. Shop.*

Hunterian Museum

Royal College of Surgeons of England, 35-43 Lincoln's Inn Fields, WC2A 3PE (7869 6560/ www.rcseng.ac.uk/museums). Holborn tube. **Open** 10am-5pm Tue-Sat. **Admission** free; donations appreciated. **Credit** (over £5) MC, V. **Map** p318 M6. 4+
John Hunter (1728-93) was a pioneering surgeon and anatomist, appointed physician to King

National Army Museum. *See p105.*

Soldiers can be cooks

Sightseeing

George III. He amassed many thousands of medical specimens, and after he died, the collection was enhanced and expanded by others; today it can be viewed in this museum at the Royal College of Surgeons. Among the grislier exhibits are the brain of mathematician Charles Babbage and the freakish skeleton of 'Irish Giant' Charles Byrne, who stood 2.2m (7ft 7in) tall in his socks. *See also p96* **The yuck factor**. Children can make drawings using art material, peruse the books, or try on the skeleton suit and test their knowledge of human anatomy in the fabric body-part game. The programme of workshops aimed at school groups and families is set to expand, with the introduction of more actor-based events. Temporary exhibitions are held in the College Library and Inner Hall.

Buggy access. Disabled access: lift, toilet. Nearest picnic place: Lincoln's Inn Fields. Shop.

Old Operating Theatre, Museum & Herb Garret

9A St Thomas's Street, SE1 9RY (7188 2679/ www.thegarret.org.uk). London Bridge tube/ rail. **Open** 10.30am-5pm daily. Closed 15 Dec-5 Jan. **Admission** £5.45; £4.45 reductions; £3 6-16s; free under-6s; £13.25 family (2+4). **No credit cards. Map** p319 Q8. 7+

Why is there an operating theatre squeezed into the roof space of a baroque church? Because the south wing of St Thomas's Hospital was built around St Thomas's Church. Britain's only surviving 19th-century operating theatre was used from 1822, mainly for amputations and the treatment of superficial wounds, before being boarded up and forgotten about until 1956. The rest of the museum displays instruments and images of early surgical procedures, as well as bunches and jars of dried herbs in the atmospheric 300-year-old herb garret. *See also p96* **The yuck factor**.

Buggy access. Nearest picnic place: Southwark Cathedral Gardens. Shop.

Royal London Hospital Archives & Museum

St Philip's Church, Newark Street, E1 2AA (7480 4823/www.bartsandthelondon.nhs.uk/ museums). Whitechapel tube. **Open** 10am-4.30pm Mon-Fri. Closed bank hols & adjacent Tue. **Admission** free. 7+

Down a backstreet and some barely noticeable steps is the entrance to this fascinating museum, which chronicles the history of the hospital on parallel Mile End Road, once the biggest general hospital in the UK. The 1934 X-ray control unit could have been created by a mad inventor from a sci-fi B-movie, but the museum is mostly a serious-minded affair. The development of nursing and childcare is traced through displays of starchy uniforms such as those worn by Florence Nightingale and war heroine Edith Cavell; there's a replica of the specially made hat worn by former patient Joseph Merrick (the 'Elephant Man'), and a forensics case with a copy of Jack the Ripper's notorious 'From Hell' letter. Most entertaining, however (and a welcome respite if you've been dragging children about all day), are the plummily-narrated documentaries on a video screen, which date from the 1930s to the 1960s. These show, for example, children wearing pilot's goggles receiving doses of ultra-violet light at a time the London smog prevented the natural synthesis of vitamin D.

Buggy access. Café (in hospital). Disabled access: lift, ramp, toilet. Nappy-changing facilities (in hospital). Shop.

St Bartholomew's Hospital Museum

West Smithfield, EC1A 7BE (7601 8152/ www.bartsandthelondon.nhs.uk/museums). Barbican or St Paul's tube. **Open** 10am-4pm Tue-Fri. *Tours* (Church & Great Hall) 2pm Fri. **Admission** free. *Tours* £5; £4 reductions; free under-16s accompanied by adult. **No credit cards. Map** p318 O6. 12+

The original St Bart's was built in 1123 by Rahere, a courtier of Henry I, after a near-death brush with malaria; the museum here recalls the hospital's origins as a refuge for chronically sick people hoping for a miraculous cure. The exhibits include leather lunatic restraints, a wooden head used by medical students to practise their drilling techniques on and photographs documenting the slow progress of nurses from drudges to career women. Don't miss the huge painting by local lad William Hogarth on the stairs.

Café (in hospital). Nearest picnic place: hospital grounds. Shop.

Science Museum

Exhibition Road, SW7 2DD (7942 4454/ booking & information line 0870 870 4868/ www.sciencemuseum.org.uk). South Kensington tube. **Open** 10am-6pm daily. **Admission** free; charges apply for special exhibitions. **Credit** AmEx, MC, V. **Map** p313 D9. 4+

The children's play areas and simulator rides make this huge place feel more like a theme park than a museum – yet it's also home to such luminous exhibits as the Apollo 10 capsule and Babbage's prototype calculator. The flagship

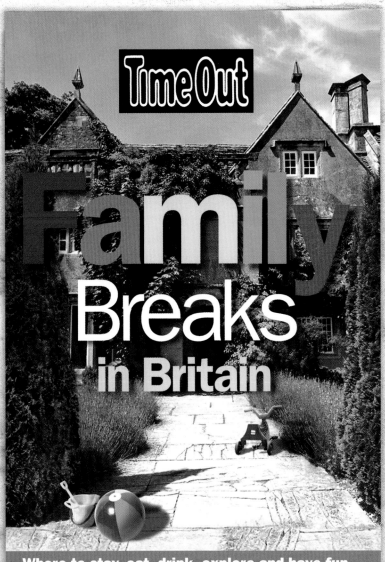

Time Out

Family Breaks
in Britain

Where to stay, eat, drink, explore and have fun.

The yuck factor

A shrunken head. A shrivelled mummy. Amputation saws. The skeleton of an Irish giant. All these objects are proudly displayed in London's medical museums. You might think kids would be scared away by all these body parts and freakish medical implements, but the truth is quite the opposite: youngsters can't get enough of the squelchy side of human anatomy. Fortunately for them, London's medical museums rise to the challenge with gusto. The **Wellcome Collection** (*see below*) has droppings from Dolly, the first cloned sheep, and a paper-thin slice of a human being; **St Bartholomew's Hospital Museum** (*see p94*) displays restraints for lunatics and tools for drilling holes in skulls; and the **Hunterian Museum** (*see p93*) has Churchill's false teeth and a whole cabinet of tumours in jars.

It all sounds pretty gruesome, but there are sound educational reasons for teaching youngsters about the frailties of the human body. For one thing, kids tend to be less disturbed by the intricacies of anatomy than many adults, and learning how the body works is a good first step towards maintaining a healthy body into adulthood. The ideal age group for trips inside the human body is six and up: younger children may find some of the exhibits a little too scary.

Although the subject matter is fairly, dare we say it, visceral, all of London's medical museums strive to educate as well as fascinate younger visitors. The Wellcome Collection uses medical specimens and art inspired by human maladies to assess contemporary subjects like obesity and the ethics of the human genome project; kids can pick up a Young Explorers pack full of entertaining health-related activities, and there are regular tours and workshops examining the questions raised by the collection, including behind-the-scenes tours on the first and last Friday of each month. Meanwhile, the Royal College of Surgeons' Hunterian Museum has the most extensive collection of medical specimens and surgical tools on public view. To bring the collection to life, there are regular talks for children at weekends and school holidays. The popular talks on 17th-century surgery are presented by an actor dressed as a Napoleonic Barber

children's gallery is the expanded Launchpad, which contains 50 experiments for children to attempt alone, with the help of an Explainer or, as often happens, with impromptu friends. The Launchpad theatre has absorbing shows tied to the national curriculum, free, daily and on the hour; in the school hols the shows are broadened for wider age range, and the whole family can join in with the Super Game Show.

The area for the under-eights is Pattern Pod, and under-sixes have free run of the wonderful Garden play areas, stocked with giant Lego, tiny boats and computerised flowers. In the IMAX cinema and simulators (over-fives), children not content to just read about space travel in the galleries can now experience how it feels to zoom into the cosmos (or indeed chase dinosaurs or ride roller coasters). There's a charge for these, but museum membership allows a year of free films and rides. The museum is hectic in the school holidays: book for films and arrive at Launchpad by 10am, or you'll be queuing for an hour. The best refueling option is Deep Blue Café. Science Night sleepovers (eight- to 11-year olds) are very popular; note that you need to book two months ahead. For more information, *see also p50* **Life in the past lane.**

Surgeon, complete with a jar of live leeches. The museum also offers special family events, including terrific mummification days run in partnership with the **Petrie Museum of Egyptian Archaeology** (*see p75*).

The **Old Operating Theatre & Herb Garrett** (*see p94*) at St Thomas's was founded as a centre for medical education, and this is still true today. Vivid re-enactments of Victorian operations are carried out in the old operating theatre for school groups, and members of the public are welcome to drop in. During the school holidays, there are special themed family events exploring such diverse subjects as body-snatching, making your own apothecary bag and the medicinal uses of chocolate.

There are plenty more educational experiences to be had at many of the small museums attached to London's teaching hospitals. The small **Royal London Hospital Archives & Museum** (*see p94*) has some fascinating displays on celebrities associated with the hospital, including Florence Nightingale, Jack the Ripper and Joseph (John) Merrick, the Elephant Man. St Bart's Hospital Museum does not offer any specific activities for children, but the well-displayed collection of Victorian medical implements will keep children suitably engrossed. One hospital museum that ties in neatly with the school curriculum is the **Alexander Fleming Laboratory** (*see p93*) at St Mary's Hospital, where penicillin was discovered. For more medical museums, visit www.medicalmuseums.org.

Buggy access. Cafés. Restaurant. Disabled access: lift, toilet. Nappy-changing facilities. Nearest picnic place: Hyde Park, museum basement and 1st floor picnic areas. Shop.

Wellcome Collection

183 Euston Road, NW1 2BE (7611 2222/ www.wellcomecollection.org). Euston Square tube/Euston tube/rail. **Open** 10am-6pm Tue-Wed; 10am-10pm Thur; 11am-6pm Sun. **Admission** free. **Credit** MC, V. **14+ (parental advisory)**

This newcomer is welcome indeed: it's modern, well laid out and stuffed to the brim with eye-opening exhibits. Founder Sir Henry Wellcome, a pioneering 19th-century pharmacist and entrepreneur, amassed an idiosyncratic collection of artefacts, implements and curios relating to the medical profession, a tiny proportion of which is displayed in the permanent Medicine Man section. Some of the items are too grisly (the vicious, bladed torture chair, the slips of real human skin) or too saucy (Japanese sex aids, phallic amulets) for sensitive young minds, but older children will get a kick out of seeing Napoleon's toothbrush, George III's hair, a case full of artificial limbs and another full of grim-looking obstetric forceps. Medicine Now presents the works of contemporary artists, all guided by themes of sickness and health: a Marc Quinn sculpture of a woman with HIV, made out of the drugs used to treat the illness, is one example. The permanent sections are bolstered by a programme of excellent temporary exhibitions that examine various aspects of life and death; the events programme, suitable for teenagers, includes talks and microscopy workshops. There's also a good bookshop, and a superb Peyton & Byrne café on the ground floor, serving meals, fabulous cakes and a good selection of teas.

Buggy access. Café. Disabled access: lift, toilet. Nappy-changing facilities. Nearest picnic place: Gordon Square. Shop.

SPECIALIST

Bank of England Museum

Entrance on Bartholomew Lane, off Threadneedle Street, EC2R 8AH (7601 5491/cinema bookings 7601 3985/ www.bankofengland.co.uk). Bank tube/DLR. **Open** 10am-5pm Mon-Fri. Closed bank hols. **Admission** free; £1 audio guide. **Credit** MC, V. **Map** p319 Q6. 5+

The history of the Old Lady of Threadneedle Street is told through a re-creation of an 18th-century banking hall (with bewigged and bestockinged mannequins) and displays of notes, coins and early handwritten cheques. A film describes the bank's origins, and there's an interactive foreign exchange desk. Special events take place throughout the year: there are calligraphy lessons, and workshops where kids design their own bank notes or make fridge magnets. Consistently popular is the gold bar: put a hand into a perspex case and try to lift the bar encased within. Its weight – 12.7kg (28lb) – comes as a shock to anyone who has ever fantasised about scarpering with a sack full of bullion.

Great Days Out
Chelsea

It's hard to believe that Chelsea was once a a fishing village (albeit as far back as the 15th century), because it seems that this area was always destined for greater things: from the late 18th until the early 20th century the area became popular with artists and writers – Dante Gabriel Rossetti and TS Eliot were among the creatives who lived here. During the '60s, it had a bohemian air and in the '70s the Kings Road became a punk hangout. Nowadays, the area is synonymous with wealth, style and culture. Sloane Square, home to the acclaimed Royal Court Theatre, is the place to start a tour of Chelsea. The nearby Duke of York Square – taking its name from the Grand Old Duke, Frederick, second son of George III and Commander-in-Chief of the British Army – hosts a wintertime ice rink, fountains in summer and several upmarket cafés.

LUNCH BOX

Also in the area: Pizza Express.
Benihana *77 King's Road, SW3 4NX (7376 7799/www.benihana. co.uk).* Japanese teppanyaki.
Big Easy *332-334 King's Road, SW3 5UR (7352 4071/www.bigeasy.uk. com).* Cajun fare for sharing: steaks, sticky ribs, crab, lobster...
Gelateria Valerie *Duke of York Square, King's Road, SW3 4LY (7730 7978).* Italian-style gelato in 24 flavours.
Great Escape Café *National Army Museum, Royal Hospital Road, SW3 4HT (7730 0717/www.national-army-museum.ac.uk).* Meatballs, fish, chips.
Itsu *118 Draycott Avenue, SW3 3AE (7590 2400/www.itsu.com).* Japanese.
Left Wing Café *9 Duke of York Square, SW3 4LY (7730 7978/www.patisserie-valerie.co.uk).* Part of the Pâtisserie Valerie cake-and-café chain.
Manicomio *85 Duke of York Square, King's Road, SW3 4LY (7730 3366/ www.manicomio.co.uk).* Pasta, pizza.
Paul *134 King's Road, SW3 4X8 (7581 9611/www.paul-uk.com).* French bakery.

War – what is it good for?

More information on the Duke and his exploits up and down hills – as well as more recent battles – can be found at the **National Army Museum** (*see p106*) and the Chelsea Royal Hospital, where the Chelsea Flower Show is held, are a short walk away. Don't be put off by the rather severe modern exterior of the museum. Some eccentric exhibits and displays, together with an exciting programme of family events, make this friendly museum dedicated to the British Army's 500-year history far more entertaining than you would think.

Sure, there are a number of dry displays of regimental items – old uniforms, kit bags and the like – but there are also fascinating highlights: the Road to Waterloo, a version of the battle starring 75,000 toy soldiers; the skeleton of Napoleon's beloved mount, Marengo; and Florence Nightingale's lamp. Children love the bizarre exhibits, such as the frostbitten fingers of Major 'Bronco' Lane, conqueror of Mount Everest. The Redcoats Gallery starts at Agincourt in 1415 and ends with the redcoats in the American War of Independence; The Nation in Arms covers both World Wars, with reconstructions of a trench in the World at War (1914-1946) exhibition, and a D-Day landing craft. There's more military hardware, including a hands-on Challenger tank simulator, up in the Modern Army exhibition.

Some of the exhibitions are not suitable for younger children. Faces of Battle includes previously unseen photographs and footage of Britain's faceless war wounded, displayed alongside contemporary uniform sculptures tracing their surgery, rehabilitation and recovery.

WAACS at War looks at the role of the women who 'did their bit' for the war effort. Their roles included cooking and waiting on officers, serving as clerks, telephone operators, store-women, drivers, printers, bakers and cemetery gardeners. There is also information on the fascinating women who disguised themselves as men to go and fight.

Themed weekend events (check the website for details), which usually involve costumed interpreters and craft activities, have gone a long way to broadening the museum's appeal, as has the Kids' Zone – a free interactive learning and play space. It's the sort of place you can bring all your troops to, as its attractions include construction, reading, art activity and board-game areas all tailored for under-tens, including a soft-play area for babies. It can be booked for birthday parties.

Gardeners' world

Also in the neighbourhood is the **Chelsea Physic Garden** (*see p107*). It can be reached via Flood Street, one of the many attractive side roads branching off King's Road. The garden was set up in 1673, but the key phase of development was under Sir Hans Sloane in the 18th century. Its beds contain healing herbs and rare trees, dye plants and medicinal vegetables; plants are also sold. Public opening hours are restricted because this is primarily a centre for research and education. That said, the education department organises activity days with interesting botanical themes over the Easter and summer holidays. Activity days should be pre-booked, and are suitable for seven- to 11-year-olds (although there are some for four- to six-year-olds and nine- to 13-year-olds) and cost £5 per child per day. For a full list of dates, phone or email education@chelsea physicgarden.co.uk. Educational visits and teacher-training days can also be arranged.

Shop... to the end of the world

The King's Road has a wealth of shopping opportunities. The western end – known as World's End – was once the home of Vivienne Westwood's shop (No.430), with its backwards-spinning clock. If you've walked all the way here, you deserve to rest your tired legs in Cremorne Gardens, a riverside park with uplifting views east to Old Ferry Wharf and west to exclusive Chelsea Harbour.

Great Days Out

Buggy access. Disabled: ramp, toilet. Nappy-changing facilities. Nearest picnic place: St Paul's Cathedral Garden. Shop.

Clink Prison Museum

1 Clink Street, SE1 9DG (7403 0900/ www.clink.co.uk). London Bridge tube/rail. **Open** *June-Sept* 10am-9pm daily. *Oct-May* 10am-6pm Mon-Fri; 10am-9pm Sat, Sun. *Tours* pre-booking essential; minimum 10 people. **Admission** £5; £3.50 5-15s, reductions; free under-5s; £12 family (2+2). *Tours* phone for prices. **Credit** MC, V. **Map** p318 P8. 5+ (parental advisory)

The original Clink prison (so called, it's said, because the inmates clanked their chains) was in operation from 1247 until 1780, the year it burned down, and was where thieves, prostitutes, debtors and priests did time. The museum stands on the spot, and much of its material is generally interesting and well-presented, albeit unsettling: a few waxwork models and props, like old beds with straw mattresses, help bring scenes to life, and there are several unsavoury devices – such as a 'scolds bridle' and execution blocks, fetters and foot crushers, thumb screws and chains.
Buggy access. Nearest picnic place: Southwark Cathedral Gardens. Shop.

SPORT

London's four biggest football clubs – Arsenal, Chelsea, Tottenham and West Ham United – all offer stadium tours that take fans behind the scenes at their grounds, as does Wembley Stadium, home of the England team and host of cup finals in several sports and of major pop concerts. Arsenal and Chelsea also have made space for club museums. The latter, with its Mourinho and Gullit memorabilia , is currently closed for a refurb, see www.chelseafc.com for details. Obviously, these appeal most to partisan supporters of the teams in question, but London's football has a fascinating history, and these museums would have plenty to interest fans of other teams as well.

Arsenal Museum

Northern Triangle Building, Drayton Park, N5 1BU (7704 4504/www.arsenal.com). Arsenal or Holloway Road tube/Drayton Park rail. **Open** 10am-6pm Mon-Sat; 10am-5pm Sun. *Match days* 10am until 30mins before kick-off. **Admission** £6; £3 reductions, under-16s; free under-5s.

British Museum. *See p74.*

Tour & museum £12; £6 reductions, under-16s. *Legends tour* £35, £18 reductions, under-16s. No tours matchdays. **Credit** MC, V. 7+
Housed in the North Triangle Building directly opposite the north entrances to the Gunners' impressive new stadium, this museum offers a lavish celebration of all things Arsenal. There are plenty of video clips of memorable triumphs and players from the club's recent and distant history, as well as trophies, medals, shirts, boots and footballs from down the ages. Among the most interesting sections are those that deal with how the club developed. Visitors can pick up a phone to hear an account of the club's early days, initially as Dial Square FC, after its formation by workers at the Woolwich Arsenal munitions factory. The club's more recent triumphs are marked in audio-visual displays, signed shirts, medals and other memorabilia. There are also sections on the Gunners' all-conquering women's team and on the club's FA Cup and European adventures.
Buggy access. Disabled access: lift, toilet. Nearest picnic place: Finsbury Park. Shop.

Lord's Cricket Ground & MCC Museum

St John's Wood Road, NW8 8QN (7616 8500/ tours 7432 1033/www.lords.org). St John's Wood tube/13, 46, 82, 113, 274 bus. **Open** Tour *Oct-Mar* noon, 2pm daily. *Apr-Sept* 10am, noon, 2pm daily. Closed matches & preparation days; phone for details. **Admission** £12; £7 reductions; £6 5-15s; free under-5s; £31 family (2+2). **Credit** MC, V. 8+
This cricketing treasure trove, situated behind the pavilion at cricket's HQ, is best enjoyed as part of one of the ground tours, which take place twice daily, Mon-Fri, and three times a day at weekends. Though relatively small in size, the museum has a rich variety of artefacts, from early bats, balls, paintings and scorecards – some going back more than 200 years – to mementoes of modern times. There are Shane Warne's boots, Brian Lara's bat, but the must-see exhibit, of course, is the original Ashes urn. This was first presented following what a *Sporting Times* newspaper reporter called the 'death of English cricket' after the victorious Australian tourists condemned the England side to their first ever defeat at the Oval in 1882. When England went 2-0 up in the four-match series in Australia, a group of Melbourne society women burned a bail from the top of some cricket stumps, placed the ashes inside the urn and presented them to the visiting captain.
The ground tour offer visitors a look around the famous pavilion, its long room and committee rooms and, of course, the home and away dressing rooms and their balconies, as well as the media centre, grandstand and cricket centre.
Buggy access. Disabled access: toilet, lift. Nappy-changing facilities. Nearest picnic place: St John's churchyard playground. Shop.

Wimbledon Lawn Tennis Museum

All England Lawn Tennis Club, Church Road, SW19 5AE (8946 6131/www.wimbledon. org/museum). Southfields or South Wimbledon tube, then 493 bus. **Open** 10.30am-5pm daily. During championships spectators only. *Tours* phone for details. **Admission** *Museum* £8.50; £7.50 reductions; £4.75 5-16s; free under-5s. *Museum & tour* £15.50; £13.75 reductions; £11 5-16s; free under-5s. **Credit** MC, V. 8+
There's much to fascinate the tennis enthusiast in this well-equipped and user-friendly museum, based at the iconic summer sporting venue. Visitors are given a history of how tennis developed from real tennis (at which Henry VIII apparently excelled) and rackets before the sport we know today as lawn tennis took off in the 1870s. Early exhibits include the original men's singles trophy and a 19th-century equipment box and a mock-up of a 1901 changing room.
Visitors are guided through Wimbledon's history, decade by decade, as it developed into a British sporting institution. Exhibits from the modern era include plenty of audio-visual attractions, broadcast snippets from major finals and interviews with tennis legends past and present such as Chris Evert and Virginia Wade. Among the more striking features is a John McEnroe 'hologram', where a 'ghost' of the three-time Wimbledon champion reflects on his memorable career. Visitors can also try on tennis outfits from different ages, test their reflexes on the 'reaction station' and prove their knowledge of the game's laws in a 'you are the umpire' display. Audio and visual guides are also available. Recommended.
Buggy access. Café. Disabled access: lift, toilet. Nappy-changing facilities. Shop.

World Rugby Museum, Twickenham & Twickenham Stadium

Twickenham Stadium, Rugby Road, Twickenham, Middx TW1 1DZ (0870 405 2001/www.rfu.com/museum). Hounslow East tube, then 281 bus/Twickenham rail. **Open** *Museum* 10am-5pm Tue-Sat; 11am-5pm Sun. Last entry 30mins before closing, ticket holders only match days. *Tours* 10.30am, noon, 1.30pm, 3pm Tue-Sat; 1pm, 3pm Sun.

Sightseeing

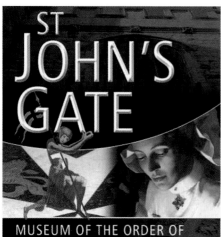

(no tours matchdays). **Admission** *Combined ticket* £10; £7 reductions, under-16s; free under-5s; £34 family (2+3). Advance booking advisable. **Credit** AmEx, MC, V. 7+

This elegantly presented museum charts the history of the game from – and indeed before – William Webb Ellis famously picked up the ball and ran with it during a football game at Rugby School in 1821. Exhibits cover the development of a proper set of rules, the split with northern clubs that led to the emergence of rugby league, and the spread of the game throughout the country and overseas. Displays include strange-shaped early rugby balls, a jersey from the first ever rugby international between Scotland and England in 1871, signed shirts from down the decades and a timeline of the history of the game, alongside major world developments. The upper floor has a library and special exhibition room, whose current display looks at the history of Harlequins RFC at Twickenham. The museum is sometimes closed after match days; phone to check.

Buggy access. Disabled access: toilet. Shop.

WAR & THE ARMED FORCES

Churchill Museum & Cabinet War Rooms

Clive Steps, King Charles Street, SW1A 2AQ (7930 6961/www.iwm.org.uk). St James's Park or Westminster tube/3, 12, 24, 53, 159 bus. **Open** 9.30am-6pm daily (last entry 5pm). **Admission** £12; £9.50 reductions; free under-16s (incl audio guide). **Credit** MC, V. **Map** p317 K9. 7+

Here below Whitehall, as if in a time capsule, you can wander the cramped corridors of Churchill's secret underground HQ, and peer in at the nooks where Britain's leaders conducted wartime business. With its low ceilings and concrete bomb protection, it's an atmospheric (if slightly stifling) installation that brings the period to life. A programme of family workshops runs during school holidays.

A larger space in the warren houses the multimedia Churchill Museum. Its centrepiece is a large timeline, an award-winning digital archive that chronicles every major incident of WSC's life, from the Boer War to his long twilight as an after-dinner speaker and recipient of awards; there's also a kind of virtual peepshow of his home in Chartwell, Kent. Churchill's voice and face and words come at you from all sides, in every possible format; this is not a museum, but a living Churchill environment that will appeal to most children, even if they end up simply playing around with all the technology. Staying here too long, though, would drive you mad: it's like being inside Winston's mind. On show for a second time in 2008, until October, is the Dig for Victory exhibition – a replica of a World War II allotment designed to teach people the virtues of recycling and healthy eating.

Buggy access. Café. Disabled access: lift, toilet. Nappy-changing facilities. Nearest picnic place: St James's Park. Shop.

Firepower Royal Artillery Museum

Royal Arsenal, SE18 6ST (8855 7755/ www.firepower.org.uk). Woolwich Arsenal rail. **Open** *Apr-Oct* 10.30am-5pm Wed-Sun (last entry 4pm). *Nov-Mar* 10.30am-5pm Fri-Sun (last entry 4pm). **Admission** £5; £4.50 reductions; £2.50 5-16s; free under-5s; £12 family (2+2 or 1+3). **Credit** MC, V. 7+

Children who love loud bangs and big guns get a kick out of the Gunners museum, which is dedicated to the soldiers of the Royal Artillery (not the North London Premiership team). It occupies a series of converted Woolwich Arsenal buildings close to the river, and the footie connection is remembered in the touching introductory film in the Breech Cinema: Arsenal FC started out as Woolwich Arsenal, when a group of armaments workers had a kickabout. After the film come the bangs, crashes and dry ice of the Field of Fire, where four massive screens relay archive film and documentary footage of warfare.

Now that the interactive weapons gallery (which children loved) has been forced to close, your only chance of getting your finger on a trigger is by paying £1.50 for a bag of paintballs to use in the Command Post section across the courtyard. There's also a rolling climbing wall (activities are supervised by friendly soldiers in fatigues), some huge tanks and guns and an Anderson shelter. The Pit Stop Café is a reasonably-priced place for rations, although if the weather's good, bring a picnic and enjoy the Thameside vista. Special events take place at Firepower throughout the year; camouflage party packages are available too. Starting in June 2008, the Out of the Dark exhibition celebrates the museum's 230th anniversary with a display of rarely seen pieces from the collection.

Buggy access. Café. Disabled access: ramp, toilet. Lift. Nappy-changing facilities. Nearest picnic place: riverside. Shop.

Sightseeing

Guards Museum

Birdcage Walk, SW1E 6HQ (7414 3430/ www.theguardsmuseum.com). Victoria tube/rail. **Open** 10am-4pm daily (last entry 3.30pm). **Admission** £3; £2 reductions; £1 ex-military; free under-16s. **Map** p316 J9. 7+
Displays in this small museum include military relics – flags, medals, uniforms, drums and weapons – covering every campaign fought by the Scots, Irish, Welsh, Grenadier and Coldstream Guards. Children will get the most out of it as a follow-up to seeing the Changing of the Guard at nearby Buckingham Palace (*see p34*). Highlights include the Grand Old Duke of York's bearskin (he commanded in peacetime, hence the nursery rhyme). Worksheets (for eight- to 14-year-olds) add an extra dimension to a visit, and staff let kids try on bearskin hats and regimental tunics: they can have their photo taken for £5. The museum shop has an impressive collection of toy soldiers.
Buggy access. Disabled access: lift, ramp. Nearest picnic place: St James's Park. Shop.

HMS Belfast

Morgan's Lane, Tooley Street, SE1 2JH (7940 6300/www.iwm.org.uk). Tower Hill tube/London Bridge tube/rail. **Open** *Mar-Oct* 10am-6pm daily. *Nov-Feb* 10am-5pm daily. Last entry 45mins before closing. **Admission** £10.30; £7.20 reductions; £6.20 disabled, carers free; free under-16s (must come with an adult). **Credit** MC, V. **Map** p319 R8. 4+
Named after the city of her birth, this cruiser was launched on St Patrick's Day 1938. Now affiliated to the Imperial War Museum, *Belfast* has been preserved to reflect the different decades of her service and the campaigns she served in. With her nine decks, the ship is a vast playground of narrow ladders, stairs and walkways. There are guided tours, but it's fun to scramble around the ship at random, from bridge to boiler room, galley, sick bay, dentist's, NAAFI canteen and mess deck; there's even an operating theatre. Models of sailors chatting, eating, cooking, and having their teeth drilled add to the entertainment. Regular activities for children include Hunt the Rat, in which you go in search of rodents, then make one out of clay. On the last weekend of every month, there are free drop-in family activities (11am-1pm and 2-4pm), which might involve craft, music or dance.
Buggy access. Café. Disabled access: toilet. Nearest picnic place: Potters Fields Park. Shop.

Household Cavalry Museum

Horseguards, Whitehall, SW1A 2AX (7930 3070/www.householdcavalrymuseum.org.uk). Embankment or Westminster tube/Charing Cross tube/rail. **Open** *Mar-Sept* 10am-6pm daily. *Oct-Feb* 10am-5pm daily. **Admission** £6; £4 5-16s and reductions; free under-5s; £15 family (2+3). **Credit** MC, V. 5+
Visitors can peer at the Household Cavalry's medals and cuirasses (kids can even try one on on the special activity days) and watch video diaries of serving soldiers. A glass wall is all that separates the museum from the stables, so you can see the magnificent horses being rubbed down. The Cavalry mounts the guard on Horse Guards Parade every day at 11am (10am on Sunday): this is a better place to see them than Buckingham Palace (*see p34*), since the crowds are thinner here, and you're not held far back from the action by railings. After the old and new guards have stared each other out in the centre of the parade ground for a quarter of an hour, if you nip through to the Whitehall side, you'll catch the departing guard's hilarious dismount choreography, which involves a synchronised, firm slap of approbation on each horse's neck before the gloved troopers all swing off.
Buggy access. Disabled access: toilet. Nearest picnic place: St James's Park. Shop.

Imperial War Museum

Lambeth Road, SE1 6HZ (7416 5320/www. iwm.org.uk). Lambeth North tube/Elephant & Castle tube/rail. **Open** 10am-6pm daily.

Admission free. Special exhibitions prices vary. **Credit** MC, V. **Map** p406 N10. 5+

The London branch of the IWM family, housed in what was the Bethlehem Royal Hospital (better known as Bedlam) has some very big guns (there's a pair of whoppers out the front), but there's far more to it than that. The collection covers conflicts, especially those involving Britain and the Commonwealth, from World War I to the present day. Tanks, aircraft and big guns are displayed on the ground floor, but, on the way to the lower floor devoted to the first and second world wars, a sobering fact pulls you up sharp. A clock, set running at midnight on 1 January 2000, when the number of lives lost during the wars of the 20th century stood at 100 million, continues to count those dying in conflicts, calculated to be two per minute; the figure on our visit stood at 107,808,351.

There's a degree of levity in the smelly Trench Experience on the World War I side, and in the stout-hearted Blitz Experience for World War II, but the mood gets blacker as you ascend through the floors. The unflinching Holocaust Exhibition, which traces the history of anti-semitism and its shameful nadir in the death camps, is not recommended for those under 14. Upstairs, Crimes Against Humanity is a minimalist space in which a film exploring genocide and ethnic violence rolls relentlessly; this is unsuitable for the under-16s. There's also a busy programme of temporary exhibitions,

Royal Airforce Museum Hendon. *See p106.*

on topics as diverse as Ian Fleming and Armistice (September 2008).

Buggy access. Café. Disabled access: lift, toilet. Nappy-changing facilities. Nearest picnic place: museum grounds. Shop.

National Army Museum

Royal Hospital Road, SW3 4HT (7730 0717/ recorded information 7881 2455/www. national-army-museum.ac.uk). Sloane Square tube/11, 137, 239 bus. **Open** 10am-5.30pm daily. **Admission** free. **Credit** *Shop* AmEx, MC, V. **Map** p313 F12. 3+

The history of the British Army as displayed here has fascinating highlights: Florence Nightingale's lamp, the Road to Waterloo, a version of the battle starring 75,000 toy soldiers; and the skeleton of Napoleon's horse. There's plenty to satisfy a child's love of things gruesome – steer younger ones away from the Faces of Battle section on World War I plastic surgery. The Redcoats Gallery shows how Brits conquered the world; the Nation in Arms covers both world wars, with a reconstruction of a World War I trench and a particularly good jungle area. We also liked the way we were exhorted to join the 1914 army by a virtual recruiting sergeant as soon as we stepped through the door.

A new exhibition for 2008 is Helmand: The Soldiers' Story, where you can feel all Prince Harry-ish in an Afghan desert camp. Themed weekend events, which usually involve costumed interpreters and craft activities, have gone a long way to broadening the museum's appeal, as has the Kids' Zone, a free, interactive learning and play space for under-10s. This is is the sort of spot you can bring all your troops to: its attractions include construction, reading, art activity and board-game areas for under-tens, and a soft-play area for toddlers; it can be booked by the hour for birthday parties. *See also p10* **Great Days Out**.

Buggy access. Café. Disabled access: lift, ramp, toilet. Nappy-changing facilities. Nearest picnic place: museum benches, Chelsea Hospital grounds. Shop.

National Maritime Museum

Romney Road, SE10 9NF (8858 4422/ information 8312 6565/tours 8312 6608/ www.nmm.ac.uk). Cutty Sark DLR/Greenwich DLR/rail. **Open** 10am-5pm daily. *Tours* phone for details. **Admission** free; donations appreciated. **Credit** MC, V. 4+

Launched in 1937, this museum dedicated to seafaring has the world's largest store of maritime art, cartography, ship's models, flags, instruments and costumes. More recent additions include, on Level 2, Your Ocean, which shows how dependent we are on the health of the world's oceans. Also on this level, in Gallery 15, is Nelson's Navy, which displays over 250 objects taken from the museum's collection of Nelsonian memorabilia; the gallery also considers the role played by Vice-Admiral Horatio Nelson and exhibits naval uniforms (including the undress coat worn by Nelson at the Battle of Trafalgar), weaponry, artefacts and art. The very hands-on Alls Hands and Bridge galleries are on Level 3: children can play with several exhibits, including Morse code machines, ships' wheels and a cargo-handling model. In the Bridge, young sea dogs can play ship's captain and steer a vessel into port using the bridge simulator.

Elsewhere in the museum, Explorers is devoted to pioneers of sea travel, and includes a small, chilling Titanic exhibition; Passengers is a paean to glamorous old ocean liners, and Maritime London tells the capital's nautical history. Seapower covers naval battles from Gallipoli to the Falklands, and Art of the Sea is the world's largest maritime art collection. A colonnaded walkway takes you to the Queen's House (*see p67*), and the Observatory and Planetarium up the hill (*see p30*) are part of the NMM complex. *Buggy access. Café. Disabled access; lift, toilet. Nappy-changing facilities. Nearest picnic place: Greenwich Park, museum grounds. Shop.*

Royal Air Force Museum Hendon

Grahame Park Way, NW9 5LL (8205 2266/ www.rafmuseum.org). Colindale tube/Mill Hill Broadway rail/303 bus. **Open** 10am-6pm daily. Closed 24-26 Dec, 1 Jan. *Tours daily;* phone for details. **Admission** free. *Tours free.* **Credit** MC, V. 8+

There has been an airfield at Hendon since 1910, hence its claim to be the birthplace of aviation in Britain. These days the aerodrome houses over 80 historic aircraft, among them a Camel, Tempest, Tiger Moth, Mosquito and Harrier – all parked at ground level or hung in dogfight poses from the rafters of the ultra-modern Milestones of Flight building. As you take a break in the café, helicopter blades jut out above your head; a little further on, miniature parachutists go up and down in a tube or drop off a wire into the hands of kids eager to learn about the laws of gravity. Other interactive games are available in the Aeronauts gallery, many in the guise of pilot aptitude tests. Only the flight simulator (over-eights only) carries an extra charge; everything else is gloriously free, so although a full tour is exhausting, you can come as often as you like. More low-key than the Milestones of Flight gallery are the atmospheric

and dimly lit Battle of Britain building and the restored Grahame-White Factory.

With this being a military museum, there is plenty of lethal hardware on display, from WWII doodlebugs to modern cluster bombs and cruise missiles; be ready to field questions about man's inhumanity to man as you walk around the galleries. Special activity days take place throughout the year, particularly on military holidays – older kids can learn the principles of rocket science while youngsters can build their own cardboard flying machines. See the website for upcoming events.

Activities for children and adults take place all year. The ever-popular workshops (book ahead) include hot-air balloon making, rocket science, and Search and Rescue role-play. Quizzes, Pulsar Battlezone interactive laser games, face-painting, aircraft displays and giant garden games are also on the cards. The Fantasy Flying Summer season (28 July to 29 August 2008) will have a witches and dragons theme, and the Wings restaurant now includes a corner for kids with books a PlayStation, beanbags and other toys. *Buggy access. Café. Disabled access: ramp, lift, toilet. Nappy-changing facilities. Nearest picnic place: on-site picnic area. Restaurant. Shop.*

Winston Churchill's Britain at War Experience

64-66 Tooley Street, SE1 2TF (7403 3171/ www.britainatwar.co.uk). London Bridge tube/ rail. **Open** *Apr-Oct* 10am-5pm daily. *Nov-Mar* 10am-4.30pm daily. Closed 24-26 Dec. **Admission** £10.45; £5.95 reductions; £4.95 5-16s; free under-5s; £26 family (2+2). **Credit** AmEx, MC, V. **Map** p319 Q8. 8+

You descend into this small, cramped and frankly rather touristy museum via an original London Underground lift, which delivers you to a mocked-up Blitz-era Underground air raid shelter, whose set – good enough to make you feel the place is still in use – includes bunks, a temporary kitchen and library, original posters and newsreel clips from the time. Other displays show the roles of women at war, the life of evacuated children and rationing. An ex-evacuee is on hand to show you his childhood photos, there's a BBC broadcasting room and a pub, and children will enjoy trying on tin helmets and gas masks in a dressing-up corner. The visit ends in a full-size street, where a bomb has just exploded – all chillingly staged to make you think the action occurred moments before. An hour or so probably suffices for the whole place. *Buggy access. Disabled access: toilet. Nearest picnic place: Southwark Cathedral gardens. Shop.*

Sightseeing

Parks & Gardens

Enough to turn you green with energy.

The average London garden might be titchy, but the number and variety of public green spaces in this city means that children can always find a place to run around, splash in puddles and climb trees. Over the last eight years many new playspaces have sprung up all over town to encourage young families outside, which means we've had no difficulty finding decent places to stretch the legs and picnic near every one of the venues listed in our Sightseeing chapters.

In these pages we list the very best of London's celebrated green lungs. They might not all be 'destination parks', like the Royals listed on p122, or stunningly laid out stately gardens, like the Botanic Gardens that kick off the chapter, but each one has special significance in its own, er, field. Some of the best loved spaces are diminutive, but precious for their suprising urban location, others may look a bit scruffy, but hugely valued for their newt, frog or bat populations. They all have an important role to play in the health and wellbeing of Londoners of all ages, and species. Check the parks' websites to check for school holiday events.

BOTANIC GARDENS

More botanic beauties can be found in **Chumleigh Gardens (Burgess Park**; *see p111*, the **Geffrye Museum herb garden** (*see p58*), **Ham House** (*see p45*), **Hampton Court Palace** (*see p36*) and **Syon House Gardens** (*see p50*).

Chelsea Physic Garden
66 Royal Hospital Road (entrance on Swan Walk), SW3 4HS (7352 5646/www.chelsea physicgarden.co.uk). Sloane Square tube/170 bus. **Open** *Mar-Oct* noon-5pm Wed-Fri; noon-6pm Sun, bank hol Mon. *Tours* times vary, phone to check. **Admission** £7; £4 5-16s, reductions; free under-5s. *Tours* free. **Credit** MC, V. **Map** p313 F12.
This lovely garden was planted in 1673, but the main development was under Sir Hans Sloane in the 18th century, when the world's first rock garden was made here with old stone from the Tower of London. *See p98* **Great Days Out**. *Buggy access. Café. Disabled access: ramp, toilet. Nappy-changing facilities. Shop.*

Royal Botanic Gardens (Kew Gardens)
Richmond, Surrey TW9 3AB (8332 5655/ information 8940 1171/www.kew.org). Kew Gardens tube/rail/Kew Bridge rail/riverboat to Kew Pier. **Open** *Apr-Aug* 9.30am-6.30pm Mon-Fri; 9.30am-7.30pm Sat, Sun. *Sept-Oct* 9.30am-6pm daily. *Late Oct-early Feb* 9.30am-4.15pm daily. *Early Feb-late Mar* 9.30am-5.30pm daily. Last entry 30mins before closing. *Tours* 11am, 2pm daily. **Admission** £13; £12 reductions, late entry (after 4.45pm); free under-17s. **Credit** AmEx, MC, V.
This lush, landscaped beauty is divided up into 47 areas, it has a massive amount of ground to cover – but small visitors tend to know what they want, and with kids aged three to nine, it's the Climbers & Creepers adventure playground. Here they can clamber into a flower, through an illuminated blackberry tangle, and dig for 'fossilised plants' while real insects buzz through see-through habitats. Climbers & Creepers is also base camp for Midnight Rambler sleepovers, which give eight to 11 year-olds and their guardians (£40 per head) the chance to track local wildlife, and earn prizes: there are half a dozen of these events between April and October; they must be booked months in advance.

The rest of Kew's half a square mile is an extraordinary array of monuments, gardens, buildings and landscapes. We love the 1848 Palm House, which has exotic plants from Africa, Asia and America, and a series of spiral staircases that lets you view them all from a gallery. Resident record-breakers enjoying old age here include the oldest pot plant in the world and the tallest palm under glass. The famous Pagoda (due to reopen in 2009) has stunning views over London, once you've climbed its 253 steps; and the £800,000 Alpine House, opened in spring 2006, is another must-see.

If you're exploring the gardens on foot, pick up a free map at the ticket office. Little ones might prefer to ride the Kew Explorer people-mover, which plies a circular route around the gardens (£3.50; £1 reductions). There are cafés and restaurants dotted here and there, but on a fine day you can't beat a picnic; and summer art shows and live music. A winter ice rink in front of the Temperate House (check website for dates) make Kew a year-round treat. Kids' Kew (£3.95), a guide book with games, crosswords, stickers and map, is sold in the gift shop. *Buggy access. Cafés. Disabled access: ramp, toilet. Nappy-changing facilities. Restaurants. Shop.*

CEMETERIES

Abney Park Cemetery & Nature Reserve

Stoke Newington High Street, N16 0LN (7275 7557/www.abney-park.org.uk). Stoke Newington rail/73, 106, 149, 243, 276, 349 bus. **Open** dawn-dusk daily. *Visitors' centre* 10am-4pm Mon-Fri. **Admission** free. **No credit cards.**

This winsomely decayed Victorian cemetery is a hub of conservation activity. There's an environmental classroom at the Stoke Newington High Street entrance, which is the scene of free workshops for children and adults: go on a mini beast hunt, examine beetles and bugs at close quarters, or take a tree tour and learn about the hundreds of different varieties on site. The visitors' centre doubles as a shop for guides to green London and other environmentally aware literature. Although still plainly the scenery of a burial ground, the worn monuments – urns, angels, Celtic crosses, saints and shepherds – add romantic interest to a local nature reserve where trees and plants are now in the ascendant. *Buggy access. Disabled access: toilet (visitors' centre). Shop.*

Brompton Cemetery

Fulham Road, SW10 9UG (7352 1201/ www.royalparks.org.uk/parks). West Brompton tube/rail. **Open** *Summer* 8am-8pm daily. *Winter* 8am-4pm daily. **Admission** free. Brompton Cemetery is full of magnificent monuments commemorating the famous and

Royal Botanic (Kew) Gardens. *See p107.*

infamous, including suffragette Emmeline Pankhurst, shipping magnate Sir Samuel Cunard and, his grave marked by a lion, boxer 'Gentleman' John Jackson, who taught Byron to box. The peace and quiet is regularly disturbed by the Chelsea FC's home games at neighbouring Stamford Bridge.
Buggy access. Disabled access.

Highgate Cemetery

Swain's Lane, N6 6PJ (8340 1834/www. highgate-cemetery.org). Highgate tube. **Open** *East cemetery* Apr-Oct 10am-5pm Mon-Fri; 11am-5pm Sat, Sun. Nov-Mar 10am-4pm Mon-Fri; 11am-4pm Sat, Sun. *West cemetery* by tour only; phone for details. **Admission** *East cemetery* £3. *West cemetery tours* £5; £1 8-15s. **No credit cards**.

With its angels, shrouded urns and broken columns, this beautiful boneyard has a romantic atmosphere of ivy-covered neglect. The fame of some of its tenants puts the cemetery on the to-see list of many a tourist, although the Friends of Highgate Cemetery, who look after the place, prefer to play down its appeal. Youngsters are discouraged from visiting unless they're coming to see the grave of a relative, but if you long to pay respects to Karl Marx, Mary Ann Evans (aka George Eliot), poet Christina Rossetti, scientist Michael Faraday, or any of the eminent figures who now repose in the Eastern Cemetery, you can bring children along, as long as they behave well. The atmospheric Western Cemetery is out of bounds to casual visitors; adults and children aged eight and over can pay (£5 and £1 respectively) for a guided tour. Both sites close for funerals, so phone before you visit.
Buggy access. Disabled access: East cemetery only.

Kensal Green Cemetery

Harrow Road, W10 4RA (8969 0152/www. kensalgreen.co.uk). Kensal Green tube/rail/18, 23, 52, 70, 295,316 bus. **Open** *Apr-Sept* 9am-6pm Mon-Sat; 10am-6pm Sun. *Oct-Mar* 9am-5pm Mon-Sat; 10am-5pm Sun. *All year* 10am-1pm bank hols. **Admission** free.

Behind the neoclassical gate is a green oasis of the dead. Kensal Green is particularly strong on towering intellects of the 19th century: Isambard Kingdom Brunel, William Thackeray, Anthony Trollope and Wilkie Collins all lie here, but the most impressive monuments are the ornate mausoleums of lesser names. There's a Greek Revivalist chapel and mysterious catacombs (over-12s only).
Buggy access. Disabled access: toilet.

Nunhead Cemetery

entrances on Limesford Road or Linden Grove, SE15 3LP (7732 9535/www.fonc. org.uk). Nunhead rail. **Open** *Summer* 8am-7pm daily. *Winter* 8am-4pm daily. *Tours* 2pm last Sun of mth. **Admission** free; donations appreciated.

A maze of Victorian commemorative statuary, tree-filled Nunhead Cemetery is a charming nature reserve with a restored chapel at its heart. From its highest points there are fine views of the city. The Friends of Nunhead Cemetery (FONC) runs guided tours on the last Sunday of each month. An annual open day takes place in May.
Buggy access.

CITY SPACES

Phoenix Garden

21 Stacey Street (entrance on St Giles Passage), WC2H 8DG (7379 3187/www. phoenixgarden.org). Tottenham Court Road tube. **Open** dawn-dusk daily. **Admission** free; donations appreciated. **Map** p315 K6.

Excavations and renovations over the last year or so have made the Phoenix, which rose from the site of a car park back in 1984, a busier garden; it's especially popular with local workers during summer lunch hours. There's a pond, a wildlife area, peaceful crooked pathways, trellises and fragmented statues, all of which come as a green surprise, tucked as they are between Shaftesbury Avenue and Charing Cross Road; the entrance is next to the playground in the garden of St Giles-in-the-Fields. As well as trees, flowers, and boxes for birds and insects, there are benches for visitors – one was donated by Sir Digby Jones, who, according to the inscription, 'takes time to smell the flowers.' The garden relies on volunteers; call for details of how you can help, or become a member. Annual membership costs £18 per household (£12 individuals, £5 reductions), and gives you advance notice of kids' events at Hallowe'en, Bonfire Night and Christmas.
Buggy access. Kiosk.

Postman's Park

Between King Edward Street & Aldersgate Street, EC1R 4JR (7374 4127/www.cityof london.gov.uk/openspaces). St Paul's tube. **Open** 8am-dusk daily. **Admission** free. **Map** p318 O6.

Peaceful, fern-filled Postman's Park (named after its proximity to a large sorting office, long since demolished) is best known for the Watts

Sightseeing

Memorial to Heroic Sacrifice, a canopy-covered expanse of ceramic plaques, inscribed in florid Victorian style, that pay tribute to ordinary people who died trying to save others. 'Frederick Alfred Croft, Inspector, aged 31', begins one typical thumbnail drama. 'Saved a Lunatic Woman from Suicide at Woolwich Arsenal Station, But was Himself Run Over by the Train, Jan 11, 1878'. Many of the dead heroes were children, who tried to rescue drowning companions; their fates make gruesome lessons for their latter-day counterparts. *Buggy access.*

St Swithin's Garden

Oxford Court, off Cannon Street, EC4N 5AD (7374 4127/www.cityoflondon.gov.uk/ openspaces). Monument tube/Bank tube/ DLR/Cannon Street tube/rail. **Open** 8am-dusk Mon-Fri. **Admission** free. **Map** p319 Q7.
This carefully tended, walled garden is the burial place of Catrin Glendwr and two of her children. Catrin was the daughter of Owain Glendwr, the fiery Welsh hero whose uprising ended bloodily in 1413. There's a memorial sculpture dedicated not only to Catrin, but to the suffering of all women and children in war. *Buggy access.*

LOCAL PARKS

Alexandra Park & Palace

Alexandra Palace Way, N22 7AY (park 8444 7696/information 8365 2121/www.alexandra palace.com). Wood Green tube/Alexandra Palace rail/W3, 144 bus. **Open** *Park* 24hrs daily. *Palace* times vary depending on exhibitions. **Admission** free.
'The People's Palace', when it opened in 1873, was supposed to provide affordable entertainment for all. It burned down 16 days later. Rebuilt, it was the site of the first TV broadcasts by the BBC in 1936; then, in 1980, it burned down again. But the third version was still upright last time we went ice-skating. Outside, the children's playground is a well-equipped and wholesome place in which to take the air; the main source of interest for children, apart from the ice rink, is the pitch-and-putt course. In all, the palace on the hill and its environs have much to offer, some tattiness notwithstanding: walking around the park affords breathtaking views of London – you get the feeling you're above the pollution levels up here – and there's plenty of space for picnics; in bad weather, try the café in the garden centre. Bonfire Night in November is

the best night of the year, with lots of pyrotechnics that can be seen for miles around. *Buggy access. Disabled access: lift, ramp, toilet. Nappy-changing facilities (ice rink). Nearest picnic place: picnic area by boating lake.*

Battersea Park

SW11 4NJ (8871 7530/www.wandsworth. gov.uk). Sloane Square tube, then 19, 137 bus/Battersea Park or Queenstown Road rail. **Open** 8am-dusk daily. **Map** p313 F13.
The riverside park laid out here in 1858 was splendidly restored in 2004. Before it, this part of London was just marshy fields, used for market gardens and, more excitingly, for duelling: the Duke of Wellington fought an abortive duel here in 1829. Facilities range from water features (a boating lake, elegant fountains and riverside promenade) to state-of-the-art sporting facilities and play areas, including a toddlers' playground and a challenging adventure playground for children aged eight to 15 (8871 7539). Tennis coaching is available on floodlit courts to anyone over eight, bikes can be hired from London Recumbents (7498 6543; open Sat, Sun, bank holidays, school holidays), and open fishing is available from mid June to mid March (for permits, contact 8871 7530). Battersea Park is also home to a rich array of wildlife, the London Wildlife Trust has nature reserves here.

The Gondola al Parco café (7978 1655) has tables overlooking the boating lake, and live music on summer evenings. The prettiest landmark is the lofty Peace Pagoda, donated in 1985 by Japanese monks and nuns to commemorate Hiroshima Day. It stands serenely opposite the Children's Zoo, in the centre of the park's northern edge. *Buggy access. Café. Disabled access: toilet. Nappy-changing facilities.*

Brent Lodge Park

Church Road, W7 3BL (07940 021183/ www.ealing.gov.uk). Hanwell rail/E1, E2 bus. **Open** 7.30am-dusk daily. *Maze & animals* May-Aug 10.30am-6pm daily. Apr, Sept, Oct 10.30am-5pm daily. Nov-Mar 10.30am-4pm daily. **Admission** *Maze and animals* £1; 50p reductions, 3-16s; free under-3s. **No credit cards.**
Walk up the hill from the Millennium Maze, planted in 1999, for the hub of activities in this sweet and well-maintained local park. There's a café and a playground with an animal centre, housing a handful of primates as well as reptiles, amphibians, birds and domestic pets such as bunnies and guinea pigs. New arrivals

include black rats and three Turkish spiny mice; four baby inland bearded dragons will be on show in a new enclosure in summer 2008. The centre organises children's activity days in summer; phone for details.

Buggy access (not animal area). Café. Disabled access: toilet. Nappy-changing facilities.

Brockwell Park

Dulwich Road, SE24 0PA (7926 0105/ www.brockwellpark.com). Herne Hill rail.
Open 7.30am-dusk daily. **Admission** free.

It may only make the headlines for the wrong reasons – a riot at a punk gig, a recent council decision to set up a designated street drinkers' area – but Brockwell Park is every inch the lungs of Lambeth, and even hosts a country show every July (albeit one with reggae soundtracking the vegetable competitions; *see p21*). Tucked away behind its grassy slopes on the Tulse Hill side is one of south London's best playgrounds, with colour-coded sections for different age groups. There's an aerial slide and massive sandpit, and nearby there are duck ponds with dense greenery screening out the council flats, and signs informing you about coots, moorhens and tufted ducks. It's a steep walk to the top of the hill, but worth it for the view north over the city, plus a long-established BMX track and all-weather tennis courts. There's also the late-Georgian Brockwell Hall country house, now a café serving great wedges of lasagne and other pasta dishes, plus own-made cakes. Down on the Herne Hill side, the recently refurbished 1930s Lido, absolutely packed in sunny weather, is known by some wags as Brixton Beach. This beautiful lido and surrounding buildings offers more than just swimming: there are music classes for kids, who, at weekends, can take a miniature railway right to the door. The busy and dedicated users' group (www.brockwelllido.com) ensures there's plenty going on.

Buggy access. Café. Disabled access: toilet. Nappy-changing facilities.

Burgess Park

Albany Road, SE5 0RJ (7525 2000/ www.southwark.gov.uk). Elephant & Castle tube/rail, then 12, 42, 63, 68, 171, 343 bus.
Open 24hrs daily. *Lake area* 8am-dusk daily. **Admission** free.

Assembled and landscaped in gradual stages since the late 1940s, Burgess Park has attractions for all ages in an area sorely needing community spaces. For young tearaways, there's a busy kart track (7525 1101), adventure playground, indoor games room and a new cycle track. Then there are Chumleigh Gardens (home to Southwark Rangers football team), which are home to a great little café with its menu of fry-ups, quiches, salads and jazz on sunny Sundays. In fine weather it's good to order a plateful of grub and take it out to one of the garden tables.

Abney Park Cemetery. *See p108.*

Sightseeing

The sense of adventure

There are loads of places in London where kids can get good and muddy and let off a lot of steam. The playgrounds in the **Royal Parks** are particularly well suited to untrammelled exertion, as they're well segregated from dog users and have some exciting equipment. The rope see-saws in **Bushy Park** are exhilarating for kids and parents, and the pirate ship in **Diana, Princess of Wales Memorial Playground** (pictured) is a firm favourite: take your bucket and spade, as it's moored in a huge sandpit. This delightful play facility also has a tree encampment with walkways and ladders, water fountains to splash in. *See p122* for all.

For a different kind of playground, the **WWT Wetlands Centre** in Barnes (*see p138*) takes some beating, with a water vole tunnel complex and astroturf slopes;

children play in the landscape rather than just on equipment, and get a real sense of adventure. Older kids will love the adventure playground at **Battersea Park** (*see p110*), with its high-level walkways, slides and rope swings (and parents will come over all nostalgic at the sight of its faded-rainbow wood).

These are just a sample of the wide range of adventure playgrounds in the city: the London Play website (www.londonplay.org.uk) lists them all, including those aimed particularly at children with disabilities. Finally, 2007's Adventure Playground of the year, **Glamis Adventure Playground** in Shadwell (*see p122*), offers indoor and outdoor activities galore, including den-building and digging in the vegetable garden as well as an amazing climbing structure.

Various garden styles are employed in the series of interconnecting plots. There's English country garden, fragrant Mediterranean, meditative Islamic, and a splendid, flamboyant Caribbean garden. The Heart Garden is a fruit and vegetable patch planted, tended and harvested by people with long-term illnesses. On Wednesdays and Thursdays, the Peckham Sure Start programme organises outdoor games and activities for families with young children (phone for information).
Buggy access. Café. Disabled access: toilet.

Clissold Park

Stoke Newington Church Street, N16 5HJ (park ranger 7923 3660/www.clissoldpark. com). Stoke Newington rail/73, 149, 329, 476 bus. **Open** 7.30am-dusk daily.
Admission free.
Stroll over the river bridge and peek through the fences at the deer, rabbits, birds and goats; there are also several ponds supporting various waterfowl, an outdoor stage for children to cavort on whenever it's not in use by bands (the annual Stokefest is held here in June), and tennis

Sightseeing

courts that parents could use while kids are in the adjoining, well-kitted-out playground. The courts are home to the Hackney wing of the City Tennis Centre (7254 4235); ring for details of its programme (family tennis evenings, coaching, and junior clubs and tournaments are all available). The playground is lovely, with modern equipment and shady picnic tables. Other events, such as circuses, take place in the summer, and Clissold House and Park have been given a £4.5 million grant for a major revamp, with work due to start late in 2008; keep an eye on the website for news.

Buggy access. Café. Disabled access (not café): toilet. Nappy-changing facilities (on request).

Coram's Fields

93 Guilford Street, WC1N 1DN (7837 6138/ www.coramsfields.org). Russell Square tube. **Open** *May-Aug* 9am-7pm daily. *Sept-Apr* 9am-dusk daily. **Admission** free. **Map** p317 L4.

Thomas Coram established the Foundling Hospital for abandoned children on this spot (*see p73*) in 1747. The building was demolished in the 1920s, and a successful campaign to set out a children's park here finally bore fruit in 1936. *See p64* **Great Days Out**.

Buggy access. Café. Disabled access: toilet. Nappy-changing facilities.

Crystal Palace Park

Thicket Road, SE20 8DT (park ranger 8778 9496/www.crystalpalacepark.net). Crystal Palace rail/2, 3, 63, 122, 157, 227 bus. **Open** 7.30am-dusk daily. **Admission** free.

Curiously, a big part of this park – and all of its little museum (staffed by volunteers, open Sundays and bank holidays) – is dedicated to something that's no longer here: William Paxton's Crystal Palace, built to house Hyde Park's Great Exhibition of 1851. It entertained visitors for 70 years before being consumed by fire, and the park has been in limbo ever since. What is does have is atmosphere and local folklore in spades. A beautifully landscaped lake complex is home to Benjamin Waterhouse Hawkins' Victorian dinosaur sculptures, which caused outrage by backing up the theory of evolution, yet continue to give pleasure to kids – especially the T-Rex, who recently got a new arm: the tree he was gripping grew, and snapped off the old one. There are also strange, headless sphinxes (remnants of the Palace's grand old Upper Terrace), London's largest maze, and a wonderfully twisty set of wide woodland paths, which, until the 1970s, played host to motor-racing by like Stirling Moss and

Jack Brabham. These days, the only engine noise comes on a Sunday, by the International Sports Centre, where enthusiasts rev their remote-controlled cars. On the Sydenham side, you can search for the remains of London's second-oldest underground railway, an 1864 compressed air-powered contraption; down at the Penge end, the park's café is decorated with one of London's best murals.

Buggy access. Café. Disabled access: toilet. Nappy-changing facilities.

Dulwich Park

College Road, SE21 7BQ (7525 2000/ www.southwark.gov.uk). North Dulwich rail/ 12, 40, 176, 185, 176, 312, P4 bus. **Open** 8am-dusk daily. **Admission** free.

The park was formally landscaped in 1890, but had served as a scenic retreat long before that; Queen Mary was a regular visitor (one of the park's four gates is named after her). Visitors today are treated to the exceptionally child-friendly Pavilion Café, a super playground, boat hire on the lake, novelty bike hire (8299 6636, www.londonrecumbents.com, open most days) and a variety of gardens (including the American Garden, home to one of London's largest collections of rhododendrons and azaleas, as well as herons, cormorants and the occasional kingfisher). Boats can be rowed on the central pond for £5.25 per half hour during the summer.

The playground is one of the best in the area, with web-like climbing facilities, swings, slides and the new Ability Whirl, a safe, robust roundabout that can be used by able-bodied and disabled children. A community officer runs a programme of children's activities from the Francis Peek Centre (phone for details).

Buggy access. Café. Disabled access: ramp, toilet. Nappy-changing facilities (café).

Hampstead Heath

NW5 1QR (8348 9908/www.cityoflondon. gov.uk/openspaces). Kentish Town tube/ Gospel Oak or Hampstead Heath rail/214, C2, C11 bus. **Open** dawn-dusk daily. **Admission** free.

The closest thing you'll find to an unspoilt natural landscape in central London, the 800-acres (320-hectare) heath is as far from the manicured flowerbeds of the Royal Parks as you could hope to find. You could spend all day hiking and playing on the heath. Grassland, woods, ponds, hedgerows and ancient trees all testify that this land was once farmland. Wildlife – from bats and fungi to kingfishers and parakeets – flourishes here.

Sightseeing

Great Days Out
Camden

Camden Town has always had a raffish air – its gaudy shopfronts, banners and street stalls lending it an atmosphere reminiscent of a seaside town. This traditionally fitted its status as the poor relation to sprauncier neighbouring districts like Primrose Hill and Belsize Park, but the cheerful shabbiness of the place is now largely an act: galloping gentrification has priced out many of the impoverished Londoners who were once drawn to Camden's cheap housing. Despite ongoing redevelopment, and the tourist-trap emporia that have taken over the High Street, the Market area retains much of its higgledy-piggledy charm and still makes a great day out.

In the market for fun

If possible, plan your trip for a weekday; at weekends the streets and markets are absurdly busy and can be so frantic that small or nervous children find the experience pretty testing. Be aware too, that Camden Town tube station is exit-only on Saturday and Sunday, which means you could have a long walk up to Chalk Farm or down to Mornington Crescent tube stations at the end of a tiring day.

Luckily, the shops and market stalls are open all week. There's so much on offer that it pays to be picky, though. Feel free to bypass the first market you come to after turning north from the tube station – the one at Buck Street bearing the legend 'Camden Market' – unless you have a teenager who is desperate for goth T-shirts and cheap tat. The Canal Market used to be a better bet, but is currently closed after the fire of February 2008, so go for **Camden Lock**, where you'll find quirky craft stalls as well as alt.fashion, accessories and jewellery. After that, explore the new-look **Stables Market**. This redevelopment has caused controversy locally, and parts of it were still under construction at the time of writing, but on current evidence, the atmosphere seems little changed – there are still plenty of jumbled displays of ethnic doo-dads, vintage clothes and furniture, and lots of child-friendly novelties and toy stalls. You'll also find all kinds of stand-up eating places – or plonk down on comfortable rug-covered seats outside the Marrakech café.

Small children are fascinated by the Lock, particularly if a boat is coming through as

Great Days Out

you pass. On your way there, stop off at Inspiral Lounge, not just for an organic drink and a splendid view across the water, but to book tickets for a canal cruise with **Jenny Wren** (7485 4433, www.walkersquay.com). These one-and-a-half hour trips take you to Little Venice and back and represent a welcome interlude of peace and tranquillity. A walk on the canal path is soothing, though if you're pushing a buggy you might prefer not to negotiate the steps you'll inevitably encounter along the way.

Round about Camden

A stroll down Parkway will take you to lovely **Regent's Park** (*see p123* and *p136*). Another airy location nearby is **Primrose Hill**, separated from its brasher neighbour to the east by a railway line and a hoick in house prices. Children like kite-flying on the hill and the cakes in the cafés on Regent's Park Road.

Apart from the all-consuming attractions of market, shops and watering holes, culture comes courtesy of one chuffing great arts venue. Down Chalk Farm Road is the **Roundhouse** (*see p178*), famous for historic early gigs and once again providing an avant garde programme of music, theatre and arts. Not bad for an old railway engine shed. Your canal trip to Little Venice will lead you to another must-see for children, the eccentric **Puppet Theatre Barge** (*see p183*), surely the jolliest place to take in a show, especially if you're under eight.

LUNCH BOX

Also in the area: Belgo Noord, Pizza Express, Strada, Wagamama.
Belgo Noord *72 Chalk Farm Road, NW1 8AN (7267 0718).* Musselbound free lunches for kids. *See p234.*
Cottons *55 Chalk Farm Road, NW1 8AN (7485 8388/www.cottons-restaurant.co.uk).* Caribbean food.
FishWorks *57 Regents Park Road, NW1 8XD (7586 9760/www.fishworks. co.uk).* Seafood, with a kids' menu.
Fresh & Wild *49 Parkway, NW1 7PN (7428 7575/www.wholefoods market.com).* Organic and wholefoods.
Gilgamesh *Stables Market, Chalk Farm Road, NW1 8AH (7428 4922/ www.gilgameshbar.com).* Ornate, oriental, a treat for older children.
Green Note *6 Parkway, NW1 7AN (7485 9899/www.greennote.co.uk).* Folksy vegetarian restaurant.
Marine Ices *8 Haverstock Hill, NW3 2BL (7482 9003).* Italian. *See p244.*

Great Days Out

A brisk walk up Parliament Hill is a good way to whet appetites for a picnic, and weary climbers will be rewarded with one of the best views in London. Parliament Hill's playground is well worth a stop-off too, still looking spanking new after its award-winning refurb, and packed with state-of-the-art equipment designed to challenge children rather than keep them boringly safe. An alternative focal point is over to the west: the listed Pergola, built in the 1920s by Lord Leverhulme to join together two parts of his estate, is free to enter and fun to explore. And at Golders Hill you'll find a free zoo (small, but well kept) and a new butterfly house in a converted former greenhouse. The Kenwood Estate, though officially part of the Heath, is run by English Heritage.

As well as the famous year-round open-air swimming ponds, fishing is available in six of the ponds (you need a rod licence and a free Heath fishing permit). Families wanting to swim often prefer the Lido at Parliament Hill, which recently had a refurb. There are also tennis courses, bat walks, nature trails, and a 'secret garden' and wildlife pond. Clowns, magicians, storytellers and puppeteers perform in various locations in the hols. No wonder the heath has a Green Flag Award, given to top-quality parks. Check the website and local press for more news of the Hampstead Heath consultation and management plan, and to check that family events are going ahead as expected.

Buggy access. Cafés. Disabled access: toilet. Nappy-changing facilities.

Highbury Fields

Highbury Crescent, N5 1RR (7527 4953/ www.islington.gov.uk). Highbury & Islington tube/rail/19, 30, 43, 271 bus. **Open** *Park* 24hrs. *Playground* dawn-dusk daily. **Admission** free.

In 1666, 200,000 Londoners fled here to escape the Great Fire, and it's still Islington's largest outdoor space today. Hidden behind Highbury Pool (which reopened after refurbishment in 2007) and a series of high bushes is an unusual playground that combines old-fashioned thrills (like a circular train requiring *Flintstones*-style propulsion, and an excitingly long and steep slide) with more recent additions, like the flying fox and giant, web-like climbing frames. The outdoor tennis courts have been refurbished and are used by the excellent Islington Tennis Centre, and a stroll across Highbury Fields takes you from busy Upper Street past imposing period terraces to Highbury Barn, a trendy enclave with several excellent food shops, restaurants and child-friendly cafés.

Buggy access. Café.

Clissold Park. *See p112.*

Holland Park

Ilchester Place, W8 6LU (7471 9813/Ecology Centre 7471 9809/www.rbkc.gov.uk). Holland Park tube/9, 27, 28, 49 bus. **Open** 8am-dusk daily. **Admission** free. **Map** p314 A9.

Holland Park is one of London's finest green spaces, and one of the most densely wooded. Its paths takes you past imperious peacocks and plenty of squirrels and rabbits, a smart Italian café and an open-air theatre; the peaceful Japanese Garden has a pond full of koi carp, which fascinate children, and the adventure playground keeps the over-fives entertained. Of most interest to youngsters is Whippersnappers (7738 6633, www.whippersnappers.org), which puts on weekly musical and puppet workshops. Then there's the Ecology Centre, which provides site maps, nets for pond-dipping and information; it also hosts half-term and holiday activities of the local Wildlife Watch group, the junior branch of the Wildlife Trust (www.wildlondon.org.uk). Also in the park are tennis courts and two art spaces, the Ice House and the Orangery. The North Lawn is busy with families and picnickers throughout the summer.

Buggy access. Café. Disabled access: toilet. Nappy-changing facilities. Restaurant.

Mile End Park was 50 years in the making (work started in the 1940s), and is for many Londoners the quintessential modern urban park. The south end of the park has a great playground (funded by HSBC to the tune of £2m), with rope slide, scrambling wall, complicated climbing frame, swings and see-saw, as well as a dedicated area for under-fives. New apparatus installed in the playground is designed especially to appeal to children with disabilities, as well as to their able-bodied playmates, with a huge, bird-nest-style swing and a ramped bridge. The interactive play structure is made from a forest of uprights with hooks and catches, so that children can attach ropes, canvases and scramble nets. There's a refreshments kiosk and toilet, and the Play Pavilion hosts 'stay and play' sessions (phone for details). A little to the north, the go-kart track provides thrills and spills. During the school holidays there are structured events for children.
Buggy access. Café. Disabled access: toilet. Nappy-changing facilities.

Morden Hall Park

Morden Hall Road, Morden, Surrey SM4 5JD (8545 6850/www.nationaltrust.org.uk). Morden tube. **Open** 8am-6pm daily. **Admission** free.
This 125-acre (50-hectare) swathe of National Trust parkland is one of uncommon beauty. The Morden Hall of the name is run as a private restaurant, so you have access only to meadows, woodland, a network of waterways from the River Wandle and a rose garden. The Snuff Mill Environmental Centre, housed in one of several historic buildings in the park, puts on children's activities every Thursday in school holidays. Craftspeople, furniture restorers and artists occupy many of the old estate buildings. The Riverside Café is a refreshing place to take stock.
Buggy access. Café. Disabled access: toilet. Nappy-changing facilities. Shop.

Queen's Park

Kingswood Avenue, NW6 6SG (park manager 8969 5661/www.cityoflondon. gov.uk/openspaces). Queen's Park tube/rail. **Open** 7.30am-dusk daily. **Admission** free.
This Corporation of London park is a godsend to the people of Brent, and it wasn't awarded a Green Flag for nothing. It has a great playground with giant sandpit, a paddling pool, a small animal enclosure, and patrolling wardens. At the northern end is a wild, overgrown area; here a nature trail displays pictures of the small beasts you might encounter. The pleasant café serves own-made

Manor House Park

Old Road, SE13 5SY (8318 1358/www. lewisham.gov.uk). Hither Green rail. **Open** *Café & park* 9am-dusk daily. *House & library* 9.30am-5pm Mon, Sat; 9.30am-7pm Tue, Thur. **Admission** free.
The gardens and park surrounding this Manor House and library (closed for a refurb until Dec 2008) are lovely. The central lake has a raised platform, with flocks of wildfowl to feed; the handsome play area, made of natural materials, includes rocks, wooden see-saws, balance bars, climbing frames and swings. On one side of it is a wildlife garden; on the other is the very family friendly Pistachios park café, with its menu of simple, own-made hot meals, such as baked potaoes and pasta dishes, ice-cream, drinks and snacks. A farmers' market takes place here on the first Saturday of the month.
Buggy access. Café. Disabled access: toilet.

Mile End Park

Locksley Street, E14 7EJ (73644147/ children's park 7093 2253/www.tower hamlets.gov.uk). Mile End tube. **Open** 24hrs daily. *Children's park* 10am-dusk daily. **Admission** free.

Sightseeing

cakes and local Disotto's ice-cream. There's a pitch-and-putt area, pétanque enclosure and six tennis courts. Children's entertainment takes place at the bandstand during the summer holidays. The annual Queen's Park Day, which in 2008 is held on 14 September, involves fancy dress competitions, face-painting, a dog show and plenty of 'He's behind you!' puppetry. *Buggy access. Café. Disabled access: toilet. Nappy-changing facilities.*

Ravenscourt Park

Ravenscourt Road, W6 0UL (www.lbhf.gov.uk). Ravenscourt Park tube. **Open** 7.30am-dusk daily. **Admission** free.

Family-friendly Ravenscourt Park covers 32 acres (13 hectares), and its north-eastern corner has been designated an Archaeological Priority Area. In summer the packed paddling pool is the park's popular attraction, full of gambolling children in their cossies, but there are also three play areas, a big pond, a nature trail and a scented garden for the visually impaired. Kids with spare energy can use the skateboarding ramp or enjoy a game of tennis. The café is open all year and is conveniently positioned for the playground – it does good children's meals. There's a flower show and children's fair in July, and an annual Play Day in August, with bouncy castles and face-painting. *Buggy access. Café. Nappy-changing facilities.*

Southwark Park

Gomm Road, SE16 2UA (art gallery 7237 1230/www.southwark.gov.uk). Canada Water tube. **Open** *Park* 7.30am-1hr before dusk daily. *Gallery* (during exhibitions) Summer 11am-5pm Wed-Sun; noon-6pm Sat. Winter 11am-4pm Wed-Sun; noon-4pm Sat. Phone ahead to check. **Admission** free.

London's oldest municipal park was opened by the Metropolitan Board of Works in 1869. In 1998, it was given a new bandstand, bowling pavilion and children's play area, and nine years later the whole place is still looking good, thanks to the efforts of the energetic Friends of Southwark Park and the vandal-busting wardens. Sport enthusiasts have plenty yto keep their heart rates up – an athletics track (this and the astroturf pitches are often used by nearby Millwall Football Club) as well as tennis courts and football pitches. The park is surrounded by art galleries, the most accessible being the Café Gallery Project, which holds frequent exhibitions and a Saturday morning DIY family art club; check www.cafegalleryprojects.com for details of this and the summer Children's Exhibition and winter Open Exhibition. Parkside Café & Bar, just across from the Gallery, is a useful place for lunch, serving hot meals and sandwiches. Children's parties are also hosted in the park. *Buggy access. Café. Disabled access: toilet. Nappy-changing facilities (in gallery).*

The kids are all right in **Coram's Fields**. *See p113 ...*

Thames Barrier Park

North Woolwich Road, E16 2HP (www.thames barrierpark.org.uk). Pontoon Dock DLR.
Open 7am-dusk daily. **Admission** free.

When it opened in 2001, the beautiful Thames Barrier Park was London's first new park in half a century. With its sleek landscaping and view over the silver pods of the Thames Barrier, it's an unexpected delight. The Barrier's visitor centre is on the south side (*see p12* **Old Father Thames**). On one side of the park is a concrete and granite channel the width of a small motorway. Called the Green Dock, it's filled with fragrant honeysuckle and wavy yew hedges: excellent hide-and-seek potential, with the two pedestrian bridges overhead adding an extra dimension to the game. On the riverfront is the Pavilion of Remembrance, erected to remember victims of the Blitz. The flat lawns are manicured, perfect for picnics and games; there's a playground packed with apparatus; a basketball hoop and five-a-side court. Ducks, geese, swans and oyster catchers pick around on the gleaming mudflats. The park is fantastic for waterfowl watching: herons feed along the shore at low tide, and large numbers of teal, shelduck and cormorants enjoy the river's bounty. The tea pavilion serves the best coffee in Docklands, for a low price.
Buggy access. Café. Disabled access: toilet. Free parking. Nappy-changing facilities.

Victoria Park

Old Ford Road, E3 5DS (8985 1957/ www.towerhamlets.gov.uk). Mile End tube/ Cambridge Heath or Hackney Wick rail/ 8, 26, 30, 55, 253, 277, S2 bus. **Open** 8am-dusk daily. **Admission** free.

With its grand wide carriageways, ornate lampposts and wrought-iron gates, Victoria Park, opened in 1845, was conceived as the Regent's Park of the East End, and is the largest area of formal parkland this side of town. In the past, poverty-stricken locals used the park's two lakes as as their washing facilities, but now there are fish in the Western Lake (you can help deplete the stock by applying for a free fishing licence); Britain's oldest model boat club convenes around the other lake, near Crown Gate East, every second Sunday. There's a fallow deer enclosure on the east side, tennis courts and a bowling green, plus football, hockey and cricket pitches. Take refreshments at the Lakeside Pavilion Café near the busy playground and watch the geese, swans and ducks play under the fountain.
Buggy access. Café. Disabled access: toilet. Nappy-changing facilities.

Wanstead Park

Entrance via Warren Road or Northumberland Avenue, E11 2LT (8508 0028/www.cityof london.gov.uk). Wanstead tube. **Open** dawn-dusk daily. **Admission** free.

… and in **Greenwich Park**. *See p122.*

Sightseeing

Space to grow

No stinky litter trays, wet walks before school, daily brushings (and hooverings), holiday care or expensive bills. You still have the satisfaction of caring for and raising little ones, but when these tiddlers are grown, on to the plate they go. Plants are a fantastic way for children to learn about green issues and how to care for living things (with low-level damage if they're occasionally forgotten).

Gardening opportunities exist even in the most seemingly barren of boroughs. Seek inspiration from the landscaped acres of **Kew**'s botanic gardens and learn about the healing properties of plants, if dock leaves versus nettles has your child intrigued, at the **Chelsea Physic Garden**. S*ee p107* for both. Visit the **Chelsea Flower Show** (www.rhs.org.uk); the Royal Horticultural Society's show is the ultimate event in the gardening year – and it's not all blue-rinsed retirees who attend. Modern landscape gardeners like Diarmid Gavin, with his controversial installations and architectural planting, have made dirty wellies positively trendy, and there's plenty of ideas and information to be had from joining the RHS (plus free entry to their gardens).

Many urban backyards aren't large enough for more than a few gro-bags' worth of cherry toms and some herbs let alone a kitchen garden. Consider putting your name down for an allotment and don't be intimidated about managing the plot; you can always share it with friends. The popularity of allotments has rocketed in recent years and chances are you'll have a long wait (often years) as demand is high and plots are like gold dust. Contact the applications officer at your local borough for information and visit the London Allotments Network website (www.londonallotments.net) for useful advice and forums.

Don't give up you can't find an allotment; the great thing about gardening is that all you need is a patch of ground, and if a group of like-minded people band together, wonderful things can happen. Growing Communities (7502 7588, www.btinternet.com/~grow.communities), a project run by Hackney's locals, is a sustainable system of growing and selling seasonal organic veg. Food miles are reduced, small-scale farmers are supported and Hackney residents get a fruit and veg box scheme. If want to muck in, visit Growing Communities' Urban Market Gardens. Volunteering is a fantastic way to learn about growing organic produce, and the fruits of your labours are sold through the Box Scheme. Their Butterfield Green Community Orchard, only a year old, is planted with plums, peaches, quince and hazelnuts alongside apples and pears.

Gardening's great for learning about wildlife: finding minibeasts doesn't get more hands-on than when you're poking around in their patch. Primary schools can contact the London Wildlife Trust's education co-ordinator (7261 0447, www.wildlondon.org.uk) to arrange a visit and talk, help with setting up a wildlife garden and arranging trips to sites. The LWT Centre for Wildlife Gardening in Peckham (*see p128*) welcomes volunteers. Check their website for activities. While you're at it, visit www.thegardeners-directory.co.uk and www.gardenersclub.co.uk to search for organisations and clubs to join; many are family-friendly. What better excuse is there for getting absolutely covered in dirt!

Sightseeing

Managed by the City of London as part of Epping Forest (*see p128*), Wanstead Park is a heavily wooded green space with several beautiful water features: the Ornamental Water and the three ponds – Perch, Heronry and Shoulder of Mutton. At the fenced-off end of the Ornamental Water is a ruined grotto, built in the early 1760s with a boathouse that is now all tumble-down romantic. The other important ruin in the park is the Temple, once a fancy summerhouse, which has the park toilets to one side; it's open one week a month in the summer (phone for dates, and for details of summer outdoor theatre, community operas and guided walks). Adults might like to know that the grotto and Temple are both Grade II-listed, but children will prefer the ball-throwing and kite-flying possibilities on the extensive grassy area between the Temple and the tea stall. The park's Wildlife Group (www.wrengroup.fsnet.co.uk) is a good point of contact.
Buggy access. Café. Free parking.

Waterlow Park

Highgate Hill, N6 5HG (8348 8716/café 8341 4807/www.lauderdalehouse.co.uk). Archway tube/143, 210, 271, W5 bus. **Open** 11am-4pm Tue-Fri; noon-5pm Sun; phone to check weekend openings. *Café* 9am-dusk Tue-Sun. **Admission** free.
Waterlow Park was donated to the public by low-cost housing pioneer Sir Sydney Waterlow. The pretty, 16th-century Lauderdale House, once home of Nell Gwynne, is the park's centrepiece, and in the summer, weather permitting, the parkland surrounding it plays host to open-air entertainments. Whatever's on, it's lovely to sit on the terrace of the café and admire the view over a coffee and ice-cream or an Italian meal; book ahead if you fancy having Sunday lunch here. The Grade II-listed park, with its lakes and toddler playground, has a 17th-century terrace garden whose depot building contains an activities room and toilets; there's a year-round programme of kids' activities, ranging from dance and drama to craft workshops and various seasonal jollies.
Buggy access (café ground floor only). Café. Disabled access: toilet (café ground floor only).

West Ham Park

Upton Lane, E7 9PU (8472 3584/www.cityof london.gov.uk). Stratford tube/rail/104, 238 bus. **Open** 7.30am-30mins before dusk daily. **Admission** free.
West Ham Park is an East End treasure, and was voted best park in the South East in 2005's Britain's Best Park contest. It opened in 1874, and is still as neat and civilised as ever, with pretty ornamental gardens, superb roses and lovely trees; it's one of the few London parks to have its own plant nursery (the flowerbeds are quite spectacular in the summer as a result) and full-time park attendants. The playground has some impressive climbing apparatus, a wooden prairie locomotive to clamber on, and a Wendy house corner. There are 12 tennis courts (lucky locals have access to the annual tennis clinic, which is held in June), three cricket nets (Essex CCC runs free training for under-16s in July), two match-quality cricket tables, two football pitches (one all-weather), a running track and a rounders area. The pre-war paddling pool (late May to August) is another attraction. From late July to August there are children's events on Monday and Friday afternoons; a very popular bouncy castle appears on Wednesday; and there are occasional Sunday concerts. An ice-cream van takes up position near the playground (from noon daily, Easter to October) but it also has healthy snacks on offer.
Buggy access. Disabled access: toilet. Nappy-changing facilities.

Wimbledon Common

Rangers office, Windmill Road, SW19 5NR (8788 7655/www.wpcc.org.uk). Putney rail, then 93 bus/85 bus. **Open** 24hrs daily. **Admission** free.
The countryside in the midst of urban sprawl, Wimbledon Common is truly massive: almost twice the size of Hampstead Heath. It's a haven for anyone who loves the outdoors, with sports grounds, cottages, golf courses, woodland, lakes, ravines, and around 16 miles (10km) of riding trails. There's never any shortage of things to do, particularly in spring and summer, when nature trails for the public, schools and other groups are organised. Pick up a copy of the small guide book from the ranger's office, and set off to spot the trees, shrubs, wildflowers and birds listed within. The common is patrolled by a number of rangers, both on horseback and on foot, and they're a mine of information about this common and nearby Putney Heath, both of which are designated as SSSIs (Sites of Special Scientific Interest). They're based in the Information Centre, which is open seven days a week, where postcards and Christmas cards are sold and there are leaflets to tell you about the plant and animal life on the common, as well as the history of the area. Best of all is a video microscope showing insects and other items in minute detail; specimens are changed regularly, and you can insert your own for display.
Buggy access. Café. Disabled access: toilet. Nappy-changing facilities (café).

PLAYGROUNDS

Kimber Adventure Playground in Wandsworth's King George's Park (8870 2168) is closed until autumn 2008.

Diana, Princess of Wales' Memorial Playground

Near Black Lion Gate, Broad Walk, Kensington Gardens, W8 2UH (7298 2117/recorded information 7298 2141/ www.royalparks.gov.uk). Bayswater tube/ 70, 94, 148, 390 bus. **Open** *Summer* 10am-7.45pm daily. *Winter* 10am-4pm daily. Times vary; phone or check website for changes. **Admission** free. Adults & over-12s must be accompanied by a child. **Map** p310 C7.

For children, this commemorative play area with its pirate ship and mermaids' fountain is the best bit of Kensington Gardens. There's a programme of free entertainment, such as visits by clowns or storytelling sessions; check the website for details. Beyond the shipshape features lies the tepee camp: a trio of wigwams, each large enough to hold a sizeable tribe; a tree-house encampment has walkways, ladders, slides and 'tree phones'. The area's connection with *Peter Pan*'s creator JM Barrie is remembered in scenes from the story, etched into the glass in the Home Under the Ground. Many of the playground's attractions appeal to the senses (scented shrubs, whispering willows and bamboo are planted throughout), and much of the equipment has been designed for use by children with special needs, including those in wheelchairs. There's plenty of seating for parents; unaccompanied adults aren't allowed in, but they can view the gardens between 9.30am and 10am. The café has a good children's menu. *See also p76* **Great Days Out**.
Buggy access. Café. Disabled access: toilet. Nappy-changing facilities.

Glamis Adventure Playground

Glamis△ Road, E1W 3DQ (7702 8301/ www.glamisadventure.org.uk). Shadwell DLR. **Open** *Termtime* 3.15-7pm Mon-Fri; 10am-4pm Sat. *School holidays* 10am-5.30pm Mon-Fri. **Admission** free.
Winner of Adventure Playground of the year 2007. *See p112* **The sense of adventure**.
Buggy access. Disabled access: toilet.

Lady Allen Adventure Playground

Chivalry Road, Wandsworth Common, SW11 1HT (7228 0278/www.kids-online.org.uk). Clapham Junction rail. **Open** *Wandsworth borough term times* 10.30am-5pm Tue (under-8s only); 3-5pm Wed-Fri; 10am-noon Sat. *School holidays* 10am-noon Mon, Wed-Fri; 10am-3pm Tue. **Admission** £1; accompanying carers free. **No credit cards**.
The most northerly tip of Wandsworth Common is home to this purpose-built playground for Wandsworth children with special needs. Tuesday is for the under-fives and their carers; the rest of the time, it's open to all children under 15. Children have access to a play room, a computer room and soft play area; outside, there's a large adventure playground with a variety of fixed equipment. The operation is staffed by Kids London volunteers, and you should phone ahead before visiting; able-bodied children are also welcome.
Buggy access. Disabled access: toilet. Nappy-changing facilities.

ROYAL PARKS

Bushy Park

Hampton Court Road, Hampton Court, Surrey, TW12 2EJ (8979 1586/www.royal parks.gov.uk). Hampton Wick, Hampton Court or Teddington Rail/111, 216, 265, 411, R68 bus. **Open** *Pedestrians* Jan-Aug, Oct, Dec 24hrs daily. Sept, Nov 8am-10.30pm daily. *Vehicle access* 6.30am-dusk daily. **Admission** free.

It's possible to drive right through Bushy, the second largest Royal Park, in ten minutes, and wonder what all the fuss is about. But park the car and wander along its scrubby avenues, past secluded ponds and wonderful walled wooded section, and you'll find it an excellent alternative to Richmond. On a recent visit, we got up close to a reclining deer, which was having grubs picked from its fur by a magpie. There's a decent kids' playground, and notices about this former Hampton Court extension's history and ecosystem. The park's most glamorous section is Chestnut Avenue, with the Arethusa 'Diana' Fountain forming the centrepiece.
Buggy access. Café. Disabled access: toilet.

Greenwich Park

Blackheath Gate, Charlton Way, SE10 8QY (8858 2608/www.royalparks.org.uk). Cutty Sark DLR/Greenwich DLR/rail/Maze Hill rail/1, 53, 177, 180, 188, 286 bus/riverboat to Greenwich Pier. **Open** 6am-dusk daily. **Admission** free.
See p124 **Great Days Out**.
Buggy access. Cafés. Disabled access: toilet. Nappy-changing facilities.

Hyde Park & Kensington Gardens

*W2 2UH (7298 2100/www.royalparks.gov.uk).
Hyde Park Corner, Knightsbridge, Lancaster
Gate or Marble Arch tube/2, 8, 10, 12, 23,
73, 94 bus.* **Open** *Hyde Park* 5am-midnight
daily. *Kensington Gardens* 5am-dusk daily.
Admission free. **Map** p311 E7.
See p76 **Great Days Out**.
*Buggy access. Cafés. Disabled access: toilet.
Nappy-changing facilities.*

Regent's Park

*NW1 4NR (7486 7905/boating lake 7724
4069/www.royalparks.gov.uk). Baker Street,
Camden Town, Great Portland Street or
Regent's Park tube.* **Open** dawn-30mins before
dusk daily. **Admission** free. **Map** p314 G3.
See p136 **Great Days Out**.
*Buggy access. Cafés. Disabled access: toilet.
Nappy-changing facilities.*

Richmond Park

*Holly Lodge, Richmond, Surrey TW10 5HS
(8948 3209/www.royalparks.gov.uk). Richmond
tube/rail.* **Open** *Summer* 7am-30mins before
dusk. *Winter* 7.30am-30mins before dusk.
Admission free.
Sprawling Richmond Park, eight miles (13km)
across at its widest point, is the biggest city park
in Europe, and along with Epping Park the
nearest London gets to wild countryside. Herds
of red and fallow deer roam freely, a source of
much fascination to children (but don't let them
get too close). The park is also home to
numerous varieties of bird, and fish and to 1,000
species of beetle. Tucked away in the middle is
the Isabella Plantation, a tranquil woodland
garden with streams, ponds and bridges.
Planted with camellias, azaleas and
rhododendrons, it's best seen in all its glory in
early summer or late September. There are
plenty of benches and grassy glades where you
can picnic, and the park's Petersham Gate has a
playground. From the top of nearby King Henry
VIII's Mound, you get a spectacular view right
across London. Alternatively, you could stroll
along Terrace Walk, a Victorian promenade that
runs from the philosopher Bertrand Russell's
childhood home, Pembroke Lodge (now a
licensed café, and a good lunch spot), and
beyond the park to Richmond Hill. A well-kept
cycle path follows the perimeter; hire kids' bikes
and adult bikes with tag-alongs or children's
seats from Roehampton Gate (7581 1188). Like
all the Royal Parks, Richmond hosts a summer
events programme for families, see the notice at
the gate lodge, or the website.
Café.

Green, serene **Regent's Park**.

Great Days Out
Greenwich

Historic maritime Greenwich is a UNESCO World Heritage Site with a wealth of attractions, as well as one of the most wonderfully sited parks in London. River trips (Thames Cruises, Catamaran Cruises; *see p9*) take you to Greenwich Pier, just by the old tea clipper, the *Cutty Sark*. The Docklands Light Railway (DLR) offers sightseers the Rail & River Rover (www.dlr.co.uk), a family pass also valid on City Cruises.

The **Cutty Sark** (www.cuttysark.org.uk) brought tea from China and wool from Australia. Now a museum, the vessel has the builders in following a fire – but she's still entertaining visitors. Work isn't due to be finished until October 2008. You can visit an exhibition centre that details the history and revamping of the ship. Hard-hat tours are available on request. Tea tasting is also available. Once reopened and raised up from the ground, the ship will have a new keel and main deck, accessed by lift, with a small auditorium. Below will be an exhibition space for Robert Burns memorabilia (his poem gave the ship her name) and the famous figurehead collection.

A walk in the park

From the riverside it's a ten-minute walk to **Greenwich Park** (*see p122*). For two centuries (between around 1450 and 1650), England's principal royal palace, the Palace Of Placentia, stood in Greenwich. It was the birthplace of King Henry VIII and the Queens Mary and Elizabeth I. In the late 17th century the palace was torn down and replaced by Sir Christopher Wren's **Old Royal Naval College** (*see p89*).

Today visitors to the Park can enjoy fab views, teeming wildlife, roly-poly hills, an observatory at the top and a museum at the bottom, an excellent café, playgrounds, boating and fun. It's the oldest Royal Park, whose proud connections go back to Tudor times. Henry VIII hunted here and there's an ancient husk of an old oak tree, which

the monarch is said to have danced around with his then paramour, Anne Boleyn. The dead tree has a more vigorous neighbour: a new oak planted on the site by Prince Philip to mark his wife's Golden Jubilee.

A grassland enclosure near the Flower Garden is a wildlife sanctuary. It's home to the Greenwich Park Secret Garden Wildlife Centre, where a hide has been built to let kids get close-up views of wild red and fallow deer that live in Greenwich Park. Just outside the top gates, across Charlton Way, a group of donkeys give rides to children on sunny weekends – fitting for a park that's going to host the equestrian events at 2012's Olympics. Free fun for under-tens is provided by the Royal Parks' summer programme, including alfresco theatrical workshops.

The park is also home to the bright and lively

National Maritime Museum (*see p105*) where the nation's seafaring history is covered over three floors. At weekends and during school holidays, amiable staff invite children to take part in various maritime-themed artistic endeavours, trails, games and storytelling sessions. But just wandering around the place is a lark. No young pirate can leave without plundering the gift shop, which runs the vaguely nautical gamut from dolphin water pistols to models of *HMS Victory*.

Stars in their eyes

Later, you could walk (or take the park's shuttle bus) up the steep slopes to the **Royal Observatory** (*see p30*). This has a dome housing Britain's largest refracting telescope – and the eighth largest in the world. In the courtyard is the Prime Meridian Line: star of a billion snaps. The 120-seater Peter Harrison Planetarium contains an advanced digital laser projector. This unique building has a shape that reflects its own astrological position; a semi-submerged, bronze-clad cone tilts at 51.5 degrees, the latitude of Greenwich, so it points to the north star and its reflective disc is aligned with the celestial equator. The planetarium shows are presented by a Royal Observatory astronomer and special shows are available for children daily (suitable for over sixes; shows for kids aged three to six take place at weekends and school during holidays; check the website).

The building looks all the more stunning at night thanks to its bright-green Meridian Line Laser marking the

place where the world is divided into the east and west hemispheres.

From Greenwich the Thames Path can take you to the Greenwich Peninsula, dominated by the structure formerly known as the Millennium Dome, now rechristened the **O2**. The area around the O2 is being regenerated too. Work has begun on the construction of Millennium Square, all part of the plan to make this once derelict stretch of the riverscape a new town and offshoot of Olympics 2012 action. Keep walking toward the posh flats to find the really wild **Greenwich Peninsula Ecology Park** (*see p127*).

St James's Park

*SW1A 2JB (7930 1793/www.royalparks
.org.uk). St James's Park tube/3, 11, 12, 24,
53, 211 bus.* **Open** 5am-midnight daily.
Admission free. **Map** p317 K8.

Pelicans have lived in St James's Park ever since
the Russian ambassador donated two live
pelicans to King Charles II as a gesture of
Anglo-Russian friendship in 1662, and their
daily feeding on Duck Island is probably the
most child-friendly spectacle in the West End.
The current pelican residents come from
Eastern Europe and America. At certain times
of year, park staff run guided tours of the
island, with visits to nests and roosts; once dates
are confirmed, they go on the park website. If
you can't time your visit to coincide with
pelicans' tea, you can feed more familiar birds
at stations dotted around the shore of the lake.
The range includes dozens of varieties of
ducks, geese and seagulls, black and white
swans, coots, moorhens, teals and grebes; the
honking cacophony has to be heard to be
believed. The park squirrels are tame enough to
take food from your hand, although that
perhaps should not be encouraged – they can be
vicious little blighters.

Duck Island is the headquarters of the
London Historic Parks & Gardens Trust (7839
3969, www.londongardenstrust.org), which
aims to promote and enhance London's parks
and green spaces for families and young people.
*Buggy access. Disabled access: toilet. Kiosk.
Nappy-changing facilities. Restaurant.*

WILDLIFE SANCTUARIES

Camley Street Natural Park

*12 Camley Street, NW1 0PW (7833 2311/
www.wildlondon.org.uk). King's Cross tube/rail.*
Open 10am-5pm daily. Closed 20 Dec-1 Jan.
Admission free. **Map** p315 L2.

The flagship project of the London Wildlife
Trust, Camley Street Nature Park was created
on the site of a former coal yard behind King's
Cross Station in 1984. Today, it's a small but
thriving green space in an area better known for
massive transport projects and urban grit. Set
beside the canal are winding nature trails,
experimental gardens, a visitor centre with
nature displays and resident rabbits, and a large,
bulrushed pond full of frogs, newts and other
slimy creatures that kids adore. From 10am to
3pm on Saturday and Sunday, children can come
pond-dipping and insect-hunting, assisted by
park volunteers. The wood-cabin visitor centre
is used by the London Wildlife Trust's Wildlife

Watch Club – there are special events for kids
throughout the year.
*Buggy access. Disabled access: toilet.
Nappy-changing facilities.*

East Ham Nature Reserve

*Norman Road, E6 4HN (8470 4525). East
Ham tube/Beckton DLR.* **Open** 10am-5pm
Tue-Fri. **Admission** free.

The East Ham Nature Reserve combines a
funny little museum with the largest churchyard
in London, which has beguilingly shaggy nature

A purple patch of **St James's Park**.

trails. The museum comprises a small room dotted with stuffed birds and mammals, all looking a little on the weary side, plus a case each of beetles and butterflies.
Buggy access. Disabled access: toilet.

East Sheen Common Nature Trail

East Sheen Common, Fife Road, SW14 7EW (Borough Ecology Officer 8831 6125/www. richmond.gov.uk). Hammersmith tube, then 33 bus/Mortlake rail, then 15min walk. **Open** dawn-dusk daily. **Admission** free.
This nature trail runs through 13 areas of woodlands, ponds and streams marked with orange posts. A wildlife-watching leaflet tells you about the animals and insects that live around here; you'll be lucky to see the badgers, but visit in spring and you should hear frogs croaking and woodpeckers tapping. Summer brings butterflies to the meadow flowers and woodland floor; autumn provides berries for the birds. Contact the ranger for details of children's activities and guided walks.

Greenwich Peninsula Ecology Park

Thames Path, John Harrison Way, SE10 0QZ (8293 1904/www.urbanecology.org.uk). North Greenwich tube/108, 161, 422, 472, 486 bus. **Open** 10am-5pm Wed-Sun. **Admission** free.
This pond-dipping, bird-watching haven is run by the Trust for Urban Ecology. The park is reserved for schools on Mondays and Tuesdays; the rest of the week, you'll have this wetland area, with woodland, marsh, meadow, lakes and streams, all to yourself. *See also p138.*
Buggy access. Disabled access: toilet. Nappy-changing facilities.

Gunnersbury Triangle Nature Reserve

Bollo Lane, W4 5LW (8747 3881/www.wild london.org.uk). Chiswick Park tube. **Open** *Reserve* 24hrs daily. *Information Cabin* June-Sept 10am-4.30pm Tue-Sat. Oct-May 10am-4.30pm Tue, Sun. **Admission** free.
Run by the London Wildlife Trust and enclosed by railway tracks, this stretch of woodland, marsh and meadow is the scene of much ecological activity. Conservation workshops are supplemented by free, drop-in activities for kids: craft workshops, mask-making sessions, and mini safaris. When the small information cabin is open you can pick up trail leaflets, find out about tours, and hire a net for pond-dipping.
Buggy access.

Highgate Wood/Queen's Wood

Muswell Hill Road, N10 3JN (8444 6129/ www.cityoflondon.gov.uk/openspaces). Highgate tube/43, 134, 263 bus. **Open** 7.30am-dusk daily. **Admission** free.
This 70-acre (28-hectare) park, originally part of the Forest of Middlesex, is so thickly forested with oak and hornbeam that it's easy to feel you're miles from the city and rambling through a wild wood. Keep to the wide paths and you can enjoy a leisurely stroll with a buggy, or head into the less well-trodden areas for a proper adventure. The centrepiece of Highgate Woods is its large, well-equipped playground, complete with enormous sandpits, climbing equipment of various levels of difficulty and a flying fox ride that gets very busy at peak times. Great thought has gone into providing fun and challenges for the various age groups, and there's also a separate area for tiny tots to call their own. The playground benefits in summer from its shady situation – cooler for all concerned, as well as making hats and suncream less of a repetitive chore. Highgate's other great asset is its café, reached by crossing the cricket pitch. The food is the usual park fare – soups, pasta dishes and cake predominate – but the quality is a cut above what you find elsewhere. The menu makes much of the fact that food is sourced locally where possible, and the big own-made burgers are highly recommended by locals.
Throughout the year an imaginative set of activities is offered in the woods, from outdoor storytelling to evening bat watches: consult the website before setting out, however, as some events require pre-booking.
Buggy access. Café. Disabled access: toilet. Nappy-changing facilities.

Islington Ecology Centre

Gillespie Park Nature Reserve, 191 Drayton Park, N5 1PH (7354 5162/www.islington. gov.uk). Arsenal tube. **Open** *Park* 8am-dusk Mon-Fri; 9am-dusk Sat; 10am-dusk Sun. Closed Arsenal FC home matches. *Centre* varies; phone to check. **Admission** free; donations appreciated.
Islington's largest nature reserve was fashioned from derelict railway land. It has woods, meadows, wetland and ponds, and the Ecology Centre is its educational heart. Staff are endlessly enthusiastic and helpful on the subject of all natural things in the borough. The events programme includes events suitable for families, from moth evenings to craft sessions. Nature-themed workshops run in the holidays; ring for details.
Buggy access.

Sightseeing

London Wildlife Trust Centre for Wildlife Gardening

28 Marsden Road, SE15 4EE (7252 9186/ www.wildlondon.org.uk). East Dulwich rail. **Open** 10.30am-4.30pm Tue-Thur, Sun. **Admission** free.

The London Wildlife Trust has been reclaiming derelict land for nature reserves for over 20 years. This centre – set up on a disused bus depot – is one of its best, with areas of wildlife-friendly woodland, marshland, a herb garden, a pond area and a nursery for plants and trees. Local families can fill their own gardens with plants grown here, giving a donation to the LWT; for children, there's a play area, sandpit and parent-and-toddler group, and the visitors' centre has tanks of fish and stick insects. Green-fingered children should join the LWT's Wildlife Watch Club for eight- to ten-year-olds (£15 per year), which runs all sorts of outdoor activities, like pond-dipping and bat walks.

Buggy access. Disabled access: toilet. Nappy-changing facilities. Shop.

WIDE OPEN SPACES

Epping Forest

Information Centre, High Beech, Loughton, Essex IG10 4AF (8508 0028/www.cityof london.gov.uk/openspaces). Wanstead tube/Chingford rail. **Open** *Information Centre* Summer 11am-6pm daily. Winter 10am-3pm daily. *Forest* 24hrs daily. **Admission** free.

The biggest public space within London's boundaries, Epping Forest is a gift for walkers, riders and cyclists, not to mention wildlife fans. It is 12 miles long and 22 miles across (19 by 35 kilometres) and was saved from development by the Corporation of London in 1878. Commoners still have grazing rights and, each summer, English Longhorn cattle can be seen chewing the cud. The forest contains Iron Age earth-works and two listed buildings – the Temple in Wanstead Park and the fully restored, 16th-century Queen Elizabeth's Hunting Lodge (Rangers Road, E4 7QH, 8529 6681; under-16s must be accompanied by an adult). The latter has a quiz trail, weekend craft activities and Tudor-themed dressing up; in the kitchen area, you can smell food made from 400-year-old recipes – ring for details.

If you're coming to Epping Forest by public transport, be prepared for some exercise. Chingford railway station gives access to the Hunting Lodge and some lovely strolls. Loughton and Theydon Bois (Central line) are the forest's nearest tube stops, though it's a two-mile (three-kilometre) uphill walk from both. The best advice is to get a map and plan your route in advance – or use the car. At High Beech car park there's a small tea hut, as well as the Epping Forest with a children's area. For a real back-to-nature feeling, between May and September you can pitch your tent at the Debden House campsite (Debden Green, Loughton, Essex IG10 2NZ, 8508 3008; £7/night, £3.50/night under-16s, free under-3s) and listen to the owls hoot.

Buggy access. Disabled access: toilet. Nappy-changing facilities. Shop.

Lee Valley Regional Park

Head office: Lee Valley Regional Park Authority, Myddelton House, Bulls Cross, Enfield, Middx EN2 9HG (01992 717711/ www.leevalleypark.org.uk). Turkey Street rail. **Open** 10am-4.30pm daily. **Admission** £3; £2.50 reductions, 5-16s; free under-5s. **Credit** MC, V.

Starting east of Hackney and heading north-east all the way into Hertfordshire, Lee Valley Regional Park is a 26-mile (42km) network of lakes, waterways, parks and countryside areas that covers a vast area on either side of the River Lee. There's plenty to do, though a gentle guided walk is a good way to start. The park's ideal for picnics, walking or fishing; it's well signposted and open year-round. It's also a nature lover's paradise. There are said to be 32 species of mammals making their home in the park, and 21 species of dragonfly. Waymarked walks, some providing easy buggy access, take you to see orchids, grasshoppers and water lilies. The birdwatching is excellent: winter brings 10,000 migrant waterbirds from chillier climes, and summer is the time to enjoy the kingfishers.

Other attractions include the Lee Valley Riding Centre (71 Lea Bridge Road, E10 7QL, 8556 2629, www.leevalleypark.org.uk). The erstwhile Lee Valley Cycle Circuit has been handed over to the Olympic builders to become a velopark in time for 2012. Lee Valley Boat Centre (Old Nazeing Road, Broxbourne, Herts EN10 6LX, 01992 462085, www.leevalleyboats. co.uk) hires boats by the hour and organises narrowboat holidays. The fascinating town of Waltham Abbey has plenty of cafés and shops and an Augustinian abbey, founded in 1060 by King Harold. The exciting Royal Gunpowder Mills (Beaulieu Drive, Waltham Abbey, Essex EN9 1JY, 01992 707370, www.royalgunpowder mills.com) and Epping Forest (*see above*) are but a ten-minute drive from the town.

Buggy access. Disabled access: toilet. Kiosk. Nappy-changing facilities.

Meet the Animals

Beastly goings-on in the heart of the city.

Rats, foxes and pigeons aside, there are thousands of wild and domesticated furry, scaly and feathered friends in this city that can't wait to make your aquaintance. Below we list the best places, from aquariums to zoos, for petting, feeding, mucking out and even adopting some of them. But there is much more on offer: there are opportunities to learn about food production and how to cook, be a farmer for a day, take a blacksmithing class, drive a tractor, watch sheep-shearing or goat-milking, ride a donkey or a shire horse, and take part in historical re-enactments. Animal lovers should also beat a path to the open spaces with wildlife and pet enclosures listed in **Parks & Gardens** (*see p107*).

AQUARIUMS

Horniman Museum

100 London Road, SE23 3PQ (8699 1872/ www.horniman.ac.uk). Forest Hill rail/176, 185, 197, 356, P4 bus. **Open** 10.30am-5.30pm daily. **Admission** free; donations appreciated. **Credit** MC, V.

The aquarium in this most diverse of museums (*see p74*) is amazing. More than 200 species of aquatic animal and plant are housed in 14,000 litres of water across seven distinct zones. Visitors working their way round explore the diverse nature of ecosystems from around the world and read about the threats such fragile environments face. Endangered aquatic ecosystems covered include British pond life, Devonshire rockpools, Fijian coral reefs, mangrove swamps and South American rainforest. Live exhibits include British seahorses, jellyfish and tropical monkey frogs among others. Children enjoy the tank-viewing dens and interactive displays and are particularly mesmerised by the jellyfish. Check the website for details of events and activities.

Buggy access. Café. Disabled access: lift, toilet. Nappy-changing facilities. Nearest picnic place: museum gardens. Shop.

London Aquarium

County Hall (riverfront entrance), Riverside Building, SE1 7PB (7967 8000/tours 7967 8007/www.londonaquarium.co.uk). Westminster tube/Waterloo tube/rail. **Open** 10am-6pm daily (last entry 5pm). *Tours* (groups of 10 or more) phone for details. **Admission** £13.25; £11.25 reductions; £9.75 3-14s; £8.25 disabled children; free under-3s; £44 family (2+2). **Credit** MC, V. **Map** p317 M9.

County Hall no longer displays London's unemployment figures on its roof as two fingers to the government. Instead, almost every square inch has been turned into a wealth-creating exercise in parting tourists from their money. It isn't cheap and you may baulk at all the inducements to sample (lesser) attractions (some, like Fright Club, even sharing the same foyer). However, no one with a passing interest in Davy Jones' Locker could fail to be fascinated here. The 14 themed zones are arranged over two floors of the Hall's basement. Toddlers especially love rampaging around the wide, rubber-floored corridors, stopping now and then to gaze in awe at the sand tiger sharks, nurse sharks, zebra shark, giant groupers and shoals of shimmering bream in the central, million-litre tank.

Smaller aquatic attractions from sticklebacks to seahorses are equally fascinating, though, and dads will appreciate the open river reconstructions bringing them face to face with familiar British residents like rudd, barbel and perch. A touch pool lets you (gently) stroke the uppers of giant rays bobbing up to meet the visitors, and don't miss the surprisingly pretty, silver sequin-like scales of the piranhas. There's a pleasing randomness to the side exhibits (one is dedicated to old junk dredged from the Thames) and if you're still quibbling at the price, it's worth noting that there are a further 125 tanks behind the scenes for breeding endangered species, including coral. To get the best value, time your visit for Saturdays, Tuesdays and Thursdays when you can see divers hand-feed the sharks at 2.30pm. If you're pushing a buggy, enter and leave from the London Eye side; you'll avoid McDonald's and the tricky steps up to Westminster Bridge.

Buggy access. Disabled access: lift, ramp, toilet. Nappy-changing facilities. Nearest picnic place: Jubilee Gardens. Shop.

FARMS

Deen City Farm & Community Garden
39 Windsor Avenue, SW19 2RR (8543 5300/ www.deencityfarm.co.uk). Colliers Wood tube, then 200 bus. **Open** 10am-4.30pm Tue-Sun, bank hol Mon. **Admission** free; donations welcome. **No credit cards.**
This doesn't really feel like a city farm at all, situated as it is on the edge of Morden Hall Park. It's got fields to keep its pigs, cows and sheep happy, and a big area for pony rides (Wednesdays, Saturdays, Sundays and school holidays). The farm is a member of the Rare Breeds Survival Trust and has a wide range of unusual species. Make sure you don't miss the spectacular white peacocks near the entrance, shacked up with a particularly exhibitionist turkey. There are ducks and geese galore, alpacas, and a huddle of rabbits and guinea pigs that you can handle at certain times (check as you arrive). The

---

The best
Animal antics

Deen City Farm
Guinea pig whispering. *See above.*

Greenwich Peninsula Ecology Park
Frog Day in spring. *See p139.*

London Zoo
Birds and butterflies. *See p138 & p140.*

Spitalfields City Farm
Donkey rides. *See p135.*

Stepping Stones Farm
Petting the friendly sheep. *See p135.*

Surrey Docks Farm
Fending off the goats. *See p135.*

WWT Wetland Centre
Watching Easter hatchings. *See p139.*

---

cheerful café – toasties, baked potatoes, chips, and the like – is refreshingly cheap.
Buggy access. Café. Disabled access: toilet. Nappy-changing facilities. Nearest picnic place: Morden Hall Park. Shop.

Freightliners City Farm
Paradise Park, Sheringham Road, off Liverpool Road, N7 8PF (7609 0467/ www.freightlinersfarm.org.uk). Caledonian Road or Holloway Road tube/Highbury & Islington tube/rail. **Open** *Summer* 10am-4.45pm Tue-Sun, bank hol Mon. *Winter* 10am-4pm Tue-Sun. **Admission** free; donations appreciated. **No credit cards.**
In the heart of Islington is a real working farm. The half-hectare site of Freightliners is home to rabbits, cows, sheep, goats, cats, geese and pigs, as well as all kinds of poultry. The collection of animals, many of them rare breeds, is impressive. Giant Flemish rabbits are the biggest you'll see anywhere; guineafowl run amok in other animals' pens; exotic cockerels with feathered feet squawk in your path; bees fly around their hives. You can buy hen and duck eggs of all hues, plus seasonal, own-grown fruit, veg and plants. There's a weekly gardening club on Wednesdays, an organic market on Saturdays, and the farm even runs an 'Adopt an Animal' scheme. Playschemes run in summer are popular, and you can even hold a party on the farm. The farm is setting up a beekeeping club and teens (14- to 19-year-olds) can have beekeeping instruction and gain a qualification here.
Buggy access. Café. Disabled access: toilet. Nappy-changing facilities. Nearest picnic place: farm picnic area. Shop.

Hackney City Farm
1A Goldsmiths Row, E2 8QA (7729 6381/ www.hackneycityfarm.co.uk). Cambridge Heath Road rail, then 26, 48, 55 bus. **Open** 10am-4.30pm Tue-Sun, bank hol Mon. **Admission** free; donations appreciated. **Credit** MC, V.
For more than 20 years the city farm in Hackney has been a delight. The muted cacophony of clucking, quacking, honking and squeaking is rightly therapeutic: turkeys, geese, ducks, donkeys, rare breed pigs (including Bella the Saddleback), cattle, rabbits and guinea pigs are housed around the courtyard or swish their tails in the fields. There are also plenty of activities to get involved in, from environmental projects to pottery classes and stone carving. A host of other wholesome entertainments ensure the venue is lively summer and winter. The award-winning organic café, Frizzante, is a great place

to enjoy quality Mediterranean food. Outside, the farm garden, with a plant nursery attached, is lovely in summer. Many fitness and craft activities aimed at parents (include Low-Impact Living Initiative courses) take place in the evenings in the new lime-rendered, straw-bale farm building; children's workshops run throughout the holidays and at weekends. The free Mini Farmers' Club is held every Saturday for eight to 12-year-olds. The meeting room is available for children's parties.

Buggy access. Café. Disabled access: ramp, toilet. Nappy-changing facilities. Nearest picnic place: gardens. Shop.

Hounslow Urban Farm

A312 at Faggs Road, Feltham, Middx TW14 0LZ (8751 0850/www.hounslow.info/ urbanfarm). Hatton Cross tube, then 15min walk or 90, 285, 490 bus. **Open** 10am-4pm daily. **Admission** £4.50; £3.75 reductions; £3 2-16s; free under-2s; £13 (2+2) family. **No credit cards**.

Covering 29 acres, London's largest community farm offers plenty of petting and feeding (3.30pm daily) opportunities. There are pigs, goats, ducks, Exmoor ponies, alpacas and chipmunks, and some of the animals are rare, endangered and historic breeds that the farm has reared as part of a conservation programme. Turn up at the right time of year and you could be lucky enough to see brand-new lambs, goats or a litter of piglets. You can even buy a small animal – such as a rabbit or a guinea pig – and get some helpful care advice. Activities are held daily and throughout the school holidays, such as animal handling, scarecrow-making and pig racing, with a children's entertainer on bank holiday Mondays and every Tuesday during the holidays. Orphan lambs need to be bottle-fed and children are sometimes allowed to help. There's a playground (with pedal tractors), a picnic area and a café for coffees and snacks.

Buggy access. Café. Disabled access: toilet. Nappy-changing facilities. Nearest picnic place: farm picnic area.

Kentish Town City Farm

1 Cressfield Close, off Grafton Road, NW5 4BN (7916 5421/www.ktcityfarm.org.uk). Chalk Farm tube/Kentish Town tube/rail/ Gospel Oak rail. **Open** 9am-5.30pm daily. **Admission** free; donations appreciated. **Credit** MC, V.

London's oldest city farm was founded over 30 years ago and stretches way beyond the farmyard into precious pasture and well-tended

What's up duck? **Hackney City Farm**.

Sightseeing

Kentish Town City Farm. *See p131.*

vegetable gardens by the railway line. Livestock includes farmyard ducks, goats, pigs, horses, cows, chickens and sheep, including some rare breeds. As well as petting the animals, children can get involved with their care and can help to muck out (arrive by 9am) and feed them (with supervision), and take care of the site. During the holidays there is a host of activities held in the farm centre, such as felt-making, photography, and games. Parties can be held here (including use of the kitchen). There are after-school clubs too: practical city farming, pottery and cookery classes. A pond with a dipping platform is full of frogs, and a riding school (home to the Camden Pony Club) is the scene of weekend pony rides (1.30pm Sat, Sun, weather permitting, £1). The energetic education officer welcomes school visits from all boroughs, and anyone can come to the May Day celebrations (dancing around a maypole, making hats for the procession, farm olympics), Easter egg hunt, and Apple Day. *Buggy access. Disabled access: ramp, toilet. Nappy-changing facilities. Nearest picnic place: farm grounds.*

Lee Valley Park Farms

Stubbins Hall Lane, Crooked Mile, Waltham Abbey, Essex EN9 2EG (01992 702200/ www.leevalleypark.org.uk). Broxbourne or Cheshunt rail. **Open** *Mar-Oct* 10am-5pm daily. Closed Nov-Feb. **Admission** £6.50; £5 reductions, 3-16s; free under-3s; £24.50 family (2+3). **Credit** MC, V.

In the middle of Lee Valley Country Park you get two farms for the price of one. Hayes Hill is a traditional farm and rare-breeds centre on a 17-acre site. There's a 'Tudor Barn' for sheltered picnics, a pet centre housing small mammals and reptiles, and an adventure play area. Children can meet Tallulah the Tamworth and Barbara the Berkshire pig, as well as Tinkerbell and Maurice (Golden Guernsey goats). In the spring there are new lambs and piglets. Visitors can watch the milking of cows (from 2.30pm daily) and learn about the making of dairy products at the nearby commercial farm, Holyfield Hall. Livestock includes sheep, goats, cows, llamas and even water buffalo. There are guided tours for school parties, and tractor-trailer rides (1.45pm weekends, school holidays, Apr-Oct, weather permitting). New in 2008 is 'Rabbit World', a vegetable plot, and a new café and shop. *Buggy access. Café. Disabled access: ramp, toilet. Nappy-changing facilities. Nearest picnic place: farm picnic areas. Shop.*

Mudchute City Farm

Pier Street, Isle of Dogs, E14 3HP (7515 5901/www.mudchute.org). Crossharbour, Mudchute or Island Gardens DLR. **Open** 9am-5pm daily. **Admission** free; donations appreciated. **No credit cards.**

You really can feel like Heidi here as you and the kids chase a flock of sheep around a hilly meadow (albeit one that's right under the shadow of Canary Wharf). This is the largest urban farm in the city, built over spoil from the creation of Millwall docks, and the pampered pigs and goats really have a taste of the country, thanks to some sensitive landscaping which blocks out the urban sprawl. Indeed, the farm's well-established woods and hedgerows are one of the last London outposts of the once-common sparrow. You can feed many of the animals – goats, geese and horses – which adds to the excitement for the children. And, though this is undoubtedly the only spot in Docklands to offer the opportunity to picnic among llamas, for most parents the wonderful farm café will be the highlight of the day, with farm-grown produce cooked on the premises. Breakfast comes with a hefty slab of wholemeal fried bread and even own-made baked beans. Or time your visit for three o'clock: that's when the scones come out of the oven.

Buggy access. Café. Disabled access: toilet. Nappy-changing facilities. Nearest picnic place: farm grounds. Shop.

Newham City Farm

Stansfeld Road, E6 5LT (7474 4960). Royal Albert DLR/262, 300, 376 bus. **Open** *Summer* 10am-5pm Tue-Sun, bank hol Mon. *Winter* 10am-4pm Tue-Sun. **Admission** free; donations appreciated. **No credit cards**.

Set up over 30 years ago, Newham is one of London's oldest city farms. As well as the usual farmyard poultry, sheep, pigs and goats, you can see Blaze the shire horse, and taste the honey made by bees from the farm's hives. There are also littler chaps (rabbits, guinea pigs,

---

Taking kids to the farm

When you stumble upon them on a country walk, farms can sometimes seem unwelcoming places: you're never quite sure whether you're allowed to cut through the farmyard, holding your nose as you pass great piles of fertiliser while trying to avoid the gaze of the rather disapproving farmer in flat cap and bodywarmer. That's because, in order to make any money, farming has to be done on an industrial scale, rendering obsolete your children's-book visions of the ruddy-faced farmer's wife scattering feed for the chickens. To their credit, London's city farms embrace this dichotomy, offering toddlers the chance to live out their Farmer Barleymow fantasies among the pigs and hens while subtly teaching them the reality of where the ham in their sandwiches actually comes from.

Of the ones we've visited recently, Surrey Docks Farm is the best for getting up close to the animals in the farmyard, while Vauxhall City Farm gives city types the most opportunity to literally muck in. For a genuine taste of the country, the meadows of Mudchute are the best; its sensitive landscaping will make you oblivious to the fact you're on the Isle of Dogs and, once you've sampled a farm breakfast in the café, you might want to come back every week. Staffed by volunteers and often fiercely defended from the demands of developers,

London's city farms play a vital role in teaching city kids about animals, agriculture and food production; and, while a one-off visit is fun, imagine your youngsters' satisfaction in seeing their favourite pig rear a litter or following the progress of their own crop on the farm's allotments. Whichever one you choose, you'll find it a whole lot more welcoming than the real thing. And the animals are probably happier too.

Sightseeing

and two ferrets) and a twittering house of finches and a kookaburra. The visitor's centre holds plenty of holiday activities, such as the popular 'Be a Farmer for a Day' sessions (book in advance) and other drop-in sessions. There are picnic areas and a recently opened café serving teas, coffees and light snacks. Fun days offer the likes of sheep-shearing demonstrations, rides on a shire horse-drawn cart on most bank holidays, and children's activities, such as felt-making. For information, phone and leave a message and someone will call you back, or check the Newham Council website.
Buggy access. Café. Disabled access: toilet. Nappy-changing facilities. Nearest picnic place: farm picnic area. Shop.

Spitalfields City Farm

Buxton Street, off Brick Lane, E1 5AR (7247 8762/www.spitalfieldscityfarm.org). Whitechapel tube. **Open** *Summer* 10am-4.30pm Tue-Sun. *Winter* 10am-4pm Tue-Sun. **Admission** free; donations appreciated. **No credit cards**.

This is more than just a community farm. Established in 1978 after local allotments were lost to property developers, the farm currently has geese honking about, a daily goat-milking demo, mice and rabbits for stroking, and a full complement of cows, pigs and sheep. Children can take part in workshops and learn where milk and eggs come from, as well as about healthy eating and sustainability and (part of the

Newham City Farm. *See p133.*

national curriculum) animal welfare. Poultry, gardeners and all the livestock produce free-range eggs, seasonal vegetables and manure (in that order). Keen eight- to 13-year-olds can join the Young Farmers Club, which runs a play scheme on Saturdays; there's also a jolly parent and toddler group for under-fives (Tue, Sun). The Healthy Living Project provides education as well as an inspiring green space for relaxing and a way of teaching children how vegetables grow. The Coriander Club offers twice-weekly classes to local Bangladeshi women who grow veg and learn how to cook them. Young visitors can often enjoy donkey rides (£1), and special annual events include various open days, the Spitalfields Show (September) and Apple Day (October).

Buggy access. Disabled access: toilet. Nappy-changing facilities. Nearest picnic place: Allen Gardens. Shop.

Stepping Stones Farm

Stepney Way (junction with Stepney High Street), E1 3DG (7790 8204/www.stepping stonesfarm.org.uk). Stepney Green tube. **Open** 10am-4pm Tue-Sun, bank hol Mon. **Admission** free; donations appreciated. **No credit cards**. Delightfully chaotic, with possibly the friendliest sheep in England jostling for attention, and a pair of amiable donkeys greeting visitors from their paddock by the gate, this farm is all the more miraculous for its carefree use of a huge tract of highly desirable land close to the City. Near the ramshackle allotments and old railway carriages used as feed stores stands a ruined building surrounded by yet more pasture land sustaining cattle, pigs, goats. Poultry and ducks are in little enclosures near the café area. The farmers, ably assisted by junior volunteers, are as friendly as the beasts and never tire of running jolly events for local children, such as Easter egg hunts, animal-themed treasure hunts and summer holiday activities, as well as regular workshops (egg decorating, face painting, clay modelling, composting and recycling).
Buggy access. Café. Disabled access: toilet. Nappy-changing facilities. Nearest picnic place: Stepney Green Park. Shop.

Surrey Docks Farm

South Wharf, Rotherhithe Street, SE16 5ET (7231 1010). Canada Water tube, then 381, C10 bus. **Open** 10am-5pm Tue-Sun. **Admission** free; donations appreciated. **No credit cards**.
Hemmed in by two identikit gated developments and the defiantly newtown-ish community of Surrey Quays, this is part farm, part sculpture park. Sheep, goats and chickens mooch around a central farmyard, tolerating and providing endless entertainment for hordes of excitable youngsters. Out in the pens, there are organically-reared cows, pigs, donkeys and horses too, many fenced in by delightful wrought metal railings provided by the farm's other tenant, creative blacksmith Kevin Boys, who teaches classes in his forge. It's all part of a vision set in motion by city farm pioneer Hilary Peters in 1975, who wanted all schoolchildren to have an appreciation of food production and the skills connected with agriculture (ideas which seem especially prescient in the light of recent campaigns by Jamie Oliver and Hugh Fearnley-Whittingstall).

Sightseeing

Great Days Out
Marylebone

This is a lovely day out for enjoying parks and animals. If you don't want to shell out too much money on admission prices, we suggest you head straight to **Regent's Park** (*see p123*) – once Henry VIII's hunting land – to admire the flower beds, the lake and its herons, the café and the open-air theatre and the free concerts in the bandstand. Sporty types appreciate the park for the Hub, the name given to the biggest outdoor sports facility in central London, with tennis and netball courts, an athletics track, football and hockey pitches and a sports pavilion. There are four playgrounds, each with a sandpit and toilets. The shallow boating lake has rowing boats to hire by the hour (£6.50) or pedalos for smaller children (£3/20min).

Combat gear

After a picnic in the park, walk past the serene squares off Marylebone High Street to the glorious gilded **Wallace Collection** (*see p70*) of paintings, furniture, and, best of all, the biggest collection of armour in Britain. On the first Sunday of the month there is the Little Draw, a free event in which families can get sketching with help from the gallery's in-house artist. There are regular armour workshops (when kids can find out how heavy the armour and weapons are, and handle items such as 3,000-year-old bronze swords and oriental daggers). Check the website for other daily events.

Walk to the animals

Rather more expensive, the inimitable Zoological Society of London (aka **London Zoo**, *see p140*), is essential viewing. We're all of a flutter over the latest addition: the Blackburn Pavilion (*see p138* **Flight of fancy**). One thing that hasn't changed since its inception in 1826 is its ability to 'interest and amuse the public' (Sir Stamford Raffles, Founder). ZSL is a charity, whose ethical work – conservation, ecotourism, biodiversity and education – is partly financed by this huge city zoo's role as public entertainment. Indeed, as many of the bigger animals (elephants, hippos) have been moved on to more spacious quarters at ZSL Whipsnade, and ongoing work continues to 'bring down the bars' in the remaining wild-animal enclosures, such as Gorilla Kingdom, the zoo seems a far jollier place these days.

Once you've shelled out for admission, there's no need to spend more. Bring a picnic to one of the many attractive settings to avoid expensive eating concessions (where the children's lunchbox is, we'll admit, reasonably good

LUNCH BOX

Also in the area: Ask, Carluccio's Caffè, Giraffe, Pizza Express, Tootsie's Grill, Wagamama.

Eat & Two Veg *50 Marylebone High Street, W1U 5HN (7258 8595/www. eatandtwoveg.com)*. Meat-free fare.

Golden Hinde *73 Marylebone Lane, W1U 2PN (7486 3644)*. Good fish and chips; kids' portions too.

Honest Sausage *Broadwalk, off Chester Road, Regent's Park, NW1 4NU (7224 3872/www.honest sausage.com)*. Brilliant bangers and bacon butties (organic and free range).

Le Pain Quotidien *72-75 Marylebone High Street, W1U 5JW (7486 6154)*. Breakfast baskets, substantial salads.

Paul *115 Marylebone High Street, W1U 4SB (7224 5615/www.paul-uk.com)*. Fantastic French bakery-café.

value for £4.95) and just say 'no' to the pricey merry-go-round and bouncy castle. There's a fine free play area just behind them. We've never been able to divert small children from the huge and gorgeous shop, though. We like it as much as the kids do.

If you're planning on taking a trip along the canal, you'll save on the combined ticket prices with the **London Waterbus Company** (*see p9*), whose boats tie up alongside the zoo.

Great Days Out

Flight of fancy

Be sure to arrive at the Blackburn Pavilion at **London Zoo** (*see p140*) on the hour. The astonishing clock outside shows how time flies with an entertaining clockwork bird display. The short drama shows figures in antique headgear gaping as birds take flight, and is a tribute to the Victorian fascination with wildlife that saw the founding of the Zoological Society of London. Inside the building, originally intended as a reptile house, there are more tributes to great natural scientists as well as an intriguing cabinet of birds eggs. The real fun starts when you walk through several plastic and beaded curtains into the steamy, jungly tropical home for about 50 species of birds. Jewel-coloured roul-roul partridges and bluebellied rollers hop about around your feet and fly freely in the shrub canopy.

Since using Dog & Duck Passage to graze her goats, she's seen this former shipyard site grow to two acres, with a full-time teacher and farmer living in situ. Raise a glass of cordial to her on the sun-trap terrace of Café Nabo, which serves up hearty Mediterranean-style grub, cooked to order. And, if you're making a day of it, the museum celebrating the magnificent engineering folly of Marc Brunel's first tunnel is nearby too (*see p81* **Brunel Engine House & Tunnel Exhibition**).
Buggy access. Café. Disabled access: ramp, toilet. Nearest picnic place: riverside. Shop.

Vauxhall City Farm

165 Tyers Street, SE11 5HS (7582 4204). Vauxhall tube/rail/2, 36, 44, 77 bus. **Open** 10.30am-4pm Wed-Sun. Closed 1wk in late summer, phone to check. **Admission** free; donations appreciated. **No credit cards**.
The volunteering spirit is strong in Vauxhall. At the nearby Bonnington Café locals take it in turns to cook up welcoming vegetarian grub, while this tiny sliver of the countryside – overlooked by council flats – has been staffed by the community since 1977. Many of the animals – Poppy and Pepper, a pair of Anglo Nubian goats, plus their black Wensleydale sheep friends – inhabit a specially constructed straw-bale animal house, built by Barbara Jones in 2001 with sedums on the roof to attract bees (plus Metal Billy, a scrap-metal goat). The rabbits are just as pampered, there's a mini lake for ducks and geese, plus an authentically unctuous pond full of frogs. The farm runs pony-riding sessions in nearby Spring Gardens park, hosts the Ruby Rhymes under-fives singing group on Fridays, and there are gardening therapy programmes for outpatients from the Maudsley Hospital. Facilities are fairly basic – and the chatter of the radio can spoil the bucolic feel – but, together with the slippery pathways, cloying mud and occasional dollop of horse muck, this gives a passable representation of a working farm. There's no café, but you can change babies in the classroom toilet. And, while Vauxhall might not be the most obvious place for a day out, it's worth noting that the amphibian Duck Tours set out from just across Spring Gardens too (*see p8*).

Toucans squawk and clack their beaks, hooded pitas and the Sorocco dove (extinct in the wild and now bred only in captivity) call across the waterfall. You walk along a boardwalk among all this into another, more enclosed area, where the Blackburn's pièce de résistance, the tiny Amazilian hummingbirds, which have people pressing their noses up to the mesh to see those wings whirr as they hover, fly backwards and up and down. They're the only hummingbirds on show in the UK.

The restoration of the tropical bird house was made possible through the support of the Blackburn family, hence the name. David Blackburn OBE helped support the board of London Zoo, playing an important part in shoring up the zoo when it was faced with closure back in 1992. The family stepped in again when finance that was earmarked for the renovation of the tropical birdhouse needed to be redirected following the terrorist bombs in 2005. Without the generosity of people like this, the Zoo would probably have gone the way of the dodo.

Buggy access. Disabled access: toilet. Nappy-changing facilities. Nearest picnic place: Spring Gardens.

Woodlands Farm

331 Shooters Hill, Welling, Kent DA16 3RP (8319 8900/www.thewoodlandsfarmtrust.org). Falconwood rail/89, 486 bus. **Open** 9.30am-4.30pm daily. **Admission** free; donations appreciated. **No credit cards**.

Close to Oxleas Wood, Woodlands is a community farm covering 90 acres between the boroughs of Greenwich and Bexley. It's a working and educational farm that is aiming for organic status. It has a lovely, award-winning cottage garden, a wildlife garden created by year 10 work-experience pupils, orchards and meadows, and livestock includes some noisy geese, hens, a flock of sheep (four different breeds), Neptune and Daisy the British White cows, Vietnamese pot-bellied pigs Doris and Iris, Biskit the goat and a Shetland pony called Bob. Volunteers are welcome to don their gumboots and help with the Garden Group (Tue, Sun). The farm hosts educational group visits, giving

lessons on farm-animal care, conservation, composting, and the history of farming. Keep an eye on the events diary to see what's in the offing. The spring show includes tug-of-war, period costume re-enactments and the sale of country crafts and local produce. The farm also sells logs, manure and hay at good prices.

Buggy access. Café (weekends). Nearest picnic place: farm grounds. Shop (weekends).

WETLAND RESERVES

Greenwich Peninsula Ecology Park

Thames Path, John Harrison Way, SE10 0QZ (8293 1904/www.urbanecology.org.uk). North Greenwich tube/108, 161, 422, 472, 486 bus. **Open** 10am-5pm Wed-Sun. **Admission** free.

A wetland area with woodland, marsh, meadow, lakes and streams, it supports frogs, toads, newts, dragon-, damsel- and butterflies, and many bird species. Hides allow you look at the birdlife close up, and staff host regular activities involve pondlife, mud and gumboots. There are themed quiz trails, prize trails, word searches and art (using collage, pastels and watercolour pencils), and Frog Day is usually held on the first weekend in March. A popular summer play event runs from the end of July to early September, and there are regular evening bat walks.

Buggy access. Disabled access: toilet. Nappy-changing facilities. Nearest picnic place: southern park.

WWT Wetland Centre

Queen Elizabeth's Walk, SW13 9WT (8409 4400/www.wwt.org.uk/london). Hammersmith tube, then 33, 72, 209 (alight at Red Lion pub) or 283 bus (Duck Bus direct to Centre). **Open** *Summer* 9.30am-6pm daily. *Winter* 9.30am-5pm daily (last entry 1hr before closing). *Tours* 11am, 2pm daily. *Feeding tours* 3.30pm daily. **Admission** £8.95; £6.70 reductions; £4.95 4-16s; free under-4s; £25 family (2+2). *Tours* free. **Credit** MC, V.

As if Barnes didn't feel rural enough – with its scrubby common and the wonderful Sun Inn on the village green – this stretch of managed wetland habitat is now a Designated Site of Scientific Heritage, guaranteeing our feathered friends protection from the rapacious development taken for granted elsewhere along the Thames. Carved from a number of small reservoirs in 2001, the Centre is home to rare international breeds like New Zealand's beautiful black swans and white-faced whistling ducks, while every season brings new migratory

Sightseeing

visitors, including lapwings, hobbies and ospreys. Every good spot is faithfully recorded in the six observation hides, the largest of which, the Peacock Tower, even has a lift for wheelchair and buggy users to get to the third storey and take in the full 105-acre panorama. You can book guided tours with your own personal bird-, or on summer evenings, bat-watcher and, if the weather's soggy, the Discovery Centre is a game attempt at recreating wetland habitats such as mangrove swamps indoors, fibre glass crocodiles and all. There's plenty of space – though high chairs can prove elusive – at the tempting, cake-laden self-service Water's Edge restaurant while kids aged three to 11 will happily play for hours amid the water vole tunnels, climbing the walls and zip wires of the Explore Adventure playground. The Duck shuttle bus 283 is the best way to get back on to the tube network but, after an afternoon here, Hammersmith – a mile as the bittern flies – will seem like another world *Buggy access. Café. Car park. Disabled access: lift, toilet. Nappy-changing facilities. Nearest picnic place: centre picnic areas. Shop.*

ZOOS

Battersea Park Children's Zoo
Queenstown Road, Battersea Park, SW11 4NJ (7924 5826/www.batterseazoo.co.uk). Sloane

Battersea Park Children's Zoo

Square tube, then 19, 137 bus/Battersea Park or Queenstown Road rail/156, 345 bus. **Open** *Summer* 10am-6pm daily. Last entry 5pm. *Winter* 10am-dusk daily. **Admission** £6.50; £4.95 2-15s; free under-2s; £20.50 family (2+2). **Credit** MC, V. **Map** p313 F13.
Looking like a full-size zoo to small people, Battersea Park zoo is tucked away by the riverside and full of excitement. Kids can laugh along with Rocky the cheeky monkey, watch house mice running around in their own doll's house, and crawl down a pair of tunnels, popping up in a bubble in the meerkats' den. New Zealand kune kune pigs provide vocal entertainment with top-volume snorting to amuse the toddlers, and the mynah birds might talk to you if you're lucky. The Lemon Tree café provides basic lunch fare and there's a pretty good playground. One warning: you have to enter and leave via the gift shop, so get your excuses in early.
Buggy access. Café. Disabled access: ramp, toilet. Nappy-changing facilities. Nearest picnic space: zoo picnic area. Shop.

London Zoo
Regent's Park, NW1 4RY (7722 3333/www.zsl.org). Baker Street or Camden Town tube, then 274 or C2 bus. **Open** *Mar-late Oct* 10am-5.30pm daily (last entry 4.30pm). *Late Oct-Feb* 10am-4pm daily (last entry 3pm). Check website for any changes. **Admission** (including £1.60 voluntary contribution) £17; £15.50 reductions; £13.50 3-15s; free under-3s; £55.50 family (2+2 or 1+3). **Credit** AmEx, MC, V. **Map** p314 G2.
Pick up a schedule from the main gate and plan your day. Enjoy the insect talks and demonstrations at BUGS (the biodiversity centre with its ant empire and cockroach quarters) or the acrobatic, freeflying parrots and birds of prey that have their own shows in the Animals in Action amphitheatre and Predatory Birds display lawn. More beautiful birds flutter in the gorgeous Blackburn Pavilion (*see p138*). In between these there are more talks in the Clore Rainforest Lookout, the chance to meet uncaged monkeys in their own walk-through jungle, feeding penguins in their big pool (the architecturally admired Lubetkin one isn't right for the zoo's current colony). That's before you've been entertained by the otters and meerkats, the farm animals and the big walk-through Butterfly Paradise, where flutterers of every hue land on their visitors. With so much to see and do, this is a day out well worth its admission charge.
Buggy access. Café. Disabled access: ramp, toilet. Nappy-changing facilities. Nearest picnic space: zoo picnic areas. Restaurant. Shop.

Activities

cartoonito
™

'Smile' with Fireman Sam every day on Cartoonito!

HiT entertainment

Sky 619
cartoonito.co.uk

Parties

… and how to survive them.

Choosing what to do for a child's birthday is guaranteed to get parents in a lather. To make life easier, our party directory lists a wide range of activity organisers, entertainers, cake-makers and shops for partyware and dressing-up gear. Where possible, we've given a rough guide to the cost, but as most entertainers and organisers prefer to tailor their service, prices need to be negotiated on application. Remember that personal recommendations are helpful – and many kids enjoy the familiarity of something they've experienced before.

The venue is another consideration. If you don't have enough space at home (or want to preserve your sanity), consider hiring a church hall or sports centre or hosting the party in a park. The earlier you book, the better deal you'll get. Economise by ordering decorations from websites, or visit street markets and pound shops.

As for feeding the hordes – keep it simple. Yes, most children are happy to stuff themselves silly with sugary snacks, but you risk the wrath of other parents. You can always go overboard with a spectacular cake. Just remember to check with parents about allergies and dietary requirement. Party on…

ACTIVITIES

Arts & crafts

For more artistic options, *see p193.*

Crawley Studios
39 Wood Vale, SE23 3DS (8516 0002/ www.crawleystudios.co.uk). Forest Hill rail. **Open** by appointment daily. **No credit cards**.
Marie-Lou's studio is attached to her home where pottery-painting parties are organised for small groups of children. The cost usually depends on what's to be painted; selections range from popular animal ornaments (around £8) to cups and bowls (£10-£15 including firing charge). Items are ready for collection a week later. Refreshments are provided free (tea and coffee, and hot chocolate for the kids).

Pottery Café
735 Fulham Road, SW6 5UL (7736 2157/ www.pottery-cafe.com). Parsons Green tube/ 14, 414 bus. **Open** 11am-6pm Mon; 10am-6pm Tue, Wed, Fri, Sat; 10am-10pm Thur; 11am-5pm Sun. **Credit** MC, V.
Among the first to offer a paint-your-own crockery deal, these studios have added another string to their bow with the Little Toy Shop, selling classic playthings such as puppets, ride-on wheelies, wooden cars and Jellycat cuddlies. Children's parties can be arranged for £19.95 per head, which includes invitations, party food (bring your own cake) and all the necessary materials and staff. Alternatively, you can bring your own sandwiches. You collect the children's works of art after they've been glazed and fired. The café also sells fruit juices, Byron Bay cookies and Union coffee.
Buggy access. Café. Disabled access. Nappy-changing facilities. Shop.
Other locations 322 Richmond Road, Twickenham, Middx TW1 2DU (8744 3000).

Soap & Bubble Company
0845 430 0130/www.soapandbubble.com.
Looking for a creative party? We like the sound of this squeaky clean one. Children make their own soap, bubble and bath treats to take home. Creations include floating duck soap, bath bombs, chocolate lip balm, body glitter and Flower Power bath salt. You can book a photographer to capture all the special moments for an extra fee, so that each party guest will receive a record of the day. The party package costs £175 for up to eight children. Older kids and teens can take part in workshops on skincare and facial scrubs. Spotty teens: cleanse, tone, exfoliate!

Cookery

For cookery lessons and workshops, *see also p196* **Kids' Cookery School** and **Munchkins**.

Cookie Crumbles

8876 9912/www.cookiecrumbles.net.
Carola Weymouth and her team provide a wide range of cooking activities for young people aged from four to 18. They have taught more than 10,000 children to cook since CC was set up just over seven years ago. The well-run cooking workshops offer an enjoyable introduction to food preparation. During the nourishing parties children have a load of fun creating their own celebration tea. Menus are tailored to suit very little chefs and Ms Weymouth has devised some great ideas for sophisticated teen dinner parties for the 14-18 age range too. A two-hour party starts at £165 (plus VAT) for six kids; the price covers everything, including shopping and mopping up all the flour and sugar children have been crunching underfoot. Bonus!

Gill's Cookery Workshop

7 North Square, NW11 7AA (8458 2608).
Golders Green tube.
Gill Roberts's parties cater for 12 to 20 children who can decide on their own themes or menus to make on the day. There are two-day holiday classes for six to 13 year-olds and Saturday morning sessions for three- to eight- year-olds. Phone for prices.

Face-painting & make-up

Magical Makeovers

01932 244347/07957 681824/www.magical makeovers.com.
If your partygoers are girly girls (aged six to 16), MM can put at their disposal a friendly beauty therapist with good child skills and a big bag of make-up, nail polishes, hair equipment and endless patience to prettify the celebrants (usually between five and 12 girls). The children are given hair accessories to keep. Prices start at £150 for eight participants for

Cake heaven for chocoholics at **Choccywoccydoodah**. *See p146.*

up to two hours. The new spa party package (for 11-18s) offers gentle facials, make-up lessons, manicure and pedicure.

Mini Makeovers
8398 0107/www.minimakeovers.com.
With a staff-to-child ratio of one to four, hypo-allergenic cosmetics, disco lights and music as part of the package and a pink stretch limo an optional extra, Mini Makeovers provides beauty parties with added bells and whistles. Girls aged ten to 15 can indulge fairy and princess fantasies, or learn dance routines or preening. Guests receive a party bag with hair accessories, bracelet or necklace. Prices start at £160 for eight children. French manicures, a catwalk and a photo shoot are also available.

Performance
For more clubs and companies that run term-time music and drama courses, as well as staging parties, *see chapter* **Arts & Entertainment**.

Blueberry Playsongs Parties
8677 6871/www.blueberry.clara.co.uk.
Children aged one to five enjoy 45 minutes of guitar-led singing and dancing. Prices start at £85 for up to 20 children. Puppets, balloons and parachute games are included, and there's a gift for the birthday child. *See also p174.*

Club Dramatika!
8883 7110.
Vicky Levy offers fun-packed drama parties for birthday kids with thespian leanings. Parties cost £80 for one hour, £150 for two. Phone for details of after-school sessions in north London for children aged from five.

Dramatic Dreams
8741 1809/www.dramaticdreams.com.
Arwen Burnett and team send out a questionnaire to find out all about the birthday child. On the day, two actors (for up to 20 children) bring round props, face-paints and a script. The children (aged from five) play warm-up games, the actors tell them the plot, then everyone acts it out. This costs £350 for two hours. DD also offers after-school and holiday drama workshops in south-west London.

Little Actors Theatre Company
0800 389 6184/www.dramaparties.com.
As well as running drama clubs in south-east and east London, Little Actors provides role play, storytelling and games to get the party

started for children aged from three. Actors guide the children in activities based around the usual suspects – princesses, pirates, fairy tales, superheroes – or your suggestions. Little Actors party invitations, thank-you cards and stickers come with the booking; party bags cost from £2. Parties (London-wide) start at £130 an hour.

MovieParty
7387 4341/www.youngfilmacademy.co.uk.
The Young Film Academy runs filmmaking courses as well as being the sole provider of movie parties in the capital. The MovieParty concept – planning, shooting, editing and screening a film in a single day – costs £1,200 (plus VAT).

Tiddleywinks
8964 5490/www.tiddleywinks.co.uk.
Kate Gielgud-Killick's drama parties are action-packed (acting's in the blood; she's Sir John's great-niece). Costumes and props are provided for plays that may have James Bond or various supermodels in their plots; younger children may prefer *Sleeping Beauty* or *Chitty Chitty Bang Bang*. Prices start at £300 for two hours (four- to seven-year-olds) and from £330 for three hours for eights to 13s.

Science

Mad Science
0845 330 1881/www.madscience.org.uk.
Children of all ages have a blast at these excellent science-based parties. Two mad scientists come to you, bearing a portable laboratory. They entertain the troops with bubbling potions, indoor fireworks, rocket launchers and other irresistible tours de force. Choose from Super Cool and Mega parties; prices start from £285. Party bags start at £4.99.

Science Boffins
0800 019 2636/www.scienceboffins.com.
Science Boffins organise parties that are reassuringly empirical in both style and content. A team of boffins (in reality, trained professionals with backgrounds in teaching, science and theatre) arrives at your chosen venue to provide a meticulously conceived party experience with no danger or mess, including exciting demonstrations, and interactive experiments and races. Keeping children from five years to pre-teens entertained with scientific wonders such as self-inflating balloons and light that bends, it's all about educational fun that aims to inform as well as entertain.

Activities

Sport

Campaign Paintball

Old Lane, Cobham, Surrey KT11 1NH (01932 865999/www.campaignpaintball.com). Effingham Junction rail.

The junior wing of this warlike outfit in the heart of rural Surrey is called Campaign Young Gunz. Paintballing days for ten- to 15-year-olds take place at weekends and school holidays (see the website for details). For £24.95 per child including 300 paintballs (£34.50 for 500 balls) you receive seven to nine games, tuition, a battlesuit, semi-automatic paintball guns and a barbecue lunch. Campaign trophies and team photographs are handed out after all the fun.

Delta Force

01483 211194/www.paintballgames.co.uk.

Paintball giant Delta Force has several branches near enough to the M25 to be convenient for Londoners (choose from Billericay, Oakwood, Upminster, Reading, Effingham and Sevenoaks). Children have to be over 11 to don their fatigues and participate in the fun. They get 150 paintballs to fire between 9.15am and 4pm, plus a barbecue lunch, for £17.50 per head. If you're planning a large manoeuvre, every 15th person goes free.

League One Sports Academy

8446 0891/www.leagueone.co.uk.

Coach Danny Grant and his team organise sporty activities for children aged between three and 12, ranging from basketball, football and cricket to mini Olympics. Varying skill levels aren't generally a problem, as the coaches will cater for everyone's needs. Prices (phone for details) cover equipment, coaches' fees and a winner's trophy for the birthday child. Venue hire can be arranged for an extra charge. League One also offers after-school, Saturday morning and holiday courses in the Hampstead area. Partner Dramarama (*see p180*), runs children's parties of a more theatrical nature.

Pro-Active 4 Parties & Entertainment

0845 257 5005/www.proactive4parties.co.uk.

Hyperactive coaches keep children (aged from four) jumping, shooting and scoring in sports-themed parties. Prices vary (more children, more dosh), but start at about £200. Activities may include ultimate frisbee and circus skills, depending on the birthday child's proclivities. More sedentary pursuits include makeover and face-painting parties, balloon modelling and 'Who Wants to be a Millionaire'. Pro-Active can set up parties in homes, but most sports events take place in more spacious venues.

CAKES

Amato Caffè/Pasticceria

14 Old Compton Street, W1D 4TH (7734 5733/www.amato.co.uk). Leicester Square or Tottenham Court Road tube. **Open** 8am-10pm Mon-Sat; 10am-8pm Sun. **Credit** AmEx, DC, MC, V. **Map** p315 K6.

This legendary Soho café can make the bespoke cake of your child's dreams, or dress up one of its renowned chocolate cream numbers (about £20) with a birthday plaque. The marzipan animals are sweet in every sense.

Buggy access. Delivery service.

Cake Store

111 Sydenham Road, SE26 5EZ (8778 4705/www.thecakestore.co.uk). Sydenham rail. **Open** 8am-5.30pm Mon-Sat. **Credit** MC, V.

The number of artistically led designs for children in Cake Store's catalogue is mind-boggling. We fell in love with an elaborately coiled viper in lurid colours for £69. Standard 8in (20cm) models, decorated with a 'Happy Birthday' and your child's name, cost from £19.95, but you'll doubtless be tempted to go for the more showstopping offerings.

Buggy access. Delivery service. Disabled access.

Cakes4Fun

100 Lower Richmond Road, SW15 1LN (8785 9039/www.cakes4fun.co.uk). Putney Bridge tube/Putney rail/14 bus. **Open** 10am-5pm Mon-Sat. **Credit** MC, V.

The splendid shop has a section devoted to baking with children, and making your own sugar-craft delights, but most people order from celebrity cake queen Carolyn and her team. There's a formidable selection of designs to suit all age groups, or you can discuss specific requirements. Decorations include sugarcraft figures and flowers, models and edible photos, as well as 2D and 3D cake sculptures. Prices start at £60 for an 8in (20cm) round cake. Book well ahead for the cake of your child's dreams, as this place is popular.

Buggy access. Delivery service. Disabled access.

Choccywoccydoodah

47 Harrowby Street, W1H 5EA (7724 5465/www.choccywoccydoodah.com). Edgware Road or Marble Arch tube. **Open** 10am-2pm, 3-6pm Fri; 11am-6pm Sat. **Credit** MC, V. **Map** p311 F5.

Activities

Peter Pan? Batman? Fairy or prince? **Lydie's Children's Parties**. *See p156*.

Activities

Ask the entertainer

Ali Do Lali
See p154.
What's your speciality? All-round performer, magician, fire-eater and illusionist.
How many years in the business? 30 years.
Preferred age group? No preference, first birthdays through to teens.
Preferred venue? Don't mind, I have worked everywhere.
Biggest pleasure? This is what I always wanted to do.
Biggest gripe? Parking in London.
Worst experience? None, it's always wonderful.

Boo Boo
See p154.
What's your speciality? All-round entertainment for a range of ages.
How many years in the business? Ten years.
Preferred age group? One to seven years – but all age groups are possible.
Preferred venue? Halls are good for parking, but houses have more intimacy.
Biggest pleasure? A love of performing and the feedback from the audience.
Biggest gripe? Parking problems.

Worst experience? Being given the wrong venue by a company.

Christopher Howell
Pictured below. See p154.
What's your speciality? Magic.
How many years in the business? 13 years.
Preferred age group? Three to eight years.
Preferred venue? All work well.
Biggest pleasure? Seeing the magic in children's eyes, and the magic in the stories.
Biggest gripe? Parents not getting involved.
Worst experience? Being shut in a room with no adults and many children on a sugar high.

Jenty the Gentle Clown
Pictured right. See p154.
What's your speciality? Being gentle, especially with one- to three-year-olds
How many years in the business? More than ten.
Preferred age group? From one to six.
Preferred venue? Don't mind.
Biggest pleasure? Being part of a celebration, a happy occasion.

Activities

Biggest gripe? Parking.
Worst experience? I like to forget those; 99 per cent are fine!

John Styles
Pictured top right. See p154.
What's your speciality? Punch and Judy show.
How many years in the business? 58, with an MBE for services to arts.
Preferred age group? Fives and above.
Preferred venue? Indoors in a house is more intimate, but outdoors is fun too!
Biggest pleasure? Lifting people's spirits and making them laugh.
Biggest gripe? Disrespectful adults.
Worst experience? Shows in halls when adults are talking and children can't hear.

Lee Warren
Pictured above. See p156.
What's your speciality? Magician.
How many years in the business?

20 years.
Preferred age group? Four to eight years is the best age for magic.
Preferred venue? Private home or any decent space.
Biggest pleasure? Making children laugh.
Biggest gripe? Adults talking during a performance.
Worst experience? Asking for the magic word and getting swear words.

Professor Fumble
See p157.
What's your speciality? Slapstick comedy.
How many years in the business? 15 years.
Preferred age group? Three to seven years.
Preferred venue? There's more scope in a hall.
Biggest pleasure? Enjoying what I do.
Biggest gripe? Travel, petrol costs, acoustics in modern buildings, parents talking during shows.
Worst experience? At a venue with 55 children and all the parents in the next-door bar. It turned into a riot and they flushed my equipment down the loo.

Westway – for sport, for fun, for everyone

From Perfect Parties to Training for Excellence plus open after-school and weekend sessions for all!

Climbing age 5 up | Handball – learn Eton Fives – age 8 up
Football age 5 up | Tennis age 3 up (lessons, coaching, open sessions)
Term-time and holiday programmes in all sports

Westway Sports Centre:

England's largest indoor climbing centre, 12 tennis courts, 6 football pitches, 4 Eton fives handball courts, basketball, netball, gym and more.

Westway is an LTA High Performance Tennis Centre with London's leading junior development programme

020 8969 0992
www.westway.org/sports

New at Westway

Westway hosts a number of performance programmes for young people demonstrating sporting promise. The newest of these is the **Frutina Westway Performance Academy**

To find out more about participation, sponsorship or supporting young sportspeople from under-privileged backgrounds call **020 8962 5735**

The Westway Development Trust is registered charity no. 112312

Crazy name – and a crazy place to come if chocolate's off the menu – because that's the kind of delicious cake produced here. Choccywoccy cakes are dark, dense, moist chocolate sponges layered with chocolate truffle, either sporting the child's name and message, or, if you're minded to have something really eye-catching, some gorgeous choccy decorations. The smallest house cake (£28.50) yields eight to ten portions. Prices go way higher than that, of course. *Buggy access.*

Chorak

122 High Road, N2 9ED (8365 3330). East Finchley tube/263 bus. **Open** 8am-6pm daily. **No credit cards**.
Handmade party cakes embellished with icing versions of cartoon heroes come in two sizes, with the price also depending on whether you opt for a flat cut-out design or a 3D shape. Small cakes contain around 20 portions and cost from £40; large creations (40 portions) begin at £78. *Buggy access. Disabled access.*

Dunn's

6 The Broadway, N8 9SN (8340 1614/ www.dunns-bakery.co.uk). Finsbury Park tube/rail, then W7 bus/Crouch Hill rail/41, 91 bus. **Open** 6am-6pm Mon-Sat; 9am-5pm Sun. **Credit** MC, V.
Standard sponges cost from £25.30, and feed about 14 children. Personalised ones decorated with your child's photograph or Tweenies, Teletubbies and so on, cost from £42.35. *Buggy access. Delivery service.*

Jane Asher Party Cakes

22-24 Cale Street, SW3 3QU (7584 6177/ www.jane-asher.co.uk). South Kensington tube/ 11, 19, 211 bus. **Open** 9.30am-5.30pm Mon-Sat. **Credit** AmEx, MC, V. **Map** p313 E11.
Ever the darlings of the tea-time confectionery world, Ms Asher's team will bake you a cake and decorate it to your spec, or sell you a standard design (there are loads to choose from, costing from £60). Some cake mixes and Jane Asher sugarcraft materials are sold in the shop. *Buggy access. Delivery service. Disabled access. Mail order.*

Maison Blanc

102 Holland Park Avenue, W11 4UA (7221 2494/www.maisonblanc.co.uk). Holland Park tube. **Open** 8am-7pm Mon-Sat; 8.30am-6pm Sun. **Credit** MC, V.
Distinctive, delicious and very French, a Maison Blanc gateau can be made birthday-child friendly with elaborate writings, sugarcrafted decorations

or by the addition of a pivotal figure, such as Peter Rabbit. They're beautifully presented. *Buggy access. Disabled access.* **Other locations** throughout town.

Margaret's Cakes of Distinction

224 Camberwell Road, SE5 0ED (7701 1940). Elephant & Castle tube/rail, then 12, 35, 45, 68, 171, 176 bus. **Open** 9am-5pm Mon-Sat. **No credit cards**.
Margaret's turns out fairly priced personalised cakes in both Caribbean and English styles. A simple round sponge cake sandwiched with buttercream or jam can be embellished with cute marzipan figurines; it costs from £25.24. *Buggy access. Disabled access.*

Primrose Bakery

69 Gloucester Avenue, NW1 8LD (7483 4222/ www.primrosebakery.org.uk). Chalk Farm tube. **Open** 8.30am-6pm Mon-Sat; 10am-5pm Sun. **Credit** MC, V.
Martha Swift and Lisa Thomas, famous for their cupcakes, are top women for beautifully baked children's party creations. They use organic eggs, have a way with sugarcraft, and their layer cakes, especially the 70% cocoa versions, can be embellished with delectable edibles. Many parents go for a plateful of personalised cupcakes for the party. Prices are £1.15-£1.75 per cupcake, or £18 for a simple sandwich sponge. *Buggy access. Delivery service.*

COSTUMES

Mail order

Hopscotch

8696 1313/www.hopscotchdressingup.co.uk.
From Roman soldiers to disco dollies, Hopscotch can cater for most dressing-up requirements, and provides all the accessories (crowns, fezzes and wands). We adore the dinosaur at £24.95, but serviceable outfits sell from just £7. For parents who want to avoid that nightmare-before-nativity needlework, your Mary, Joseph, kings and shepherds can be tricked out by Hopscotch.

J&M Toys

01274 599314/www.jandmtoys.co.uk.
Firefighters, lollipop men and ladies, fairies, witches, pirates, cowgirls, Vikings, dragons, police officers, nurses – Jim and Melanie's stock includes more than 150 dressing-up costumes, available in age ranges three to five and five to eight. J&M are medieval enthusiasts, so regal

Activities

Cooking up a party storm

If children's cooking conjures up images of sticky fingers and messy faces in a trashed kitchen, think again. Cooking parties, organised by those who know and care about teaching children to cook, can be surprisingly civilised affairs, with children reaping the many benefits of learning to prepare their own meals. With so many current concerns about children and food, from obesity rates to advertising bans, it's a great way to raise kids' awareness about what to eat.

Fiona Hamilton-Fairley, who runs the ever-busy charity **Kids' Cookery School** (*see p196*), points out that cooking is 'about understanding that food is more than a packet on a supermarket shelf. Cooking from scratch is a life skill.' Joy Neal launched her thriving agency **Munchkins** (*see p196*) precisely because her teaching background showed her that 'so many children don't and can't cook, yet the benefits to doing so are huge. It's fantastic for self-esteem and helps with learning group skills, communication skills, developing concentration and attention, plus understanding maths and science.'

robes, Robin Hoods and knights' armour, with wooden swords and shields, are also here. It's all surprisingly cheap; most costumes cost no more than £15, with discounts on group purchases.

Natural Nursery

0845 890 1665/www.naturalnursery.co.uk.
Some of the most gorgeous partywear we've seen. The ladybird and bee tutu-like dresses are adorable (from £17.99). This family-run business specialises in natural, sustainable and eco-friendly materials, so dress 'em up with a clear conscience.

Shops

For more toyshops and boutiques with dressing-up gear, *see p279*.

Angels

119 Shaftesbury Avenue, WC2H 8AE (7836 5678/www.fancydress.com). Leicester Square or Tottenham Court Road tube. **Open** 9.30am-5.30pm Mon, Tue, Thur, Fri; 10.30am-7pm Wed. **Credit** AmEx, MC, V.

Carola Weymouth, the woman behind top company **Cookie Crumbles** (pictured; see p144), which has taught cooking to thousands of children, explains: 'I've met many children who have never touched or cooked food.'

These are serious issues, but they are secondary to the simple pleasures and rewards of cooking. As Neal says: 'Children are more likely to try new food if they're involved in its preparation; at parties they have fun because they feel safe – it's a structured event where they're free to be creative and express themselves.'

And structure is key, right from explaining to parents how the event will work, to children cooking three-course meals, to ensuring a safe environment throughout and a clean kitchen afterwards. Parents don't need to worry whether their own kitchen is up to scratch; trained staff will arrive at homes with their own equipment or – perhaps better still – the party is held in a specially equipped venue.

'Many declare that the party is the calmest they've ever seen,' says Neal, 'as the children aren't overwrought on a sugar high.' Weymouth adds: 'It's a myth that cooking is a girls' thing; everyone enjoys it, and they're often so proud, they want to show their parents before eating the food!'

There is scope for children to start cooking when they're as young as 18 months, with parties then catering for children cooking around a theme to teenagers managing dinner party menus. Now there's a thought for harassed parents everywhere.

Angels has costumes, props and make-up for kids and adults, covering many themes. There are angels and fairies, animals and superheroes, witches and skeletons. Prices start at £13. *Buggy access. Disabled access. Mail order (0845 054 8854).*

Escapade
150 Camden High Street, NW1 0NE (7485 7384/www.escapade.co.uk). Camden Town tube. **Open** *10am-7pm Mon-Fri; 10am-6pm Sat; noon-5pm Sun.* **Credit** *AmEx, MC, V.*

Located at the other end of Camden High Street from the market, Escapade is a tiny costume shop that's been running for 25 years. The down-at-heel interior houses an absorbing array of costumes, masks, props, jokes and theatrical cosmetics. The shop is always rammed with customers checking out wacky outfits of all types for all ages, and there's a dressing room too. Wonderfully gory rubber masks line the shop shelves. Ready-made kits cost from around £10 and costumes may be hired. *Buggy access. Delivery service. Disabled access. Mail order.*

Harlequin
254 Lee High Road, E13 5PR (8852 0193). Hither Green or Lewisham rail/DLR/21, 261 bus. **Open** *10.30am-5.30pm Mon; 10am-5.30pm Tue, Thur-Sat; 10am-1pm Wed.* **Credit** *MC, V.*

Garb for all the superheroes, from Batman to Spidey (£29.95), is here. Cheaper alternatives come in the form of Indians, pirates, princesses and ninjas or a set of sheriff accessories. The kid's Elvis jumpsuit (£14.95) is a blast. *Buggy access.*

Pantaloons
119 Lupus Street, SW1V 3EN (7630 8330/www.pantaloons.co.uk). Pimlico tube. **Open** *11am-5pm Mon, Tue; 11am-6pm Wed; 11am-7pm Thur; 11am-8pm Fri; 10am-6pm Sat.* **Credit** *AmEx, MC, V.*

A dressing-up and balloon specialist that caters for adults and children, Pantaloons can make sure your party animal looks like an animal, if she should require it, or like a pirate, fairy, soldier, prince, nurse – you name it. Budget costumes cost from £10, but you're more likely to hand over £35 for the full Disney regalia. *Buggy access. Delivery service. Mail order.*

Preposterous Presents
262 Upper Street, N1 2UQ (7226 4166). Highbury & Islington tube/rail. **Open** *10am-6pm Mon-Sat.* **Credit** *MC, V.*

A quirky shop full of party fripperies, plus jokes of the whoopee cushion, itching powder and fake blood school of humour. Fancy dress includes stage make-up, latex heads, stick-on wizards' beards and costumes (expect to pay £10-£22 for a dalmatian or fairy outfit). *Buggy access. Disabled access.*

Deals on wheels

Party Bus
07836 605032/www.childrenspartybus.co.uk.

A converted coach bedecked with stars is one way of keeping party debris out of the house. It holds up to 24 children (without adults). On-board events, such as games, magic or a disco, are tailored to the age group (from fours to nines). The bus parks outside for two hours and costs from £350, including catering (you provide the cake). Venues within the Low Emission Zone (roughly within the M25) have to pay a surcharge of £200.

ENTERTAINERS

Ali Do Lali
01494 774300/www.alidolali.com.
The celebrated Do Lali's career spans over 30 years. He has routines to suit from three years and up, and all situations. He lives in a magic lamp, as would be expected. Prices available on application.

Amigo's Magic
8480 8176/www.amigosmagic.co.uk.
Simple Simon, Magic Circle member and all-round top joker and balloon modeller, is the child-friendly face of Amigo's. Prices start at £125 for an hour (£185 for two).

Billy the Disco DJ
8471 8616/07949 936864/www.billythedisco dj.co.uk.
These popular disco parties for ages five to 11 may include limbo contests, temporary tattoos, bubble machines, pop quizzes, dancing competitions and karaoke. Billy costs £190 for two hours, and can take care of party bag needs for a little bit extra.

Boo Boo
7727 3817.
Sean Hampson dons spectacular trousers, steps out of the dry ice and is Boo Boo at parties for threes to eights. His shows include music, balloon-modelling, bubbles, smoke, dancing and lots of comedy. Phone for a quote.

Christopher Howell
7993 4544/www.christopherhowell.net.
A member of the Magic Circle, Howell uses magic, music and storytelling, in which the children play a part. The story is followed by a balloon-model game. Hour-long parties for four- to six-year-olds start at around £150; £5 of the fee is donated to the Roald Dahl Foundation.

Foxy the Funky Genie
7692 5664/www.foxythefunkygenie.com.

Foxy is an accomplished magician and balloon modeller and his show gets everyone dancing with balloon limbo, disco and karaoke. He also puts on a puppet show for the under-fives. Shows cost from £95 for 45 minutes.

Jenty the Gentle Clown
8527 4855/07957 121764/www.jentythe gentleclown.com.
Parties for children aged one to 11 include singing, banjo, guitar, magic, storytelling, face-painting, balloon-modelling and limbo dancing. Choose activities to suit your child's tastes. Jenty charges £145 for one hour, £195 for two.

John Styles
8300 3579/www.johnstylesentertainer. co.uk.
Kids are enthusiastic devotees of the antique art of ventriloquism as practised by Mr Styles and his team; he also does a Punch and Judy show, balloon modelling and magic for children aged three years and above.

Juggling John
8938 3218/0845 644 6659/www.juggling john.com.

Nellie Shepherd Events. *See p158.*

Circus skills (including plenty of juggling), action-packed storytelling and all sorts of other fun stuff are included in Juggling John's one- or two-hour shows. Prices from £125 for an hour, with ages starting at one year.

Just George
8442 0739/07944 863961.
George McAllister's two-hour parties include parachute games, music, magic and balloon models. All this goes down well with three- to eight-year-olds. The cost is about £180; phone for price details.

Laurie Temple the Party Wizard
8951 9469/07951 596240/www.theparty wizard.co.uk.
Well known on the London party circuit, Laurie Temple can wave his magic wand and make the party happen. He and his team of conjurers, jugglers, balloonologists, DJs, puppeteers and magical storytellers can entertain children from as young as two for one or two hours.

Lee Warren
8670 2729/07973 337575/ www.sorcery.org.uk.
Lee combines sorcery with audience participation. The hour-long shows – for four- to eight-year olds – cost from £130 for a performance in your own home or £140 in a hired hall, and Lee says he's able to deal with nearly any size of audience (minimum eight).

Little Blisters
8392 9093/www.childrensentertainment-surrey.co.uk.
Ava de Souza has created the characters of Flossie Bella the Fairy, Sea Lily the Mermaid and Kitty Willow the Magical Cat for her shows with stories, music and optional face-painting. Her productions are for three- to seven-year-olds and cost from £100 (for one hour).

Lydie's Children's Parties
7622 2540/www.lydieparties.com.
Bubbly Lydie has a vast repertoire of themes for boys and girls (from Pocahontas to Batman) and promises to turn your home into a magical, musical world for up to 26 children. Lydie arrives five hours in advance, to set up for the two-hour show, then, like the trooper she is, stays another two hours to dismantle her set and clear up the house. Parties cost from £400.

Magic Mikey
0808 100 2140/www.magicmikey.co.uk.
Disco, magic, balloon modelling, games and the hyperactive Rocky the Super Racoon make up the two-hour Magic Mikey bash for children up to 12 years old. A seasoned professional, with plenty of cruise ship experience under his magic belt, Magic Mikey is strong on slapstick and high-energy discos. Prices are available on phone application.

Merlin Entertainments
8866 6327/01494 479027/www.merlinents. co.uk.
If you're not sure what kind of entertainment you want at the party, talk to Merlin, a one-stop shop for entertainers of all types, from mad scientists to sane clowns. An animal encounters show, Punch and Judy theatres, face-painters and makeover artists can also be sought through Merlin. Prices start at £135 for a one-hour performance, or £155 for two hours.

Preposterous Presents. *See p153.*

Activities

Mr Squash

8808 1415/07939 252241/www.mr-squash. co.uk.

Mr Squash travels all over London with his musical puppet show, balloon tricks, singalongs and funny stories. Well known on the playgroup circuit, he's experienced in engaging the very young (two- and three-year-olds), but his parties are suitable for children aged up to six. His puppets, performing in a booth, invite audience participation, especially from the birthday child. Mr Squash charges £150-£180 for a one-hour set.

Pekko's Puppets

8575 2311/www.pekkospuppets.co.uk.

Stephen Novy's puppet plays are aimed at children aged three to 12, with shows for under-fives packing in two shorter tales presented by Pekko, a lively and cheerful bird; there's plenty of singing and audience participation. The repertoire for older children includes Celtic folk tales, popular classics, humorous verse and chillers like Dracula, all enacted from one of Mr Novy's two mobile booths. Prices start at £150 for one hour.

Professor Fumble

01395 579523/www.professorfumble.co.uk.

The Professor can put on a 30-minute balloon modelling party for tinies (aged two to four), an hour-long clowning, slapstick, balloon modelling and circus workshop party, or the two-hour Super Dooper Wizzo with added workshops, prizes and party games galore (and exhausted children guaranteed) for three- to eight-year-olds. Prices are from £135 for one hour (£195 for two).

Silly Millie the Clown

7823 8329/www.sillymillietheclown.co.uk.

Purple-haired Silly Millie was born in 2001, when Faith Tingle started her training as a special clown working in hospitals with sick children. Cuddly, crazy parties for three- to nine-year-olds include magic, balloon animals, singalongs and puppets – all wrapped up in general daftness. Prices start at £85 an hour.

EQUIPMENT HIRE

Disco

Young's Disco Centre

2 Malden Road, NW5 3HR (7485 1115/ www.steveyoungdisco.co.uk). Chalk Farm tube. **Open** by appointment 9am-7pm Mon-Sat. **Credit** MC, V.

Not just sounds, such as turntables, but sights too, including coloured lights, bubbles and smoke. Young's will also hire you a DJ and turntables or iPod systems; otherwise, a DIY children's party package with a sound system and disco lights costs £95.

Buggy access. Delivery & set-up service. Disabled access.

Fairground

PK Entertainments

01344 626789/07771 546676/ www.fairandfete.co.uk.

All the fun of the fair (well, village fete) can be hired from PK. If you have the room, this outfit can provide the hoopla, swingboats, bouncy castles, candy floss and popcorn – even the bucking bronco. PK can also provide clowns, magicians and face-painters. Check out the price list online.

Marquee

Sunset Marquees

Unit 5, Glenville Mews, Kimber Road, SW18 4NJ (8741 2777/www.sunsetmarquees.com). Southfields tube. **Open** 8am-6pm daily. **No credit cards.**

Hire a tent, fill it with children and protect your home from attack. Sunset supplies mini marquees as well as very large ones (prices from £190 for a weekend). For an extra charge it will also provide lighting, furniture, candy-floss machines, heating and carpeting.

ORGANISERS

See also p281 **Mystical Fairies**.

Action Station

0870 770 2705/www.theactionstation.co.uk.

This agency's books brim with magical storytellers, face-painters, clowns, dramatists, cheerleaders and magicians. Children of all ages are catered for. Prices start at £170 per hour, £258 for two hours.

Adam Ants

8959 1045/www.adamantsparties.com.

Entertainers, party accessories, including ball ponds and bouncy castles and kid-o-gram characters, can be hired from Ants. Catering can also be organised. Phone for prices.

Birthday Dreams

7700 2525/www.birthdaydreams.co.uk.

Activities

Offering an integrated, bespoke party service, Birthday Dreams will 'take the mess and stress' out of party planning. It hosts events at its own venue, Kinloch Castle, where the 3D storybook interior, encompassing art murals, grass underfoot and a tree decorated with fibre-optics, is used to full effect for parties with special characters. Prices start from £450. Birthday Dreams can also organise a party at your home or assist with elements including entertainers, invites, cakes and cleaning. It is similarly flexible about themes, with packages from fairytale and film characters to arts and crafts, plus parties organised around a desired theme.

Boo! Productions
7287 9090/07825 310780/www.booparties.com.
Bespoke parties from Boo! include the entire organisation of your event – all you have to do is discuss your plans. If you only need an entertainer, Boo! will supply one; prices start at around £170 for two hours.

Nellie Shepherd Events
07710 479852/www.nellieshepherdevents.com.
A dedicated, well-established company with high-profile, returning clients extending across the corporate, entertainment and celebrity worlds, Nellie Shepherd Events brings energy and expertise to children's parties. Favourite themes include Snow Princess, Animal Art, Space, and Pink Ballerina. With the emphasis on imagination and creativity, Nellie can organise anything and everything you can dream up, from *Doctor Who* and Underwater World to Cowboys and Circus, for children of any age.

Puddleduck Parties
8893 8998/www.puddleduckparties.co.uk.
Puddleduck puts together flexible packages that encompass all those party necessities such as catering (including tableware), decorations and entertainers. Teddy bears' picnics can be arranged for smaller children; otherwise, there's drama, sport or disco parties for all ages, starting from around £200 for two hours of fun.

Taylor-Made Entertainment
07974 901215/www.taylor-made entertainment.com.
This organisation puts together bespoke two-hour party packages. It can provide discos (with lights, scented smoke, bubbles and karaoke) and bring makeover artists, face-painters, musicians and party MCs. Supplying entertainment for young and easily bored guests at weddings is another speciality.

Theme Traders
8452 8518/www.themetraders.com.
High-end (from £3,500) party organisers renowned for their contribution to the Queen's 'Party at the Palace' for 2,000 children a few years back. Clients are invited to visit showrooms to firm up the theme and budget and view portfolios of previous events. This is usually followed by a site visit and the drawing-up of plans. Theme Traders also offers a prop rental service, starting at £150.

Twizzle Parties
8789 3232/www.twizzle.co.uk.
Beloved of London's celebrity parents, Twizzle earned itself the number-one slot in a *Harper's Bazaar* party survey, and continues to organise glittering children's 'film première' and photo-shoot parties. Themed events for all ages start with simple sing-along parties for toddlers and go glamorous with all sorts of pop-starry, street-dancey shenanigans. Twizzle also runs a performing arts school during the holidays. Prices start at about £165 for one hour.

PARAPHERNALIA

Mail order

Baker Ross
0844 576 8922/www.bakerross.co.uk.
Fantastic ideas for craft parties and an inspired range of multi-pack toys (pirate pens, colour-in magnets, glitter tattoos) perfect for party bags.

CYP
08700 340010/www.cyp.co.uk.
Are you in charge of the music for the tot party? Check out the selection of party tapes, CDs and downloads for traditional games such as pass the parcel or musical chairs. Prices from £4.99.

Party Directory
01252 851601/www.partydirectory4kids.co.uk.
Themed tableware (costing from 10p to £2.75), party bags and boxes, plus trinkets, toys and gorgeous little chocolate novelties to put in them, make the Party Directory a top stop for children's parties. You can even sign up for party-planning email reminders when your children's big days are looming large on the horizon.

Party Pieces
01635 201844/www.partypieces.co.uk.
Tableware (from around 25p per item) is themed around the film or programme of the moment

Activities

Fears of a clown

They're characterised by their red noses, unfeasibly large footwear, whacky trousers and squirty flowers. Their sole aim is to make people laugh, but they have to guard against scaring the pants off children. They've made subversive behaviour into an art form, but they're obliged to keep gaggles of excited small children under control. There's no doubt that choosing 'clown' as a career path is something of a challenge.

Making people laugh is a serious business and no one knows that better than top clown **Mattie Faint** (www.clowns-international.co.uk), in the business for 37 years, and newer clown **Silly Millie** (pictured; see p157). Clowning is, they say, specialised work underpinned by lifelong training in performance skills, plus extensive experience – none more important than working in the wards of children's hospitals. Both clowns have honed their craft as clown doctors to the most vulnerable children, so can bring their knowledge and sensitivity to parties.

'A good clown loves their job and loves children,' says Faint. 'It's about creating a strong, individual character. The costume is valuable, and I use other elements, such as puppets and bubbles, but it's mainly about talking and improvisation.'

There's an art to clowning, so it's worth booking the right person; word-of-mouth recommendations are best. It's also wise to heed the clown's advice on the day, about changing the running order, for example: the clown appearing before the children have indulged in the customary party-tea sugar rush can make all the difference to a party's success. It's a relationship of mutual respect: a professional clown won't bring messy props into a home to wreck the soft furnishings. For their part, parents should not forget that it's their responsibility to maintain a semblance of discipline: getting mellow with wine and friends while your kids mob the clown is not helpful. Fine-tuning the entertainment to the correct age group is crucial, of course. Says Silly Millie: 'I employ nursery rhymes, magic and music with younger children. Meanwhile, older children enjoy close-up magic such as cards, and learning to do the tricks for themselves. But everyone – children and parents alike – is happy when a room is filled with bubbles, music and laughter – it's organised chaos.' Happiest of all is the clown, a figure not of ridicule but of fun, whose work is a true vocation. As Faint simply says: 'Make 'em laugh!'

Activities

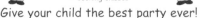

(*Cars, Pirates of the Caribbean, Power Rangers*), fairies, football and the like. Then there are party-bag fillers, traditional games (a 'pin the eyepatch on the pirate' version of the donkey's tail original is £2.45), and a whopping range of banners, balloons and assorted decorations.

Your Party by Post

01293 575314/www.yourpartybypost.co.uk. Stockists of themed children's partyware – everything from *Charlie and Lola* to *High School Musical* – as well as goody bag gifts, banners, balloons, piñatas and games. And thank-you notes for afterwards.

Shops

Balloon & Kite Company

613 Garratt Lane, SW18 4SU (8946 5962/ www.balloonandkite.com). Earlsfield rail. **Open** 9am-6pm Mon-Fri; 9am-5.30pm Sat. **Credit** AmEx, MC, V.
Balloons in rubber or foil, bearing pictures of any number of favourite screen heroes, or personalised for your child, can be ordered here. There's also themed paper tableware and banners, kites and goody bag stuff.
Buggy access. Delivery service. Disabled access. Mail order.

Balloonland

12 Hale Lane, NW7 3NX (8906 3302/ www.balloonland.co.uk). Edgware tube/ Mill Hill Broadway rail/221, 240 bus.

Open 9am-5.30pm Mon-Fri; 9.30am-5.30pm Sat. **Credit** AmEx, MC, V.
A super soaraway choice of inflated latex and foil – as well as all sorts of balloon-based services, from helium hire to venue decorating – explains this shop's name, but Balloonland is a fab general party shop too. All the themes in children's tableware and party bags, from Dora (Explorer) to Spongebob (Squarepants) await your offspring's pleasure.
Buggy access. Delivery service. Disabled access. Mail order.

Bouncing Kids Party Shop

127 Northfield Avenue, W13 9QR (8840 0110/ www.bouncing-kids.com). Northfields tube/ West Ealing rail/E2, E3 bus. **Open** 9am-5.30pm Mon-Wed, Fri, Sat; 9am-6pm Thur. **Credit** MC, V.
Paperware, balloons, fancy dress and party bags fill the shop, but you can also hire bouncy castles, tables and chairs from here. Check the website for more information.
Buggy access. Delivery service. Disabled access. Mail order.

Circus Circus

176 Wandsworth Bridge Road, SW6 2UQ (7731 4128/www.circuscircus.co.uk). Fulham Broadway tube. **Open** 10am-6pm daily. **Credit** AmEx, MC, V.
Staff here can find you caterers, entertainers and bouncy castle specialists. They'll also show you around what seems like hundreds of themes in tableware and party stationery, a

Who thinks **Foxy the Funky Genie** is magic? *See p154.*

Activities

dressing-up department and a load of booty for party bags. They've thought of everything.
Buggy access. Delivery service. Disabled access. Mail order. Play area.

Just Balloons

8560 5933/www.justballoons.com.
You can't have too many helium-filled balloons at a party. Just Balloons supplies the wherewithal (including hiring out canisters of helium gas), and also has a lucrative line in balloons emblazoned with messages or photographs (£125 for 100). Delivery in central London costs around £15.

Mexicolore

7622 9577/www.mexicolore.co.uk
Mexicolore makes proper piñatas (not the cheapo cardboard ones you can buy at supermarkets). The decorated papier mâché comes in a number of designs that can be filled by parents with goodies, then hung up ready for frenzied bashing by the children. Prices start at about £20.

Non-Stop Party Shop

214-216 Kensington High Street, W8 7RG (7937 7200/www.nonstopparty.co.uk). High Street Kensington tube/10, 27, 391 bus. **Open** 9.30am-6pm Mon, Tue, Thur-Sat; 10am-6pm Wed; 11am-5pm Sun. **Credit** MC, V. **Map** p312 A9.
This large shop comprises a basement connecting two ground-level stores: one for cards and wrapping, the other for fancy dress and accessories, including some fun inflatables. The basement houses all other party essentials, with an especially good range of themed tableware and stationery. With eight stores in the South East, Non-Stop is a big name in partyware. A balloon service includes printing, inflating and decorating party premises.
Delivery service. Mail order.

Oscar's Den

127-129 Abbey Road, NW6 4SL (7328 6683/www.oscarsden.com). Swiss Cottage tube/West Hampstead tube/rail/31, 138, 189 bus. **Open** 9.30am-5.30pm Mon-Sat; 10am-2pm Sun. **Credit** AmEx, MC, V.
The shop of award-winning party supplies outfit Oscar's Den is rammed with party stuff: there's an incredible amount of balloons, plus everything you need for a big event, from bubbles, bouncy castles and super slides, to paper ware, party tricks, play equipment, face-paints and fancy dress. Staff are friendly and capable; they'll take on the whole project if you

want them to (they have catered for numerous personalities, including Prime Minister Gordon Brown). Fireworks are a speciality.
Buggy access. Delivery service. Disabled access.

Party Party

3 & 11 Southampton Road, NW5 4JS (7267 9084/www.partypartyuk.com). Chalk Farm tube/Gospel Oak rail/24 bus. **Open** 9.30am-5.30pm Mon-Sat. **Credit** MC, V.
You'll find balloons, banners and decorations at No.3 and, a few doors down at No.11, party bags, costumes and tableware. Party Party also has a bespoke piñata service; otherwise their brightly coloured off-the-peg bashables come in number shapes or fashioned into clowns, bees, butterflies, fish and donkeys.
Buggy access. Delivery service. Disabled access. Mail order.

Party Party

9-13 Ridley Road, E8 2NP (7254 5168/www.ppshop.co.uk). Dalston Kingsland rail/30, 38, 56, 67, 76, 149, 236, 242, 243, 277 bus. **Open** 9am-5.30pm Mon-Thur; 9am-6.30pm Fri, Sat. **Credit** AmEx, MC, V.
A no-frills party shop offering all the trimmings, based in bustling Dalston, this prince among party shops is a friendly place that's all about cheap and cheerful. There are three floors. The ground floor covers basics from paper plates and wrapping paper to banners. The first floor is devoted to cake making, with a huge range of equipment, decorations and ingredients. The new basement area is fancy-dress nirvana, with stock running the gamut from good fun to bad taste, including plenty of wigs, costumes and props.
Mail order.

Party Superstore

268 Lavender Hill, SW11 1LJ (7924 3210/www.partysuperstores.co.uk). Clapham Junction rail/39, 77, 345 bus. **Open** 9am-6pm Mon-Wed, Sat; 9am-7pm Thur, Fri; 10.30am-4.30pm Sun. **Credit** AmEx, MC, V.
The ground floor of the glittering Superstore stocks children's party accessories, fancy-dress costumes (from £7.99), eye-masks and novelty hats (from £1.99) and wigs (from £4.99). There are also more than 50 themed tableware collections (many of which are suitable for children), as well as practical jokes, balloons in latex and helium, costume jewellery, party-bag fillers and cake decorations and candles.
Buggy access. Delivery service. Disabled access. Mail order.
Other locations 43 Times Square, High Street, Sutton, Surrey SM1 1LF (8661 7323).

Arts & Entertainment

Celebrating the city's creative spirit.

This section is all about learning and fun. The two go together swimmingly in the embarrassment of cultural riches that is London. Keeping the children entertained, educated and informed need not be the job of home computers and multi-channel tellies. London has so many centres for the arts and sciences, running workshops and activities to suit all tastes, that kids could do something different every day of the year if they so wished.

The creative spirit is nurtured and celebrated in London's premier cultural venues, many of which are listed under **Museums & Galleries** (*starting on p58*), and **Attractions** (*starting on p30*). Many workshops, shows and activities are free at weekends and during school holidays, but dedicated arts educational establishments, such as **Perform** and **Stagecoach** (for both, *see p183*), charge a fee each term. Where possible, we've tried to indicate the price of children's dance, drama and music classes, but do check websites for more details.

Many of London's major galleries include free arty activity packs to enhance the experience for young visitors; it's always worth asking about these. Also check for information on children's activities, workshops and family events at **Tate Modern** (*see p69*) and the **Hayward Gallery** (*see p60*) on the South Bank, Westminster's **National Gallery** (*see p62*) and **Tate Britain** (*see p69*), the **Royal Academy of Arts** (*see p67*) in Piccadilly, the **Wallace Collection** (*see p70*) in Marylebone and the **Dulwich Picture Gallery** (*see p58*) in south-east London.

ARTS CENTRES

Barbican Centre

Silk Street, EC2Y 8DS (box office 7638 8891/ cinema hotline 7382 7000/www.barbican. org.uk). Barbican tube/Moorgate tube/rail. **Open** *Box office* (in person) 9am-8pm Mon-Sat; 11am-8pm Sun. *Gallery* 11am-8pm Mon, Thur-Sun; 11am-6pm Tue, Wed; until 10pm 1st Thur of mth. **Admission** *Library* free. *Exhibitions, films, shows, workshops* phone for details. **Membership** (BarbicanCard) £20-£25/yr. **Credit** AmEx, MC, V. **Map** p318 P5.

Study the maps and follow the notices on the walkways, and you need not get lost in this rather complex arts complex. It's a very desirable place to live too, with 6,500 handsome flats. There are some pockets of pleasant calm for everyone to enjoy: the fountains in the inner courtyard; the Waterside Café, with its children's menu; the exotic plants and lazy koi carp in the conservatory (open to the public on Sunday afternoons); and the library, with its extensive children's section. The Barbican's range of cultural offerings is certainly extensive. A programme of family-oriented activities includes the weekly Family Film Club (tickets £3.50-£5.50) with a diverse mix of international movies, workshops, goodies and events. Screenings for kids aged five to 11 and their parents are at 11am on Saturdays; book ahead. The Barbican also hosts mini-seasons and events for families, including the Animate The World! animation-fest in May, and the London Children's Film Festival in November. The children's classic concerts enchantingly combine music and storytelling.

Buggy access. Cafés. Disabled access: lift, toilet. Nappy-changing facilities. Nearest picnic place: Barbican lakeside terrace. Restaurants. Shops.

Rich Mix

35-47 Bethnal Green Road, E1 6LA (7613 7498/www.richmix.org.uk). Bethnal Green or Liverpool Street tube/rail. **Open** 9am-11pm Mon-Fri; 10am-11am Sat, Sun. **Admission** prices vary; phone for details. **Credit** MC, V.

The Rich Mix building is a vast former garment factory turned cross-cultural arts and media centre, with an artsy, East End flavour. It houses a three-screen cinema;café, broadcasting centre and exhibition areas; a 200-seat performance venue; education and work spaces. The cinema offers a good-value family ticket, available before 5pm Mon-Fri, all day Sat, Sun, for £12-£16 (under-2s go free). Occasional parent/baby screenings are held; check the website for more information.
Buggy access. Cafés. Disabled access: lift, ramp, toilet. Nappy-changing facilities.

Southbank Centre
Belvedere Road, SE1 8XX (box office 0871 663 2500/www.southbankcentre.co.uk). Embankment tube/Waterloo tube/rail. **Open** *Box office & foyer* 10am-8pm daily. *Hayward Gallery* 10am-6pm Mon-Thur, Sat, Sun; 10am-10pm Fri. **Admission** prices vary; phone for details. **Credit** AmEx, MC, V. **Map** p317 M8.
The Southbank Centre encompasses four spaces: the Royal Festival Hall, Queen Elizabeth Hall, Purcell Room and Hayward Gallery. The 3,000-capacity Royal Festival Hall reopened in summer 2007 after a £90m renovation. Access is now easier, acoustics are better and, most importantly, there's a new music learning space,

Spirit Level. It includes a technology area, where young people can experiment with composition and sound-making, and a special gamelan studio. The Clore Ballroom is the venue for regular school holiday events and family activities, with treasure trails, performances, storytelling and large-scale drawing escapades – usually all free. Philharmonia Family Days (www.philharmonia.co.uk) take place regularly in the Queen Elizabeth Hall, making music fun for everyone over five.
Buggy access. Cafés. Disabled access: infra-red hearing system, lift, toilet. Nappy-changing facilities. Restaurants.

Tricycle Theatre & Cinema
269 Kilburn High Road, NW6 7JR (box office 7328 1000/www.tricycle.co.uk). Kilburn tube/ Brondesbury rail. **Open** *Box office* 10am-9pm Mon-Sat; 2-8pm Sun. *Children's shows* 11.30am, 2pm Sat. *Children's films* 1pm Sat. **Tickets** *Theatre* (Sat) £5; £4 advance bookings. *Films* (Sat) £4.50; £3.50 reductions, under-16s. **Credit** MC, V.
A venue with a real community feel, the Tricycle has a programme of children's shows, events, films and workshops hailed by the *Times Educational Supplement* as 'one of the best reasons for living in and around Kilburn'. There

Southbank Centre

Activities

are also after-school classes covering drama, dance and performance. Half-term and holiday workshops allow kids to get creative with everything from screenprinting to producing a play in a day.
Buggy access. Disabled access: lift, ramp, toilet. Nappy-changing facilities. Restaurant.

CINEMAS

For a blockbuster multiplex blowout, with absurdly priced buckets of popcorn and pop, go to Leicester Square, W1. It's home to the glitzy West End flagships of **Vue** (0871 224 0240, www.myvue.com), the **Odeon** (0871 224 4007, www.odeon.co.uk), and the **Empire** (0871 224 4007). Some of these big boys also do their own version of Watch with Baby screenings, as pioneered at the **Clapham Picturehouse** (*see p166*) and now in all Picturehouses.

The **London Children's Film Festival**, now in its fourth year and billed as the biggest family film event in London, takes place 22-30 November 2008. The nexus of operations is the **Barbican** (*see p163*), but 15 other cinemas across London are involved too.

BFI London IMAX

1 Charlie Chaplin Walk, SE1 8XR (0870 787 2525/www.bfi.org.uk/imax). Waterloo tube/rail. **Open** varies; phone or check website for details. **Admission** £8.50-£12.50; £6.25-£9.75 reductions; £5-£8 4-14s; free under-4s; add-on IMAX film £6 extra per adult, £4 extra per child. **Credit** AmEx, MC, V.
This London landmark at the bottom of Waterloo Bridge houses the biggest cinema screen in the UK, soaring over 20m (65ft) high and 26m (85ft) wide. Kids enjoy wearing 3D glasses to watch films such as *Dinosaurs 3D* and *Deep Sea 3D*, where the storylines tend to be secondary to the fantastic effects that seem to leap from the screen. Note that some films can be a bit intense for very young viewers. Non-IMAX mainstream films are also shown. The big number for 2008 is *Speed Racer: The IMAX Experience*.
Bar. Buggy access. Café. Disabled access: lift, toilet. Nappy-changing facilities.

BFI Southbank

National Film Theatre, Belvedere Road, SE1 8XT (box office 7928 3232/www.bfi.org.uk). Embankment tube/Waterloo tube/rail. **Open** *Box office* (in person) 11am-8.30pm daily (by phone from 11.30am). *Film club* times vary;

Activities

usually Sat, Sun, school hols. **Tickets** £8.60 non-members; £7.60 members; phone for children's prices. **Membership** £35/yr; £20/yr reductions. **Credit** AmEx, MC, V. **Map** p317 M8.

The revamped BFI is a lovely place, with its arts spaces, installations, comfortable Benugo café-bar and four screens, as well as the Mediatheque where you can watch film and television clips for free. Bring the family on Saturday mornings, when beautifully remastered junior screenings combine classic and current hits. The BFI is just around the corner from the IMAX.
Buggy access. Café. Disabled access: ramp, toilet. Nappy-changing facilities. Restaurant.

Clapham Picturehouse

76 Venn Street, SW4 0AT (0871 704 2059/ www.picturehouses.co.uk). Clapham Common tube/35, 37 bus. **Open** *Box office (by phone) 9.30am-8.30pm daily; (in person) noon-8.30pm daily. Film club activities 11.15am, screening 11.45am Sat.* **Tickets** £6.50-£8.50; £5 3-15s; reductions for film club. **Membership** £4/yr. **Credit** AmEx, MC, V.

Kids' film clubs and parent-and-baby screenings were pioneered at this stylish cinema. Parents can bring infants under one year to the long-running Big Scream! club (10.30am Thursday) to watch a movie from an updated roster of blockbuster and art-house films without having to worry about disturbing the audience. The Kids' Club offers Saturday matinées for three- to ten-year-olds. Staff organise craft and activity workshops before the show and prize competitions after. Young members can go into the projection room and start the film as a birthday treat.
Buggy access. Café. Disabled access: toilet. Nappy-changing facilities.

Electric Cinema

191 Portobello Road, W11 2ED (7908 9696/ www.the-electric.co.uk). Ladbroke Grove or Notting Hill Gate tube/52 bus. **Open** *Box office 9am-8.30pm Mon-Sat; 10am-8.30pm Sun. Children's screenings Sat; phone to check times.* **Tickets** *Children's films* £5 over-3s. *Workshops* £3. **Credit** AmEx, MC, V. **Map** p310 A7.

With its luxurious trimmings (leather seating, footstools and tables), this is a most attractive cinema. Become a member (call for prices) to get access to the restaurant and private rooms and two free tickets for every Kids' Club screening; otherwise, you can just pay per film. Electric Scream! parent-and-baby shows are held at 3pm on Mondays (except bank holidays).
Buggy access. Disabled access: lift, toilet.

Greenwich Picturehouse

180 Greenwich High Road, SE10 8NN (08707 550056/www.picturehouses.co.uk). Cutty Sark DLR/Greenwich rail/DLR. **Open** *Box office (by phone) 9.30am-8.30pm daily; (in person) 11am-10pm daily. Kids' Club 11am Sat.* **Tickets** £5-£10; £5 under-14s; reductions for film club. **Membership** £4.50/yr. **Credit** AmEx, MC, V.

The four-screen Greenwich branch of the right-on Picturehouse chain has a tapas bar, and a children's club on Saturday mornings, with Big Scream! at 11.30am on Wednesday and Friday.
Buggy access. Café. Disabled access: lift, toilet. Kiosk. Nappy-changing facilities. Restaurant.

Rio Cinema

103-107 Kingsland High Street, E8 2PB (7241 9410/www.riocinema.co.uk). Dalston Kingsland rail/Liverpool Street tube/rail, then 67, 77, 149 bus. **Open** *Box office 2-8pm daily. Film club 4.15pm Tue; 11am Sat.* **Tickets** £6-£8; £5 2-16s; reductions for film club. **Credit** AmEx, MC, V.

The Rio is an affordable place where Kids' Club members are given a card to be stamped on each visit, (free visit after ten stamps). A parent-and-baby club operates on some Tuesday and Thursday lunchtimes. In the holidays there's a daily matinée for five- to 15-year-olds.
Buggy access. Café. Disabled access: ramp, toilet.

Ritzy Cinema

Brixton Oval, Coldharbour Lane, SW2 1JG (0870 755 0062/www.picturehouses.co.uk). Brixton tube/rail. **Open** *Box office (by phone) 9.30am-9.15pm daily; (in person) 12.15-9.15pm daily. Film club 10.30am Sat.* **Tickets** £6.50-£8.50; £4.50-£5 under-14s; reductions for film club. **Membership** £3/yr. **Credit** AmEx, MC, V.

Opened in 1911, Brixton's Ritzy has survived numerous owners, near-demolition and development in the 1990s to become one of London's finest. Now it's in the Picturehouse family. The Big Scream! is on Fridays at 11am, open to parents with under-ones.
Buggy access. Café. Disabled access: lift, toilet. Nappy-changing facilities.

Stratford East Picturehouse

Theatre Square, Salway Road, E15 1BX (0870 755 0064/www.picturehouses.co.uk). Stratford tube/rail/DLR. **Open** *Box office (by phone) 9am-9pm daily. Film club 10.30am Sat.* **Tickets** £6-£7; £4.40 18mths-14s; reductions for film club. Half-price all day Mon. **Membership** £4/yr. **Credit** AmEx, MC, V.

Musical youth

In a perfect world, all children would receive a stimulating musical education at school. Sadly, that's rarely true in these SAT-obsessed days. If you're less than impressed by your child's music classes at school, encourage the head to visit www.musicplatform.co.uk. The good people of the Platform go into schools to explore music with those who wouldn't normally get the opportunity. They promise 'a fun experience' in 'an engaging, lively setting that is as enjoyable for the teachers and parents as it is for the children involved. Laughing, shouting, cheering are all part of the experience.'

Otherwise, here are our top tips for a great musical education outside school.

Centre for Young Musicians
See p174.
The Saturday classes at this college-based centre for children who have already begun to learn an instrument are highly prized. You can also book for family concerts (£6-£9) at Morley College; running from 10.30am to 12.30pm on one Saturday a month from October to May, they are open to all ages.

Junior Guildhall
See p176.
Advanced training in music and drama is provided for pupils between four and 18 years. Aimed at skilled pupils who are looking to develop careers in music, around 250 students attend the main music course, which runs from 9am to 6pm on Saturdays. Other weekly classes and workshops feature jazz, composition, vocals, music awareness and electronic studio classes, all of which can lead to performances as part of the Junior Guildhall String Ensemble, the Symphony Orchestra, Brass Band and a series of ensemble groups for flute, piano, clarinet and other instruments.

Junior Trinity
See p176.
Sitting in the historic grounds of the Old Royal Naval College at Greenwich, this is a consistently popular option for Saturday schooling. Open for three- to 19-year-olds, a broad range of classes take place in over 70 practice and teaching rooms, with small and large ensembles performing for weekly lunchtime concerts. The main

learning programme encompasses 30 teaching weeks a year (with a week off for half term), with classes running from 8 or 9am to 5pm. String Time for three- to 11-year-olds combine musical technique, creative musicianship and ensemble playing. Learning string instruments begins with the String Starters level and progresses through to Stepping Stones and Rhythm Runners for classes in the viola, double bass or harp. Full-body music training comes under the tongue-twisting title of Dalcroze Eurythmics and features full-body movement to music to connect the ear, brain and limbs so that the mind and body learns to react to music to increase creative development.

Music House for Children
See p176.
Music House's philosophy of 'Music for life' matches its comprehensive approach to music, with sessions for newborns, toddlers, children and young adults. Small classes in popular instruments – guitar, keyboards, percussion and drums – are available, as are beginner-sized harps, which can be hired for £40 for three

months. There's also one-to-one home tuition in piano, violin, viola, cello, double bass, clarinet, oboe, guitar and drums, and in-house classes for small groups. Pupils can go on to graded exams or solo performances in the Edwardian hall.

Suzuki Method
See p176.
Violinist Shinichi Suzuki invented his learning process in the mid 20th century. The method promotes music learning for young children who are taught to play instruments in the same way as language learning. At the London Suzuki Group, listening, absorbing and copying are encouraged by specially trained teachers. Courses in violin, piano and cello take place in teaching groups in venues across London – all at £125 a term. Five years of age is the usual starting point and, in the way that books are usually presented to children a long while after they've grasped the notion of speech, much of the initial Suzuki experience involves young children watching and listening to older children playing. Showcase concerts take place in the spring, often at Cadogan Hall, SW1.

Activities

Music House for Children

Attractions for families and children include a film club where creative activities, fun and games take place before a screening. The club is suitable for three- to ten-year-olds and membership entitles you to the first film free. *Bar. Buggy access. Disabled access: lift, ramp, toilet. Nappy-changing facilities.*

DANCE

Discos & clubs

Over the last couple of years underage discos, especially parent-and-baby grooves, have exploded on to the scene. Sceptics might say it's a sign that children are growing up too fast while their parents can't bear to grow up at all. Whatever. Anyway, everyone's raving, babbling, dribbling and boogieing away, thanks to the organisations below. Note that clubs, underage or otherwise, are naturally transient affairs, so check the website to see where special events are taking place if no venue has been listed.

Babygroove
www.babygroove.co.uk.
Launched in 2007, this showcases funky house sounds for families in venues around town.

Baby loves disco
www.babylovesdisco.co.uk.
Parent-and-baby bopping organised by BLD takes place once a month at the Clapham Grand (21-25 St John's Hill, SW11 1TT, 7223 6523).

Disco Loco
Chats Palace Arts Centre, 42-44 Brooksby's Walk, E9 6DF (8533 0227/www.chatspalace. com). Homerton rail. **Tickets** £1; £4 3-10s.
A hip and hugely popular second-Sunday-of-the-month event underpinned by the belief that adults and children really can enjoy good music together. Food and drink are available too.

Mothers' Pride
Enquiries 0333 444 0321.
Funk, hip hop, indie, house music for five to 12-year olds, a bar selling own-made burgers and ice-cream, all organised by DJs Sarah and Vicky, both mummies who work in the music industry. MP was due to launch as we went to press (Sat 5 July 2008 official launch date) at Dingwalls, Camden and continue on selected Saturdays (ring for details). Admission is £10.

Planet Angel
www.planetangel.net.
Planet Angel Chilled has been running in north London since 2001. It aims to create a positive, safe, social environment for children of all ages.

Whirl-Y-Gig
www.whirl-y-gig.org.uk.
A collective that has has welcomed families to its festival-club events for more than 26 years. A favourite venue is Jacks Club (7-9 Crucifix Lane, SE1 3JW). Under-18s can attend with a parent, but this needs to be arranged in advance.

Tuition

Chisenhale Dance Space
64-84 Chisenhale Road, E3 5QZ (8981 6617/www.chisenhaledancespace.co.uk). Mile End tube. **Fees** £36/£24 reductions 2-8s; £54/£32 reductions 9-11s. **Credit** MC, V.
This long-running east London specialist in movement arts and independent dance offers a range of creative dance classes for children aged two to eight, as well as Performance Project (jazz, urban, contemporary salsa and more) for ages nine to 11. See the website for details on skills and confidence-building.

Dance Attic
368 North End Road, SW6 1LY (7610 2055/ www.danceattic.com). Fulham Broadway tube. **Fees** £2/day, £40/6mths, £70/yr; £15/6 mths, £25/yr 13-16s; free under-13s. **Classes** £5-£6. *Children's ballet £50-£62/11wk term.* **Credit** MC, V.
Ballet (for over-threes) goes from beginner to Intermediate Foundation level, with RADA exams at each level. There's also a shop stocking dancewear for children.

Danceworks
16 Balderton Street, W1K 6TN (7629 6183/ www.danceworks.net). Bond Street or Marble Arch tube. **Classes** times vary; phone for details. **Fees** *Membership* £2-£2.50/day; £69/year. *Classes* £5-£8/class. **Credit** AmEx, MC, V.
Europe's largest selection of dance classes (as well as pilates and martial arts) take place in six studios in this listed building.

Diddidance
07973 982790/www.diddidance.com.
Songs, actions, dancing games exploring all styles of dance and movement for two- to four-year-olds, taking place in venues throughout the city. Diddidance parties can also be arranged.

East London Dance

*Stratford Circus, Theatre Square, E15 1BX
(8279 1050/www.eastlondondance.org).
Stratford tube/rail.* **Classes** times vary; phone
for details. **Fees** free. **No credit cards**.
Brazilian samba, street dance and creative,
contemporary styles are favoured by this
creative community.

Greenwich Dance Agency

*Borough Hall, Royal Hill, SE10 8RE (8293
9741/www.greenwichdance.org.uk). Greenwich
rail.* **Classes** times vary; phone for details
Fees *Drop-in* £2.50 13-20s; £3.80 under-5s.
Courses £19-£26.60/term 6-12s. **Credit** MC, V.
This popular dance agency in South-east
London offers a programme of activities for
children and young people called NRgDANCE.
Activities are organised according to age-
groups, from zero to 20. The aim is to let
participants, especially the young who get bored
easily, to try out a variety of dance styles. The
focus is on creativity and having fun.

Laban

*Creekside, SE8 3DZ (8691 8600/www.laban.
org). Cutty Sark DLR/Deptford rail.* **Classes
& fees** times & prices vary; phone for details.
Credit MC, V.
This is the largest and best equipped
contemporary dance school in Europe. There's
a long waiting list to join the performance,
contemporary dance and music classes, for all
ages, that run throughout the week. The award-
winning modern building, designed by Herzog
& de Meuron, which shimmers handsomely
next to muddy old Deptford Creek, is a pleasure
to visit. Once your child is in a class, however,
the educational experience is fantastic. Young
children are encouraged to explore inventive
movement, and the annual Children's Show
presents work by students aged four to 14, is
always booked up by proud parents. Laban has
twinned with Trinity College of Music *(see
p176)* in Greenwich to form Trinity Laban, the
UK's first conservatoire for music and dance.

London Dance Network

www.londondance.com.
A useful one-stop resource for all things to do
with dance in the capital, including a directory
of venues and organisations across the city that
offer classes for children of all ages and abilities.

Pineapple Performing Arts School

*7 Langley Street, WC2H 9JA (8351 8839/
www.pineapplearts.com). Covent Garden tube.*

Classes *Drop-in* 1-2pm (under-13s), 2-3pm
(12-16s) Sat; 1-2pm (12-16s), 2-3pm (under-13s)
Sun. *Term classes* 11am-noon (3-4s), 11am-
2pm (5-12s), 2-5pm (14-18s) Sun. **Fees** £90/
12wk term 3-4s; £295/12wk term over-4s;
£6 drop-in session; £195 holiday course.
Trial class £25. *Registration fee* £30-£35.
Credit MC, V. **Map** p315 L6.
Drop-in street-dancing classes are held here
every weekend; you just turn up, pay £6 and
dance in these legendary Covent Garden studios.
Otherwise, children can sign up for a lively
Sunday School, comprising Pineapple Chunks
for tiny dancers, junior classes for kids and early
teens, and senior classes for 14- to 18-year-olds.
There are also dance courses held during the
Easter and summer holidays.

The Place

*17 Duke's Road, WC1H 9PY (box office 7121
1100/classes 7121 1090/www.theplace.org.uk).
Euston tube/rail.* **Classes** times vary; phone
for details. **Fees** from £85-£95/11wk term;
£5 discount for 2nd or subsequent class taken
by same student or a sibling. **Credit** MC, V.
Map p315 K3.
Parents and children queue up to use this 300-
seat dance venue and studios. The ethos is that
anyone can learn to dance; the centre is
accessible to all ages, as well as to the disabled.
There is, however, a waiting list. The Saturday
programme offers classes, with live music, for
five- to 18-year-olds, combining imaginative,
free-form expression with fundamental dance
techniques. Shift, an exciting company of young
dancers aged between 13 and 19, meets twice
weekly during term time (Monday and
Thursday, 6-8pm) to perform work by a range
of choreographers. Auditions are held every
September. For more on kids' classes, phone or
email children@theplace.org.uk.

Royal Academy of Dance

*36 Battersea Square, SW11 3RA (7326
8000/www.rad.org.uk). Clapham Junction rail.*
Classes times vary; phone for details.
Fees £6-£12.50/class; £60-£154/term.
Credit AmEx, MC, V.
All sorts of dance styles, from boogie to ballet,
are offered at the RAD, whose services cover
kids aged from two to 16. They hold summer
workshops, private lessons and courses.
Activities include West End Jazz for eight- to 18-
year-olds, tap for nine- to 16-year-olds, creative
dance for little ones aged five to nine,
contemporary for ten- to 16-year-olds and an
awful lot more. Check out www.radacadabra.org
for more information.

Activities (sidebar)

It's more than just a wonderful life at the **BFI Southbank**'s Fun Day. *See p165.*

Venues

See also **Chisenhale Dance Space**
(*see p170*), **Laban** and **The Place**
(for both, *see p171*).

Royal Opera House

*Bow Street, WC2E 9DD (box office 7304
4000/www.royaloperahouse.org). Covent
Garden tube.* **Open** *Box office* 10am-8pm Mon-
Sat. *Tours* daily (times vary, book in advance).
Tours £9; £7 9-16s. **Credit** AmEx, MC, V.
Map p317 L6.
Home of the Royal Ballet as well as one of the
world's great opera houses, the ROH is
anything but stuffy. Its glass ceilings make it a
bright and airy space; free recital tasters
happen regularly and the upstairs café offers
terraced seating with fantastic views over the
crowds and street entertainers in Covent
Garden. Look out for child-friendly Christmas
shows such as the *Nutcracker*.
*Bar. Buggy access. Café. Disabled access: lift,
toilet. Nappy-changing facilities. Nearest
picnic place: St Paul's Churchyard.
Restaurant. Shop.*

Sadlers Wells

*Rosebery Avenue, EC1R 4TN (0844 412
4300/www.sadlerswells.com). Angel tube.*
Open *Box office* 9am-8.30pm Mon-Sat.
Credit MC, V.
Sadlers Wells is the epicentre of dance in
London. The dazzling complex also provides a
home for Matthew Bourne's New Adventures
and Wayne McGregor's Random Dance. The
adjacent Lilian Bayliss Theatre offers new work
and theatre on a smaller scale and the Peacock
Theatre (Portugal Street, WC2A 2HT, 0844 412
4322) is a satellite venue for Sadlers Wells,
where family shows take place every Christmas.
Check the website for details of occasional
family workshops.
*Bar. Buggy access. Cafés. Disabled access:
infra-red hearing system, lift, toilet. Nappy-
changing facilities. Restaurant.*

Siobhan Davies Dance Studios

*85 St George's Road, SE1 6ER (7091 9650/
www.siobhandavies.com). Elephant & Castle
tube/rail.* **Open** 9am-9pm Mon-Fri; 9am-4pm
Sat, Sun. **Credit** MC, V.
This beautiful new dance centre was opened in
2006, when it won an architecture award. Check
the website for details of shows.
*Buggy access. Disabled access: lift, toilet.
Nappy-changing facilities.*

LITERATURE

Libraries

See also p188 **And now read on…**

British Library

*96 Euston Road, NW1 2DB (7412 7676/
Learning 7412 7797/www.bl.uk). Euston or
King's Cross tube/rail.* **Open** 9.30am-6pm
Mon, Wed-Fri; 9.30am-8pm Tue; 9.30am-5pm
Sat; 11am-5pm Sun, bank hols. **Credit** MC, V.
Map p317 K3.
In the digital age, libraries are no longer the
magnet for kids that they once were, but the
British Library bucks the trend. The national
library has a collection of more than 154 million
pieces of writing, from primitive etchings on
bone and papyrus to modern sound recordings
and handwritten lyrics from the Beatles. Every
year, the library receives a copy of everything
published in the UK and Ireland, including
books, newspapers, magazines, maps, prints
and drawings. For those who enjoy statistics,
the library contains 388 miles (625km) of
shelves and the collection spans 2,300 years of
human creativity.
 The main attraction for youngsters is not the
vast reference collection – which is kept behind
closed doors and only released to registered
readers – but the museum's unique collection of
national treasures. Displayed in the dimly lit Sir
John Ritblat Gallery are such literary wonders
as the original manuscript of *Beowulf*, Lewis
Carroll's diary and the *Codex Sinaiticus*, the
oldest bible outside the Vatican, along with
reams of illustrated medieval scriptures, framed
by writhing supernatural creatures. In the
centre of the gallery is a small room containing
the original Magna Carta signed by King John
in 1215. Lighting is kept low for conservation
purposes, but you can scroll through a digital
scan of the manuscript.
 Temporary exhibitions are held in the
Pearson Gallery – the focus for 2008 is the epic
Hindu poem, the *Ramayana*, which also forms
the basis for a series of children's workshops in
shadow puppetry and Indonesian traditional
music. From October 2008, the attention will
shift to 'Taking Liberties', exploring the concept
of citizenship and the arguments for and
against a British constitution. A smaller gallery
in the entrance hall contains interactive displays
on music and culture linked to the National
Sound Archives. Older children may be
interested in the free tours of the conservation
centre (2pm Thursday – advance booking
essential). The library education department

Activities

arranges regular storytelling sessions and hands-on workshops, for schools during term time and for families during the school holidays – see www.bl.uk/learning for more information. *Buggy access. Café. Disabled access: lift, toilet. Nappy-changing facilities. Nearest picnic place: St James's Gardens. Restaurant. Shop.*

Charlton House
Charlton Road, SE7 8RE (8856 3951/ www.greenwich.gov.uk). Charlton rail/53, 54, 380, 422 bus. **Open** *Library* 2-7pm Mon, Thur; 10am-12.30pm, 1.30-5.30pm Tue, Fri; 10am-12.30pm, 1.30-5pm Sat. *Toy Library* (term time only) 9.30am-12.30pm, Mon, Tue, Fri (2-5s); 9.30am-12.30pm Thur (under-2s). **Admission** free. **No credit cards.**
One of Britain's finest examples of Jacobean domestic architecture, this handsome house was built between 1607 and 1612 by Sir Adam Newton. These days it's a community centre and library, but glimpses of its glorious past can be seen in the creaky oak staircase, marble fireplaces and ornate plaster ceilings. The library has a good children's section (activities take place 10.30am Mon) and is also home to the Charlton Toy Library (8319 0055, www.charlton toylibrary.co.uk). The mulberry tree outside, dating from 1608, still bears fruit that sometimes finds its way into crumbles, cakes and chutneys that are sold in the Mulberry Café. Visit at 1pm on a Friday and you'll be treated to a free concert by musicians from the Trinity College of Music, who also puts on a soaring Christmas concert.
Buggy access. Café. Disabled access: lift, ramp, toilet. Nappy-changing facilities. Nearest picnic area: Charlton House grounds.

Idea Store
321 Whitechapel Road, E1 1BU (7364 4332/ www.ideastore.co.uk). Whitechapel tube. **Open** 9am-9pm Mon-Thur; 9am-6pm Fri; 9am-5pm Sat; 11am-5pm Sun.
This striking, rectangular building is one of several Idea Stores, a flagship project of Tower Hamlets Council. The ultra-modern interior offers a café and state-of-the-art learning and information services. For children over 16-years old, Idea Stores offer over 900 courses in subjects such as dance, music, languages, cookery, creative arts, textiles and fashion.
Buggy access. Café. Crèche. Disabled access: lift, toilet. Nappy-changing facilities.
Other locations 1 Gladstone Place, Roman Road, E3 5ES (7364 5775); 1 Vesey Path, East India Dock Road, E14 6BT (7364 1502); Churchill Place, E14 5RB (7364 1260).

Peckham Library
122 Peckham Hill Street, SE15 5JR (7525 0200/www.southwark.gov.uk). Peckham Rye or Queen's Road rail/12, 36, 63, 171 bus. **Open** 9am-8pm Mon, Tue, Thur, Fri; 10am-8pm Wed; 10am-5pm Sat; noon-4pm Sun. **No credit cards.**
Family activities that take place inside Will Alsop's unusual-looking library include creative baby and toddler sessions and the Sure Start reading group for under-fives. Monday and Friday bring in the Homework Club (4-7pm), and craft sessions are held on Tuesday after school. In addition, there are monthly meetings of the Teenage Reading Group. An extended programme of holiday workshops is also run. The square outside hosts a regular farmers' market on Sundays (9.30am-1.30pm).
Buggy access. Disabled access: lift, toilet. Nappy-changing facilities.

MUSIC

Tuition
See also p168 **Musical youth.**

Blackheath Conservatoire
19-21 Lee Road, SE3 9RQ (8852 0234/ www.conservatoire.org.uk). Blackheath rail. **Fees** from £96/term. **Credit** MC, V.
Children aged from five can enrol to learn a musical instrument. They are taught in groups of three or four and also receive a free book and CD, so they can practise at home. Kids can also join the choir and take part in music, drama and art courses all year round.

Blueberry
Contact Centre, 60 Hambalt Road, SW4 9EH (8677 6871/www.blueberry.clara.co.uk). Clapham South tube. **Fees** from £60/10-wk term. **No credit cards.**
These lovely little music groups take place in many areas across London. In the weekly parent-and-toddler groups (ages nine months to three years), parents have a good sing-song and guide their offspring through the actions. Big Kids Blueberry (two- to four-year-olds) builds on the singing with more games, but without the aged Ps. For Blueberry birthday parties, *see p145.*

Centre for Young Musicians
Morley College, 61 Westminster Bridge Road, SE1 7HT (7928 3844/www.cym.org.uk). Lambeth North tube. **Classes** 9am-5pm Sat term-time only. **Fees** vary. **No credit cards.**

Activities

families
Have great days out at Tate

A visit to Tate is child's play...

Let your children's imagination run riot at Tate! Whether it's your first visit with your children or you've been before, there's loads to do for everyone.

Sign up for free families email bulletins at www.tate.org.uk/bulletins

Tate Britain
Millbank
London SW1P 4RG
⊖ Pimlico or Vauxhall
🚤 Millbank Pier

Daily 10.00–17.50

BP British Art Displays 1500–2008

Supported by BP

Tate Modern
Bankside
London SE1 9TG
⊖ Southwark or Blackfriars
🚤 Bankside Pier

Sun – Thurs, 10.00–18.00
Fri and Sat, 10.00–22.00

Opening up art
Tate Modern Collection with UBS

 UBS

Call 020 7887 8888
www.tate.org.uk/families

The Main Centre and its two satellite annexes – Notre Dame High School (three minutes' walk from Morley College) and Johanna Primary School (percussion faculty only) – are open to children who already play an instrument and are attending school, or are in a gap year. Students have to audition for a place, and auditions are held at all stages of learning, although absolute beginners are discouraged from applying.

Guildhall School of Music & Drama

Silk Street, EC2Y 8DT (7628 2571/www. gsmd.ac.uk). Barbican tube/Moorgate tube/rail. **Classes** 9am-6pm Sat. **Fees** basic course from £2,090/term. **Credit** MC, V.

This world-class conservatoire runs the coveted Junior Guildhall instrumental training for gifted children on Saturday mornings. Entry is by audition, and standards are extremely high. A String Training Programme for newcomers aged four to 11 includes instrumental training and music appreciation. Talented musicians who can't afford the fee can apply for local authority grants or Guildhall scholarship funding. The Guildhall's Drama Course (13- to 18-year-olds) involves a more informal audition process.

London Suzuki Group

01372 720088/www.londonsuzukigroup.co.uk. **Fees** from £30/hr. **No credit cards**.

Dr Shinichi Suzuki's belief that talent is inherent in all newborn children inspired a ground-breaking school of music in Japan. This led to the foundation of the London Suzuki Group in 1972; its teachers (covering violin, cello and piano) apply Dr Suzuki's methods to enhance the natural ability of children aged from three. The key is learning through listening, and then playing for pleasure. Classes are held after school and at weekends, and are for members only. A Day Bonanza for kids includes group lessons and musical games. To find a teacher in your area, check the website.

Musical Express

Southfields Methodist Church, 423 Durnsford Road, SW19 8EE; Wimbledon Rugby Club, Barham Road, Copse Hill, SW20 0ET (8946 6043/www.musicalexpress.co.uk). **Classes** times vary; phone for details. **Fees** 1st session free, then from £6/lesson. **No credit cards**.

Flautist and music therapist Jenny Tabori's music groups are for babies and pre-schoolers, giving tinies the means to express themselves and develop social skills, with instruments and 'action songs'. Parents and carers stay and share the experience throughout each session, lasting 40-60 minutes. Musical Jolly Phonics on Wednesday, in which children learn their initial sounds with an accompanying action, are an entertaining way of introducing reading skills in young children.

Music House for Children

Bush Hall, 310 Uxbridge Road, W12 7LJ (8932 2652/www.musichouseforchildren.co.uk). Shepherd's Bush tube. **Classes** times vary; phone for details. **Fees** £6/drop-in class; from £45/5wk course. **Credit** MC, V.

From drop-in music and movement classes for toddlers to music technology Saturday clubs for teens – with classes in piano, percussion, recorder, violin, guitar and music appreciation in between – the Bush House is a broad musical church. The Music House has over 200 home tutors on its books. Holiday workshops encompass many age groups and interests.

Royal College of Music

Prince Consort Road, SW7 2BS (7589 3643/ www.rcm.ac.uk). South Kensington tube/9, 10, 52, 452 bus. **Open** 9am-5pm Mon-Fri. **Classes/fees** phone for details. **Credit** MC, V. **Map** p313 D9.

The RCM's junior tuition is aimed at students 'of an exceptionally high standard'. Applications (for children aged eight to 17) are by audition and are heavily oversubscribed. Lessons – 8am-5pm Saturday, run in conjunction with the school term – focus almost exclusively on classical instruments. For inspiration, check the website for details of (usually free) performances staged by pupils throughout the year.

Buggy access. Café. Disabled access: lift, toilet.

Trinity College of Music

King Charles Court, Old Royal Naval College, SE10 9JF (8305 4444/www.tcm.ac.uk). Cutty Sark DLR. **Classes** 9am-6pm Sat. **Fees** £650/term. **No credit cards**.

Trinity College was the first UK conservatoire to open its doors to schoolchildren on Saturdays, back in 1906. Junior Trinity (for three- to 19-year-olds) encourages the creative aspects of music-making, in improvisation, composition and vocal work. String Time, a special programme for young players aged from three to 11, also takes place on Saturday mornings. Groups are divided by age into Trinity Teenies, Stepping Stones and Fast Fiddlers. Open Days, in which you can see Junior Trinity in action, take place every term. Auditions are held in March and May.

Activities

Play's been framed

It started with the humble ball pool. Then someone decided to attach a slide, a tunnel, some punching bags, a climbing frame… until you have what is known as a play frame. These indoor playgrounds are scattered around the capital – *see p178* **Indoor play centres** for details. Most, such as **Zoomaround**, **Bramley's Big Adventure** and the huge **Discovery Planet** are big venues filled with play frames; some, like **Eddie Catz** and **It's A Kids Thing** have classes and workshops alongside; and others, like **Gambado** and **Kidspace** have enlarged the play frame into an all-round adventure, with go-karts and fairground rides.

It seems you either love them or hate them. Fans cite the exhausting exercise their children get without encountering rain or gravel; the safety of an enclosed soft play area; and most valuable of all, the chance to let kids play while you get quality time with your partner or friends. Or even with your laptop, as most play frames have wireless internet access.

Detractors point out that the play frames get grubby and noisy, and children can run riot and overheat in these unsupervised dens. Also, with the city's free parks, playgrounds and One O'Clock Clubs – why pay to entertain your child?

It's possibly an age thing. Parents of children old enough to run about without assistance appreciate being freed up to read the newspaper, and declare that playframes are magic for birthday parties. Parents of toddlers, however, may be overwhelmed by the wild atmosphere of weekends, and disheartened by the lonely pottering of weekdays.

Safety campaigners are concerned that the frames lull parents into a false sense of freedom. It is rare to climb inside these structures without finding some crying child hidden in a corner while mummy reads the latest Martina Cole elsewhere. In the US, ball pools are hastily being removed from play centres because of cleanliness concerns. That's not to say that the great outdoors is any safer – no matter how dirty a ball pool gets, it's not as insanitary as falling in a duck pond.

The experience is often improved if you climb in with your kids. Kidspace is, unusually, made of wood, and has been made precarious on purpose to force parents to get in and play with their children. This may seem totally against the point for those who prize their peaceful cappuccino, but the atmosphere is strikingly happier. It is not unusual to see kids having lunch while dad is still rolling around the Thunderball City.

The Kidspace website predicts a future of high-street play centres competing for our membership just like adult gym chains. At least with play frames you won't have to force yourself to go – instead, you'll have an enthusiastic child dragging you down twice a week.

Activities

Venues

English National Opera

The Coliseum, St Martin's Lane, WC2N 4ES (education 7632 8484/box office 7632 8300/www.eno.org). Leicester Square tube. **Open** *Box office* 10am-8pm Mon-Sat. **Tickets** £10-£83. **Credit** AmEx, MC, V. **Map** p315 L7.
Given the doughty ENO's beginnings as an artistic outlet for the poor (thanks to the 19th-century philanthropist Lilian Baylis and her aunt), it seems only right that the institution should have a reputation for sparky accessibility. Central to the outreach work of the ENO Baylis department are its enjoyable Family Days, and dedicated Clore Education Room. Workshops offer kids aged seven and above, their families and carers a chance to explore the ENO's current production. Family opera packages are also available for the matinée performance. Check the website for details of courses, such as 'takepart!', a music theatre programme for those aged seven to 18, based at St Marylebone School in Central London (7935 9501).
Buggy access. Disabled access: lift, ramp, toilet.

Roundhouse

Chalk Farm Road, NW1 8EH (7424 9991/ box office 0870 389 1846/www.roundhouse .org.uk). Chalk Farm or Camden Town tube. **Open** *Box office* 11am-6pm Mon-Sat. **Tickets** £10-£25. **Credit** MC, V.
In the 1960s and '70s, this former railway engine shed became legendary for staging concerts by the likes of Led Zeppelin and Jimi Hendrix. While not all the shows in its latest sleek incarnation are for families, creative opportunities for young people lie at the heart of the Roundhouse Studios. *Bars. Café. Disabled access: ramp, toilet. Nappy-changing facilities.*

Royal Albert Hall

Kensington Gore, SW7 2AP (7589 8212/ www.royalalberthall.com). South Kensington, Knightsbridge tube. **Open** *Box office* 9am-9pm daily. **Tickets** £5-£150. **Credit** AmEx, MC, V. **Map** p313 D9.
This 5,000-capacity rotunda, built as a memorial to Queen Victoria's beloved husband, hosts the annual BBC Proms from July to September. Two Blue Peter Proms and the outdoor Proms In The Park extend this classical music extravaganza to younger audiences. The smart education department has projects aimed at children and local students.
Bars. Buggy access. Café. Disabled access: lift, ramp, toilet. Nappy-changing facilities. Restaurants. Shop.

Wigmore Hall

36 Wigmore Street, W1U 2BP (7935 2141/ education 7258 8227/www.wigmore-hall. org.uk). Bond Street or Oxford Circus tube. **Open** *Box office* 10am-5pm daily (8pm on performance nights). **Tickets** £10-£25. **Credit** AmEx, DC, MC, V. **Map** p314 H5.
This art deco recital hall has endured a great deal over the years, not least two world wars. Thankfully, the interior remains virtually unaltered, with marble, wooden panelling and plush red seating. There's a programme of family, community and outreach projects. Chamber Tots – music and movement classes for two- to five-year-olds – is the best-known series, and always sells out. For fives and over, two family-themed activity days are held each term (£3 children, £6 adults). These include such highly praised events as Discover Your Voice, where choral leader Gillian Dibden teaches vocal techniques to families, through works ranging from African music to modern classical songs.
Buggy access. Disabled access: toilet. Nappy-changing facilities. Restaurant.

PLAYTIME

See also p177 **Play's been framed** and *p194* **Telling stories**.

Indoor play centres

Bramley's Big Adventure

136 Bramley Road, W10 6TJ (8960 1515/ www.bramleysbig.co.uk). Latimer Road tube. **Open** *Term-time* 10am-6pm Mon-Fri; 10am-6.30pm Sat, Sun. *Holidays* 10am-6.30pm daily. **Membership** £15/yr. **Admission** *Members* £2/£2.50 under-2s; £3.50/£4 2-5s; £4/£4.50 over-5s. *Non-members* £3/£3.50 under-2s; £4.50/£5 2-5s; £5/£5.50 over-5s. Under-1s free with older child. **Credit** AmEx, MC, V.
Silence is unheard of at Bramley's, the largest indoor playground in central London. For a start, it's under the Westway flyover. But the real noise comes from inside, where a huge three-level play frame with slides, ball pools, swings, climbs, spooky den, giant balls and sound effects makes it tot paradise. There are separate under-fives and baby areas, and the café offers organic and healthy grub. Ask about children's parties, which include meals and party bags. Parents can catch up on work while the children run wild; there's free Wi-Fi.
Buggy access. Café. Disabled access: toilet. Nappy-changing facilities.

Activities

Discovery Planet

1st floor, Surrey Quays Shopping Centre, Redriff Road, SE16 7LL (7237 2388/ www.discovery-planet.co.uk). Canada Water tube. **Open** 10am-6pm Mon-Sat; 11am-5pm Sun. **Admission** 2-10s £3.99 Mon-Fri; £4.99 Sat, Sun; under-2s £3.49 Mon-Fri; £4.49 Sat, Sun. **Credit** (over £10) MC, V.

This huge indoor area filled with brightly coloured tubes, tunnels, ball ponds and slides gives children two-hour sessions of climbing, sliding, bashing and throwing themselves about. Check the website for party information.
Buggy access. Disabled access: lift, toilet. Nappy-changing facilities.

Eddie Catz

68-70 High Street, SW15 1SF (0845 201 1268/www.eddiecatz.com). Putney Bridge tube. **Open** 9.30am-6.30pm Mon-Sat; 10am-5pm Sun. **Admission** £5.50 over-3s; £5 under-3s; £4 under-2s; free under 8mths. **Credit** MC, V.

This first-floor play centre and café is a big, bright, clean space, bordered by windows and mirrors, where children have access to interactive video games, table ice-hockey and a themed adventure play frame. An innovative workshop programme includes 'Mad Science', which gives kids a chance to build rockets and robots – themes vary, so check the website. Eddie Catz has also taken over Wimbledon's Tiger's Eye.
Buggy access. Café. Disabled access: lift, toilet. Nappy-changing facilities. Shop.
Other locations 42 Station Road, SW19 2LP (8288 8178).

Gambado

7 Station Court, Townmead Road, SW6 2PY (7384 1635/www.gambado.com). Fulham Broadway tube/391 bus. **Open** 9.30am-6.30pm daily. **Admission** (2.5hr session) £2.50 adults; £9.45 3-10s; £7.45 1-2s; free under-1s. **Credit** MC, V.

Located near the new Imperial Wharf development, Gambado's is very popular – at weekends the place is usually full of birthday parties – even though it's expensive (this is Fulham, after all). There's a giant multi-level climbing frame, ball ponds, slides (enclosed twirly tunnels plus bumpy ones large enough for parents to join in), trampolines, assault courses and even mini dodgems. Tinies get a soft-play section with big Lego bricks and face-painting. You can refuel at the café, and there's free internet access for the adults.
Buggy access. Café. Disabled access: toilet. Nappy-changing facilities.

It's a Kid's Thing

279 Magdalen Road, SW18 3NZ (8739 0909/ www.itsakidsthing.co.uk). Earlsfield rail. **Open** 9am-6pm daily. **Admission** £5 over-2s; £4 under-2s; £2 siblings under 2yrs. Prices of activities vary; check website for details. **Credit** MC, V.

An award-winning family-run indoor adventure play centre, with a two-tier playzone and a soft-play area. Parents can keep a watchful eye from the café, which offers nursery food for all ages, or bury themselves in the free daily papers. There's also an fun programme of activities (such as capoeira, and 'soca tots' for 6-month olds) and a party room. It's a popular spot, so book ahead.
Buggy access. Café. Disabled: toilet. Nappy-changing facilities.

Kidspace

Colonnades, 619 Purley Way, Croydon, Surrey CR0 4RQ (8686 0040/www.kidspace adventures.com). Waddon rail/119, 289 bus. **Open** *Term-time* 9.30am-7pm Mon-Thur; 9.30am-8pm Fri; 9am-8pm Sat; 9am-7pm Sun. *Holidays* 9am-7pm Mon-Thur, Sun; 9am-8pm Fri, Sat. **Admission** *Weekdays* £5.50; £2.50 adults; free under-1s. Adult with sole under-1 £3.50. *Weekends & holidays* £8.50 over-3s; £5.50 under-3s; £5.50; under-1s free. Adult with sole under-1 £3.50. **Credit** AmEx, MC, V.

The biggest indoor play centre in London, this is an unusually tasteful-looking place where the apparatus is made out of wood.
Buggy access. Café. Disabled access: lift, ramp, toilet. Nappy-changing facilities. Shop.

Kidzmania

28 Powell Road, E5 8DJ (8533 5556). Clapton rail. **Open** 10am-6pm daily. **Admission** £4.50 4-12s; £3.50 under-4s; free adults. **No credit cards.**

An indoor adventure centre perfect for use as a children's party venue and activity centre. Kidzmania has full on-site catering (special party menus can be prepared). There are ball rooms, slides and bouncy castles.
Buggy access. Café. Nappy-changing facilities.

Zoomaround

46 Milton Grove, N16 8QY (7254 2220/ www.zoomaround.co.uk) Highbury & Islington tube/rail, then 393 bus/73, 141, 236, 341, 476 bus. **Open** 10am-6.15pm daily. **Admission** £2 under-1s; £3.50 1-3s; £4.50 over-4s; free adults & siblings (under-1s). **No credit cards.**

Activities

This huge multi-level play area is filled with ball ponds, slides, rope swings, climbing nets and tunnels – all made of brightly coloured, padded plastic. Bouncing, crawling and climbing (up, down, across, inside and out) are the order of the day. Toddlers have their own separate area and carers can either squeeze through the child-size nooks and crannies in hot pursuit of little ones, or sit and look on, with some cake and a cappuccino, from the café. There's a fine-weather garden too.
Buggy access. Café. Disabled access: toilet. Nappy-changing facilities.

THEATRE

Tuition

Allsorts
Office: 34 Pember Road, NW10 5LS (8969 3249/www.allsortsdrama.com). **Classes** phone for details. **Fees** £90-£180/10wk term; from £75 3-day workshop; from £120 5-day workshop; 20% sibling discount. **Credit** MC, V.
Classes bring role playing and improvisation, encouraging young imaginations to run free. Group sizes are kept small, and previous drama experience isn't necessary to join up for Saturday classes and holiday workshops (held at various school venues). It's all about boosting communication skills and confidence through lively role-playing. Ages range from four to 16; bespoke drama workshops at home can also be booked.

Dramarama
8446 0891/www.dramarama.co.uk. Holiday courses: South Hampstead High School, Maresfield Gardens, NW3 5SS. Term-time classes: South Hampstead Junior School, Netherhall Gardens, NW3 5RN. Finchley Road & Frognal rail. **Fees** phone for details. **No credit cards**.
Jessica Grant's Dramarama outfit, for children of all abilities, runs Saturday workshops for kids aged three and above. More intensive theatrical tuition leads 11- to 14-year-olds into their LAMDA (London Academy of Music & Dramatic Art) speech and drama exams; these are recognised qualifications in drama and can be converted into university-entrance UCAS points. Half-term and holiday workshops, in which participants devise and perform a play of their own, last for five days. There's also a birthday party service for six- to 14-year-olds.

Helen O'Grady's Children's Drama Academy
Office: Northside Vale, Guernsey, GY3 5TX (01481 200250/www.helenogrady.co.uk). **Classes** times vary; phone for details. **Fees** £66/12wk term. **No credit cards**.
Children aged five to 17 attend a one-hour workshop each week, with courses spread across three terms. The lower and upper primary groups (five to eight and nine to 11, respectively) learn self-esteem through clear speech and fluent delivery. The Youth Theatre (for 13-17s) develops more progressive technique (improvisation and monologues). A production is held at the end of every third term. Check the website to find your nearest group.

Hoxton Hall
130 Hoxton Street, N1 6SH (7684 0060/www.hoxtonhall.co.uk). Old Street tube/rail. **Classes** times vary; phone for details. **Fees** £20/12wk term. **No credit cards**.
In this unusual venue – a refurbished Victorian music hall – eight- to 11-year-olds experiment and compose at leisure in the junior music class, working individually or in groups. They can also perform in front of an audience or record their work on a CD. The parallel junior arts class encourages fledgling talent by using varied resources and materials. Both the junior drama (eight to 11s) and youth drama (11-18s) groups give young people a free hand in writing and producing a performance for the main hall.

Lewisham Youth Theatre
Broadway Theatre, Catford Broadway, SE6 4RU (8690 3428/box office 8690 0002/www.lewishamyouththeatre.com). Catford or Catford Bridge rail/75, 181, 185, 202, 660 bus. **Classes** *Junior Youth Theatre* (8-11s, 11-15s) 90 mins Wed, Sat. *Senior Youth Theatre* (15-21s) Oct-Apr 6pm Mon 120 mins. *ROAR! Children's Theatre* (2-8s & families) Oct-Mar 11.30am Sat. **Fees** free with £5 refundable deposit. **Tickets** £4. **Credit** *Box office* MC, V.
Driven by the admirable conviction that theatre should be fully accessible (free, with no auditions), LYT's youth programmes have a solid reputation for innovation, variety and high standards. All classes work towards full productions. Junior Youth Theatre is divided into two groups, but there's some crossover with the Senior Youth Theatre. Most recruitment takes place through schools, but some places are allocated on a first come, first served basis. Workshops take place after school and at weekends.

London Bubble Theatre Company

*5 Elephant Lane, SE16 4JD (7237 4434/
www.londonbubble.org.uk). Bermondsey,
Canada Water or Rotherhithe tube.* **Open**
Box office July-Sept 10am-6pm Mon-Fri.
Classes phone for details. **Fees** £38/11wk
term. **Credit** MC, V.
There was a bit of a panic in 2008 when the
Arts Council announced that it would withdraw
Bubble's grant, but fortunately it received a
stay of execution in the form of transitional
funding and increased support from Southwark
Council. Which means that the company can
continue its exemplary arts programme. There
are theatre groups for various ages: five to
sevens (4.30-6pm Tuesday; there's a waiting list)
and 13-17s. Youth drama members take part in
the annual summer show.

Millfield Theatre School

*Silver Street, N18 1PJ (box office 8807 6680/
www.millfieldtheatre.co.uk). Silver Street
rail/34, 102, 144, 217, 231, W6 bus.* **Open**
Box office 10am-6pm Mon-Sat. **Classes** (4-5s)
10.30am-noon, (6-7s) 12.30-2pm, (8-16s) 11am-
2pm Sun; (14-25s) varies. **Fees** (4-5s, 6-7s,
14-25s) £100/10wk term; (8-16s) £185/10wk
term. **Credit** MC, V.

Millfield Arts Centre presents a regular
calendar of musicals, comedies and drama, as
well as some perky touring shows, in its 362-
seat venue. The Millfield Youth Theatre is
divided into three age groups, honing the
dramatic instincts of local thesps aged from
four to 19. Auditions take place in September.
Courses run in term time, on Friday or Sunday,
with performances throughout the year,
including a panto. Sunday 4 Kidz is on the last
Sunday of the month.

National Youth Music Theatre

*Head office: 2-4 Great Eastern Street, EC2A
3NW (7422 8290/www.nymt.org.uk) Old
Street tube/rail.* **Classes** phone for details.
Fees prices vary; phone for details. **Credit**
MC, V.
With alumni like Toby Jones, Matt Lucas and
Jude Law, the NYMT's starring role in the
world of youth arts would seem assured, yet it
is constantly battling against extinction.
Nonetheless, the company continues to
audition young hopefuls for its amazing shows.
Details of auditions and regional workshops
are held on the website. Stage-management
opportunities appeal to those keen to work
behind the scenes.

Activities

'Come on, let's go and have some fun' at **Eddie Catz**. *See p179.*

Artfully messy

Let the spirit of October's Big Draw (www.campaignfordrawing.org) inspire your children throughout the year. It's easy enough in London, where almost all galleries and spaces run some sort of art workshop during the school holidays. Expression through bursts of colour and the use of quirky materials can have a lasting impact on children's well-being, and adult sanity is preserved by keeping homes free from permanent markers, acrylic paints and enthusiastic handprints on the furnishings.

North Finchley's **artsdepot** (pictured; *see p184*) is a brilliant one-stop spot for all ages. Those at the youngest end of the scale (six months to two years) are well catered for with Messy Play activities (£6 a session) using colour, texture and games. Fives to sevens can explore photography, sculpture, illustration and screen-printing.

Arty activities are also a great way to interest youngsters in the nation's top collections. The **National Portrait Gallery** (*see p62*) runs first come, first served

Family Art Workshops for children aged five and over. Next door, at the **National Gallery** (*see p62*), the education centre links children with sculptors, printmakers and other artists to learn different techniques based on the gallery paintings.

The Art Trolley at **Tate Britain** (*see p69*) is packed with activities and materials to take into the galleries, and children can have their work photographed for display in the new Art Trolley Gallery on the Families website, where online activities include Becoming an Art Detective and Creating an Imaginary City. The all-day BP Saturdays returns on 15 September 2008, with Secret Tate, a chance for all ages to explore secret spaces and architecture, re-creating paintings using a range of materials, and looking at art through spy holes.

Young Tate offers 13- to 25-year-olds a holistic opportunity to develop their skills in art, marketing, events and their overall creative confidence through a series of paid and free events (all require pre-booking). Led by a forum of 25 young artists, Young Tate has events and workshops throughout the year; past themes have included urban myths, art bingo, rap and grime. Artists Online includes the Jake Chapman blog, while Mobilography features a world of images explored by young people, through the world of technology.

Tate Modern (*see p69*) has weekend drop-in sessions for over-fives. Led by the Start team, who do a fine job of inspiring children to spot artworks in the galleries, kids draw what they see using a range of wet or dry materials. There's also a Young Tate group, called Raw Canvas. Run by young adults for young adults (aged 15 to 23), it provides a full year's programme of art-related activities.

It's not just the big galleries either. The diminutive **Dulwich Picture Gallery** (*see p58*), offers after-school workshops (five days over five weeks) for 11- to 14-year-olds, which allow children to build up their own sketchbooks. The **Wallace Collection** (*see p70*) has weekend classes and sponsors the Little Draw, where practising artists introduce young children to the 18th- and 19th-century paintings that are on display.

Perform

Office: 49 Chalton Street, NW1 1LT (0845 400 4000/www.perform.org.uk). **Classes** phone for details. **Fees** £130/10wk term (weekday); £185/10wk term (weekends); free trials. **Credit** MC, V.

Ideal for very young children, Perform concentrates on encouraging the natural potential of four- to eight-year-old children, with fun, creative workshops. For even tinier talents, there are Mini Ps classes, which cater for 'Crawlers, Walkers and Talkers' from six months upwards. The workshops take place at more than 100 venues across London and the South East. They're geared towards building up the four Cs: confidence, communication, concentration and coordination. Sessions include movement games, singing and improvisation. Phone or see the website for details of the party service.

Stagecoach Theatre Arts

Head office: Courthouse, Elm Grove, Walton-on-Thames, Surrey KT12 1LZ (01932 254333/www.stagecoach.co.uk). **Fees** £308/ 12-13wk term (6-16s); £155.50/12-13wk term (4-7s). **Credit** MC, V.

This huge, global concern has an attendant performers' agency for children and young people that's now the biggest of its kind in the UK. Of course, this part-time theatre school with 60 branches in London cannot guarantee celebrity, but it does offer a solid grounding in dance, drama and singing, through three hours' tuition a week in small groups. Two shows are given annually, and parents receive a written report twice a year. Some students work towards exams in their second or subsequent year, while third-year pupils can audition for the Stagecoach National Showcase Production in London. School holiday workshops are also organised. Sportscoach is a sister organisation for sporty children.

Sylvia Young Theatre School

Rossmore Road, NW1 6NJ (7402 0673/ www.sylviayoungtheatreschool.co.uk). Baker Street tube/Marylebone tube/rail. **Classes** phone for details. **Fees** *Classes* £68-£91/12wk term. *Summer school* (10-18s) £275/wk. **Credit** MC, V.

Sylvia Young's alumni span stage, screen and pop charts (Billie Piper, Matt from Busted and numerous *EastEnders* actors). The full-time stage school (with around 150 pupils aged from ten to 16) and Saturday school (fours to 18s) are famously oversubscribed; there are also evening classes on Thursdays. During the summer holidays there are theatre-skills and musical-theatre workshops for kids aged from eight.

Puppet theatres

Little Angel Theatre

14 Dagmar Passage, off Cross Street, N1 2DN (7226 1787/www.littleangeltheatre.com). Angel tube/Highbury & Islington tube/rail, then 4, 19, 30, 43 bus. **Open** *Box office* 10am-6pm Mon-Fri; 11am-4pm Sat, Sun. **Tickets** £8-£10; £6-£8 under-16s. **Credit** MC, V.

Established by John Wright in 1961, this atmospheric little place is London's only permanent puppet theatre. The Little Angel is highly respected for the quality of its puppetry, and for innovative programming, staging productions that use every type of puppet. Themes, styles and stories are drawn from a range of cultural traditions, from fairytales to folk tales. The theatre also plays host to visiting puppet companies. Most productions are aimed at kids aged five and over, with occasional shows for the very young. A Saturday Puppet Club runs in conjunction with most major productions. There's also a LAT Puppet Academy.

Buggy access. Disabled access: ramp, toilet. Nappy-changing facilities. Shop.

Puppet Theatre Barge

Opposite 35 Blomfield Road, W9 2PF (7249 6876/www.puppetbarge.com). Warwick Avenue tube. **Open** *Box office* 10am-8pm daily. **Tickets** £8.50; £8 under-16s, reductions. **Credit** MC, V.

One of the capital's most enchanting assets, the Puppet Theatre Barge offers a unique combination of puppet shows (courtesy of Movingstage Productions) and unusual location. It's a diminutive venue with just 50 seats, moored on the scenic towpath in Little Venice between November and June. A variety of performances are staged, such as *Red Riding Hood* and various *Brer Rabbit* tales, at 3pm on Saturday and Sunday. More frequent daytime and evening shows take place in the school holidays. Between July and October, the barge floats off on a tour of the Thames, stopping to perform at riverside towns (Henley, Clifton, Marlow and Richmond) at 2.30pm and 4.30pm.

Touring companies

Kazzum

7539 3500/www.kazzum.org
Since its inception in 1989, Peter Glanville's Kazzum collective has toured schools, theatres,

Activities

libraries, parks and festivals. Its diverse projects include works aimed at under-sixes, reworkings of international classics, and interactive installations for under-11s.

Oily Cart
8672 6329/www.oilycart.org.uk.
Oily Cart's forte is in brilliantly innovative, multi-sensory productions for two theatrically excluded groups: very young children and children with special needs. Shows involve large multi-sensory spaces, where groups of children can become part of the performance. The new show for 2008/9 is *How Long is a Piece of String?*, an interactive production with live music and a maze, exploring the wonders of string. A Christmas run at the Unicorn Theatre (*see p190*) is planned.

Pop-Up Theatre
7609 3339/www.pop-up.net.
Founded in 1982, the pioneering Pop-Up has made a name for itself creating multimedia theatre for audiences aged under 11. Its Equal Voice interactive theatre sessions tour schools, opening up the art form to kids from all backgrounds. As we went to press, Pop-Up was reeling from the loss of its Arts Council funding – see the website for details.

Quicksilver Theatre
7241 2942/www.quicksilvertheatre.org.
This collective has toured new plays for children across the UK during the past 25 years. Joint artistic directors Guy Holland and Carey English commission, produce and collaborate with other companies, such as Indefinite Articles, with whom they have produced their new show, *La Di Dada*. They're determined that their recent cut in Arts Council funding will not hold them back.

Theatre Centre
7729 3066/www.theatre-centre.co.uk.
Founded in 1953 by the late Brian Way (a pioneering director, educator and writer), Theatre Centre works internationally, in schools, colleges, theatres, arts centres and community spaces. The company has a reputation for excellence and technical invention, and also champions more challenging writing.

Theatre-Rites
7953 7102/www.theatre-rites.co.uk.
Founded by the late Penny Bernand, continued by puppet supremo Sue Buckmaster and installation artist Sophia Clist, Theatre-Rites is an unusual company. A reputation for site-specific work was cemented by 1996's astounding *Houseworks*, which took place in a Brixton home. Site-specifics are still a speciality; the company has one planned for Germany later in 2008.

Venues

Albany
Douglas Way, SE8 4AG (8692 4446/ www.thealbany.org.uk). Deptford rail/21, 36, 47, 136, 171, 177, 188, 225, 453 bus. **Open** *Box office* 9am-9pm Mon-Fri; 10am-5pm Sat; 2hrs before performance Sun. **Tickets** *Family Sunday* £5.50; £4 under-16s, reductions. **Credit** MC, V.
Serving Deptford since the late 19th century, this now-multimedia arts centre retains a lively neighbourhood focus. Its regular Family Sunday performances (3pm) may include specially written pieces or musical stories with sing-along songs. The Albany is also a party venue. *Buggy access. Café. Disabled access: lift, ramp, toilet. Nappy-changing facilities.*

artsdepot
5 Nether Street, N12 0GA (8369 5454/ www.artsdepot.co.uk). West Finchley or Woodside Park tube. **Open** *Box office* 9am-5.30pm Mon-Fri; 10am-5.30pm Sat; noon-5.30pm Sun (later during performances). **Tickets** free-£18. **Credit** MC, V.
The stylish artsdepot houses the 400-seat Pentland Theatre, but most children's performances take place in the 150-seat studio; shows are held on Sunday at noon and 3pm. A learning programme involves all ages from one-year-olds to adults, and has courses ranging from drama to visual arts. Bright Sparks Theatre Company (8-12 years) meets on Friday; younger age groups do drama and story making on Saturday. Dance and movement classes for pre-schoolers, as well as the terrific Messy Play, take place through the week. Check the website for details of the summer circus school. *Buggy access. Café. Disabled access: lift, ramp, toilet. Nappy-changing facilities.*

BAC (Battersea Arts Centre)
Lavender Hill, SW11 5TN (7223 2223/ Puppet Centre 7228 5335/www.bac.org.uk). Clapham Common tube, then 345 bus/ Clapham Junction rail/77, 77A, 156 bus. **Open** *Box office* 10am-6pm Mon-Fri; 2.30-6pm Sat, Sun. *Puppet Centre* phone for details. **Tickets** £3.50-£15. **Membership** suggested discretionary donation of £30-£250/yr. **Credit** MC, V.

That's the way to do it. Puppetry at the **Little Angel Theatre**. *See p183.*

Activities galore for children at **Lauderdale House**. *See right.*

Ground-breaking theatre is BAC's stock in trade. Shows developed here continue to make the leap to the West End. The BAC's Young People's Theatre groups take those aged 12 to 25, working towards an end-of-term performance. *Buggy access. Café. Disabled access: lift, toilet. Nappy-changing facilities.*

Broadway Theatre
Catford Broadway, SE6 4RU (8690 0002/ www.lewishamyouththeatre.com). Catford or Catford Bridge rail/75, 181, 185, 202, 660 bus. **Open** *Box office* 10am-6pm Mon-Sat. **Tickets** £3.50-£22. **Credit** MC, V.
Home to Lewisham Youth Theatre (*see p180*), this listed art deco building is Catford's pride and joy. ROAR! performances are presented to three- to eight-year-olds and their families on Saturday mornings. These usually take place in the intimate 100-seater studio, although the main auditorium (400 seats) has been used for family entertainment such as the rumbustious pantomime and big school-holiday shows. There are also film screenings on 'dark' nights between shows. *Buggy access. Café. Disabled access: lift, toilet. Nappy-changing facilities.*

Chickenshed
Chase Side, N14 4PE (8292 9222/www. chickenshed.org.uk). Cockfosters or Oakwood tube. **Open** *Box office* 10am-6pm Mon-Fri; 10am-5pm Sat. **Tickets** *Shows* £3.70-£18. *Workshops* phone for details. **Credit** MC, V.
Chickenshed was founded in 1974, on the premise that the performing arts belong to everyone who wants to join in. This inclusive policy has attracted around 700 members from every background. Performances are held in one of four spaces, including, in summer, an outdoor amphitheatre. Tales from the Shed (Friday and Saturday morning) is aimed at under-sevens, bringing stories, both original and traditional, to life. *Bar. Buggy access. Café. Disabled access: lift, toilet. Nappy-changing facilities. Shop.*

Colour House Children's Theatre
Merton Abbey Mills, Watermill Way, SW19 2RD (8542 5511/www.colourhouse theatre.co.uk). Colliers Wood tube. **Open** *Box office* 10am-5pm daily; 1hr before show. **Shows** 2pm, 4pm Sat, Sun. **Tickets** £7. **Credit** MC, V.

Tucked in amid Abbey Mills' weekend craft market, this bijou riverside venue regularly lends a zany twist to classics, with irresistible titles such as *Robinson Crusoe in Space*. Children's theatre workshops and groups are run by the Colour House Theatre; call the school on 8623 9600 for details of classes. After-show birthday parties with a mini disco can be arranged.
Buggy access. Disabled access: toilet. Nappy-changing facilities (in Merton Abbey Mills). Shop.

Hackney Empire
291 Mare Street, E8 1EJ (box office 8985 2424/www.hackneyempire.co.uk). Hackney Central rail/38, 106, 253, 277, D6 bus. **Open** *Box office* 10am-6pm Mon-Sat; 1hr before show Sun. *Tours* 1st Sat of mth; phone for times. **Tickets** prices vary; phone for details. **Tours** £10; £7 reductions. **Credit** MC, V.
This East End variety theatre dates back to 1901 – Charlie Chaplin performed here – and was lovingly revamped in 2004. The education programme offers professional-run workshops as well as the Artist Development Programme for 12- to 16-year-olds. The annual panto is always a hit.
Buggy access. Disabled access: toilet. Nappy-changing facilities.

Half Moon Young People's Theatre
43 White Horse Road, E1 0ND (7709 8900/ www.halfmoon.org.uk). Limehouse DLR/rail. **Open** *Box office* 10am-6pm Mon-Fri; 9am-4pm Sat. **Tickets** £4.50. **Credit** MC, V.
A full season of dramatic events – from weekend children's theatre to professional and participatory productions for young people – runs at the Half Moon from September to April. Kids are encouraged to join in regardless of race, sex, ability or financial situation; an estimated 32,000 individuals take part. The fully accessible theatre hosts performances for kids from birth up to 17 years. Plays for under-11s are held on Saturdays, with midweek performances for under-sevens, and on Thursday evenings for elevens upwards. Children can join one of seven youth theatre groups, which meet weekly during term-time (phone for fee details), working towards a show.
Buggy access. Disabled access: lift, ramp, toilet. Nappy-changing facilities.

Jackson's Lane
269A Archway Road, N6 5AA (8341 4421/ www.jacksonslane.org.uk). Highgate tube.

Open *Box office* 10am-10pm Tue-Sat; 10am-5pm Sun. **Tickets** £5-£12. **Credit** MC, V.
This handsome red-brick gothic church conversion is home to a 170-capacity theatre, a dance and rehearsal studio and four other rehearsal and workshop spaces. Countless courses in dance, drama and performance skills take place throughout the year; details on the website.
Bar. Buggy access. Café. Disabled access: ramp, toilet. Nappy-changing facilities.

Lauderdale House & Waterlow Park
Highgate Hill, Waterlow Park, N6 5HG (8348 8716/www.lauderdalehouse.co.uk). Archway tube, then 143, 210, 271, W5 bus. **Open** *Box office* 30mins before performance. **Tickets** £4.50; £3 reductions. **No credit cards**.
Set in ornamental gardens on the edge of peaceful Waterlow Park, the 16th-century Lauderdale House was once the home of Nell Gwynne, the mistress of Charles II. Exhibitions of arts and crafts take place regularly in the lobby of the mansion, but the big lure for parents is the jam-packed programme of activities for kids. During term-time, most of the action takes place at weekends: every Saturday, there are panto-style children's shows and sing-a-long sessions at 10am and 11.30am, while Sunday mornings are set aside for family-friendly concerts designed to promote interest in classical music amongst the iPod generation. Toddlers can get in on the musical action on Monday and Friday with drop-in sessions for babies and parents. Pre-schoolers can burn off energy at the Thursday dance and movement sessions, and get an early introduction to classical music at the Tuesday Mini-Mozart sessions. During the school holidays (including half-term) there are special workshops in arts, dance and drama for kids of all ages; call for details or pick up a copy of the Bizzy Kids brochure for upcoming events.
Surrounding Lauderdale House, Waterlow Park is a rolling green space with a play-park and a huge central pond full of tufted ducks that kids can feed from a wooden platform. The park was founded in 1889 by Sir Sidney Waterlow as a 'garden for the gardenless' and families still make good use of it today. The Heritage Lottery-funded Waterlow Park Centre offers its own weekend activities for kids who like to get their hands dirty, including pond-dipping and conservation days. Meanwhile, parents can kick back at the restaurant that looks out over the gardens from the rear terrace of Lauderdale House.
Buggy access. Café. Disabled access: toilet.

Activities

And now read on...

London's libraries are changing. They've had to. Fewer people than ever are reading, so the old-fashioned local library has become a temple to the information god. Which is a good thing: kids don't actually care about the format – paper or disc or webpage – but their minds want feeding. Libraries now proudly vaunt their free Wi-Fi status as well as their copies of the latest Ian McEwan. They have become customer-focused; their spaces are relaxed and comfy rather than forbidding. Banishing the old cliché of a grim-faced librarian telling you to 'Shush!' is bound to appeal to kids, after all.

And libraries are stuffed to the gills with ideas designed to lure children in, get them reading and keep them reading. Among the options now available across the capital are: Bookstart (your baby's first reading list), Chatter Books (a reading group for children), baby and toddler sessions, speech and language drop-ins for under-fives, craft sessions, storytelling, a children's chess club, TRG (teenage reading group), story tapes, story CDs, children's DVDs, Bookstart Plus Workshops in the children's 'pod', Ripples (a reading list – slogan: 'One good book leads to another'), graphic novels, the

Activities

Lyric Hammersmith Theatre

Lyric Square, King Street, W6 0QL (0871 221 1722/www.lyric.co.uk). Hammersmith tube. **Open** *Box office* 9.30am-7pm Mon-Sat (until 8pm on performance days). **Tickets** £9-£27; £10 under-16s, reductions; £9 students, 16-25s (restrictions apply). **Credit** MC, V.
The glassy modern façade here belies the antique auditorium with its gorgeous Victorian proscenium arch. The Lyric remains one of London's most future-focused theatres for children's programming. A pioneering Creative Learning schedule gives 11- to 19-year-olds access to high-quality arts provision to develop their creative and personal skills and gain qualifications. It includes talks, workshops and teacher-training. The studio is also the venue for most kids' events: Saturday morning theatricals, school holiday workshops and pre-schooler specials in the week. Messy Play is a new interactive post-show workshop after selected Saturday shows. The Summer Party – a free theatre festival for all the family – takes place on Saturday 12 July 2008.
Buggy access. Café. Disabled access: lift, toilet. Nappy-changing facilities.

Booked Up scheme (to encourage Year 7 readers by offering each of them a free book), the RaW scheme (read more and write better with the BBC), a homework help club, multi-coloured beanbags and free bookmarks.

The **Barbican Centre** (*see p163*) has a sweet kids' library attached to its main library. And a very empty one: only 56 children were born in the City last year. The well-known **Peckham Library** (*see p174*) offers everything a 21st-century library can come up with, as well as good views over the city. Like many London libraries, it's attuned to the ethnic make-up of the local area. Unfortunately, the design is awful, cramming everything into a fourth-floor open-plan space the size of an airport. The relaxed calm familiar to library-lovers is lost; it feels like being in the middle of Tesco's.

The best kind of design is illustrated by the **Idea Store** (*see p174*) based in Whitechapel (but with branches all over London), where they have actually thought through what people want and provided it. Children's computers are positioned closer to the floor; you can check out books by machine; there's a café, a crèche and water-coolers; areas are divided into useful categories, such as Teen Choice and Sight & Sound; surfers are separate from book-browsers – and the result is five wonderfully quiet floors, full of people happily doing different things alongside each other. Whether many of those people have even considered that they are spending their precious leisure time in a library is precisely the point.

National Theatre

South Bank, SE1 9PX (box office 7452 3000/information 7452 3400/www.national theatre.org.uk). Waterloo tube/rail. **Open** *Box office* 9.30am-8pm Mon-Sat. **Credit** AmEx, MC, V. **Map** p317 M8.

The three world-class theatres (the Olivier, the Lyttleton and the Cottesloe) making up the NT show primarily adult-oriented material, although a few productions are specifically for families. Occasional half-term shows are supplemented by school holiday specials;

summer sees the Word Alive! Storytelling festival. You can catch free music concerts Monday to Friday in the early evening before the plays begin; the bands perform both at lunchtime and in the evening on Saturday. The outdoor space – Theatre Square – has done much to draw families' attention toward Sir Denys Lasdun's landmark concrete theatre complex. It's the home of the terrific Watch This Space summer season (4 July-14 September 2008), which includes street theatre and comic shows suitable for families at lunchtime and in the early evening. The New Connections programme is designed to encourage schools and youth theatres nationwide to produce new plays, commissioning some of the best playwrights to write specifically for young performers; the culminating event is a week-long festival at the National. The National Theatre Young Company is made up of performers aged 11 to 19, who meet once a week; check the website for details on how to join. You can also join a backstage tour (£7, £5 under-18s; £13 family; not suitable for under-sevens). Tours take in the rehearsal rooms, the workshops where costumes and props are made, dressing rooms and the stages.

Café. Disabled access: lift, toilet. Nappy-changing facilities. Nearest picnic place: Bernie Spain Gardens. Restaurants. Shop.

Nettlefold Theatre

West Norwood Library, 1 Norwood High Street, SE27 9JX (7926 8070/www.lambeth. gov.uk). West Norwood rail/2, 68, 196, 468 bus. **Open** *Box office* 9am-9pm Mon-Fri; 9.30am-6pm Sat. **Tickets** £5. **Credit** MC, V.

This 200-seat theatre is built into West Norwood Library and runs one child-oriented show a month (usually on a Saturday at 2pm). Another draw is the Bigfoot Theatre Company (0870 011 4307, www.bigfoot-theatre.co.uk), which runs drama, singing, and dance and movement classes for eights and over between 10am and noon every Saturday during term time.

Buggy access. Disabled access: lift, toilet. Nappy-changing facilities.

New Wimbledon Theatre

The Broadway, SW19 1QG (0870 060 6646/ www.theambassadors.com/newwimbledon). Wimbledon tube/rail. **Open** *Box office* 10am-6pm Mon-Sat (until 8pm on performance days). **Credit** MC, V.

A glimmer of the West End on a suburban high street, the New Wimbledon Theatre presents a steady flow of touring hits. Family-friendly highlights in 2008 so far include *Angelina*

Activities

Ballerina and *Flashdance,* and *Cinderella* at Christmas. The end-of-year panto is always jolly. *Bar. Buggy access. Disabled access: lift, toilet. Shop.*

Open Air Theatre
Inner Circle, Regent's Park, NW1 4NU (box office 0844 826 4242/www.openairtheatre. org). Baker Street tube. **Open** *Apr, May* 10am-6pm Mon-Sat. *June-Sept* 10am-8pm Mon-Sat. **Tickets** £8-£42; £18 under-18s. **Credit** AmEx, MC, V. **Map** p314 G3.

There's nothing to beat hearing Titania hold forth as the surrounding trees rustle their approval on a summer's evening. And that's exactly what you'll get from 8 July to 2 August 2008, when *A Midsummer Night's Dream* is 're-imagined for everyone aged six and over'. Other Shakespeare plays being performed in 2008 in this lovely open-air theatre include *Romeo and Juliet* and *Twelfth Night,* for the over-11s. If rainy weather stops play, tickets will be exchanged for a later performance – subject to availability – but umbrellas and blankets are always advisable. *Buggy access. Café. Disabled access: toilet.*

Polka Theatre
240 Broadway, SW19 1SB (8543 4888/www. polkatheatre.com). South Wimbledon tube/ Wimbledon tube/rail, then 57, 93, 219, 493 bus. **Open** *By phone* 9.30am-4.30pm Mon; 9am-6pm Tue-Fri; 10am-5pm Sat. *In person* 9.30am-4.30pm Tue-Fri; 10am-5pm Sat. **Tickets** £6.50-£11.50. **Credit** MC, V.

This exceptional young persons' theatre has earned its place in generations of young hearts since it launched in 1979. Daily shows are staged by touring companies in the main auditorium (10.30am, 2pm), with weekly performances – often puppet-based – taking place in the Adventure Theatre, dedicated to babies and toddlers. There are also in-house productions, workshops and storytelling sessions for families and schools. Book for school-holiday workshops, or enrol at the Polka Youth Theatre (£80 per term, subsidised places available), where in once-a-week sessions kids aged from three are taught performance skills and learn to put on their own production with Polka professionals. The wonderful day-long workshops (£30), based on the show in the auditorium (participants see this in the afternoon), are a treat for children in the school holidays. We love the little playground, the gorgeous Teddy Bear Museum, moved here from Stratford (look out for Blair's bear) and the cheerful café is a top place for lunch. Check the website for literature events featuring children's authors such as Jacqueline Wilson. Christmas 2008 promises to be a laugh with the main theatre show for over-sixes *Pinocchio*, adapted by Michael Rosen. *Buggy access. Café. Disabled access: lift, toilet. Nappy-changing facilities.*

Shakespeare's Globe
21 New Globe Walk, SE1 9DT (7401 9919/ tours 7902 1500/www.shakespeares-globe.org). Southwark or Mansion House tube/London Bridge tube/rail. **Open** *Box office* (theatre bookings until 5 Oct 2008, then from March 2009) 10am-6pm daily. *Tours* May-Sept 9am-12.30pm daily. Oct-Apr 10am-5pm daily. **Tickets** £5-£33. *Tours* £9; £7.50 reductions; £6.50 5-15s; free under-5s; £25 family (2+3). **Credit** AmEx, MC, V. **Map** p318 O7.

Young kids won't be inclined to sit – or stand – through the shows at this reconstructed venue, but older children might like to know that the plays staged in 2008 will be *King Lear, The Merry Wives of Windsor* and *A Midsummer Night's Dream.* The building captures the imagination of any age group, and the Globe has a dedicated education department. A huge range of talks, tours and activities – many conducted by staff wearing full period costume – takes place with schools during term time, while holiday workshops and excellent seasonal events open the floor to families. *Café. Disabled access: lift, toilet. Nappy-changing facilities. Restaurant. Shop.*

Unicorn Theatre for Children
147 Tooley Street, SE1 2HZ (0870 053 4534/ www.unicorntheatre.com). London Bridge tube/ rail. **Open** *Box office* 9.30am-6pm Mon-Fri; 10am-6pm Sat; noon-5pm Sun. **Tickets** £9.50-£14.50. **Credit** MC, V. **Map** p319 R9.

This bright, bright building near More! London, with its holographic images of children's authors like Anne Fine and Michael Morpurgo, and its huge white unicorn in the foyer, is the result of a three-year collaboration with local school children, whose thoughts have been incorporated into the £13m design. The two performance spaces include the 300-seater Weston Theatre and more intimate Clore Theatre; so far they have hosted a vibrant, critically acclaimed programme for audiences aged four and above. Family Days get everybody together for performances and themed workshops, and cost £24 per person. The Christmas show for 2008 is based on the story of *Sleeping Beauty*. *Buggy access. Café. Disabled access: lift, toilet.*

Activities

Warehouse Theatre

*62 Dingwall Road, Croydon, Surrey CR0 2NF
(8680 4060/www.warehousetheatre.co.uk).
East Croydon rail.* **Open** *Box office* 10am-6pm
Mon; 10am-8.30pm Tue; 10am-10pm Wed-Sat;
3-7pm Sun. **Tickets** £8-£15; £4.50 2-16s.
Credit AmEx, MC, V.
Easy to miss, the Warehouse is tucked into a
converted Victorian warehouse behind East
Croydon station – but once found, you won't
forget it. Theatre4Kidz shows take place every
Saturday at 11am (£6; £4.50 children), while a
variety of touring shows entertain those as
young as two. Croydon Young People's Theatre
(CRYPT) offers a creative base for 13- to 16-year-
olds; it meets 2-5pm every Saturday during term
time, and puts on an annual summer show. The
fee per term is currently only £12; application
forms are available online.
*Bar. Buggy access. Café. Disabled access: lift,
toilet (bar only).*

West End shows

With the exception of *Billy Elliot*, the
shows listed below are suitable for young
children. Less-developed attention spans
may find some more suitable than others
(many clock in at over two hours). If
you've got young children in your party,
we'd recommend avoiding the West End
altogether and going instead to a more
intimate kid-specific venue in another
part of town, where plays are shorter,
house lights brighter and the bangs less
likely to scare.

The **Society of London Theatres**
(SOLT, 7557 6700, www.officiallondon
theatre.co.uk), gives a great introduction
to Theatreland with **Kids Week**
(www.kidsweek.co.uk). Every year during
the last two weeks of August (15-29 Aug
2008), children aged five to 16 can go free
to West End shows, provided they are
accompanied by a paying adult; up to two
additional children can get in at half-price.
They can also go backstage, meet the
stars and take part in workshops. For
more on Kids Week and the best family-
friendly theatre information in London,
subscribe to the free family bulletin on the
SOLT website.

Billy Elliot the Musical

*Victoria Palace Theatre, Victoria Street,
SW1E 5EA (0870 895 5577/www.billyelliott
hemusical.com). Victoria tube/rail.* **Times**
7.30pm Mon-Sat. *Matinée* 2.30pm Thur, Sat.

Tickets £17.50-£60. **Credit** AmEx, MC, V.
Map p316 H10.
The musical version of the BAFTA-winning
film, about the motherless miner's son who
discovers a talent for ballet, has 17 songs by
Elton John. Its website has a warning that it
contains strong language and scenes of
confrontation, which gave the film a 15 rating.
Not for under-eights.

Grease

*Piccadilly Theatre, 4 Denman Street, W1V
8DY (0844 412 6666/www.theambassadors.
com). Piccadilly Circus tube.* **Times** 7.30pm
Mon-Thur, Sat; 8.30pm Fri. *Matinée* 3pm Sat;
5pm Fri. **Tickets** £15-£55. **Credit** AmEx,
MC, V. **Map** p316 J6.
More TV talents ham it up as Sandy and Danny
and sing the songs we all know and love.

Hairspray

*Shaftesbury Theatre, 210 Shaftesbury
Avenue, WC2H 8DP (7379 5399/www.hair
spraythemusical.co.uk). Holborn or Tottenham
Court Road tube.* **Times** 7.30pm Mon-Sat.
Matinée 3pm Thur, Sat. **Tickets** £20-£60.
Credit AmEx, MC, V. **Map** p315 K6.
Loveable chubby heroine Tracy Turnblad teams
up with the black kids from Special Ed to
overthrow 1960s racial prejudice and fulfil her
dreams. Cheesey, preposterous and insanely
uplifting stuff for older kids.

Joseph & the Amazing Technicolor Dreamcoat

*Adelphi Theatre, Strand, WC2E 7NA
(0871 297 0749/www.josephthemusical.com).
Charing Cross tube/rail.* **Times** 7.30pm Mon,
Wed-Sat; 7pm Tue. *Matinée* 3pm Wed, Sat.
Tickets £15-£49.50. **Credit** AmEx, MC, V.
Map p317 L7.
A new audience drawn in by the TV show's
search for a star will love the psychedelic and
arch camp polish, but the Sunday school
wholesomeness and great songs make it a
wonderful family show.

Les Misérables

*Queen's Theatre, Shaftesbury Avenue, W1D
6BA (0870 950 0930/www.lesmis.com).
Leicester Square or Piccadilly Circus tube.*
Times 7.30pm Mon-Sat. *Matinée* 2.30pm
Wed, Sat. **Tickets** £15-£55. **Credit** AmEx,
MC, V. **Map** p315 K6.
An enduring musical adaptation of Victor
Hugo's tale of revolution in 19th-century France;
20 years since its London première, *Les
Misérables* is still impressive. The Les Miz Kids'

Activities

Club also runs here twice a month, and gives children aged eight- to 15-years old a chance to tour backstage and re-enact a scene from the show the princely sum of £15.

Lion King
Lyceum Theatre, Wellington Street, WC2E 7RQ (0844 844 0005/www.disney.co.uk/ musicaltheatre). Covent Garden tube/ Charing Cross tube/rail. **Times** 7.30pm Tue-Sat. *Matinée* 2pm Wed, Sat; 3pm Sun. **Tickets** £20-£59.50. **Credit** AmEx, MC, V. **Map** p317 L7.
Most children are familiar with the film version of this Disney classic. The beauty of the stage production lies in the elaborate staging. Expect awesome set designs, a combination of puppetry and live actors (there are 25 different animals represented in the show) and a fabulous cocktail of West End choruses and African rhythms. Parents enjoy it as much as children.

Mamma Mia!
Prince of Wales Theatre, Coventry Street, W1V 8AS (0844 482 5115/www.mamma-mia.com). Piccadilly Circus tube. **Times** 7.30pm Mon-Thur, Sat; 8.30pm Fri. *Matinée* 5pm Fri; 3pm Sat. **Tickets** £20-£59. **Credit** AmEx, MC, V. **Map** p317 K7.
It may be thin on story, but what *Mamma Mia!* lacks in dramatic development it more than makes up for with feel-good musical numbers.

Sound of Music
London Palladium, Argyll Street, W1F 7TF (0871 297 0748/www.soundofmusiclondon. com). Oxford Circus tube. **Times** 7.30pm Mon, Wed-Sat; 7pm Tue. *Matinée* 2.30pm Wed, Sat. **Tickets** £25-£55. **Credit** AmEx, MC, V. **Map** p314 J6.
An old-fashioned musical in which the melodic children are adorable. The plot might seem a tad absurd in this day and age, but the spirit of the show is exhilarating. The saccharin content has been adeptly reduced by director Jeremy Sams.

Stomp
Ambassadors Theatre, West Street, WC2H 9ND (0844 811 2334/www.stomp.co.uk). Leicester Square tube. **Times** 8pm Mon, Thur-Sat; 5.30pm Sun. *Matinée* 3pm Thur, Sat; 2pm Sun. **Tickets** £20-£45. **Credit** AmEx, MC, V. **Map** p315 K6.
Kids who like smashing pans together will adore this hyperactive show. The cast finds music in the most obscure objects – including the kitchen sink – and the whole noisy extravaganza is a blast.

Wicked
Apollo Victoria, Wilton Road, SW1V 1LG (0844 826 8000/www.wickedthemusical. co.uk). Victoria tube/rail. **Times** 7.30pm Mon-Sat. *Matinée* 2.30pm Wed, Sat. **Tickets** £15-£60. **Credit** AmEx, MC, V. **Map** p316 H10
The Wicked Witch of the West wasn't really wicked at all according to this enjoyable answer to the *Wizard of Oz*. For eights and above.

WORKSHOPS & ACTIVITIES

Brilliant Kids
7 Station Terrace, NW10 5RT (8964 4120/ www.brilliantkids.co.uk). Kensal Green tube/ Kensal Rise rail. **Open** 8am-6pm Mon-Fri; 9am-5pm Sat; 10am-4pm Sun. **Fees** £5-£7/ class. **Credit** MC, V.
A sociable little art and activities club with a café (*see p223*), where children aged from six months can have fun with painting sessions, cookery clubs, gardening and nature activities and then have a brilliant lunch afterwards. Outside companies put on classes such as Mini Picasso throughout term time. Classes take place every hour.

Maggie & Rose
58 Pembroke Road, W8 6NX (7371 2200/ www.maggieandrose.co.uk). Earl's Court or West Kensington tube. **Classes** times vay; phone for details. **Fees** £500/yr membership; £180/12wk course. **Credit** MC, V.
A 'lifestyle members' club' for families that aims to introduce children to a host of exhilarating activities to help build their confidence through play. Activities (term time and holiday) for kids aged from six months to seven years include Cheflets Cookery, Green Fingered Gardening and Messy Masters Art. Parties can also be arranged in the bright double studio.

That Place on the Corner
1-3 Green Lanes, N16 9BS (7704 0079/ www.thatplaceonthecorner.co.uk). Highbury & Islington tube/rail/Canonbury rail/21, 73, 141, 276, 341, 476 bus. **Open** 10.30am-5.30pm Mon-Fri; 10.30am-2.30pm Sat, Sun. **Credit** MC, V.
A much-loved family-friendly café (*see p231*) that also offers a host of classes – from Rucksack Music and Tip Toes dance to Angelina Ballerina's Dance Academy. Check the website for full details.

Activities

Archaeology

Young Archaeologists Club @ UCL

Institute of Archaeology, 31-34 Gordon Square, WC1H 0PY (7679 4717).
The Institute of Archaeology supports a children's club for eight- to 16-year-olds which meets on the third Saturday of each month, from 11am till 1pm; call first before going.

Museum of London Archaeology Service

7410 2200/www.museumoflondon archaeology.org.uk.
The Museum of London's Archaeology Service (MoLAS) also runs digs and activities for families. Its Young Archaeologists Club, for eights to 16s, has branches in central London (meeting on the third Saturday of the month) and in Rotherhithe (meeting on the last Saturday of the month). Activities include walking the foreshore to collect objects washed up at low tide on the Thames; identifying animal bones; mosaic making; and creating Saxon costumes based on reconstructions from archaeological evidence.

Art & crafts

All Fired Up

34 East Dulwich Road, SE22 9AX (7732 6688/www.allfiredupceramics.co.uk). East Dulwich or Peckham Rye rail. **Open** 9.30am-6pm Mon, Tue, Sat; 9.30am-10pm Wed-Fri; 10.30am-4.30pm Sun. **Fees** *Studio* £3/day. *Workshops & courses* phone for details. **Credit** MC, V.
AFU has shelves of plain white ornaments (cartoon characters, animals, fairies), crockery and pots to paint at tables equipped with palettes, sponges, water and brushes. Friendly staff give advice and there's a little coffee bar from which to buy salads, sandwiches and pastries. Painted objects are glazed, fired, gift-wrapped and ready for collection within ten days. 'Picasso Birthday Parties' (£10-£12.50 per child) are run for groups of eight or more children aged five to 15.

Art 4 Fun

172 West End Lane, NW6 1SD (7794 0800/www.art4fun.com). West Hampstead tube/rail. **Open** 10am-6pm Mon, Wed-Sun; 10am-8pm Tue. **Fees** *Studio* £5.95/day. *Workshops & courses* phone for details. **Credit** MC, V.

Activities

Polka Theatre. *See p190.*

Telling tales

Take a step over the threshold at Discover and enter a world of stories. Billed as the UK's first creative learning centre for young children, the venue was developed in collaboration with the local community in Stratford; families, community groups, teachers and children all gave their thoughts on the venture to the architects and designers.

The result is magical. Outside, the Story Garden is a handsome playground with monster's tongue-slide, raised stream, wooden play ship and futuristic space vehicle. Inside, the principal character is a baby space monster called Hootah; children are told she is visiting from a faraway planet, Squiggly Diggly, on a mission to collect new stories and take them home. Kids are invited to stand in Hootah 'cones', a sort of hairdryer affair that plays sample stories and records anything that the user cares to invent. Kids can also go on a trail involving a 'Lollipopter', an indoor river full of twinkling lights and a wooden footbridge that shouts 'Trip', 'Trap', baas like a sheep and gobbles like a troll. Inside the low, softly lit 'caves' are machines that allow you to hear your own echo, manipulate string puppets or appear instantly on screen in a film shot in the garden.

The team at Discover have always recognised that a childhood furnished with colourful stories – particularly those told by their parents or teachers – opens up a world of creative possibilities. As Sally Goldsworthy, the centre's director, puts it: 'Stories have power. They wrap us in words and ideas, allow us to explore different places and situations, experience emotions, connect to our past and prepare for the future. Stories help us play, question and imagine a million possibilities. In an uncertain world stories provide the sense and sparkle in children's lives.'

To this end, regular drop-in activities at weekends include Stories in a Bag, during which children and a 'Story Builder' create a tale using a random selection of objects, while bookable events for half-terms and holidays may include mask-making and own-made puppet shows. Discover also offers parties, at the gratifyingly low price of £6.50 per head.

The Story Den – a new feature – hosts interactive exhibitions based on stories

Art 4 Fun is ideal for large groups of children intent on getting creative by painting on to a ceramic, wood, glass, paper or fabric item of their choosing. Mosaic-making is another option. Items for painting cost from £4.50; the studio fee is for the glazing and finishing. Workshops run throughout the year for kids and adults, and include sand-painting, tie-dyeing and stamp-making. Parties are also a speciality. You can buy refreshments such as hot drinks and cakes, but customers are also allowed to bring in their own snacks.

Art Yard

318 Upper Richmond Road West, SW14 7JN (8878 1336/www.artyard.co.uk). Mortlake rail/33 bus. **Classes** *Term-time* 9am-6pm Mon-Fri. *School hols* 9.30am-3.30pm Mon-Fri. **Fees** £8/session; £100-£130/term. **Credit** MC, V.

After-school art clubs, drop-in sessions for pre-school tinies and school holiday courses for ages five to 11 are all offered at this busy (and pleasingly messy), Ofsted-registered outlet. Many children come for two-day workshops, costing £33, (bring a packed lunch and wear old clothes) during the school holidays, and have great fun creating improvised art works (from painting to collage and papier-mâché) and listening to music. Five-day workshops at £145 are also available. Themed events include preparations for Easter and Christmas during the relevant school holidays.

Children's Workshops in Clay

Lewisham Arthouse, 140 Lewisham Way, SE14 6PD (8694 9011/www.shirley-stewart.co.uk). New Cross, Deptford or Greenwich rail. **Fees** £7 drop-in; £60/term. **Credit** phone for details.

Lewisham Arthouse is a cooperative based in a handsome Grade II listed building with an amazing marble staircase. Artists rent studio space here, and Shirley Stewart is among them. Her throwing and studio pottery workshops for children aged from five are held during term time only, but extra sessions can be arranged for the holidays. Pottery parties are also available for £12 per child, which includes the cost of materials and firings.

Smarty Paints

85 Nightingale Lane, SW12 8NX (8772 8702/ www.smarty-paints.com). Clapham South tube/ Wandsworth Common rail. **Open** 10am-6pm Mon-Wed, Fri, Sat; 10am-9pm Thur; 11am-6pm Sun. **Fees** *Studio* £6. **Credit** MC, V.

A bright new ceramic painting studio next to Munchkin Lane children's café.

from around the globe. The element of capturing memories is created in the current exhibition, City of Stories (until 31 August 2008), which mixes tales and legend with recollections from six of east London's most prominent communities. Aimed at five- to 12-year-olds, it highlights Bengali, Polish Roma, African, Albanian, English and Tamil communities, all of which have their own specific rhythm and depth of storytelling that blend with their unique senses of tradition, myth and language. Educational packs tie in with the exhibition, allowing local schools to delve into what the installation has to offer, and let the different cultures explore commonality and individuality.

Discover

1 Bridge Terrace, E15 4BG (8536 5563/ www.discover.org.uk). Stratford tube/ rail/DLR. **Open** *Term-time* 10am-5pm Tue-Sun. *Holidays* 10am-5pm daily. **Admission** *Garden* free. *Story Trail* £4; £3.50 reductions; free under-2s; £14 family (2+2). **Credit** MC, V.

Buggy access. Disabled access: ramp, toilet. Nappy-changing facilities. Shop.

Activities

Stitchclub

www.stitchclub.co.uk
Sewing classes for children aged from eight at venues throughout south-west London.

Circus skills

Albert & Friends' Instant Circus

Riverside Studios, Crisp Road, W6 9RL (8237 1170/www.albertandfriendsinstantcircus.co.uk). Hammersmith tube.
Albert the Clown's Instant Circus workshops teach children skills such as juggling, diabolo and stilt-, ball- and wire-walking. Many of his students go on to join the Albert & Friends' performing troupe – the UK's largest youth circus theatre, which also tours abroad.

Circus Space

Coronet Street, N1 6HD (7613 4141/www.the circusspace.co.uk). Old Street tube/rail.
There's a Sunday morning 'Little Top' course for eight- to 12-year-olds at this well-known circus school. Older children can choose static and flying trapeze, juggling, trampoline and acrobatics.

Cooking

We're all licking our lips with anticipation about the proposed new food school at Borough Market, which promises cookery courses for all ages (*see p230* **Eating lessons**). For details, visit www.borough market.org.uk and click on 'Community', then 'No.1 Cathedral Street'.

Cooking Village

3039 4002/www.thecookingvillage.com.
Cooking clubs in the usual north London locations (Crouch End, Hampstead, Muswell Hill and Highgate) introduce children to the delights of cooking fun, healthy and tasty food. A variety of programmes for twos to 11s include courses for under-fives and their parents, after-school and holiday clubs and themed parties. Check the website for times, places and fees.

Kids' Cookery School

107 Gunnersbury Lane, W3 8HQ (8992 8882/www.thekidscookeryschool.co.uk). Acton Town tube. **Open** *Office* 9am-5.30pm Mon-Fri. **Fees** *School hols* £15/75mins; £30/2.5hrs; £50/5hrs incl lunch. **No credit cards**.
A company that grew from Fiona Hamilton-Fairley's kitchen into a highly inclusive charity with its own space in west London, the Kids' Cookery School is an organisation dedicated to

bringing cooking into young people's lives. On-site classes and workshops run throughout the week, while parties for children aged five and over are held on Saturdays (£28 per child). Groups of eight to 12 children do several hours of cooking, learning to cook three-course meals chosen by the birthday boy or girl. The school can also provide party bags, and they'll do all the cleaning up.

Munchkins

8269 1331/www.munchkinskidscooking.co.uk.
Munchkins runs children's cooking parties as well as courses and private classes in both term time and during the holidays. Set up by former teacher and lifelong cook Joy Neal, whose background means she has a winning way with children, the parties are staffed by professional primary and cookery school teachers. Munchkins is known for working wonders with fussy eaters, as well as delivering smoothly run group events.

Unicorn Theatre for Children. *See p190.*

Choose from baking parties or making-your-own-meal parties with optional extras such as face-painting and games. Prices start from £110 for six children.

Film & new media

Film Club
www.filmclub.org.
An outfit that aims to put film on the (extra) curriculum by setting up after-school film clubs, running specially devised seasons and grouping films into interesting themes, giving member children and their teachers the chance to rate and review films and share their views with others. The goal is to have actors, directors, writers and other leading film industry figures visiting many schools giving personal talks about their experiences. The website also gives a useful list of films categorised by age group.

Film London
www.filmlondon.org.uk.
London's film and media agency, supporting projects across the capital.

Filmsteps
*St Christopher's School, Belsize Lane, NW3 5AE (0870 024 2522/www.filmsteps.com).
Belsize Park tube.* **Fees** from £235/term; siblings from £160. **No credit cards**.
A variety of filmmaking activities for seven- to 16-year-olds are held for two hours every Saturday year-round. The Summer Term is the 'film term', when young crews have ten weeks to make their own mini feature film; the results are screened at a red-carpet premiere at the Screen on the Hill cinema. School-holiday events, such as summer schools, family workshops, behind the scenes at the BBC and animation days, are also organised

First Light
www.firstlightmovies.com.
UK Film Council-funded scheme for five- to 18-year-olds. First Light invests over £1 million annually, offering a range of courses across the country via schools and educational groups. Its subsidiary website Film Street (www.filmstreet. co.uk) is a user-friendly resource providing a starting point for children exploring filmmaking, while the First Light Awards every February is an inspiring 'mini-Oscars' event, set in London.

Mouth That Roars
www.mouththatroars.com.
East London charity that offers training in video production and gives free membership to under-19s who attend its workshops.

Youth Culture TV Centre
79 Barlby Road, W10 6AZ (8964 4646/ www.yctv.org). Ladbroke Grove tube.
No credit cards.
A highly alternative centre for further education in the broadcast meedja that aims to give 11-to 20-year-olds a head start in television by training them in multimedia, graphics, animation, production, camera handling, editing and more.

Young Film Academy
Parish House, St Mary of the Angels Catholic Church, Moorhouse Road, W2 5DJ (7387 4341/www.youngfilmacademy.co.uk). Notting Hill Gate tube. **Fees** from £95/day; £390/4 day course. **Credit** phone for details.
The YFA's expanding programme of courses, workshops, schools events, parties and charitable programmes across London has

Activities

earned it gigs as official workshop provider for various international film festivals, including the London Children's Film Festival (*see p26*). The Academy has helped more than 600 young people make their first films, with one- to four-day courses (in west London) for children aged seven to 16. The four-day courses culminate in a premiere for friends and family in a West End screening room; students on every course receive a DVD copy of their film to keep.

Modern languages

Club Petit Pierrot

(7385 5565/www.clubpetitpierrot.uk.com). **Classes** phone for details. **Fees** from £96/term). **No credit cards**.
Children from eight months to nine years old learn with Club PP. Pupils are taught in small groups, in French, by native teachers, with an emphasis on learning through play. The lessons, planned for each age group around diverse themes, include, for the under-fives, songs, rhymes, dances, storytelling, arts and crafts and puppets. Over-fives test their mettle with songs and puppets too, as well as language games, exercises and role-play. Parent and toddler groups (during the week), Saturday and holiday clubs come highly recommended. Private tuition in the home is also available. PP also offers a free trial lesson for new children.

Easy Mandarin

Lower Belgrave Street, SW1W 0NL (7828 2998/www.easymandarinuk.com). Victoria tube/rail. **Classes** *3-5s, 6-8s* 9.30-10.30am, 10.30-11.30am Sat; *9-14s, 15-18s* 11.30am-1pm Sat. **Fees** vary; phone for details. **No credit cards**.
Thrusting parents are racing to sign up their children for these classes. It's just as well that Miss Jin, Miss Fei and their colleagues run such fun-filled Knightsbridge- and Victoria-based Saturday morning Chinese classes for ages three to 18.

French & Spanish à la Carte

97 Revelstoke Road, SW18 5NL (8946 4777/www.frenchandspanishalacarte.co.uk). Wimbledon Park tube/Earlsfield rail. **Classes** phone for details. **Fees** from £115/term. **No credit cards**.
This language school gives south London's ambitious two- to five-year-olds a head start with its weekly playgroups (Tuesday and Thursday, or Wednesday and Friday mornings), involving an hour of activity and an hour of free play while a teacher chats to them in French or

Spanish. After-school and holiday courses from £35 per session are offered for older children.

Le Club Tricolore

Office: 10 Ballingdon Road, SW11 6AJ (7924 4649/www.lecubtricolore.co.uk). **Classes** phone for details. **Fees** from £170/term; £30/yr membership. **No credit cards**.
Teresa Scibor and her team of native French speakers teach Tricolore tots (aged three to five) and Tricolore Juniors (fives to 12s) by means of role-playing or sing-alongs. Classes after school and during school holidays combine cookery, crafts and treasure hunts in a uniquely French atmosphere. The club operates mainly in Wandsworth, Clapham and Knightsbridge.

WILDLIFE

Oasis Children's Nature Garden

Larkhall Lane & Studley Road, SW4 2SP (7498 2329). Stockwell tube. **Open** *After-school Club* 3.30-5.30pm Tue-Fri. *Term time* 10am-3.30pm Sat. *School hols* 10am-noon, 2-4pm Tue-Sat. **Admission** 50p.
Reclaimed from wasteland, the Nature Garden is one of three projects run by the Oasis Children's Venture (the others are cycling and karting centres). It provides a serene environment in an inner-city area, and has a highly popular after-school club where activities include pond-dipping and gardening, as well as arts and crafts and woodwork. Environmental workshops are run on Saturdays, in school holidays or during term time after school.

Roots & Shoots

Walnut Tree Walk, SE11 6DN (7587 1131/www.roots-and-shoots.org.uk). Lambeth North tube. **Open** 10am-4pm Mon-Fri; phone before visiting. **Admission** free; donations welcome.
This half-acre wildlife garden, a peaceful haven in the heart of the city, is tended by a charity that has offered vocational training for young people for 25 years. Roots & Shoots introduces the pleasures of urban gardening to lots of London's youngsters, many of them with disadvantages and/or disabilities. The site is also a popular destination for school groups; an outreach worker guides them through the garden's diverse insects, animals and wild flowers, and explains how London honey is collected from the resident bees. The centre is home to the much-loved London Beekeepers' Association. The honey – fantastically flavoured because of the diversity of plants available from a million city gardens – is occasionally sold, but runs out quickly.

Sport & Leisure

Run, jump, pedal or swim – whatever you do, get active.

With the bulldozers grinding up and down in the east of the city, it's time for London to start training its 2012 Olympic players. The government's curriculum target of at least two hours of sport and recreation a week is all very well, but even if all schools reached it (and there's a suspicion that many don't), children need to run around for longer than that to burn off the calories. The Department of Health recommends that children between five and 18 take at least one hour of moderate exercise every day – and because schools can't fit that into the daily timetable, it's up to parents to keep their offspring active.

Fortunately, families have a wider choice of public greenery and sports facilities in London than elsewhere in the country. Almost everyone has a park that's a brisk walk or bus ride (free for kids) away. And even with London's much-publicised swimming pool crisis (there aren't enough to go round, let alone train our Olympic competitors), new sports and leisure centres are being built.

It's important to build physical activity into children's lives at an early age. The best sports teacher is the parent who can run races, climb trees and play in the park, but there are plenty of experts who can inject sport into youngsters' lives. The secret is to start 'em young and make it fun. Early-years activity clubs that do just that include Tumbletots (www.tumbletots.com) and Crechendo (www.crechendo.com).

Check your local council website for details of affordable (often free) sports camps in the school holidays. Many independent schools host private youth sports organisations that put on intensive rugby, football, tennis and cricket coaching when term ends. Such courses are more expensive than their council counterparts, but they're well worth it for seriously sporty kids. To find a specific club or venue near you, try your council website, or contact the individual sport's governing bodies, whose contact details we list on p211.

CLIMBING

Castle Climbing Centre
Green Lanes, N4 2HA (8211 7000/www. castle-climbing.co.uk). Manor House tube.
Children's classes are on Monday and Tuesday, and during the holidays. The Gecko Club (www.geckos.co.uk), for private tuition, is based here (£40/hr plus £10 admission). Phone for details of the party service.

Mile End Climbing Wall
Haverfield Road, E3 5BE (8980 0289/www. mileendwall.org.uk). Mile End tube.
Children's beginner sessions (£6) on Friday evenings, and other sessions on Saturday and Sunday mornings. Birthday parties can be held here, and there's a summer holiday programme.

CRICKET

Brit Oval
Kennington, SE11 5SS (7582 7764/www. surreycricket.com). Oval tube. **Admission** *Surrey matches £12-£20; £6-£10 under-16s.* **Credit** MC, V.
The Oval, home to Surrey County Cricket, is a world-class ground with fewer airs and graces than Lord's and a good youth programme.

Lord's Cricket Ground
St John's Wood Road, NW8 8QN (Middlesex 7289 1300/www.middlesexccc.com; MCC 7432 1000/www.lords.org). St John's Wood tube/13, 46, 82, 113, 274 bus. **Admission** Middlesex matches £14-£20; £5-£7 under-16s, reductions. **Credit** MC, V.

Any child interested in cricket will have heard of Lord's, the home ground of Middlesex. Tours give visitors a sneak peek at the historic ground; you can visit the long room, which boasts an art gallery depicting the great and the good of the sport. Fans can also have a look at the players' dressing rooms and the MCC Museum. For more details, *see p101*.

Playing cricket

There have been various initiatives to turn children on to cricket following a decline in cricket in state schools. Fortunately, many of the clubs listed below have stepped in to promote coaching for 16s and under. Try the following indoor centres:

Ken Barrington Cricket Centre
Brit Oval, Kennington, SE11 5SS (7820 5739). Oval tube.

MCC Indoor School
Lord's Cricket Ground, St John's Wood Road, NW8 8QN (7432 1014/www.lords.org/kids). St John's Wood tube/13, 46, 82, 113, 274 bus.

Middlesex County Cricket Club
East End Road, N3 2TA (8346 8020/ www.middlesexccc.com). Finchley Central tube.

CYCLING

In some European countries, as many as 60 per cent of children cycle to school. In Britain, a mere three per cent do – and a UK cyclist is 12 times more likely to be killed or injured than a Danish one. Safe Routes to Schools supports projects that encourage cycling and walking to school, by improving street design, calming traffic and linking with the 5,000-mile (8,000-kilometre) National Cycle Network. Most local authorities include Safe Routes to Schools schemes in their local transport plans. Sustrans (www.sustrans.org.uk) is the pressure group that is working to create a safer environment for cycling.

Parents who want to learn more about cycle training or Bike to School Week, can visit www.bikeforall.net for information, and log on to the websites below.

Go-Ride (www.go-ride.org.uk) is a British Cycling initiative where under-18s can learn track riding, BMX and mountain biking. It's delivered through a national network of clubs, including Lee Valley Youth Cycle Club (contact Greg Nash 7553 9494) and Sutton Cycling Club (www.suttoncycling.co.uk).

Cantelowes Skatepark is wheely cool. *See p209.*

Activities

Bikeability
www.bikeability.org.uk.
Bikeability is designed to give young cyclists the skills and confidence to ride their bikes on the roads. Kids are encouraged to achieve three levels of proficiency.

Cycle Training UK
7231 6005/www.cycletraining.co.uk.
CTUK's instructors offer individual tuition anywhere in Greater London. Accompanied journeys to school are also available. Of its participants, 81% have said they cycle more often and more confidently.

Cycling Instructor
www.cyclinginstructor.com.
Cycling instruction in schools for adults and children. The training organisation delivers Bikeability qualifications (*see above*) too.

Herne Hill Velodrome
Burbage Road, SE24 9HE
(www.vcl.org.uk/hernehill). Herne Hill rail.
The venerable home of track cycling since 1892. Many children begin their cycling careers here.

London Recumbents
Battersea Park 7489 6543/Dulwich Park
8299 6636/www.londonrecumbents.co.uk.
Both London Recumbents have a wide range of bikes, including those with a little front trailer for tots for hire (and sale).

London School of Cycling
7249 3779/www.londonschoolofcycling.co.uk.
Private tuition for all ages and abilities, as well as cycle-maintenance workshops.

FOOTBALL

Playing football
All the professional clubs in London run Football in the Community coaching courses, fun days and skills clinics. These are suitable for boys and girls aged six and over, and are staffed by FA-qualified coaches. Check the club websites listed on p203 (details are usually listed on the 'Community' pages) for venues and dates.

Most soccer schools cater equally for boys and girls, and many clubs run girls' teams. The FA have created a resource, 'Girls United', which includes a club finder facility: visit www.thefa.com/girlsunited.

David Beckham Academy
East Parkside, Greenwich Peninsula, SE10 0JF (82694620/www.thedavidbeckham academy.com). North Greenwich tube.
Two huge indoor pitches, highly qualified coaches and an impressive array of Becks memorabilia guarantee interest from children. The football camps run Monday to Friday in school holidays and follow the same lines as the schools education programme, plus coaching and skills sessions. Courses are non-residential and cost £180 (three days) or £265 (five days). That might seem pricey, but all children receive a package of adidas kit, including footwear, as well as healthy lunches and refreshments. There are also single day and after-school sessions; call or check the website for details.

Elms Football School
8954 8787/www.theelms.co.uk.
Based in Stanmore, the Elms offers Saturday and Sunday coaching, holiday courses and a school of excellence.

European Football Academy
www.footballcamps.co.uk.
The Academy runs week-long residential and day camps in England, Ireland, Scotland, Germany and Luxembourg, as well as Safari camps in Zambia and Malawi and F1 camps in Bahrain. They take place in school holidays for girls, boys and teams aged eight to 18.

Football Academy
Langston Road, Loughton, Essex IG10 3TQ (0870 084 2111/www.footballacademyuk.com). Debden tube.
Ten all-weather, floodlit, five-a-side pitches are available for hire at this new centre (you can see it from the M11). Holiday and weekend sessions are led by FA-qualified coaches under the guidance of former West Ham star John Moncur and several other ex-professionals.

Goals Soccer Centres
www.goalsfootball.co.uk.
All-weather, floodlit pitches with junior leagues, birthday parties and coaching at weekends and school holidays; there are 12 around London.

Lambeth Dribblers
(8677 6888).
Chelsea FC has helped fund this project, which provides free coaching for young children on the astroturf at Brixton Recreation Centre, while enabling enthusiastic dads (sorry, women, it's specifically aimed at fathers, not mothers) to have a kickaround as well.

Activities

Little Kickers

01235 859250/www.littlekickers.co.uk.
Parents of football-crazy infants love Little Kickers. The classes, developed by a group of FA-qualified coaches and nursery-school teachers for pre-schoolers (18 months and up), are a gentle introduction to football. The programme operates all over London and incorporates a number of early-learning goals.

London Football Academy

8882 9100/www.londonfootballacademy.co.uk.
Holiday courses, skill schools and birthday parties in Alexandra Park.

North London Girls League

07912 050374/email
natalie.huntley@londonfa.com.
Based in Regent's Park, this is a dynamic organisation for female footie fans to join – it caters for players aged nine and up.

Peter Hucker Soccer

8536 4141/www.peterhucker-soccer.com.
This highly rated scheme is run by former Queens Park Rangers goalkeeper Peter Hucker. Based in Barking and Wanstead, it offers weekly pay-and-play coaching sessions, matchplay and football parties for fives to 16s. Hucker also founded the East London & Essex Small-Sided Soccer League (07961 867501, 01375 650833, www.eleleague.com).

Powerleague

www.powerleague.co.uk.
There are 13 Power League centres around the capital, each providing all-weather, floodlit pitches. You can book a pitch for a kickabout or a party, and most also offer coaching with mini matches at weekends and during holidays, plus junior leagues.

Sharpshooters Football

07873 583366/www.sharpshooters
football.co.uk.
Sunday pay-and-play sessions on Tooting Bec Common and other venues in south-west London for four- to 11-year-olds, plus holiday courses and footie-themed birthday parties. Talented youngsters can progress to 'Sharp Shooter Select' sessions.

South East London & Kent Girls League

www.selkent.org.uk.
Specialises in girls' football for under-tens to under-16s. The website includes a very useful 'players wanted' section.

South London Special League

07946 879562/www.sl-sl.co.uk.
Helps players with special needs enjoy football. The London FA website (www.londonfa.com) has an extensive section devoted to opportunities for children with physical and learning disabilities. Many of the community programmes run by London's professional clubs cater for special needs.

Watching football

The season runs from August to May, and club websites include regularly updated ticket information. Ticket prices and membership packages are far too numerous to list for each club; as a rule, a seat at a Premier League match will cost £30-£60 for an adult, around half that for kids (if discounts are offered), and at reduced rates for members. Coca-Cola Championship and Coca-Cola League prices are around £15-£40, with reductions for children and club members.

Barclays Premiership

Arsenal

Emirates Stadium, Ashburton Grove, N7 7AF (7704 4000/www.arsenal.com). Arsenal tube.
For the club's museum, *see p100.*

Chelsea

Stamford Bridge, Fulham Road, SW6 1HS (0871 984 1955/www.chelseafc.com). Fulham Broadway tube.
For information on the museum, *see p100.*

Fulham

Craven Cottage, Stevenage Road, SW6 6HH (0870 442 1222/www.fulhamfc.com). Putney Bridge tube.
Stadium tours are also available. *See p204.*

Tottenham Hotspur

White Hart Lane, Bill Nicholson Way, 748 High Road, N17 0AP (0844 499 5000/www.spurs.co.uk). White Hart Lane rail. **Tours** 11am, 1pm non-match Sats. **Admission** *Tours* £8; £5 under-16s, reductions. **Credit** MC, V.
Book in advance for tours of pitch-side, tunnel, changing rooms, boardrooms and press rooms. Don't turn up on spec, as they don't always run. Spurs tours usually last for an hour or more, although this depends on how chatty the punters are feeling.
Buggy access. Disabled access: toilet. Shop.

Football crazy

England's latest failure to qualify for a major international tournament has prompted yet another round of footballing introspection. Too many foreigners in the Premier League? Too much money swilling at the top end of the game and not enough trickling down to the grassroots? Too little development and too much win-at-all-costs thinking? Too few decent coaches? Too many shouty parents?

Despite these setbacks, football is still exciting to play – in London there are more than 80 leagues and dozens of soccer schools catering for children – and to watch. The capital's 13 professional clubs illustrate the full spectrum of ambition, from Arsenal and Chelsea's triumphs to Barnet's battle simply to survive.

Finding a club

When helping your child to find a soccer school or club, it's important to do some research first. There's nothing more likely to demoralise than, say, thrusting a child who will never be more than an enthusiastic hacker into a group of high-achievers. Apply the following guidelines.

● The FA Charter Standard is a nationally recognised quality benchmark. If a club hasn't reached this standard (check the London Football Association website, www.londonfa.com), ask if it's working towards it. If not, why not?

● Ask if the coaches hold FA qualifications, have received training in child protection and emergency first aid, and hold an enhanced Criminal Records Bureau (CRB) disclosure.

● Watch a session to see it's well run.

● Find out the number of children in each age group. Large memberships may mean only the best get to play regularly.

● Do children play in a format appropriate to their age? Minikickers is aimed at pre-school kids; Mini Soccer, the next step up, can vary from four-a-side for the youngest to seven-a-side for under-10s.

● Consider the atmosphere and ethos: is this 'sport for all' or all about winning?

● Are parents yelling advice (or abuse) from the touchline, or are they encouraged to leave coaching to qualified personnel?

Holiday courses

All professional clubs in London (*see p203*) run extensive 'Football in the Community' holiday courses, fun days and skills clinics. These are suitable for boys and girls aged six and up, and are staffed by FA-qualified coaches. Some have nice

West Ham United

Boleyn Ground, Green Street, E13 9AZ (8548 2794/www.whufc.com). Upton Park tube.

Coca-Cola Championship

Charlton Athletic

The Valley, Floyd Road, SE7 8BL (8333 4000/www.charlton-athletic.co.uk). Charlton rail.

Crystal Palace

Selhurst Park, Whitehorse Lane, SE25 6PU (8768 6000/www.cpfc.co.uk). Selhurst rail.

Queens Park Rangers

Loftus Road, South Africa Road, W12 7PA (8743 0262/www.qpr.co.uk). White City tube.

Watford

Vicarage Road, Watford, Herts WD18 0ER (0845 442 1881/www.watfordfc.com). Watford High Street rail.

add-ons: the courses run by Fulham, for example, include two tickets to a home game. Check on the clubs' websites; details are usually listed under the 'Club' or 'Community' headings.

Spectating and stadium visits

As far as watching football is concerned, it has become increasingly difficult for young fans to watch Barclays Premier League football live, rather than on TV. Top clubs have two or three times more members than their ground can hold, and discounts are few and far between. Point your Man U-obsessed kids towards your local team. They will have a much better chance of watching live football. Your wallet will benefit too, as most local clubs encourage youngsters with cheap tickets and special deals.

Finally, what better treat than a look behind the scenes at your favourite club? **Arsenal**'s museum (*see p100*) has interactive treats. **Chelsea** has the Centenary Museum with its collection of Chelsea memorabilia. **Fulham**'s Craven Cottage is a most charismatic ground; tours take in the dressing rooms, dugouts, the Cottage balcony and press facilities. **Tottenham Hotspur** tours (for all of the above, *see p203*) reveal White Hart Lane in all its glory.

Finally, the national stadium at **Wembley** runs a 90-minute tour of the changing rooms and warm-up zone, VIP reception area, the royal box (where you can lift a replica of the FA Cup), the dugouts, treatment rooms and media suites. Tours run 9.30am-4.30pm daily. Tickets cost £15; £8 under-16s, reductions; £38 family (2+2). Full details on www.thestadiumtour.com/home.aspx.

Coca-Cola League

Barnet
Underhill Stadium, Barnet Lane, Herts, EN5 2DN (8441 6932/www.barnetfc.premium tv.co.uk). High Barnet tube. Division 2.

Brentford
Griffin Park, Braemar Road, Brentford, Middx TW8 0NT (0845 345 6442/www.brentfordfc. premiumtv.co.uk). Brentford rail. Division 2.

Leyton Orient
Matchroom Stadium, Brisbane Road, E10 5NE (0871 310 1881/www.leytonorient.com). Leyton tube. Division 1.

Millwall
The Den, Zampa Road, SE16 3LN (7232 1222/www.millwallfc.co.uk). South Bermondsey rail. Division 1.

GOLF

The English Golf Union (*see p211*) has developed Tri-Golf for six- to 12-year-olds, and is introducing the game in primary schools. Children can play golf as part of the Duke of Edinburgh's Award.

A driving range is a top place at which to introduce a child to the basics; course professionals may offer lessons to get them into good habits early. The **TopGolf** system (www.topgolf.co.uk) is a point-scoring game using balls with a microchip inside. TopGolf is played at its centres in Addlestone (01932 858551), Chigwell (8500 2644) and Watford (01923 222045).

Beckenham Place Park
The Mansion, Beckenham Place Park, Beckenham, Kent BR3 5BP (8650 2292). Beckenham Hill rail. Juniors can use this course at a reduced rate all day during the week and after noon on Saturday (before noon the cost is £23). Lessons are on Saturdays at 10am (£3). It costs £10 for juniors to play a round at weekends, £8 on weekdays.

KARTING & MOTOR SPORTS

Karting is thrilling for any child over eight. The little buggies zip around at speeds exceeding 30mph (50kmph), but modern karts are easy to drive: there are two pedals (stop and go) and no gearbox to confuse the issue. These venues welcome children and can be booked for parties.

Brands Hatch
Fawkham, Longfield, Kent DA3 8NG (01474 872331/www.motorsportvision.co.uk). Swanley rail, then taxi. Brands Hatch has loads of things to do on two and four wheels, including YoungDrive!, which puts over 13s in control of a Renault Clio.

Activities

Playscape Pro Racing

390 Streatham High Road, SW16 6HX (8677 8677/www.playscape.co.uk). Streatham rail.
This centre can be booked for children's parties (over-eights only) or for half-hour taster sessions. Those who become addicted can join the Cadet School, or the RAC's Association of Racing Kart Schools, which operates on the first Saturday of each month (8.30am-1pm, £35).

MARTIAL ARTS

All martial arts impart self-confidence, body awareness, assertiveness and resilience. Most local sports centres will be home to at least one martial arts club; many more are based in church halls and community centres. Look for evidence of a lively but disciplined atmosphere, with well-organised and age-appropriate teaching. Ask instructors about their qualifications: the grading systems in judo and karate, for example, help ensure teachers are of a suitable standard. Note, however, that a black belt is not a teaching qualification. And ask for proof of insurance cover: martial arts usually involve physical contact, and accidents can happen.

The following venues offer classes for children in a number of disciplines.

Bob Breen Academy

16 Hoxton Square, N1 6NT (7729 5789/ www.bobbreen.co.uk). Old Street tube/rail.
Children aged seven to 16 can learn kick-boxing skills and effective self-defence techniques at this well known and highly respected academy.

Hwarang Academy

Swiss Cottage Community Centre, 19 Winchester Road, NW3 3NR (07941 081 009/www.taekwondo-london-2012.com). Swiss Cottage tube.
Youngsters aged four and up can learn the Korean martial art of tae kwon do, now an Olympic sport.

London School of Capoeira

Units 1 & 2, Leeds Place, Tollington Park, N4 3RF (7281 2020/www.londonschoolofcapoeira. co.uk). Finsbury Park tube/rail.
Kids aged six to 16 can learn this Brazilian martial art, which combines acrobatics and dance, and in which creative play is a strong element. It is believed to have developed in the sixteenth century by native and African slaves.

Moving East

St Matthias Church Hall, Wordsworth Road, N16 8DD (7503 3101/www.movingeast.co.uk). Dalston Kingsland rail.
Judo and aikido (as well as dance and capoeira) classes for children are held at this friendly centre devoted to Japanese martial arts.

Shaolin Temple UK

207A Junction Road, N19 5QA (7687 8333/ www.shaolintempleuk.org). Tufnell Park tube.
Thirty-fourth-generation fighting monk Shi Yanzi and several other Shaolin masters teach traditional kung fu, Chinese kick-boxing, meditation and t'ai chi. Weekly classes for children are also given.

RIDING

Anything to do with horses is expensive, but riding is one of the most rewarding sports going. Riders who learn as children often develop a passion that lasts a lifetime. Many riding stables in Greater London can be reached easily by public transport, and some are tucked away in surprising places – the Isle of Dogs and Catford can both boast their very own riding school. There are stunning surrounds in which to hack out, notably the wide open spaces of Richmond Park and Hyde Park. If you ring in advance, some establishments will happily show you around or let you watch a lesson; ask the stables whether there are 'taster' sessions for newcomers.

Riding lessons and hacks must be booked in advance. Riders must always wear a BSI-approved hard hat (establishments can usually lend or rent you one if you don't have your own) and boots with a small heel rather than trainers or wellies. If your child decides to take up riding seriously and needs to buy some kit, make a trip to **Decathlon** (*see p278*). This sports store in Surret Quays has a huge range of inexpensive equipment and clothes for pony lovers. Some centres run 'own a pony' days and weeks, and offer birthday party packages. Many stables can cater for riders with disabilities, though not all have equipment to winch riders on to horses or ponies. All the establishments listed below are British Horse Society-approved (http://bhs.org.uk); it is not advisable to ride at non-BHS approved centres.

Deen City Farm & Riding School

39 Windsor Avenue, SW19 2RR (8543 5858/ www.deencityfarm.co.uk). Colliers Wood tube, then 20min walk/Phipps Bridge tramlink/200 bus. **Lessons** £20/45min (group); £21/30min (individual).

This friendly establishment offers lessons to children aged eight and over in flatwork and jumping (there's no hacking), from beginners to advanced. Over-12s can volunteer at the yard at weekends and in school holidays. 'Own a pony' days for eight- to 12-year-olds cost a reasonable £18 per day (without ride) or £28 (with ride), and competitions are held throughout the year. The school is a Pony Club Centre, and is approved by the Riding for the Disabled Association. The farm is also home to cows, sheep, pigs and other animals.

Ealing Riding School

17-19 Gunnersbury Avenue, W5 3XD (8992 3808/www.ealingridingschool.biz). Ealing Common tube. **Lessons** £24/hr (group); £30/hr (individual).

Riders aged five and up can learn to ride from scratch or, if they have previous experience, improve flatwork or jumping; lessons are held in an outdoor manège. Pony days (£55), in school holidays, include two hours of lessons and four hours learning stable management such as mucking out and grooming.

Hyde Park & Kensington Stables

63 Bathurst Mews, W2 2SB (7723 2813/ www.hydeparkstables.com). Lancaster Gate tube. **Lessons** £49-£55/hr (group); £69-£85/hr (individual).

Children aged five and up can enjoy an hour-long lesson (prices reflect the glamorous location) with patient, streetwise ponies. The stables is a Pony Club Centre with a membership of around 50 children.

Kingston Riding Centre

38 Crescent Road, Kingston-upon-Thames, Surrey KT2 7RG (8546 6361/www.kingston ridingcentre.com). Richmond tube/rail, then 371 bus/Norbiton rail then 10min walk. **Lessons** £35-£36/hr (group); £27-£29/30min (lead-rein); £30-£75 (individual).

This well-equipped yard, with 25 horses, is suitable for all levels of rider. There's hacking in Richmond Park, and the owners organise regular events, competitions and popular courses for children (£165 for four days). Facilities include a floodlit indoor school, an outdoor arena and, in summer months, a cross-country course. Closed Mondays.

Lee Valley Riding Centre

71 Lea Bridge Road, E10 7QL (8556 2629/ www.leevalleypark.org.uk). Clapton rail/48, 55, 56 bus. **Lessons** £18.20-£21/hr (group); £31-£37/30min, £42-£47/45min (individual); £10-£12.60/30min (taster session).

The placid ponies at the friendly Lee Valley Riding Centre enjoy the open spaces of Walthamstow Marshes and delight a devoted band of regulars. The superb facilities include one indoor and two outdoor arenas; experienced riders can use the cross-country course. Children aged five and over can participate in group lessons; children from three-and-a-half years old can have private lessons. Children over ten who have some riding and pony-handling experience can become stable helpers.

London Equestrian Centre

Lullington Garth, N12 7BP (8349 1345/ www.londonridingschool.com). Mill Hill East tube. **Lessons** £25/30min (group); £24-£30/30min (individual).

This yard has 30 horses and ponies, and caters for riders of all abilities. The centre is affiliated to the Pony Club, and runs pony days and weeks in school holidays. Birthday parties are held here, and the staff can organise pony rides for three-to-four-year-olds. Young people aged from 13 can help out at the yard in return for rides.

Mount Mascal Stables

Vicarage Road, Bexley, Kent DA5 2AW (8300 3947/www.mountmascalstables.com). Bexley rail. **Lessons** £18/hr (group); £30/hr (individual).

The busy centre is well-equipped and teaches all riders over five on its 40 horses and ponies. The centre has two indoor schools, two outdoor grass arenas and two outdoor all-weather manèges. More experienced riders can hack out in the stunning Joyden's Wood. Birthday parties for six to 12 kids can be arranged for weekends or in school holidays.

Mudchute Equestrian Centre

Mudchute Park & Farm, Pier Street, E14 3HP (7515 0749 /www.mudchute.org). Mudchute, Crossharbour or Island Gardens DLR/D3, D6, D7, D8 bus. **Lessons** £18-£22/hr (group); £30-£35/45min (individual).

This establishment on the Isle of Dogs is friendly, down-to-earth and very welcoming to new riders. Lessons are some of the most reasonably priced in the London, and are available to children over seven. It's a Pony Club Centre, enabling local kids who don't own a pony to study for badges and certificates.

Activities

Ross Nye's Riding Stables

*8 Bathurst Mews, W2 2SB (7262 3791).
Lancaster Gate tube.* **Lessons** *£50/hr (group);
£60/hr (individual).*
The Hyde Park branch of the Pony Club;
membership gives reduced prices for lessons.
Clients aged from six learn to ride in Hyde Park.

Stag Lodge Stables

*Robin Hood Gate, Richmond Park, SW15
3RS (8974 6066/www.ridinginlondon.com).
East Putney tube/Putney rail, then 85 bus/
Kingston rail then 85 bus.* **Lessons** *£30-
£35/hr (group); £45-£60/hr, £25-£30/30min
(individual).*
Riders travel across the capital to mount one of
this centre's 40 or so horses and ponies (ranging
from Shetlands to Irish hunters) in historic
Richmond Park. Threes to sevens can enjoy
half-hour lead-rein rides through the park (£20-
£25); jumping or flatwork lessons for all abilities
take place in one of the two outdoor manèges.
There are pony weeks for the over-sixes in
school holidays and half term (£250 for four
days) – book well ahead.

Trent Park Equestrian Centre

*Bramley Road, N14 4XS (8363 9005/www.
trentpark.com). Oakwood tube.* **Lessons**
*£23-£30/hr (group); £38-£42/hr, £20/30min
(individual).*
The leafy acres of Trent Park (£28 per hour for
hacking) and a caring attitude towards young
riders (over four) make this a popular place to
ride. Pony days (£60) and weeks (£220) are held
in the school holidays.

Willowtree Riding Establishment

*The Stables, Ronver Road, SE12 0NL (8857
6438/www.willowtreeridinglondon.co.uk).
Grove Park or Lee rail.* **Lessons** *from£9/
30min, £17.50/hr (group); from £18/30min
(private).*
There are 25 ponies at this friendly yard, where
children over four can learn to ride. The Welsh
native ponies are particularly popular, though
there are also good-natured Arabs and
thoroughbreds. Lessons (flatwork only) take
place in a covered, full-size indoor arena. There
are some evening lessons, but most teaching is
at weekends and holidays.

Wimbledon Village Stables

*24A-B High Street, SW19 5DX (8946 8579/
www.wvstables.com). Wimbledon tube/
rail.* **Lessons** *£55/hr, £28/30min (individual).*
This quintessential village stables is a slice of
the countryside in the city, and although it

largely caters for adult riders, children are
welcome. The centre has a small selection of
quiet, safe ponies and a popular holiday scheme
for five- to ten-year-olds (£160 for three
afternoons). Riding takes place on leafy
Wimbledon Common, where the centre has use
of two outdoor arenas for flatwork and jumping
lessons. Riders must become members to ride
regularly. No group lessons for kids.

RUGBY UNION

The top London rugby union clubs have
a slew of internationals in their line-ups,
and taking the kids to a match is a bargain
compared to football. The season runs
from September to May.

Guinness Premiership

Saracens

*Vicarage Road, Watford, Herts WD18 0EP
(01923 475 222/www.saracens.com). Watford
High Street rail.* **Admission** *£15-£50;
£5-£10 2-16s.*

Harlequins

*Twickenham Stoop Stadium, Langhorn Drive,
Twickenham, Middx TW2 7SX (8410 6000/
www.quins.co.uk). Twickenham rail.*
Admission *£17-£40; £8-£10 2-16s.*

National League

London Welsh

*Old Deer Park, Kew Road, Richmond, Surrey
TW9 2AZ (8940 2368/www.london-welsh.
co.uk). Richmond tube/rail.* **Admission** *£12-
£17; £6-£8.50 reductions; free under-16s.*

SKATEBOARDING & BMX

BaySixty6 Skate Park

*Bay 65-66, Acklam Road, W10 5YU (8969
4669/www.baysixty6.com). Ladbroke Grove
tube.* **Membership** *free.* **Prices** *£6/5hrs
Mon-Fri, 4hrs Sat, Sun; £3 beginners
10am-noon Sat, Sun.*
Sheltered beneath the A40, this famous and
enormous park includes a vert ramp, a medium
half-pipe, a mini ramp and many funboxes,
grind boxes, ledges and rails. Some skaters
mutter that it's a poor show having to pay £6
when it's free to skate everywhere else in
London – but the high quality of the ramps goes
some way to making up for it.

Cantelowes Skatepark

Cantelowes Gardens, Camden Road, NW1 (www.cantelowesskatepark.co.uk). Kentish Town tube/rail/Camden Road rail.
This phenomenally popular park re-opened in May 2006 as part of a £1.5m redevelopment.

Harrow Skatepark

Christchurch Avenue, Wealdstone, Middx HA3 5BD (www.harrowskatepark.co.uk). Harrow & Wealdstone tube/rail.
This park has a clover-leaf, kidney bowls and a challenging concrete half-pipe.

Meanwhile

Meanwhile Gardens, off Great Western Road, W10 (www.mgca.f2s.com). Westbourne Park tube.
Three concrete bowls of varying steepness and size, but no flatland, so it's not for beginners.

SKATING

On ice

Temporary skating rinks spring up in various museums, galleries and shopping centres around the city at Christmas time. Session times at London's permanent rinks vary, but venues are generally open from 10am until 10pm.

Alexandra Palace Ice Rink

Alexandra Palace Way, N22 7AY (8365 4386/ www.alexandrapalace.com). Wood Green tube/ Alexandra Palace rail/W3 bus.
Courses for children aged five to 15 run in the lofty ice arena on Saturday mornings and early on weekday evenings.

Broadgate Ice Arena

Broadgate Circle, Eldon Street, EC2A 2BQ (summer 7505 4000/winter 7505 4068/www. broadgateice.co.uk). Liverpool Street tube/rail.
This tiny outdoor rink is open from late October to April. It's very child-friendly and usually isn't as crowded as the other outdoor rinks, so it's a good place to learn.

Lee Valley Ice Centre

Lea Bridge Road, E10 7QL (8533 3154/ www.leevalleypark.org.uk). Clapton rail.
The disco nights are a big hit at this modern, well-maintained and comparatively warm rink. It's never too busy, and the ice rink is a good size. Lessons are also offered.

Michael Sobell Leisure Centre

Hornsey Road, N7 7NY (7609 2166/ www.aquaterra.org). Finsbury Park tube/rail.
Children over four are welcome at this small rink, which runs popular after-school sessions and six-week courses. Children can also have ice-skating parties here – all the necessary equipment is provided.

Activities

They'll warm to **Hampton Heated Open Air Pool**. *See p213.*

Queens

17 Queensway, W2 4QP (7229 0172/
www.queensiceandbowl.co.uk). Bayswater
or Queensway tube.
The disco nights on Fridays and Saturdays are
legendary, but beginners and families are also
nicely looked after at this well-known ice rink.

Somerset House

Strand, WC2R 1LA (78454600/
www.somersethouse.org.uk). Holborn or
Temple tube.
Every winter, the courtyard at Somerset House
is iced over to become a most attractive rink,
open (usually) from late November until late
January. *See also p68.*

Streatham Ice Arena

386 Streatham High Road, SW16 6HT
(8769 7771/www.streathamicearena.co.uk).
Streatham rail.
The combined attractions of ice rink, karting
track (Playscape, *see p206*) and bowling lane
(*see p216*) are known as the Streatham Hub.
Locals have campaigned for improvements,
with particular concern for the future of the rink
(Streatham has had one since 1931); see
Streatham Ice Skating Action Group's website
at www.sisag.org.uk. The rink offers six-week
courses for all ages, as well as classes for
'toddlers' aged up to four.

On tarmac

Citiskate (7228 2999, www.citiskate.
co.uk) teaches hundreds of Londoners
how to skate in parks, leisure centres
and schools. The instructors all hold
qualifications from UKISA (United
Kingdom Inline Skating Association);
lessons are available daily. Citiskate's
weekly Sunday Rollerstroll (www.roller
stroll.com) and Battersea Park's Easy
Peasy skate on Saturday (www.easy
peasyskate.com) are popular family-
friendly group skates around the streets .

SKIING & SNOWBOARDING

If you're thinking of taking a mixed-
ability group to a dry ski slope for an
open session, bear in mind that the
minimum requirement is to be able to
perform a controlled snowplough turn
and use the ski lift.

Bromley Ski Centre

Sandy Lane, St Paul's Cray, Orpington, Kent
BR5 3HY (01689 876812). St Mary Cray rail/
321 bus.
Two lifts serve the 120m (394ft) main slope, and
there's also a mogul field and nursery slope.
Skiing and snowboarding taster sessions cost
£17. Booking is essential.

Sandown Sports Club

More Lane, Esher, Surrey KT10 8AN
(01372 467132/www.sandownsports.co.uk).
Esher rail.
The 120m (94ft) main slope, 80m (262ft) nursery
area and 90m (295ft) snowboarding slope are
closed during race meetings. Lessons only:
tuition for under-sevens (£24/30mins) and
seven-year-olds upwards (£43/hr).

Snozone

Xscape, 602 Marlborough Gate, Milton
Keynes, Bucks MK9 3XS (0871 2225670/
www.xscape.co.uk, www.snozoneuk.com).
Milton Keynes Central rail.
This is one of the UK's largest indoor snow
domes, with three slopes (in reality they're
joined, so they resemble one wide slope): two of
170m (558ft) and one of 135m (443ft), with
button lifts running all the way to the top. The
place can feel a bit like a big fridge, but it's a
good place to find your ski legs.

SWIMMING

Most local authority pools run lessons for
children, plus parent-and-baby sessions
to develop water confidence in those as
young as three months. These are
extremely popular so may have long
waiting lists; ask at your local pool for
details. Most of the pools recommended
below are open daily; phone for times.

Barnet Copthall Pools

Champions Way, NW4 1PX (8457 9900/
www.gll.org). Mill Hill East tube.
Three pools and a diving area, with coaching
and clubs to join if you fancy taking the plunge.

Brentford Fountain Leisure Centre

658 Chiswick High Road, Brentford, Middx
TW8 0HJ (0845 456 2935/www.hounslow.
gov.uk). Gunnersbury tube/Kew Bridge rail.
A nicely kept leisure pool with a warm, shallow
teaching pool, exciting 40m (130ft) aquaslide,
underwater lighting and wave machine.

Activities

Governing bodies

Amateur Boxing Association of England
www.abae.co.uk

Amateur Rowing Association
82376700/www.ara-rowing.org

Amateur Swimming Association
01509 618 700/
www.britishswimming.co.uk

Badminton Association of England
01908268 400/
www.badmintonengland.co.uk

BaseballSoftballUK
7453 7055/www.baseballsoftballuk.com

British Canoe Union
0845 370 9500/www.bcu.org.uk

British Dragon Boat Racing Association
www.dragonboat.org.uk

British Fencing Association
8742 3032/www.britishfencing.com

British Gymnastics
01952 820330/
www.british-gymnastics.org

British Mountaineering Council
01614 456111/www.thebmc.co.uk

British Orienteering Federation
01629 734042/
www.britishorienteering.org.uk

British Tenpin Bowling Association
8478 1745/www.btba.org.uk

British Waterski
www.britishwaterski.org.uk

England Squash
01612314 499/
www.englandsquash.com

England & Wales Cricket Board
www.ecb.co.uk

English Basketball Association
0114 223 5693/
www.englandbasketball.co.uk

English Golf Union
01526 354500/
www.englishgolfunion.org

English Table Tennis Association
01424 722525/
www.englishtabletennis.org.uk

Football Association
7745 4545/www.thefa.com

Lawn Tennis Association
8487 7000/www.lta.org.uk

London Baseball Association
www.londonsports.com/baseball

London Sports Forum for Disabled People
7717 1699/
www.londonsportsforum.org.uk

London Windsurf Association
01895 846707/
www.lwawindsurfing.co.uk

National Ice Skating Association
0115 988 8060/www.iceskating.org.uk

Royal Yachting Association
0845 345 0400/www.rya.org.uk

Rugby Football Union
8892 2000/www.rfu.com

Ski Club of Great Britain
8410 2000/www.skiclub.co.uk

Wheelpower
01296 395995/www.wheelpower.org.uk
The umbrella body for 17 wheelchair sports, from archery to rugby.

Activities

Hoofing it in the city

For London-based children who live, breathe and dream ponies, learning to ride might seem a distant dream. Yet it's surprisingly easy to find a British Horse Society-approved centre in this city.

OK, so riding isn't the most wallet-friendly activity. Lessons cost around £20, sometimes significantly more. If you're considering buying, loaning or even part-sharing a pony, there'll be livery bills (£25 per week for DIY, £70 for full livery), vet bills, shoeing (£50 every six weeks), feed and hay, bedding and equipment such as rugs and tack. However, there are ways pony-mad young Londoners can get a thrifty horse fix. And just because there aren't open fields to gallop across doesn't make for dull riding. 'If you can ride in London, you can ride anywhere,' says Catherine Brown, manager of **Hyde Park & Kensington Stables** (*see p207*). 'Because horses react to their environment – which, in the city, can mean lots of distractions – riders learn to cope with a variety of situations.'

Contrary to popular perception, it's not only girls who are bitten by the pony bug. 'Of the under-tens who ride with us, it's 50-50 boys to girls,' says Brown, 'though once they reach their teens it's mostly girls; boys seem to prefer motorbikes.'

There are social advantages too, for inner-city kids, according to Jo Henbrey, stable manager and instructor at **Deen City Farm & Riding School** (*see p207*). 'The helpers on our yard learn to be independent, motivated and responsible. The older kids teach the younger ones how to feed, groom and muck out. It boosts confidence and gets them into the fresh air, away from the computer.'

What are the options for kids who beg for a pony? Yards like **Mudchute Equestrian Centre**, Deen City Farm Riding School and **Lee Valley Riding Centre** (*see p207 for all*) welcome youngsters as stable helpers. In return for mucking out and grooming, kids spend time with their favourite pony. Another option are s 'own a pony' days (from £18 per day) in the school holidays. One affordable solution for kids whose parents can't bear the financial burden might be to adopt a pony through the Blue Cross animal charity (www.bluecross.org.uk). This costs from £15, and the animal stays at one of the charity's centres, of course, but the child adopting it will get updates on their chosen pony, and can visit.

For keen under-21s, joining the Pony Club (http://pcuk.org) is a beneficial way to learn horsemanship skills and meet

like-minded pals. Kids don't have to own a pony, though they will need to join at a recognised centre – in London there are 18 Pony Club-affiliated schools, including Mount Mascal Stables, Stag Lodge Stables, Mudchute Equestrian Centre and Hyde Park & Kensington Stables.

Information and events

When they're not in the saddle, there are plenty of horse-related diversions. The Pony Club website is a good place to start, as are specialist equestrian magazines such as *Horse and Pony* (www.horseandpony.com) or *Pony* (www.ponymag.com).

And there's no shortage of opportunities to watch the experts in action. Events in 2008 include the annual Horse of the Year Show (8-12 October, www.hoys.co.uk); the Hickstead Derby (26-29 June, www.hickstead.co.uk); Burleigh Horse Trials (4-7 September, www.burghley.co.uk), a top-class international event; the glamorous Cartier International polo (27 July, www.guardspoloclub.com) at the Guards Club, Windsor; and the atmospheric London International Horse Show at Olympia (16-22 December, www.eco.co.uk; *see also p26*).

Willowtree. *See p208.*

Crystal Palace National Sports Centre

Ledrington Road, SE19 2BB (8778 0131/ www.gll.org). Crystal Palace rail.
One of the capital's two 50m(160ft) Olympic-size pools; this venerable old pool has fine diving facilities (rare across the country).

Goresbrook Leisure Centre

Ripple Road, Dagenham, Essex RM9 6XW (8227 3977/www.barking-dagenham.gov.uk). Becontree tube.
Fountains, cascades and a 60m (195ft) flume, plus a small area for length swimming.

Hampton Heated Open Air Pool

High Street, Hampton, Middx TW12 2ST (8255 1116/www.hamptonpool.co.uk). Hampton rail.
When the sun's shining, Hampton is hard to beat. It's open all year round, including Christmas Day.

Ironmonger Row Baths

1-11 Ironmonger Row, EC1V 3QF (7253 4011/www.aquaterra.org). Old Street tube/rail.
Take a trip back to the 1930s at this well-preserved 30m (100ft) pool and Turkish baths (one of only three remaining in London).

Kingfisher Leisure Centre

Fairfield Road, Kingston, Surrey, KT1 2PY (8546 1042/www.kingfisherleisurecentre.co.uk). Kingston rail.
Friendly family centre with a teaching pool, and a main pool with beach area and wave machine.

Latchmere Leisure Centre

Burns Road, SW11 5AD (7207 8004/ www.latchmereleisurecentre.co.uk). Clapham Junction rail.
Lane-swimming pool, teaching pool and a beach area, with wave machine and slide.

Leyton Leisure Lagoon

763 High Road, E10 5AB (8558 8858/ www.gll.org). Leyton tube/69, 97 bus.
A flume, slides, fountains, rapids and cascades liven up and bring a splash of colour to this rather drab corner of east London.

Pavilion Leisure Centre

Kentish Way, Bromley, Kent BR1 3EF (8313 9911/www.bromleymytime.org.uk). Bromley South rail.
A large leisure pool with shallows, flumes and a wave machine, lane swimming and a separate toddlers' pool.

Activities

Queen Mother Sports Centre
223 Vauxhall Bridge Road, SW1V 1EL (7630 5522/www.courtneys.co.uk). Victoria tube/rail.
Three excellent pools in this refurbished centre mean it's always popular with school kids.

Spa at Beckenham
24 Beckenham Road, Beckenham, Kent BR3 4PF (8650 0233/www.bromleymytime.org.uk). Clock House rail.
A clean and sparkling, award-winning leisure centre with loads of sports facilities, two swimming pools, the Space Zone soft-play area for children and a crèche.

Tottenham Green Leisure Centre
1 Philip Lane, N15 4JA (8489 5322). Seven Sisters tube/rail.
This perennially popular leisure centre has lane swimming and diving in the main pool, and waves and slides in the 'beach pool'.

Waterfront Leisure Centre
Woolwich High Street, SE18 6DL (8317 5000/www.gll.org). Woolwich Arsenal rail/ 96, 177 bus.
This leisure centre near the Woolwich Ferry terminal has four pools, six slides, waves, rapids and a water 'volcano' to keep the crowds happy in Greenwich borough's flagship centre.

Open-air swimming
For full details of London's outdoor pools (and to join the campaign to reopen those that have closed), visit www.lidos.org.uk.

Brockwell Lido
Brockwell Park, Dulwich Road, SE24 0PA (7274 3088/www.thelido.co.uk). Herne Hill rail. **Open** May-Sept, check website for times. **Admission** check website for details.
This is a wonderful listed 1930s lido, whose future has been under threat in recent years. Now it has received £500,000 from the Heritage Lottery Fund for renovation, its future seems at last to be secure. As well as the swimming, there are all sorts of baby, toddler and alternative health groups based at the lido.

Finchley Lido
Great North Leisure Park, Chaplin Square, High Road, North Finchley, N12 0GL (8343 9830/www.gll.org). East Finchley tube. **Open** check website. **Admission** check website.
There are two indoor pools here, but it's the outdoor pool and sun terrace that make it such a popular draw for locals in the summer.

Hampstead Heath Swimming Ponds & Parliament Hill Lido
7485 4491/www.cityoflondon.gov.uk. Lido: Parliament Hill Fields, Gordon House Road, NW5 1LP. Gospel Oak rail. Men & women's ponds: Millfield Lane, N6. Gospel Oak rail. Mixed pond: East Heath Road, NW3. Hampstead Heath rail. **Open** check website for times. **Admission** Lido £4.30; £2.70 reductions; £12.80 family (2+2). Ponds £2; £1 reductions. Season tickets and early/late entry discounts available.
Children aged eight to 15 are allowed in the ponds if supervised. No under eights.

London Fields Lido
London Fields Westside, E8 3EU (7254 9038/ www.gll.org). London Fields rail/26, 48, 55, 106, 236 bus. **Open** phone for details. **Admission** £4; £2.30 under-16s.
Hackney Council resurrected this lovely lido, which has proved a major draw for swimmers all over London since it opened in autumn 2006.

Oasis Sports Centre
32 Endell Street, WC2H 9AG (7831 1804/ www.gll.org). Tottenham Court Road tube. **Open** 7.30am-9pm Mon-Fri; 9.30am-5.30pm Sat, Sun. **Admission** £3.60; £1.40 5-16s; free under-5s; £6.75 family (2+2).
This 28m (90ft) outdoor pool is open all year round and is a wonderful resource for all the hot, tired media folk working in the area.

Pools on the Park
Old Deer Park, Twickenham Road, Richmond, Surrey TW9 2SF (8940 0561/www.spring health.net). Richmond rail. **Open** 6.30am-7.45pm Mon; 6.30am-10pm Tue; 6.30am-9.30pm Wed; 6.30am-9pm Thur; 6.30am-8.30pm Fri; 8am-5.45pm Sat; 7am-5.45pm Sun. **Admission** £3.80; £1.60-£3 reductions; free under-5s. Prices may vary during peak season.
A 33m (110ft) heated outdoor pool (and one the same size and temperature inside).

Tooting Bec Lido
Tooting Bec Road, SW16 1RU (8871 7198/ www.slsc.org.uk/www.tootingbeclido.co.uk). Streatham rail. **Open** *Late May-Aug* 6am-8pm daily. *Sept* 6am-5pm daily. *Oct-May* 7am-2pm daily (club members only). **Admission** £4.50; £3 reductions and under-16s; free under-5s; £12 family (2+2).
At 94m by 25m, this art deco beauty is the second-largest open-air pool in Europe.

TENNIS

Tennis for Free (TFF) is a campaign to give free access to Britain's 33,000 public courts – and encourage a long overdue change in this country's white, middle-class tennis culture. Its aim is to increase participation in tennis nationwide for all ages regardless of ability, background, race and financial circumstance. The initiative set up by comedian and author Tony Hawks and fashion executive Cecil Hollwey in 2003. To learn more, visit www.tennisforfree.com.

Most London boroughs run holiday tennis courses at Easter and in the summer, but they do need booking well ahead: keep an eye on the council website and contact your local sports development team for details. The Lawn Tennis Association publishes free guides giving contacts for private clubs and public courts listed by borough or county, along with contact details for local development officers. Details of tennis holidays are also available.

Hackney City Tennis Clubs

Clissold Park Mansion House, Stoke Newington Church Street, N16 9HJ (7254 4235/www.hackneycitytennisclubs.co.uk). Stoke Newington rail/73 bus. **Open** *Mar* 10am-5.30pm Mon-Fri; 9am-5.30pm Sat, Sun. *Apr-Sept* 10am-7.30pm Mon-Fri; 9am-7.30pm Sat, Sun. *Oct, Nov* 10am-4.30pm Mon-Fri; 9am-4.30pm Sat, Sun. *Dec-Feb* 10am-3.30pm Mon-Fri; 9am-3.30pm Sat, Sun. **Court hire** £5.50/hr; £2.50 under-16s (9am-5pm Mon-Fri). Phone to check availability.
Britain's first City Tennis Club (with courts in Stoke Newington and London Fields), part of a nationwide LTA programme to make inner-city tennis facilities cheaper and easier to find. Sessions for three- to 16-year-olds are offered during term time (one hour per week, £25 for five weeks), with free racquets and balls; holiday courses are also available. There are other CTCs in Highbury Fields (Islington) and Eltham Park South (Greenwich).

David Lloyd Leisure

0870 888 3015/www.davidlloydleisure.co.uk
There are five David Lloyd clubs in the London area, combining tennis with top-of-the-range fitness facilities. All are family-friendly, if not exactly cheap, and the courts and equipment are excellent. Check out the website or phone for your nearest venue.

Islington Tennis Centre

Market Road, N7 9PL (7700 1370/www. aquaterra.org). Caledonian Road tube. **Open** 7am-11pm Mon-Thur; 7am-10pm Fri; 8am-10pm Sat, Sun. **Court hire** *Non-members* Indoor £19/hr; £8.50/hr 5-16s. Outdoor £9/hr; £4/hr 5-16s.
Developed under the LTA's Indoor Tennis Initiative, the centre offers subsidised coaching.

Redbridge Sports & Leisure Centre

Forest Road, Barkingside, Essex IG6 3HD (8498 1000/www.rslonline.co.uk). Fairlop tube. **Open** 6.30am-11pm Mon-Fri; 8am-9pm Sat; 8am-10pm Sun. **Court hire** prices vary; phone for details.
Developed by a charitable trust, this outstanding multi-sports centre has eight indoor and 18 outdoor courts, which you can use as a member or 'pay as you play'. There are holiday activities for six- to 14-year-olds and 'fun play' sessions. There's also a short tennis club for under-eights.

Sutton Tennis Academy

Rose Hill Recreation Ground, Rose Hill, Sutton, Surrey SM1 3HH (8641 6611/ www.sjtc.org). Morden tube/Sutton Common rail. **Open** 7am-11pm Mon-Fri; 7am-9pm Sat, Sun. **Court hire** *Indoor* £19; £14 under-18s. *Outdoor* £8; £6 under-18s. *Clay* £13; £9 under-18s.
This is Britain's top tennis school, with high-quality performance coaches, led by Frenchman Erich Dochterman, who has taught various ATP and WTA-ranked players. There are residential courses for players seeking professional status and a scholarship scheme linked to Cheam High School. Children can be steeped in tennis culture from the age of three with Tiny Tots classes, mini tennis, join holiday programmes and book tennis birthday parties. There are six red clay, ten acrylic and 11 indoor courts.

Westway Tennis Centre

1 Crowthorne Road, W10 6RP (8969 0992/www.westway.org). Latimer Road tube. **Open** 8am-10pm Mon-Fri; 8am-8pm Sat; 10am-10pm Sun. **Court hire** *Indoor* £16-£22.50; £10 5-16s. *Outdoor* £8-£9; £5-£7 5-16s.
Another product of the LTA's Indoor Tennis Initiative, the Westway follows a similar model to Islington (*see above*): excellent subsidised coaching and courses, short tennis and transitional tennis. There are eight indoor and four outdoor clay courts.

Activities

TENPIN BOWLING

Many family-friendly centres, such as Hollywood Bowl (*see below*) have ramps, bumpers and lightweight balls for small children, and have even devised a numeracy trail to help the kids practise their maths skills while lobbing their bowling ball down the lanes.

Admission to the following centres averages around £6 per game, including the hire of soft-soled bowling shoes. Phone for details of children's parties.

Acton Tenpin
Royale Leisure Park, Western Avenue, W3 0PA (0871 873 3150/www.megabowl.co.uk). Park Royal tube. **Open** 10am-1am Mon-Wed, Sun; 10am-2am Thur-Sat. **Credit** MC, V.

1st Bowling Lewisham
11-29 Belmont Hill, SE13 5AU (0870 118 3021). Lewisham rail/DLR. **Open** 10am-midnight Mon, Thur, Sat; noon-midnight Tue, Wed, Fri, Sun. **Credit** MC, V.

Funland
Trocadero Centre, 1 Piccadilly Circus, W1D 7DH (7292 3633/www.funland.co.uk). Piccadilly Circus tube. **Open** 10am-12.30am Mon-Thur, Sun; 10am-1am Fri, Sat. **Credit** MC, V.

Hollywood Bowl Finchley
Great North Leisure Park, Chaplin Square, off Finchley High Road, N12 0GL (8446 6667/ www.hollywoodbowl.co.uk). East Finchley tube, then 263 bus. **Open** 10am-midnight Mon-Thur, Sun; 10am-1am Fri, Sat. **Credit** MC, V.

Hollywood Bowl Surrey Quays
Mast Leisure Park, Teredo Street, SE16 7LW (7237 3773/www.hollywoodbowl.co.uk). Canada Water DLR. **Open** 10am-11.30pm Mon-Thur, Sun; 10am-midnight Fri, Sat. **Credit** MC, V.

Queens
17 Queensway, W2 4QP (7229 0172/ www.queensiceandbowl.co.uk). Bayswater or Queensway tube. **Open** 10am-11pm Mon-Sat; 10am-10pm Sun. **Credit** MC, V.

Rowans Tenpin Bowl
10 Stroud Green Road, N4 2DF (8800 1950/ www.rowans.co.uk). Finsbury Park tube/rail. **Open** 10.30am-12.30am Mon-Thur, Sun; 10.30am-2.30am Fri, Sat. **Credit** MC, V.

WATERSPORTS

The sea may be miles away, but that doesn't stop London kids messing about on the water. There are lots of canoes, dinghies or rowing boats; and for the petrol-heads, there are powerboats down Deptford way.

Ahoy Centre
Borthwick Street, SE8 3JY (8691 7606/www. ahoy.org.uk). Deptford rail/Cutty Sark DLR. This is the place to come to for sailing, rowing and powerboating on the Thames, and in Surrey and Victoria Docks. Members help run the centre, an approach that keeps prices down and fosters a strong community spirit.

BTYC Sailsports
Birchen Grove, NW9 8SA (www.btycsailsports. org.uk). Neasden or Wembley Park tube. Dinghy sailing, windsurfing, basic training and RYA courses on the Welsh Harp reservoir.

Canalside Activity Centre
Canal Close, W10 5AY (8968 4500/ www.rbkc.gov.uk). Ladbroke Grove tube/ Kensal Rise rail/52, 70, 295 bus. This centre offers canoeing lessons, as well as water safety classes.

Dockands Sailing & Watersports Centre
Millwall Dock, 235A Westferry Road, E14 3QS (7537 2626/www.dswc.org). Crossharbour DLR. **Membership** £110/yr adult; £20/yr under-17s; £220/yr family (2+3). Docklands offers canoeing, dragon-boat racing, windsurfing and dinghy sailing for over-eights. Non-members can also take part in open sessions; phone for details.

Globe Rowing Club
Trafalgar Rowing Centre, 11-13 Crane Street, SE10 9NP (www.globerowingclub.co.uk). Cutty Sark DLR/Maze Hill rail. This friendly, Greenwich-based rowing club offers competitive as well as recreational rowing and sculling on a stretch of nearly nine miles of the River Thames from Tower Bridge to the Thames Barrier.

Lea Rowing Club
Spring Hill, E5 9BL (club house 8806 8282/ www.learc.org.uk). Clapton rail. Rowing and sculling classes, and holiday courses for children aged ten or more who can swim at least 50m.

Activities

Tiger feat

What Twickenham is to England, Burgess Park (*see p111*) is to the **Southwark Tigers**, a rugby club of fierce five- to 15-year-olds who play in the shadow of the tower blocks and housing estates of Walworth, south-East London. 'It's great,' said a parent watching the Sunday morning training, 'they get muddy, they get tired and they don't get into trouble.'

Southwark Tigers is evidence of the growing appeal of the hard, physical ball game among communities who might ordinarily be expected to be passionate soccer fans. Indeed, the first Tigers recruits enjoyed the game, but refused to wear the black-and-yellow striped shirts because they lacked credibility, and insisted on wearing their Millwall or Arsenal strips to training.

'Getting club loyalty is still the hardest thing,' says another parent, 'the feeling that you're letting the side down if you don't turn up. They get it after a while. My kids love being Tigers, and have stayed with the club even though we've moved to Tulse Hill.'

Southwark Tigers was founded in 2001 by Vernon Neve-Dunn, a passionate proponent of the game he had played as a schoolboy and now wanted to pass on to others. Modest sponsorship paid for the kit, and Southwark Council responded to the initiative by providing a pitch and even a club house. A large banner on the park railings saying 'Rugby Players Wanted' did the rest.

After seven seasons, the club fields teams at every level short of the over-16 adult game, and holds its own in competitions such as the Kent Rugby Cup, which is dominated by the grammar schools of the rural south-east. There's even a girls' XV in the junior (under-16) age-group. The glass display cabinet in the club house is impressively full of trophies; a crystal rose-bowl is inscribed to Mr Neve-Dunn, the Rugby Football Union's Hero of the Year 2002, and on top of an ancient stove rests a faded, stuffed tiger's head, snarly and inspiring, a donation from one of the parents.

One colourful, noisy spin-off is the Southwark Tigers Cheerleaders, a club that has 60 members between seven and 23, in four troupes called Preps, Peewees, Juniors and Seniors. They practise at the same time as the rugby players, but are keen to insist that they are not simply decoration: they attend their own competitions and events. In Britain, cheerleading is not a recognised sport as it is in other countries, and the Southwark Tigers are vocal campaigners for its recognition. Some of the more enthusiastic members are preparing to take cheerleading exams in the summer.

To find out more about the Tigers, log on to their website, www.southwarktigers.org.

Royal Victoria Dock Watersports Centre

Gate 5, Tidal Basin Road, off Silvertown Way, E16 1AD (7511 2326). Royal Victoria Dock DLR. **Membership** *£88/6mths; £53/6mths 8-18s.*

Dinghy sailing and RYA beginners' courses take place in Victoria Dock. A scholarship scheme offers free tuition, and a holiday programme.

Shadwell Basin Outdoor Activity Centre

3-4 Shadwell Pierhead, Glamis Road, E1W 3TD (7481 4210/www.shadwell-basin.org.uk). Wapping tube.

Fairly priced sailing, canoeing, kayaking and dragon-boating for children aged from nine.

Stoke Newington West Reservoir Centre

Green Lanes, N4 2HA (8442 8116/ www.gll.org). Manor House tube/ 141, 341 bus.

A purpose-built environmental education and watersports centre for dinghy sailing.

Surrey Docks Watersports Centre

Greenland Dock, Rope Street, SE16 7SX (7237 4009/www.fusion-lifestyle.com). Canada Water tube.

Sailing, windsurfing and canoeing for over-eights take place in the sheltered dock in school holidays. RYA courses are also available.

Westminster Boating Base

136 Grosvenor Road, SW1V 3JY (7821 7389/www.westminsterboatingbase.co.uk). Pimlico tube.

Canoeing and sailing for over-tens on the tidal Thames. There's no fixed fee; the Base asks for a donation according to personal circumstances.

YOGA

Yoga is good for children, but you need to enrol your child on an approved and registered course. A splendid arrival on the London scene is the **Special Yoga Centre** (*see right*). This registered charity is the UK home for Yoga for the Special Child, a US/Brazil-based programme that offers one-to-one work with infants who have Down's syndrome, cerebral palsy, spina bifida, autism, epilepsy and ADD/ADHD.

The therapeutic aspect of yoga is also explored at the Yoga Therapy Centre (*see below*), which runs weekly sessions for children with asthma. The big stretches of some positions are thought to help to unknot the chest muscles and assist with controlled breathing and relaxation.

The biggest name in yoga for children is YogaBugs (www.yogabugs.com). Created by Fenella Lindsell, YogaBugs has been bringing yoga to three-to-seven year olds since 1997. There are now hundreds of trained YogaBugs teachers working in nursery, prep and primary schools. Classes also run at venues throughout the capital. For older children, Yoga'd up is the next step on from YogaBugs. It is an innovative way of introducing yoga to eight-to-12 year olds. Classes are designed to help children maintain their flexibility and develop strength. For more on YogaBugs teacher training, log on the website.

The following yoga centres run classes for children.

Holistic Health

64 Broadway Market, E8 4QJ (7275 8434/ www.holistic-health-hackney.co.uk). London Fields rail/26, 48, 55, 106, 236 bus.

Iyengar Institute

223A Randolph Avenue, W9 1NL (7624 3080/www.iyi.org.uk). Maida Vale tube.

Sivananda Yoga

Vedanta Centre, 51 Felsham Road, SW15 1AZ (8780 0160/www. sivananda.co.uk). Putney Bridge tube/ Putney rail.

Special Yoga Centre

The Tay Building, 2A Wrentham Avenue, NW10 3HA (8968 1900/www.special yoga.org.uk). Kensal Rise rail.

Triyoga

6 Erskine Road, NW3 3AJ (7483 3344/ www.triyoga.co.uk). Chalk Farm tube.

Yoga Junction

Unit 24, City North, Fonthill Road, N4 3HF (7263 3113/www.yogajunction.co.uk). Finsbury Park tube/rail.

Yoga Therapy Centre

90-92 Pentonville Road, N1 9HS (7689 3040/ www.yogatherapy.org). Angel tube.

Consumer

Rainforest Cafe

A WILD PLACE TO SHOP AND EAT®

Rainforest Cafe is a unique venue bringing to life the sights and sounds of the rainforest.

Come and try our fantastic menu!
With a re-launched healthy kids menu, including gluten free, dairy free and organic options.

15% DISCOUNT
off your final food bill*

Offer valid seven days a week.
Maximum party size of 6.

020 7434 3111

20 Shaftesbury Avenue, Piccadilly Circus, London W1D 7EU

www.therainforestcafe.co.uk

*Please show this advert to your safari guide when seated.
Cannot be used in conjunction with any other offer.

Eating

Food for the brood.

There are more than 6,000 restaurants serving more than 70 different types of cuisine in this city, so you'll appreciate that choosing places to put in this chapter is a bit of a challenge. We've tried to avoid over-prissiness (we know that some of our readers may favour an exclusively organic, allergen-free and vegan diet for their progeny, but the rest of us will just settle for wholesome grub) but have taken care to eschew junk food of the twizzler variety. This last has proved surprisingly difficult. Too many places list any number of thrillingly complex and carefully sourced dishes on their adult menu, only to let the side down with a nugget-and-chip-based kiddie version. How difficult is it to whip up alternative child-pleasers, such as a nice boiled egg and buttery soldiers, or a bowl of pasta and tomato sauce?

The places we recommend have compiled some wholesome offerings for their junior consumers, and many go all out to make sure their meal is fun as well as filling.

BRASSERIES

Banners

21 Park Road, N8 8TE (8292 0001/ reservations 8348 2930). Finsbury Park tube/rail, then W7 bus. **Meals served** 9am-11.30pm Mon-Thur; 9am-midnight Fri; 10am-4pm, 5pm-midnight Sat; 10am-4pm, 5-11pm Sun. **Main courses** £9.25-£14.75. **Set lunch** £6.95 1 course. **Credit** MC, V.
The vaguely Caribbean-beach-bar look, with rainbow colours, battered tables, flags and posters, gives it an unchanging boho feel; a noticeboard offers info on nannies, lost cats, homeopathy and 'metamorphosis'. Local parents come in droves because they can still feel groovy, while their nippers are bound to find something they like from the vast, globe-wandering menu, with dishes of all sizes from chicken fajitas or meze to noodles, burgers, crayfish parcels, Malay curries and loads of veggie choices. The drinks list is also a something-for-everyone mix: various coffees, standard to exotic teas, shakes, juices and floats for the kids, a huge choice of cocktails and an exotically worldwide beer and booze range. *Buggy access. Children's menu (£2.95-£4.75). Crayons. High chairs. Toys.*

Café on the Hill

46 Fortis Green Road, N10 3HN (8444 4957). Highgate tube, then 43, 134 bus. **Meals served** 8am-5pm Mon-Thur; 8am-5pm, 7-11pm Fri- Sun. **Main courses** £4.95-£12.50. **Credit** MC, V.
The menu at this Muswell Hill institution is strong on all-day breakfasts, with a short lunch menu available from midday to 4pm. A nod to the Muswell Hill muffia and their broods is a new kids' lunch menu, though portion size makes this an option only for the very small in age or appetite. The all-day breakfast is no mean feat, with 12 dishes and counting, including well-done classics – free-range eggs benedict – as well as creative new ideas: frittata with olives and chorizo served with herb salad. Other combos include main-course salads such as coriander chicken and mango, open sandwiches and panini. The range of the menu caters for all, as does the drinks menu: wines by the glass or bottle, with smoothies for the kids and wide range of teas and coffees for Grandpa. The place is always busy. Smiley service charged at ten per cent. *Buggy access. Children's menu (£2.20-£4.95). Disabled: toilet. High chairs. Tables outdoors (6, pavement). Takeaway service.*

The Depot

Tideway Yard, 125 Mortlake High Street, SW14 8SN (8878 9462/www.depot brasserie.co.uk). Barnes Bridge or Mortlake rail/209 bus. **Lunch served** noon-3pm Mon-Fri; noon-4pm Sat, Sun. **Dinner served** 6-11pm Mon-Sat; 6-10.30pm Sun. **Main courses** £9.95-£15. **Set meal** (Mon-Thur) £12.50 2 courses; £15.50 3 courses. **Credit** AmEx, DC, MC, V.

Winning ways

Every year, as part of the Time Out Eating & Drinking Awards, we at *London for Children* pick our top five family-friendly restaurants. Only one can win the award, however, and every year our panel of children and parents hotly debate the finalists' merits. All winners have to have certain things in common: children should enjoy being there; both children and their parents must enjoy the food; the restaurant's staff must be tolerant and friendly towards children and their picky parents; facilities should be baby- and toddler-friendly and a family meal should be an all-round treat. All these below fitted the bill.

2001 Giraffe
A diverse menu, and a jolly atmosphere earned Giraffe the gong this year. *See p222.*

2002 Carluccio's Caffè
The staff couldn't be friendlier, and the Italian food is terrific. *See p243.*

2003 Dexter's Grill
Super juicy burgers, organic children's meals and build-your-own puddings scored a direct hit. *See p246.*

2004 Frizzante at City Farm
You eat in a farmhouse kitchen, with poultry, pigs and cattle scenting the air outdoors. Who needs the countryside? *See p226.*

2005 Gracelands
We'd never seen such a relaxed and friendly kitchen-diner full of parents and children, and the food was inventive and excellent. *See p228.*

2006 Benihana
Those juggling, dicing, splicing chefs won the hearts of our teens and tots, who ate every scrap of their quasi-Japanese dinner. *See p244.*

2007 Tate Modern Café
Splendid use of colour in the carefully sourced dishes for all ages, with a well-thought-out and educational children's menu. *See right.*

The location, in a courtyard by the Thames, is a big part of this place's draw. But the food is similarly appealing. Expect the likes of charcuterie or asparagus for starters, and sea bass, roast duck leg and roast pork belly for mains. The children's menu includes pasta with various sauces; fish cakes, sausage or chicken strips with roast potatoes; and ice-cream for pudding. There's a monthly prize of a free meal in the 'best colouring-in' competition.
Buggy access. Children's set meal (£5.50). Crayons. High chairs. Nappy-changing facilities. Tables outdoors (8, courtyard).

Giraffe
Units 1&2, Riverside Level 1, Royal Festival Hall, SE1 8XX (7928 2004/www.giraffe.net). Waterloo tube/rail. **Open** 8am-11pm Mon-Fri; 9am-11pm Sat; 9am-10.30pm Sun. **Main courses** £6.95-£14.95. **Set dinner** (5-7pm) £6.95 2 courses. **Credit** AmEx, MC, V. **Map** p317 M8.
At lunchtimes this popular branch of the worldly-wise mini chain pulls in a substantial family crowd with its winning ways – children are given balloons and babycinos, proper small food and plenty of attention. The staff are clearly chosen for their sunny disposition and the food they serve is good – both in value and taste terms. Meals are large, colourful ensembles. A vegetarian meze plate stars falafel, houmous, beetroot, tabouleh, Tunisian ratatouille and warm pitta. Burgers are juicy and delicious. Salads are imaginative, the sunshine powerfood one is bursting with nuts, seeds and edamame beans. The brunch menu lists stacked pancakes, waffles and eggs and bacon.
Balloons. Buggy access. Children's set meal (£5.50 noon-3pm Mon-Fri). Crayons. Disabled: toilet. High chairs. Nappy-changing facilities. Tables outdoors (40, terrace). Takeaway service.
Other locations throughout town. Check website for details.

Tate Modern Café: Level 2
Second Floor, Tate Modern, Sumner Street, SE1 9TG (7401 5014/www.tate.org.uk). Southwark tube/Blackfriars or London Bridge tube/rail. **Meals served** 10am-6pm Mon-Thur, Sat, Sun; 10am-10pm Fri. **Main courses** £10.50-£12.95. **Credit** AmEx, MC, V.
Children are greeted with much enthusiasm in this gallery brasserie, winner of our award for Best Family Restaurant in 2007. Families plump for tables by the huge floor-to-ceiling windows framing the busy Thames – a sight for sore eyes of all ages. As well as the views, there are

distractions in the form of a junior menu with art and literacy activities included, handed out with a pot of wax crayons. This is a superior children's menu for a top-of-the-range gallery restaurant. Children can choose haddock fingers, pasta bolognese with parmesan or broccoli and spinach bake, with their choice of drink and an ice-cream or fruit pudding. It's top-quality food, everything is carefully sourced, regional and seasonal. The inspiration is quality over quantity, always a good idea where kids are concerned. Children can also choose half-price mains from the adult menu, which lists some inspirational light lunches, including a vivid vegetaran meze plate, or fried fish of the day with crisp, solid, chips.
Buggy access. Children's set menu (£5.95; 11am-3pm daily). Disabled access: toilet. High chairs. Nappy-changing facilities.

CAFÉS

Boiled Egg & Soldiers
63 Northcote Road, SW11 1ND (7223 4894). Clapham Junction rail. **Open** 9am-6pm Mon-Sat; 9am-4pm Sun. **Main courses** £4-£10. **Credit** AmEx, DC, MC, V.
What's perhaps the original yummy mummy café is still going strong, offering own-made soups and baguettes on the specials board, and nursery food for the kids, including the eponymous eggs. Milkshakes and smoothies go well with the own-made cakes and, if the sun is shining, there are a couple of tables outside as well (remember, though, that oversized sunglasses are de rigeur in these parts). It's not the biggest space and you may have to queue but if you can't find room at the inn you could do worse than cross the road to Crumpet (*see p225*).
Buggy access. Children's menu (£2.50-£3.50). High chairs. Tables outdoors (3, pavement; 8, garden). Takeaway service.

Brew House
Kenwood, Hampstead Lane, NW3 7JR (8341 5384/www.companyofcooks.com). Bus 210, 214. **Open** *Oct-Mar* 9am-dusk daily. *Apr-Sept* 9am-6pm daily (7.30pm on concert nights). **Credit** (over £10) MC, V.
Set in the beautiful surroundings of Kenwood House, the Brew House is a self-service café with fabulous cakes and a sunny outdoor seating area.
Buggy access. Children's menu (£2.50-£3.95). High chairs. Nappy-changing facilities. Tables outside (400-seat garden). Takeaway service.

Brilliant Kids Café & Arts Centre
8 Station Terrace, NW10 5RT (8964 4120/ www.brilliantkids.co.uk). Kensal Green tube.

Bootiful burgers at **Banners** in Crouch End. *See p221.*

Meals served 8am-6pm Mon-Fri; 9am-5pm Sat; 10am-5pm Sun. Closes 2pm Sat, Sun during birthday parties. **Main courses** £6-£7.50. **Credit** MC, V.

Filling the stomachs and feeding the imagination of local children and providing a lovely chill-out space for their parents, Brilliant is, quite simply, a brilliant place to bring kids. Many customers come for the substantial all-day breakfast, with its thick bacon rashers and sausage; and the daily special hot lunch is usually pretty special (chicken pie, shepherd's pie, curry – made with meat from Devon Rose Organics). Then there's the fact that Brilliant does a mean cappuccino, the pastry goods (especially the rough-hewn, substantial, individual quiches) are out of this world, and the salads and fillings for the bagels and loaves are fresh and imaginative. Everything chalked up on the board can be scaled down for children's portions, and there are tempting treats such as tiny rainbow-sprinkled fairy cakes and proper sausage rolls to stimulate small appetites. There's a pleasant generosity about this place. Food, and the arty workshops for children held in the studio next door (£5-£7/hr), represent value for money. A childish request for Nutella on toast yielded a nicely presented plate of fresh soft toast, an individual pot of butter and a big jar of Nutella.

Birthday parties (2-5pm Sat, Sun). Buggy access. Crayons. Disabled: toilet. High chairs. Tables outdoors (3, garden). Play area. Takeaway service.

Bush Garden Café
59 Goldhawk Road, W12 8EG (8811 1795). Goldhawk Road tube. **Meals served** 8am-6pm Mon-Fri; 9am-5pm Sat. **Main courses** £3.50-£8.50. **Credit** (over £5) MC, V.

This vintage-chic café and food shop near Shepherd's Bush is a home from home for laptop-wielding writers and young parents. A small garden with play equipment, community noticeboard advertising baby massage and Ashtanga yoga, as well as the presence of babycinos on the drinks board, suggests a strong infant customer base. Otherwise, this is standard, wholefood café fare, strong on big breakfast fry-ups (available until 11am on weekends) and soup/sandwich/salad lunches. Soups are hearty and vegetable-filled. Salads are interesting, making good use of seasonal vegetables, such as beetroot and fennel, pulses and diverse leaves. Served with quiche or frittata they make a well-rounded lunch. To drink there's a changing wine selection or virtuous freshly blended juices, for afters there are appetising fairy cakes and light fruit sponges.

Buggy access. Children's menu (£2.60-£8.50). High chairs. Nappy-changing facilities. Tables outdoors (5, garden). Takeaway service. Toys.

Cibo
Mamas & Papas, 256-258 Regent Street, W1B 3AF (01484 438476/www.mamas andpapas.com). Oxford Circus tube. **Meals served** 10am-8pm Mon-Wed, Fri; 10am-9pm Thur; 9am-8pm Sat; noon-6pm Sun. **Main courses** £6.75-£9.95. **Set dinner** (4-7.30pm Mon-Fri) £9.95 3 courses. **Credit** MC, V. **Map** p314 J6.

On the first floor of the Mamas & Papas flagship store, this calming Italian café is a symphony in coffee and cream. Staff are amenable, and Cibo's menu is tailored to the needs of pregnant women and small children. The appealing breakfast section offers organic toast, bagels and salmon and scrambled eggs; then there are lunchtime smoothies, sandwiches, salads and

Tate Modern Café: Level 2. *See p222.*

Consumer

hot meals. Children's dishes include organic burgers and fries, organic salmon fish cake and ketchup, pasta dishes and organic ice-cream. *Buggy access. Children's menu (£3.25-£4.50). High chairs. Nappy-changing facilities. Play area. Takeaway service. Toys.*

Coffee & Crayons

915 Fulham Road, SW6 5HU (3080 1050/ www.coffeeandcrayons.co.uk). Putney Bridge tube. **Meals served** 7.30am-6pm daily. **Main courses** £2.30-£6.95. **Credit** MC, V.

A quiet café and toyshop sits above a staffed ground-floor playroom with sofas where parents lounge as children play and paint. The coffee is great and, like most of the food, organic and fairtrade. Pastries, baguettes, soup and tasty meat and vegetarian pies make up much of the menu. The daily special is usually something substantial, such as lasagne (which can be served in children's portions), but dedicated children's dishes seem to be limited mostly to sandwiches. Infants-in-arms get an extensive range of Truly Scrumptious baby foods.

Play sessions cost £3.50-£4 with no time limit. Adults can sit upstairs to be unfettered grown-ups again; otherwise, the downstairs room is cosy enough to lose yourself in a magazine despite the presence of playful tots. The playroom holds music classes and Fairy School weekly, also Mum Massage. *Children's menu (£1.50-£4.25). High chairs. Nappy-changing facilities. Play area (6mths-9yrs; £4, £3.50 under 18mths). Tables outdoors (3, pavement).*

Common Ground

Wandsworth Common, off Dorlcote Road, SW18 3RT (8874 9386). Wandsworth Common rail. **Open** 9am-5.15pm Mon-Fri; 10am-5.15pm Sat, Sun. **Main courses** £3.50-£9. **Credit** MC, V.

A shady patio overlooks a cricket ground. It's a great place to relax with a sandwich, savoury tart or a few cakes. Inside, the parlour has comfy sofas, a play area and toys and a very child-friendly approach. Indulge in a beer while you tempt kids with a babycino and a fairy cake. *Children's menu (£2.25-£3.95). High chairs. Nappy-changing facilities. Play area. Takeaway service.*

Crumpet

66 Northcote Road, SW11 6QL (7924 1117/ www.crumpet.biz). Clapham Junction rail. **Open** 8.30am-6pm Mon-Sat; 9.30am-6pm Sun. **Main courses** £4.20-£7.50. **Credit** AmEx, MC, V.

Proper teas, with scones, locally baked cakes and hefty sandwiches are a Crumpet priority. Its other big interest is children, which means there are buggies and babes-in-arms everywhere. Families tend to sit in the light, airy back room, where there's a play area. The menu covers all infant tastes, from toasty fingers, crudités and a babycino on the side, to whimsical dishes called, for example, Rosy Posy pasta and Dylan's scrumptious chicken – all organic and free-range where possible. Everything is presented with great care, in generous proportions and the high quality of the ingredients shines through. Crumpet is a treat. *Buggy access. Children's menu (£1.60-£3.95). Crayons. Disabled: toilet. High chairs. Nappy-changing facilities. Play area (under-5s). Tables outdoors (2, pavement). Takeaway service.*

Deep Blue Café

Science Museum, Exhibition Road, SW7 2DD (7942 4488/www.sciencemuseum.org. uk). South Kensington tube. **Meals served** 11.30am-3pm daily. **Main courses** £7.25-£8.95 **Credit** MC, V.

Visitors to the Science Museum can expect a decent feed at the Deep Blue. The set meal for children is just £4.50, the cheapest we've found in Kensington, and consists of generous portions of, for example, chicken with chips or mash and a corn on the cob, pasta with tomato or bolognese sauce, or small portions of anything from the adult menu (veggie lasagne, pizzas, main-meal salads). The children's pudding can be jelly or ice-cream. The adult menu features massive portions, plus there's coffee and cakes. A satisfying place to eat, even if the decor is a bit headache-inducing. *Buggy access. Children's set meal (£4.50). Disabled access. High chairs. Nappy-changing facilities.*

Domali Café

38 Westow Street, SE19 3AH (8768 0096/ www.domali.co.uk). Gypsy Hill rail. **Meals served** 9.30am-11pm daily. **Main courses** £4.50-£8.90. **Credit** MC, V.

A perennial Crystal Palace favourite, Domali, with its bistro-style vibe and decor attracts a steady foot flow of couples, local traders, lone diners and often a full-complement of in-laws with parents, offspring and toddlers happily munching away at the well-priced and nicely varied menu. Free-range, organic and vegetarian options will please all palates with full breakfasts a popular choice, as well as the likes of veggie sausages, scrambled eggs and mushrooms or more occasional dishes like eggs

Consumer

benedict or hollandaise. Specials can include sweet potato pie or dover sole. Children very often go for the doorstep-sized chips or omelettes although there is a special menu with milkshakes, smoothies, pasta and omelettes. Summer sees tables snagged in the back garden space, where little ones feel free to run around theirs and other diners' tables in between fuelling up on whichever meals they've opted for.

Buggy access. High chairs. Nappy-changing facilities. Tables outdoors (10, garden).

Esca

160 Clapham High Street, SW4 7UG (7622 2288/www.escauk.com). Clapham Common tube. **Meals served** 8am-9pm Mon-Fri; 9am-9pm Sat, Sun. **Main courses** £3.95-£8.35. **Credit** MC, V.

With possibly the prettiest window display on the high street, Esca is a catch-all for sweet-toothed visitors. The fabulous cakes, buns and tarts on display feature sticky orange slices, apple crumble with ricotta, generous slabs of cheesecake and grand selections of layered cream sponges. Banks of blond wood tables surrounded by off-white walls at the back of the café are roomy enough for communal dining, and families and toddlers do very well with the selections of breakfasts, salads, pies and pasta. There's a good selection of vegetarian and vegan options in a well-thought-out menu that includes grilled halloumi and pumpkin with flaked almonds. Other choices are honey-roasted gammon, poached salmon, stuffed roast lamb or marinated chicken breast. Chilled drinks include fruit smoothies, and there's a selection of teas and coffees and 70 per cent pure hot chocolate. Also a deli, Esca has an enticing floor-to-ceiling shelved selection of sweet jams, fancy biscuits, chocolates, fruit drinks and gifts, much of which is shipped in from Italy.

High chairs. Disabled access: toilet. Nappy-changing facilities. Takeaway service.

Frizzante at City Farm

1A Goldsmith's Row, E2 8QA (7739 2266/ www.frizzanteltd.co.uk). Bus 26, 48, 55. **Meals served** 10am-5.30pm Tue-Sun. **Main courses** £4.50-£9.75. **Credit** AmEx, DC, MC, V.

A real, busy farmhouse kitchen in the heart of Hackney, what could be better? Once you've trotted around visiting poultry, pigs and sheep you can settle down to eat their relatives (or stick to the many vegetarian options). The oilcloth-covered tables are heaving with parents and their offspring tucking into healthy foods chosen from the blackboard. There's own-made lasagne, pastas, herb-crusted chicken and Frizzante's big

farm breakfasts, also served in vegetarian versions. Prices are reasonable, portions large. Our tagliatelle with grilled vegetables was a colourful, filling treat, and the children's pizzas perfectly thin crust and cheese-laden. Juicy burgers came with delicious roasted potatoes and a big salad. Drinks include smoothies, tea, coffee and juices. And check out the noticeboard – there's always something going on. On our visit it was breastfeeding classes, as well as pottery classes (£4; Tue, Wed, Sun).

Buggy access. Children's menu (£2.25-£4.25). Disabled access: toilet. High chairs. Nappy-changing facilities. Tables outdoors (12, garden). Takeaway service. **Other locations** Unicorn Theatre, 147 Tooley Street, SE1 2HZ (7645 0500).

Garden Café

Inner Circle, Regents Park, NW1 4NU (7935 5729/www.thegardencafe.co.uk). Baker Street or Regents Park tube. **Open** 9am-6pm daily. **Main courses** £8.75-£12.50. **Credit** MC, V.

Handy for the Open Air Theatre, this pleasingly retro café surrounded by rose beds has a satisfying menu (prawn cocktail, steak and chips, ratatouille), as well as a children's menu for pasta and chips. Ice-cream comes from the estimable Marine Ices, or there are cakes aplenty.

Buggy access. Children's set meal (£5.95). Disabled: toilet. Nappy-changing facilities. Tables outdoors (40, park).

Golders Hill Park Refreshment House

North End Way, NW3 7HD (8455 8010). Golders Green or Hampstead tube/210, 268 bus. **Meals served** *Summer* 9am-6.30pm daily. *Winter* 9am-dusk daily. **Main courses** £3-£7. **Credit cards** (over £10) AmEx, MC, V.

One of the nicest locations for a child-friendly café we know, the Refreshment House has a simple, good value menu of family favourites. Excellent own-made ices, serviceable salads, sandwiches and scones, croissants, muffins and a few cakes and flans fill a hole. Pasta features heavily, and children's portions are available.

Buggy access. Children's menu (£3-£5). Disabled access: toilet. High chairs. Nappy-changing facilities. Tables outdoors (25, terrace). Takeaway service.

Gracelands

118 College Road, NW10 5HD (8964 9161/ www.gracelandscafe.com). Kensal Green tube. **Open** 8.30am-6pm Mon-Fri; 9am-5pm Sat; 9.30am-3pm Sun. **Main courses** £3.95-£8. **Credit** MC, V.

delicious noodles ⏐ rice dishes
freshly squeezed juices

kids menu available

bloomsbury ⏐ borough / london bridge ⏐ brent cross ⏐ camden
canary wharf ⏐ covent garden ⏐ croydon ⏐ earls court ⏐ fleet street
haymarket ⏐ islington ⏐ kensington ⏐ knightsbridge ⏐ leicester square
mansion house ⏐ moorgate / citypoint ⏐ old broad street / bank ⏐ putney
royal festival hall ⏐ soho ⏐ tower hill ⏐ victoria ⏐ wigmore ⏐ wimbledon

positive eating + positive living

wagamama.com

Brilliant Kids Cafe & Arts Centre.
See p223.

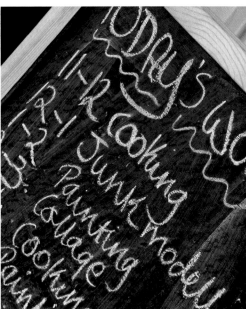

A most convivial, child-filled café. Tow-haired toddlers and bouncing babies smeared with organic sweet potato greet you at the front door. More play in the tastefully appointed home corner, presided over by mamas nursing large cappuccinos, infants, mobile phones and laptops. The staff are affability personified. Food is own-made with care, served in generous proportions. Breakfast items include big fry-ups, eggs benedict or pastries and segue into a lunchtime special hot dish, such as chicken or lentil stew, or lighter choices such as our delicious buttery, garlicky mushrooms on toast. Creative quiches (goat's cheese and sweet potato is a favourite combination) are served with chunky salads of puy lentils, tomatoes and basil and roasted veg. Children's options include pasta, risotto and sausages and there are some fine cakes and pastries to go with your babycino. The Gracelands Yard next door runs classes and creative workshops.
Buggy access. Children's set meal (£3.50). High chairs. Nappy-changing facilities. Play area. Tables outdoors (4, pavement; 6, garden). Takeaway service. Toys.

Inn The Park

St James's Park, SW1A 2BJ (7451 9999/ www.innthepark.com). St James's Park or Westminster tube. **Meals served** 8am-11pm Mon-Fri; 9am-11pm Sat; 9am-6pm Sun. *Winter times vary; phone for details.*

Main courses £12.50-£21.50. **Credit** AmEx, MC, V. **Map** p317 K8.
It's a big treat to lunch (or breakfast) here after admiring the waterbirds of Duck Island. The classic British food is locally sourced and conscientiously produced, with a children's menu of roast chicken breast and chunky chips, sausage and mash or smoked haddock fish cake with vegetables. The place is the brainchild of famous foodie Oliver Peyton.
Buggy access. Children's set meal (£7.50). Disabled access: toilet. High chairs. Nappy-changing facilities. Tables outdoors (40, patio). Takeaway service.

Konditor & Cook

10 Stoney Street, SE1 9AD (7407 5100/ www.konditorandcook.com). London Bridge tube/rail. **Meals served** 7.30am-6pm Mon-Fri; 8.30am-5pm Sat. **Main courses** £2.10-£5.75. **Credit** AmEx, MC, V. **Map** p319 P8.
It's a tiny, little café – so most locals come here for takeaway soups and salads, well-filled sandwiches, frittata, spinach and ricotta tartlets, plus hot meals and daily specials (gnocchi in fresh tomato and basil sauce with black olives, for example). Children will doubtless be unable to take their eyes off the cakes though – a lip-smacking array, such as the famous Curly Whirly double-layer chocolate cake, lemon drizzle, and the prettiest, detailed fairy cakes.

Buggy access. Tables outdoors (1, pavement). Takeaway service.
Other locations 22 Cornwall Road, SE1 8TW (7261 0456); 46 Gray's Inn Road, WC1X 8LR (7404 6300); 99 Shaftesbury Avenue, W1D 5DY (7292 1684); 30 St Mary Axe, EC3A 8BF (0845 262 3030).

Meals

1st Floor, Heal's, 196 Tottenham Court Road, W1T 7LQ (7580 2522/www.mealsrestaurant. co.uk). Goodge Street or Warren Street tube.
Meals served 10am-5.30pm Mon-Wed, Fri, Sat; 10am-7.30pm Thur; noon-5.30pm Sun.
Set meal £12.50 2 courses. **Main courses** £5.50-£9.50. **Credit** AmEx, MC, V.
Runner-up in the *Time Out* Eating Awards in the Best Design category in 2007, Meals has a very jaunty look, with marshmallow pink and white fittings that give it the look of a child's nursery. Perhaps that's why there was a collection of new mums with nursing babes enjoying a well-earned lunch when we visited. Often strangely empty, which is great for customers with young children, Meals does proper meals, at grown up prices, which might put off sandwich lunchers. If sea bass with lemon roast potatoes and veg, or a gourmet burger seems too much, plump for the daily soup or the salad special (a savoury tart or quiche with two salads). The children's menu (from £6) offers Angus beefburger with salad and fries, chicken goujons with fries or linguine with tomato sauce. The prodigiously iced fairy cakes, also sold in the Peyton & Byrne franchise on the ground floor, are pricey, but we're happy to shell out for the millionaire's shortbread.
Buggy access. Children's set meal (£6). Disabled access: lift, toilet. High chairs. Nappy-changing facilities.

Mudchute Kitchen

Mudchute Park & Farm, Pier Street, E14 3HP (7515 5901/www.mudchutekitchen.org). Mudchute DLR/D6, D7, D8 bus. **Open** 9am-5pm Tue-Sun. **Meals served** 9am-4pm Tue-Sun. **Main courses** £3.50-£8.50. **Credit** MC, V.
A smallholding fenced in by skyscrapers is a most unusual place for lunch – children love to sit in this farmhouse kitchen/café across the yard from pigs and poultry. On the menu, is suitably wholesome seasonal grub and lashings of sparkling ginger (or coffees and teas). Parents can plonk the toddlers in the book and toy corner and order food from the kitchen, There are usually four or five hot options, (available in child priced portions – about £3), such as penne

with tomato and courgette sauce and goat's cheese, or fried polenta topped with wild mushrooms, herbs and cream cheese, Plain eaters can choose home-laid eggs, own-made jam or beans on toast. The main distractions are the brilliant own-made cakes – brownies, cupcakes, flapjacks and Victoria sponges –and terrific cream teas.
Buggy access. Children's menu (£2.50-£3.50). Disabled access: toilet. High chairs. Nappy-changing facilities. Tables outdoors (15, courtyard). Takeaway service.

National Dining Rooms & Bakery

Sainsbury Wing, National Gallery, Trafalgar Square, WC2N 5DN (7747 2525/www. nationaldiningrooms.co.uk). Charing Cross tube/rail. Bakery **Meals served** 10am-5pm Mon, Tue, Thur-Sun; 11am-8.30pm Wed.
Main courses £4.50-£9.50. *Restaurant* **Lunch served** noon-3pm daily. **Dinner served** 5-7pm Wed. **Set meal** £22.50 2 courses, £27.50 3 courses. **Credit** AmEx, MC, V.
This rather grown-up dining room might seem too sombre for young families, but they are catered for handsomely. The National serves up fine British food at reasonable prices, and the all-day bakery is full of gorgeous treats. Big appetites might go for the raised pork pie or scones with Cornish clotted cream, otherwise there's a full menu of good, regional food, whose provenance is proudly stated. The children's menu includes crudités, fish and chip and chicken drumsticks.
Buggy access. Disabled access: lift, toilet. Children's menu (£2.50-£6.50). High chairs. Nappy-changing facilities.

Pavilion Café

Dulwich Park, off College Road, SE21 7BQ (8299 1383/www.pavilioncafedulwich.co.uk). North Dulwich or West Dulwich rail.
Open *Summer* 9am-6.30pm daily. *Winter* 9am-4pm daily. **Main courses** £3.50-£6.50. **Credit cards** MC, V.
Locals who want to take advantage of the top quality food in this exceptionally child-friendly café (before the onslaught of buggies and babes) come for breakfast. lunchtimes can be a bunfight, but the staff cope pretty well. There's a backroom with toys and books for children. The emphasis is on own-baked, carefully sourced, free-range and/or organic, all of which keeps the wealthy Dulwich fan base happy. Children can choose baked potatoes and stews, or delicious own-made fish fingers, chicken breast, crisp chips or pasta dishes or shepherd's pie. Then there are sandwiches, soups, French-

Eating lessons

The words 'healthy eating', 'fruit and veg' and 'school' may be enough to send junk food-addicted children waddling for the hills, but the trustees of the Borough Market aren't afraid to use such words *devant les enfants*. Keen to build on the phenomenal success of Borough Market as a renowned centre of food excellence, the trustees have come up with a big idea that will be of lasting significance to the local community. They'll need £2m, a good deal of hard work and commitment from market traders, locals, volunteers and charitable trusts, and a fair wind, but they mean to have the Borough Market Food School open by the summer of 2009.

The Food School, based at 1 Cathedral Street, across the road from Southwark Cathedral and hard by the market, will be a community education centre with the sole aim of fostering enthusiasm and excitement about food. Borough Market's traders and trustees already do much to promote an interest in healthy eating and good food by hosting barbecues for local residents and taking fresh fruit and veg into local schools to demonstrate how produce is grown, harvested and prepared. Once the school is open, it will host cookery lessons and demos for families and school groups, using market produce, as well as providing training for those who want to make a career in grub. Best of all, it will reinforce the message that food is exciting and fun – which Borough Market has been keen to promote ever since the 250-year-old market was registered as a charity back in 1999. (It was recently voted 'Best Market' by the National Association of British Market Authorities.)

When taking schoolchildren around the market and showing them stalls laden with fresh vegetables, lovely fish, cheeses, olives, jams, oils, breads, cakes and chocolates, and letting them smell, touch and taste the produce and ask questions of the traders, their enthusiasm and curiosity is all too evident. The Food School aims to harness that, and create a new generation of little Jamies and Nigellas, who understand and enjoy the business of buying, preparing and eating good food.

The five-storey building will need lift systems, demonstration kitchens, specialist catering equipment, including adjustable worktops for children and adults in wheelchairs, all manner of utensils and accessories, small tables and chairs for educational activities – the shopping list is seemingly endless. The trustees are aiming to raise the £2m through energetic fundraising and the support of various charitable and health trusts, as well as the local authority. And the clever bit? Once the school is up and running, the Food School should be self-financing.

The community education project, based in the basement, ground and first floors, won't be expected to pay, but the upper floors will be let out as meeting rooms and office space for media companies. The grooviest part of the building – the roof – with its fascinating views over the market and railway, will be turned into a corporate function space. Companies wanting to use it for promotions and parties will have to use Borough Market Food School for their refreshments – with all the profits being ploughed straight back into the community pot. A right tasty way to run a business.

inspired salads and an assortment of lovely cakes, including wheat- and dairy-free options. Further family inducements include ice-creams and frozen yoghurts. Children's parties (Mon-Fri, about £5.50 a head) are a speciality. *Buggy access. Children's menu (£1.50-£3.50). Disabled access: toilet. High chairs. Nappy-changing facilities. Play area. Tables outdoors (12, terrace). Takeaway service.*

Pavilion Café
Highgate Woods, Muswell Hill Road, N10 3JN (8444 4777). Highgate tube. **Open** *Summer* 9am-7pm daily. *Winter* 9am-4pm daily. **Main courses** £6-£8.95. **Credit** AmEx, MC, V.
Surrounded by whispering trees and looking like a rural idyll, the Pavilion has the vibe of a pub garden. For adults there are posh burgers and salads, made from carefully sourced local ingredients. There's a wide selection for kids (pasta, fish, chicken goujons), who are made welcome into the evening.
Buggy access. Children's set meal (£3.50). Crayons. Disabled access: toilet. High chairs. Nappy-changing facilities. Tables outdoors (30, garden). Takeaway service.

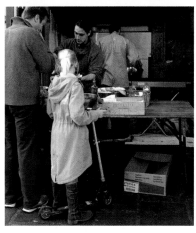

Pavilion Tea House

Greenwich Park, Blackheath Gate, SE10 8QY (8858 9695). Blackheath rail/Greenwich rail/DLR. **Open** 9am-5.30pm Mon-Fri; 9am-6pm Sat, Sun. **Main courses** £4.95-£8.50. **Credit** MC, V.

A hexagonal café with loads of outdoor tables surrounded by shady trees. Inside it's bright, clean and busy – expect lengthy queues around weekend lunchtimes. Limited space means parents are requested to leave their ginormous pushchairs outside. Their menu has a hearty range of great stoke-up food. We plumped for

scrambled eggs with smoked salmon and have never seen such a huge portion. Our mixed bean casserole was warming and tomatoey, and sandwiches are prodigiously filled. Options for children include pasta dishes and baked beans on toast.

Buggy access. Children's menu (£2.25-£2.95). Disabled access: toilet. High chairs. Nappy-changing facilities. Tables outdoors (30, patio).

S&M Café

4-6 Essex Road, N1 8LN (7359 5361/ www.sandmcafe.co.uk). Angel tube/19, 38 bus. **Meals served** 7.30am-11.30pm Mon-Thur; 7.30am-midnight Fri; 8.30am-midnight Sat; 8.30am-10.30pm Sun. **Main courses** £6.50-£9.95. **Credit** MC, V.

Friendly, efficient staff handle busy periods at this Islington stalwart well, taking names and honouring tables so customers don't actually have to queue. The decor of the former Alfredo's café is a mix of periods, with lairy blue Formica tables and tiny red leather chairs. It's cramped but mostly jovial. The all-day breakfasts are as popular as the eponymous sausage and mash, while the blackboard promotes Sunday lunch-type meals – say curried parsnip soup, roast lamb shanks, and spotted dick with vanilla custard. We enjoyed the daily special of chicken and asparagus bangers (Toulouse was another option) partnered with tasty potato, parsnip and turnip mash. The children can choose small portions of sausage and mash, or go for goujons – chicken or fish.

Buggy access. Children's set meal (£3.75). Takeaway service.

Other locations 268 Portobello Road, W10 5TY (8968 8898); 48 Brushfield Street, E1 6AG (7247 2252); Unit 9, Peninsula Square, SE10 0DX (8305 1940).

That Place on the Corner

1-3 Green Lanes, N16 9BS (7704 0079/ www.thatplaceonthecorner.co.uk). Highbury & Islington tube/rail/Canonbury rail/21, 73, 141, 276, 341, 476 bus. **Open** 9.30am-6pm Mon-Thur; 9.30-7.30pm Fri; 8.45am-2.30pm Sat; 9.30am-3pm Sun. **Meals served** 10.30am-5.30pm Mon-Thur; 10.30-7pm Fri; 10.30am-2pm Sat; noon-3pm Sun. **Main courses** £4.85-£8.25. **Credit** MC, V.

The only child-friendly café in London that won't let unaccompanied grown ups in, TPotC is a relaxed environment created for families by local mothers Sam Menezes and Virginia Fiol. The child-pleasing elements are tasteful – there's a window seat laden with brightly coloured velvet and silk cushions, a large, low velvet sofa,

Consumer

a little library, a play shop and a dressing up corner. A weekly schedule of baking, crafting, dancing, music and after-school classes is also available (*see p192*).

The menu sticks sensibly to the tried and trusted pasta/panini/big breakfast formula, with brasserie staples such as own-made burgers and fish cakes to bring further comfort. The coffee is good, the cakes and pastries come from a local bakery and the children's menu is equally trustworthy. Children can choose own-made shepherd's pie, spag bol and other pasta favourites, smaller burgers and plaice or chicken goujons, and have the option of mash, rice or chips and various vegetables to go alongside. Sunday roasts, late-night Fridays and schoolday teatime menus are all well received by local families (*see also p248* **Playing with their food**).

Buggy access. Children's menu (£4.50-£5.25). Crayons. Disabled access: toilet. High chairs. Nappy-changing facilities. Play area.

Upper Deck

London's Transport Museum, The Piazza, WC2E 7BB (7598 1356/www.ltmuseum.co.uk). Covent Garden tube. **Open** 10am-9.30pm Mon-Thur, Sat; 11am-9.30pm Fri. 10am-6pm Sun. **Main courses** £3.20-£8.50. **Credit** AmEx, MC, V. **Map** p317 L7.

Unusually good for a museum restaurant (you don't have to pay the museum admission charge to eat here), Upper Deck has a great menu of salads, soups and hot meals and a children's menu that we loved, although it was under review as we went to press, so ring to see if it's been reinstated before visiting. Adults love the own-made fish and chips and bread and butter pudding, and the fact that the café is licensed. *Buggy access. Disabled access: lift, toilet. High chairs. Nappy-changing facilities.*

V&A Café

Victoria & Albert Museum, Cromwell Road, SW7 2RL (7942 2000/www.vam.ac.uk). South Kensington tube. **Meals served** 10am-5.15pm Mon-Thur, Sat, Sun; 10am-9.30pm Fri. **Main courses** £6-£10 **Credit** MC, V.

In a museum as handsome as the V&A, stunning decor is a given. This café, taking up the Morris, Gamble and Poynter rooms, is a most attractive place for a family lunch. Happily, the menu has as much to recommend it. Children's meals are plentiful – you can pay about £5 for a sandwich and pudding option, or, for the same amount, indulge them with a mini roast dinner. Adult meals cost from about £6 for generous portions of, for example, roast peppers with stilton and a choice of salads. For simpler refreshments, there is a huge selection of teas, cakes and sandwiches. *Buggy access. Disabled access: toilet. High chairs. Nappy-changing facilities.*

CHINESE

Dragon Castle

100 Walworth Road, Elephant & Castle, SE17 1JL (7277 3388/www.dragoncastle.co.uk). Elephant & Castle tube/rail. **Meals served** noon-11pm Mon-Thur; noon-11.30pm Fri, Sat; 11.30am-10.30pm Sun. **Main courses** £5.50-£128. **Set meals** £14.80-£32.80 per person 2-3 courses (minimum 2). **Credit** MC, V.

Ever since it opened, this smart restaurant in a less than attractive area has been wowing the critics and delighting its customers. The menu includes Anglo-Canto stalwarts like lemon chicken, but also a thrilling range of more authentic dishes, deftly cooked, such as a braise of dried oysters and silky fungus, or ribbony jellyfish with cucumber or a stir-fry of roast duck, fresh lily bulb and celery. Come for dim sum in the daytime, as these savoury morsels will really appeal to children. Note that the £128 dish in the listings is for shark fin soup. *Buggy access. High chairs.*

London Hong Kong

6-7 Lisle Street, WC2H 7BG (7287 0352/ www.london-hk.co.uk). Leicester Square or Piccadilly Circus tube. **Dim sum served** noon-5pm daily. **Meals served** noon-11.30pm Mon-Thur; noon-midnight Fri, Sat; 11am-11pm Sun. **Main courses** £7.50-£10.50. **Set lunch** £10 3 courses. **Credit** AmEx, MC, V. **Map** p317 K7.

The big choice of dim sum dumplings make Hong Kong our decent Chinatown recommendation for children. The menus are plasticky, the style tacky, and the photographs of dim sum titbits amuse the kids. Service comes with a smile, and children are usually made a fuss of. Steamed dumplings stuffed with prawn and chives are nicely done. *Buggy access. Disabled access. High chairs. Takeaway service.*

Royal China

30 Westferry Circus, E14 8RR (7719 0888/ www.royalchinagroup.co.uk). Canary Wharf tube/DLR/Westferry DLR. **Meals served** noon-11pm Mon-Thur; noon-11.30pm Fri, Sat; 11am-10pm Sun. **Dim sum served** noon-4.45pm daily. **Main courses** £7-£50.

Consumer

Dim sum £2.20-£4.50. **Set meal** £30 per person (minimum 2). **Credit** AmEx, DC, MC, V. There aren't many Chinese restaurants with congenial outdoor seating, so its location, on the brink of the glittering Thames, is as good a reason as any to include Royal China. Fortunately, the extensive menu and relaxed attitude to children are a couple more pluses. We've had reliable meals here. Children adore the pasta-like dumplings on the dim sum menu, as well as the Vietnamese pancake rolls and smoked chicken slivers. Seasonal specials on our last visit included savoury beef brisket with turnip and fried beansprouts with salted fish – delicious. Staff are all smiles and very friendly towards children whenever we visit.
Booster seats. Buggy access. Disabled access: toilet. Nappy-changing facilities. Tables outdoors (23, terrace). Takeaway service.
Other locations 40 Baker Street, W1U 7AB (7487 4688); 13 Queensway, W2 4QJ (7221 2535); 805 Fulham Road, SW6 5HE (7731 0081).

Meals. *See p229.*

FISH

Belgo Noord

72 Chalk Farm Road, NW1 8AN (7267 0718/ www.belgo-restaurants.com). Chalk Farm tube. **Lunch served** noon-3pm Mon-Fri. **Dinner served** 5.30-11pm Mon-Thur; 5.30-11.30pm Fri. **Meals served** noon-11.30pm Sat; noon-10.30pm Sun. **Main courses** £8.95-£17.95. **Set lunch** £5.95 1 course. **Credit** AmEx, DC, MC, V.
Touting the Belgian speciality of moules frites and beer, Belgo Noord attracts a lunchtime crowd of workers and families. The evenings are awash with boozy birthday groups. Housed in an industrial-style basement, it has the appearance of a submarine-cum-spaceship. Kilo pots of mussels are the popular choice, ranging from marinière (white wine and garlic) to Thai green curry, and they're all organically farmed, so you don't have worry whether there's an 'R' in the month. The traditional Belgian dishes, slow-roasted with beer, prove that Belgo Noord is about more than just quick wins. Take advantage of their special offers, such as two free kids' meals per adult ordering a main course. Helpful, speedy service had us out of the door in under an hour.
Buggy access. Disabled access (call ahead): toilet. Children's menu free with adult meal. Crayons. High chairs. Nappy-changing facilities.
Other locations Belgo Bierodrome, 44-48 Clapham High Street, SW4 7UR (7720 1118);

Belgo Bierodrome, 67 Kingsway, WC2B 6TD (7242 7469); Belgo Bierodrome, 173-174 Upper Street, N1 1XS (7226 5835); Belgo Centraal, 50 Earlham Street, WC2H 9LJ (7813 2233).

Costas Fish Restaurant

18 Hillgate Street, W8 7SR (7727 4310). Notting Hill Gate tube. **Lunch served** noon-2.30pm, **dinner served** 5.30-10.30pm Tue-Sat. **Main courses** £5.20-£7.90. **No credit cards.**
An antidote to Notting Hill flummery, this no-nonsense chippy has been deep-frying since 1981. If you march past the gleaming fryer at the front, you'll enter a gratifyingly simple dining room furnished with caff-style wooden tables and chairs. There's a Hellenic accent to the menu – the restaurant is sibling to the neighbouring Greek Cypriot Costas Grill – as evidenced by houmous and taramasalata among the starters, calamares in the mains, and retsina and palatable Keo lager on the drinks list. Main courses of meaty rock salmon and delicate lemon sole, served with golden brown chips (fried in vegetable oil) and a bowlful of mushy peas were heaven on a plate. Local families, including ravenous toddlers, tuck in with abandon.
Buggy access. Takeaway service.

fish!

Cathedral Street, Borough Market, SE1 9AL (7407 3803/www.fishdiner.co.uk). London Bridge tube/rail. **Meals served** 11.30am-11pm Mon-Thur; noon-11pm Fri, Sat; noon-10.30pm Sun. **Main courses** £9.95-£22.95. **Credit** AmEx, MC, V. **Map** p317 M8.
Looking like a big conservatory facing out on to Southwark Cathedral and Borough Market, Fish! continues to reel in a cultured crowd who like to know the provenance of their fish supper. You select from the list of fish of the day, the way you want it cooked and what sauce to go with it. Starters include crisp, pink-inside Thai crab cakes served with sweet chilli and rocket, smoked haddock with cheese or fish soup. Battered (Icelandic) cod and chunky chips with mushy peas is a comforting plateful. The children's menu lists a half-portion of the fish and chips (substitute swordfish or salmon for the battered fish if necessary), chicken and chips, served with a drink and followed by an ice-cream.
Buggy access. Disabled access: toilet. Children's set meal (£6.95). Crayons. High chairs. Nappy-changing facilities. Tables outdoors (24, terrace).
Other locations fish! kitchen, 58 Coombe Road, Kingston-upon-Thames, Surrey KT2 7AF (8546 2886).

North Sea Fish Restaurant

7-8 Leigh Street, WC1H 9EW (7387 5892). Russell Square tube/Euston or King's Cross tube/rail/68, 168 bus. **Lunch served** noon-2.30pm, **dinner served** 5.30-10.30pm Mon-Sat. **Main courses** £8.95-£18.95. **Credit** MC, V. **Map** p315 L3/4.
You'll need to share portions in this traditional old fish and chippy. The 'normal sized' portions of battered cod and haddock with chips are massive, and what they lack in finesse they make up for in generosity. This isn't one of the new breed of posh chippies, but the food's enough to satisfy exhausted and whiney kids who've spent too long at the British Museum.
Buggy access. High chairs. Takeaway service.

Olley's

65-69 Norwood Road, SE24 9AA (8671 8259/www.olleys.info). Herne Hill rail/3, 68 bus. **Lunch served** noon-3pm, **dinner served** 5-10.30pm Tue-Sun. **Main courses** £8.45-£18.45. **Set lunch** £7.50 1 course. **Credit** AmEx, MC, V.
South London's multi-award winning purveyor of traditional fish and chips, Olley's, underneath the railway arches, has always been one for diversification. There are many exotic varieties of fish on offer, which can be steamed or grilled for batter-phobes. High chairs are clingfilm-wrapped (!) between each use so your child won't be picking up the last kid's peas. The children's menu consists mainly of the usual 'nuggets and chips' options, but there are also calamares and prawns. The staff can also bring small portions of the steamed dishes on request. The creamy mushy peas are the best in London, and the chips also deserve a mention, being blanched before frying.
Buggy access. Disabled access: toilet. Children's menu (£4-£4.50). Crayons. High chairs. Tables outdoors (12, pavement). Nappy-changing facilities. Takeaway service.

Rock & Sole Plaice

47 Endell Street, WC2H 9AJ (7836 3785). Covent Garden or Leicester Square tube. **Meals served** 11.30am-10.30pm Mon-Sat; noon-9.30pm Sun. **Main courses** £8-£15. **Credit** MC, V. **Map** p315 L6.
A sociable and busy little chippy with a high turnover, the R&S has feel of a beer garden and claims to be London's oldest surviving chip shop. Tourists and office workers share tables, ready to wait for the super-sized fish suppers. Chips, fried fish and mushy peas are all present and correct. Finish off with spotted dick or sticky toffee pudding.

Buggy access. Tables outdoors (7, pavement). Takeaway service.

Toff's

38 Muswell Hill Broadway, N10 3RT (8883 8656/www.toffsfish.co.uk). Highgate tube, then 43, 134 bus. **Meals served** 11.30am-10pm Mon-Sat. **Main courses** £7.95-£17.50. **Set lunch** £7.95 1 course. **Credit** AmEx, DC, MC, V.

The first thing you see at Toffs is the takeaway counter, where staff in white smocks toss chips into sizzling fryers as they cater to the constant queue of customers. But behind the bustling shop front, through a pair of saloon-style swing doors (children love them), a restaurant offers more serenity. Toff's large choice of fish can be ordered in plain batter, matzo-meal batter, or grilled for a healthier alternative (a rarity in most chippies). There's also a well-executed children's menu featuring real fish and own-made chips. For those with stamina, puddings include the likes of treacle pudding and crème caramel. There's extra seating in the style of a captain's table.

Buggy access. Children's menu (£3.50-£3.95). Crayons. Disabled access: toilet. High chairs. Takeaway service.

FRENCH

Belvedere

Holland House, off Abbotsbury Road, in Holland Park, W8 6LU (7602 1238/www. whitestarline.org.uk). Holland Park tube. **Lunch served** noon-2.15pm Mon-Sat; noon-2pm, 2.30-4pm Sun. **Dinner served** 6-10pm Mon-Sat. **Main courses** £12-£22. **Credit** AmEx, MC, V.

Around dusk, with the birds singing in the surrounding Holland Park, this is one of London's most alluring restaurants. Inside, the dining areas, one intimate and low-ceilinged, the other dramatic and opulent, seem offputtingly smart. Nevertheless, the staff are gracious with family groups. The brasserie-length menu ranges from smartly styled comfort food (plaice and chips) to luxurious treats, such as scallops and venison. If none of this turns on the children, bowls of pasta, sausage and mash or plain roast meats and fish can usually be served up for younger palates, with a reduced price ticket. Belvedere is a great place to get away from it all, without ever leaving the metropolis.

Buggy access. Disabled access (ground floor). High chairs. Tables outdoors (5, terrace).

Le Cercle

1 Wilbraham Place, SW1X 9AE (7901 9999/ www.lecercle.co.uk). Sloane Square tube. **Bar Open/snacks served** noon-midnight Tue-Sat. *Restaurant* **Lunch served** noon-3pm Tue-Sat. **Tea served** 3-6pm Tue-Sat. **Dinner served** 6-11pm Tue-Sat. **Set lunch** £15 3 dishes, £19.50 4 dishes. **Set dinner** (6-7pm) £17.50 3 dishes, £21.50 4 dishes. **Tapas** £4.50-£16. **Credit** AmEx, MC, V.

No passing trade here – the entrance, on a side road off Sloane Street, is easily missed. Word gets around, though, so the cavernous basement space (down two flights of stairs, but there is a lift) is often full. There are no high chairs, which is another reason it's not great for young children. However, the big draw is that, at lunchtime, children under 12 can eat free from a fixed menu of five smaller dishes. They have to be lunching with a paying adult, naturellement. Staff prefer to seat children on the banquettes around the edge, behind the drapes, where they are out of sight of other diners. The food comes in tapas style portions and rewards adventurous palates. Each small dish was delicious, vividly coloured and intensely flavoured, satisfying through variety rather than quantity. Highlights included cooked-then-marinated mackerel, barley 'risotto' with spinach and grilled mussels, wood pigeon breasts with a reduced pumpkin purée and an oxtail coated in a creamy blood orange sauce.

Buggy access. Disabled access: lift, toilet. Children's menu (free, lunch only, Tue-Sat).

Roussillon

16 St Barnabas Street, SW1W 8PE (7730 5550/www.roussillon.co.uk). Sloane Square tube. **Lunch served** noon-2.30pm Mon-Fri. **Dinner served** 6.30-10.30pm Mon-Sat. **Set lunch** £35 3 courses. **Set dinner** £55 3 courses. **Set meal** £60-£70 8 course tasting menu. **Credit** AmEx, MC, V.

A gastronomic destination as well as a neighbourhood place, Roussillon suits all manner of gourmands: families, elderly couples, friends out for a quiet dinner. Adults, admittedly, have to be well heeled to have this as a local. The decor is subdued, the service solicitous, and the food sublime. The menu changes with the seasons (three cheers), vegetarians have their own eight-course tasting menu. What's in it for the kids? The mini gastronomes menu offers six courses, starring such delights as scallops, truffle ravioli or smoked eel and costs £15 per child. If you call ahead, on the first and third Wednesday of each month it's free. A free lunch in Pimlico, how's that for a bargain?

Buggy access. Children's set meal (£15 lunch).

Eat down on the farm at **Mudchute Kitchen**. *See p229.*

GASTROPUBS

The Engineer

65 Gloucester Avenue, NW1 8JH (7722 0950/ www.the-engineer.com). Chalk Farm tube/ 31, 168 bus. **Open** 9am-11pm Mon-Sat; 9am-10.30pm Sun. **Breakfast served** 9-11.30am Mon-Fri; 9am-noon Sat, Sun. **Lunch served** noon-3pm Mon-Fri; 12.30-4pm Sat, Sun. **Dinner served** 7-11pm Mon-Sat; 7-10.30pm Sun. **Main courses** £12.50-£15.50. **Credit** MC, V.

History buffs might be interested to know that Brunel is believed to have have built this Grade II listed public house; it's also notable as one of the earliest boozers to go gastro (1995). As such, it has been a big success, and consistently popular with families, who favour the small walled garden when the weather's fine. A short menu that shows influences from Asian to Mediterranean lists devilled crispy whitebait, roast mushroom and aubergine tart, sea bream and chicken with chorizo, beans and harissa. Children are made welcome and given crayons and colouring books along with their own menu (sausage with chips or green beans; poached egg with chips or green beans; penne pasta with tomato sauce, followed by organic ice-cream. *Buggy access. Children's set meal (£5.50). Crayons. Disabled access: toilet. High chairs. Nappy-changing facilities. Tables outdoors (15, garden).*

House

63-69 Canonbury Road, N1 2DG (7704 7410/www.inthehouse.biz). Highbury & Islington tube/rail/Essex Road rail. **Open** 5-11pm Mon; 11am-11pm Tue-Sun. **Breakfast served** 11am-noon Sat, Sun. **Lunch served** noon-2.30pm Tue-Fri; noon-3.30pm Sat; noon-4pm Sun. **Dinner served** 5-10.30pm Mon; 6-10.30pm Tue-Sat; 6.30-9.30pm Sun. **Main courses** £12-£17. **Credit** AmEx, MC, V.

A nicely spacious street-corner terrace is one of the House's prime assets, bringing a touch of café society to Canonbury summers. Inside, the decor is mellow chic, far more restaurant than pub, but with a main dining area that can feel distinctly cramped whenever it's busy (which seems to be often). It has an upscale modern menu, listing delights such as Dorset crab spring rolls with ginger, pan-fried sea bass with ginger and lime and pork chops with spinach and mustard mash. Children are most welcome, especially on weekend lunchtimes, when they are served mini fish and chips, pasta with tomato sauce or small portions of the daily specials for £7.50. The House also opens for breakfast at weekends, so you can sit outside to sample own-baked pastries or a hefty full English using farmhouse produce. *Buggy access. Disabled access: toilet. Children's set meal (£7.50). High chairs. Nappy-changing facilities. Tables outdoors (35, terrace).*

Consumer

Pizza chains

Don't all children like pizza? They're quick, cheap and cheerful, so heading for the ubiquitous pizza chains is an obvious move – but if you think one is much like any other, think again. We've rounded up our favourites and give you the lowdown on the strengths and weaknesses to see which of the big pizza chains serves the kids best.

ASK

160-162 Victoria Street, SW1E 5LB (7630 8228/www.askcentral.co.uk). Victoria tube/rail. **Meals served** noon-11pm Mon-Sat; noon-10.30pm Sun. **Main courses** £5.60-£8.45. **Credit** AmEx, DC, MC, V.
ASK was once hailed as a serious rival to the mighty Pizza Express. This branch, with its reproduction Renaissance artwork, and elaborate cornicing, has a spiral staircase leading to a prodigiously windowed first-floor space. Pizzas are tasty, but not as crisp as those in Pizza Express. The salad, though, was good and fresh, and the ice-cream was delicious. **Total number of branches** 20. **What's in it for the kids?** The £5.95 children's menu (with colouring-in and wax crayons) is good value, giving sprogs a choice of ten pastas and pizzas (including ham and pineapple), garlic bread, salad and a scoop of top-quality ice-cream or banana split. *Buggy access. High chairs.*

Pizza Express

Benbow House, 24 New Globe Walk, SE1 9DS (7401 3977/www.pizza express.com). London Bridge tube/ rail. **Meals served** noon-11pm Mon-Sat; noon-10.30pm Sun. **Main courses** £5.65-£9.25. **Credit** AmEx, DC, MC, V.
A household name. Pizza Express's habitat is gentrified London; it also colonises heavily touristed environs, such as here, on the South Bank. This branch, a symphony in glass and chrome, gives you Thameside seating and views. The waiters are trained in child-friendliness (*see p244* **Service with a smile**). Children and youths go bonkers for the comforting dough balls and their accompanying excessive butter pot, and the chocolate fudge cake.

Total number of branches 91. **What's in it for the kids?** The Piccolo menu is superb, and must be responsible for the huge numbers of extended family groups we always find in this branch. For £5.65, the children can have their favourite – dough balls – followed by a choice of meaty or vegetarian pizza or pasta, with a mini side salad if they want it. Then comes toffee fudge sundae, chocolate sundae or strawberry sundae, rounded off with a bambinoccino (that's foamed milk and chocolate powder – no coffee). Terrific.
Buggy access (ground floor). Crayons. Disabled access: ramp, toilet. High chairs. Nappy-changing facilities. Tables outdoors (12, riverside). Takeaway service.

Pizza Paradiso

61 The Cut, SE1 8LL (7261 1221/ www.pizzaparadiso.co.uk). Southwark tube/Waterloo tube/rail. **Meals served** noon-midnight Mon-Sat; noon-11pm Sun. **Main courses** £6.10-£17.95. **Credit** AmEx, DC, MC, V.
A 1934-established, determinedly Sicilian and very mini chain, Paradiso started life as the Ristorante Olivelli and still keeps this alternate name in its official title. It isn't anything like its bigger chain rivals, though, and feels more like a neighbourhood trattoria. The food is consistently well presented, with the taste of quality Italian produce very evident. Dough balls (nine to a portion) are fantastic, pasta is as good as the pizza, and salads are perky. **Total number of branches** 5. **What's in it for the kids**? Staff will discount a quid off some pasta dishes sold in child sizes.
Booking advisable Wed-Fri. Buggy access. High chairs. Tables outdoors (4, pavement). Takeaway service.

La Porchetta

33 Boswell Street, WC1N 3BP (7242 2434). Holborn or Russell Square tube. **Lunch served** noon-3pm Mon-Fri. **Dinner served** 6-11pm Mon- Sat. **Main courses** £5.90-£11.50. **Credit** MC, V.
There are pigs displayed everywhere in La Porchetta, which is fitting, as this

Consumer

is undoubtedly the best pizza place for a big blowout. Pizzas are extremely large and the choice wide, including both porky and vegetarian options. Tables are small and tightly packed together. Party groups love it. Food is generally good, but forget about the fridge-tasting puddings – they're cheap, but not worth ordering. **Total number of branches** 5. **What's in it for the kids?** More adult in orientation than most chains. Kids can comfortably share one of the huge pizzas, or enjoy a half portion of pasta at a reduced price.
Booking advisable (5 or more people). Buggy access. High chairs. Takeaway service.

Prezzo

17 Hertford Street, W1J 7RS (7499 4690/www.prezzoplc.co.uk). Green Park or Hyde Park Corner tube. **Meals served** noon-11.30pm Mon-Sat; noon-11pm Sun. **Main courses** £5.75-£8.95. **Credit** AmEx, DC, MC, V.
This Mayfair branch of a famously sophisticated seven-year-old chain is a treat. It's oddly reminiscent of a convent dining room, with dark oak panelling and votive candles, but that image might have been prompted by our sitting next to the massive oil painting of tonsured monks enjoying a pasta dinner. The atmosphere is classy, and the menu surprisingly good value for such a swish location. Its presence amid various top-end hotels makes it popular with wealthy American families. Food is high quality, with some tempting flame-roasted chicken dishes for dough-avoiders, although our uninteresting ice-cream let the side down. **Total number of branches** 10. **What's in it for the kids?** They love the antique atmosphere and the young, Euro-poppy staff and the kids' menu – £3.95 for a choice of three pizzas/pastas, ice-cream and squash.
Booking advisable. Buggy access. Disabled access. High chairs. Takeaway service.

Strada

Riverside, Royal Festival Hall, Belvedere Road, SE1 8XX (7401 9126/www.strada.co.uk). Embankment tube/Waterloo tube/rail. **Meals served** noon-11pm Mon-Fri; 11am-11pm Sat; 11am-10.30pm Sun. **Main courses** £6.95-£16.50. **Credit** AmEx, MC, V.
When the brand first came on the scene, the contemporary, hand-stretched, wood-burning schtick earned the burgeoning chain many fans. Our last Strada meal was excellent: fresh and flavoursome Italian ingredients were enhanced by perfectly cooked spaghetti and splendid breads and pizzas. There's a buzz in this Festival Hall branch that's missing from some of the quieter venues, but the staff were unruffled by a busy Sunday lunch influx. We continue to applaud Strada for its free chilled, bottled and filtered water on every table. **Total number of branches** 27. **What's in it for the kids?** They can have a reduced-price pasta dish – say, a small bowl of spag bol – for £4.25. Other pasta accompaniments for children include mozzarella and tomato or ham.
Buggy access. Disabled access: toilet. High chairs. Tables outdoors (22, terrace). Takeaway service (pizza).

Zizzi

73-75 Strand, WC2R 0DE (7240 1717/www.zizzi.co.uk). Covent Garden or Embankment tube/Charing Cross tube/rail. **Meals served** noon-11.30pm Mon-Sat; noon-11pm Sun. **Main courses** £6.25-£11.95. **Credit** AmEx, DC, MC, V.
Part of the same family as ASK, but this swish basement branch of Zizzi exudes more warmth than its sister and seems to be run on more professional lines. Our pizzas were good, a goat's cheese bruschetta yummy and the salads fresh and well presented. We were also happy to polish off a fantastic pistachio ice-cream for pudding; the chocolate version was gorgeous too. **Total number of branches** 15. **What's in it for the kids?** The kids' menu costs £5.95 and offers breadsticks, a choice of 7 pizza/pasta dishes, and ice-cream.
Buggy access. Disabled access: toilet. High chairs. Nappy-changing facilities. Takeaway service.

Consumer

Common Ground. *see p225.*

Consumer

Prince Regent

*69 Dulwich Road, SE24 0NJ (7274 1567).
Brixton tube/rail/Herne Hill rail.* **Open** noon-11pm Mon-Thur; noon-midnight Fri, Sat; noon-10.30pm Sun. **Lunch served** noon-3pm Mon-Sat; noon-5pm Sun. **Dinner served** 7-10pm Mon-Sat; 6-9pm Sun. **Main courses** £8.85-£15. **Credit** MC, V.

A favourite with parents who can park their prams by the tables, this cheerful pub occupies an elegantly striped brick building with plenty of original features, lending an atmosphere as warm as the welcome. Adults enjoy the excellent beer selection, children love the desserts, which are worth prioritising for their generous portions, fun presentation and quality ice-creams and custard. There's no child-specific menu, but the chef is willing to serve up items from the brunch menu (eggs, smoked salmon, bacon), or small portions of gastro classics, such as sausage and mash, fish and chips or beef bourguignon. Note that children must be out by 7pm.
Buggy access. Disabled access: toilet. High chairs. Nappy-changing facilities. Tables outdoors (12, terrace).

Roebuck Pub & Dining Room

122 High Road, W4 1PU (8995 4392/www. theroebuckchiswick.co.uk). Turnham Green tube. **Lunch served** noon-3pm Mon-Fri; noon-5pm Sat, Sun. **Dinner served** 6-10.30pm Mon-Sat; 6-10pm Sun. **Main courses** £8.50-£17.50. **Set lunch** (Mon-Fri) £5 1 course. **Credit** AmEx, MC, V.

This is a reassuringly slick operation, all stripped wooden floors, chocolate suede banquettes and reclaimed church pews. The front half operates strictly as a pub with bar snacks (and no children), the back half is run as a dining room (families welcome). The whole space is light, airy and welcoming, with the back opening onto a charming walled garden – a real suntrap. An extensive, varied menu takes in gastropub classics with some experimentation (including some excellent fish dishes) but strictly no gimmicks. None of it was cheap but it was all excellent value for money. Service was swift and unobtrusive. The wine list is excellent but succinct – surprisingly limited for such a large cosmopolitan venue.
Buggy access. High chairs. Children's menu (£4.50-£6.50). Crayons. Disabled: toilet. Nappy-changing facilities. Tables outdoors (25, garden).

Stein's

Richmond Towpath, rear of 55 Petersham Road, Richmond, Surrey TW10 6XT (8948 8189/www.steins.com). Richmond tube/rail. **Meals served** noon-10pm Mon-Fri; 10am-10pm Sat, Sun. **Main courses** £7.90-£14.90. **Set lunch** (noon-4pm Mon-Fri) £5.99 1 course. **Credit** MC, V.

This is an unusual and quirky destination: a family-friendly riverside Bavarian beer garden a stone's throw from Richmond bridge. Converted from a ramshackle ice-cream parlour, Stein's consists of a kiosk with a large kitchen behind it surrounded by benches alongside the river – about half of them undercover. There is a safe, small area where under-fives can play (not under cover). The menu is 100 per cent German: this is wurst (sausage) central, and there are Bavarian specialities like roasted pork shoulder with dumplings and pork meatloaf. Bratkartoffeln – potatoes sautéed with bacon, onion and spices – is a good choice for children: simple, own-made comfort food. They also do some mean breakfasts and a vast array of strudel desserts. As you might expect, German beer flows freely and the Almdudler, an apple-flavoured herbal lemonade from Austria, is lovely. Watch out for the weather: at the slightest sign of rain, Stein's closes.
Buggy access. Crayons. High chairs. Nappy-changing facilities. Play area. Tables outdoors (28, towpath). Takeaway service.

ICE-CREAM

Don't miss Marine Ices (*see p244*), the gelateria/caff that has been fattening up Chalk Farm residents since the 1930s.

Caffè Deli Paradiso
109 Highgate West Hill, N6 6AP (8340 7818). Gospel Oak rail, then 214 bus. **Open** 8.30am-10.30pm Mon-Sat; 8.30am-9pm Sun. **Main courses** £6.20-£7. **Credit** MC, V.
Handy for Hampstead Heath, and with open French windows in summer, this Sicilian-style café and gelateria offers wonderful flavours such as tartufo (truffle), Sicilian lemon, stracciatella (with chocolate strands) and zuppa inglese (English trifle).
Buggy access. Disabled access: toilet. High chairs. Table outdoors (6, pavement). Takeaway service.

Gelateria Danieli
16 Brewers Lane, Richmond, Surrey TW9 1HH (8439 9807/www.gelateriadanieli.com). Richmond tube/rail. **Open** *Summer* 10am-10pm daily. *Winter* 10am-6pm daily. Times may vary, phone to check. **Credit** MC, V.
The queues stretch out of the door for Richmond's finest ices. Space is limited, so you might want to wander down to the Green to enjoy tubs of chocolate sorbet, or rum and raisin, plum and yoghurt, panna cotta, and pistachio ice-creams. The company also has a foothold on Oxford Street, with a kiosk on the pavement between John Lewis and House of Fraser.
Buggy access. Disabled access: ramp. Takeaway service.
Other locations Bentalls Centre, Wood Street, Kingston-upon-Thames, Surrey KT1 1TX (8141 5098); Centre Court Shopping Centre, 4 Queens Road, SW19 8YA (8946 7766); 47 Queenstown Road, SW8 3RG (7720 5784, open in summer only).

Gelateria Valerie
9 Duke of York Square, SW3 4LY (7730 7978/www.patisserie-valerie.co.uk). Sloane Square tube. **Open** 8am-7pm Mon-Sat; 10am-7pm Sun. **Credit** MC, V.
It's as though this gelateria was plucked from Rome and plonked in the middle of Chelsea. Glass walls and extensive al fresco seating add to the see-and-be-seen element. Children love the fountains outside in hot weather.
Buggy access. Disabled access. Tables outdoors (20, Duke of York Square). Takeaway service.

Oddono's
14 Bute Street, SW7 3EX (7052 0732/ www.oddonos.co.uk). South Kensington tube. **Open** 11am-11pm Mon-Thur, Sun; 11am-midnight Fri, Sat. **Credit** MC, V.
Valrhona chocolate, Sicilian pistachios and Madagascan vanilla are the type of premium ingredients favoured by this artisanal producer. Co-founder Christian Oddono was inspired by the ice-cream made by his Italian granny. We like the generous servings. There's also an Oddono's counter in Selfridges food hall.
Buggy access. Disabled access. Takeaway service. Tables outdoors (4, pavement).

Scoop
40 Shorts Gardens, WC2H 9AB (7240 7086/ www.scoopgelato.com). Covent Garden tube. **Open** 11am-9pm daily. Times may vary, phone to check. **Credit** MC, V.
Good sorbets and dairy-free ices using rice and berries also make Scoop a boon for anyone on a special diet.
Delivery service. Takeaway service.

INDIAN

Masala Zone
80 Upper Street, N1 0NU (7359 3399/www. masalazone.com). Angel tube. **Lunch served** 12.30-3pm, **dinner served** 5.30-11pm Mon-Fri. **Meals served** 12.30-11pm Sat; 12.30-

Consumer

10.30pm Sun. **Main courses** £6.50-£9. **Thalis** £7.80-£12.50. **Credit** MC, V.

This chain is especially popular with hip youngsters who come here for the buzzy vibe, reasonable prices and decent pan-Indian grub. Distinctive in looks, it's notable for earthy curries, thali selections, and zesty street snacks. The menu also offers a line in spicy burgers and chilli-flecked noodles – a sample of modern India tastes. Traditional choices include gol guppas – puffed pastry globes filled with tamarind water spiked with black salt – smoky lamb korma and chicken lazeez. Safe bets are thalis (an entire meal on one platter), which take the stress out of ordering and include daily specials of dahls and side dishes. Children's thalis are especially good value.

Buggy access. Children's set meal (£3.75). Disabled access. High chairs. Takeaway service. **Other locations** throughout town. Check website for details.

Tamarind
20-22 Queen Street, W1J 5PR (7629 3561/ www.tamarindrestaurant.com). Green Park tube. **Lunch served** noon-3pm Mon-Fri, Sun. **Dinner served** 6-11.30pm Mon-Sat; 6-10.30pm Sun. **Main courses** £14.50-£26. **Set lunch** £18.95 2 courses, £26.95 3 courses. **Set dinner** (6-7pm, 10-11pm) £24 2 courses. **Credit** AmEx, DC, MC, V.

There's a good Sunday lunch deal at this classy restaurant. Children under ten can either eat free if they're with two or more adults eating from the main menu, otherwise they can go for the £12.50 Sunday children's special menu, which lists delights such as potato cakes with lentil, or a fruity, spicy salad, followed by tandoori chicken, fried tilapia or spiced vegetable wrap, served with veg and rice, then ice-cream and seasonal fruit. Watch the highly skilled chefs at work in the open kitchen. Children must be out by 7pm.

Buggy access. Children's set meal (£12.50, Sun lunch). High chairs. Takeaway service.

INTERNATIONAL

Ditto
55 East Hill, SW18 2QE (8877 0110/www.do ditto.co.uk). Clapham Junction rail, then 37, 39, 87, 170, 337 bus/Wandsworth Town rail. **Lunch served** noon-3pm, **dinner served** 6.30-11pm Mon-Fri. **Meals served** noon-11pm Sat; noon-10pm Sun. **Main courses** £8.75-£17.50. **Credit** AmEx, MC, V.

'We always welcome children' said the manager on our arrival at Ditto. This new restaurant aims

to attract families – it has a large playroom which is publicised as perfect for coffee mornings and a well-thought-out kid's menu. For £4 children can choose from burgers or chicken with chips and salad, a roast on Sunday, or grilled fish of the day (on our visit it was a velvety piece of halibut) with steamed veg and new potatoes. Their child-friendly focus means the sophistication of the adult menu – braised rabbit and wild mushrooms, or pork belly with red cabbage in wine and vanilla – comes as a surprise. Mains are filling and only spoilt by a tendency to over-salt. For pudding juniors can tuck into ice-cream, whilst you polish off pear cheesecake or dark chocolate terrine. Some evenings the playroom closes at 5pm so the adults can be entertained with live music duos.

Buggy access. Children's set meal (£4). Crayons. High chairs. Nappy-changing facilities. Play area. Takeaway service. Toys.

Ottolenghi
287 Upper Street, N1 2TZ (7288 1454/ www.ottolenghi.co.uk). Angel tube/Highbury & Islington tube/rail. **Meals served** 8am-11pm Mon-Sat; 9am-7pm Sun. **Main courses** £9.50-£25. **Credit** AmEx, MC, V.

Children gaze openmouthed at puffy meringues the size of their heads stacked up in the window. The entrance area doubles as a

Costas Fish Restaurant. *See p235.*

bakery and deli, with colourful salads and sublime breads to take away or eat in. Choose from breakfast dishes (granola or pastries), cakes, sandwiches and other savouries. In the evening, the place shifts emphasis from café to restaurant, with a daily changing menu of small dishes 'from the counter' or 'from the kitchen' (the latter served hot). There's a Mediterranean slant in dishes like fried halibut on dahl and sweet potato mash.

Buggy access. Disabled access: toilet. High chairs. Tables outdoors (2, pavement). Takeaway service.
Other locations 63 Ledbury Road, W11 2AD (7727 1121); 1 Holland Street, W8 4NA (7937 0003). 13 Motcomb Street, SW1X 8LB (7823 2707).

Rainforest Café
20 Shaftesbury Avenue, W1D 7EU (7434 3111/www.therainforestcafe.co.uk). Piccadilly Circus tube. **Meals served** noon-10pm Mon-Thur; noon-8pm Fri; 11.30am-8pm Sat; 11.30am-10pm Sun. **Main courses** £11.20-£18.50. **Credit** AmEx, MC, V. **Map** p317 K7.
Children are as deeply thrilled by this jungle themed basement restaurant, with its animatronic wildlife, as they are by the wealth of merchandising on the ground floor. There's an unchallenging global menu of meze, pasta, seafood, ribs, steaks and burgers and, for children, organic sausages and organic salmon and pasta, alongside more predictable burgers, goujons and pizza. The children's menu is two courses, the second being a big, sticky treat involving jelly, chocolate, cream and sweeties in various permutations. Drinks are smoothies, sodas or fruit juices and are charged extra. Demand tap water. Bookings are not accepted.
Buggy access. Children's set meal (£10.90). Crayons. Entertainment: face painting, weekends and school holidays. High chairs. Nappy-changing facilities.

Shish
313-319 Old Street, EC1V 9LE (7749 0990/ www.shish.com). Old Street tube/rail. **Meals served** 11.30am-11.30pm Mon-Fri; noon-11.30pm Sat; noon-10.30pm Sun. **Main courses** £6-£11. **Credit** AmEx, MC, V.
It's easy to understand why this place packs out night after night. Food is fresh, well-sourced and reasonably priced, and staff are friendly and efficient. A good start is mixed meze – chinese beans with soy, ginger and garlic, falafel, houmous – which is also on the children's menu, alongside Mediterranean chicken, or chicken in pandana leaves, fish

cakes or falafel with rice, chips, couscous or salad, and own-made ice-cream.
Buggy access. Children's set meal (£4.25). Crayons. Disabled access: toilet. High chairs. Nappy-changing facilities. Takeaway service.
Other locations 2-6 Station Parade, NW2 4NH (8208 9290).

ITALIAN

Carluccio's Caffè
Reuters Plaza, E14 5AJ (7719 1749/www. carluccios.com). Canary Wharf tube/DLR. **Meals served** 7am-11pm Mon-Fri; 9am-11pm Sat; 10am-10.30pm Sun. **Main courses** £6.95-£13.95. **Credit** AmEx, MC, V. **Map** p314 J6.
The warmth and clatter, the great smell of coffee and cakes and the shelves of aspirational deli items bring the suited and booted office folk of Docklands galloping to this busy branch of the chain. The waiting staff are the apotheosis of Italian expansiveness, with lots of 'ciao bella's for the ladeez and extra twinkle and charm for the babies. The food is as appealing as the welcome. On the children's menu, there's grissini, pasta and sauce of choice, stuffed ravioli, lasagne or breaded chicken. To finish, there's lovely Italian ice-cream. Don't miss the fantastic baked goods and special hot chocolate.
Buggy access. Children's set meal (£5.95). Crayons. Disabled access: toilet. High chairs. Nappy-changing facilities. Tables outdoors (15, piazza). Takeaway service.
Other locations throughout town. Check website for details.

Marco Polo
Eastfields Avenue, SW18 1LP (8874 7007/ www.marcopolo.uk.net). East Putney tube/ Wandsworth Town rail. **Open** noon-11pm daily. **Main courses** £7.95-£17.95. **Set lunch** £7.95-£11.95 1-3 courses. **Credit** MC, V.
A child-pleaser by yet another modish riverside block of aspirational apartments, friendly Marco Polo is perfectly situated for Wandsworth family groups. There's a useful patch of greensward beside the numerous outdoor tables, so children can stretch their legs with impunity. Their hunger is assuaged by £4.95 pasta dishes and large, pleasantly thin pizzas, and a bowl of ice-cream to follow. This isn't just a pizza and pasta venue, however. There's a fine range of detailed, grown-up pasta dishes too.
Buggy access. Tables outdoors (20, terrace).

Consumer

Service with a smile

If you've ever wondered why it is that some places are so much better at dealing with kids than others, it will come as no surprise to discover that they don't leave it to chance. Pizza Express, for example, has introduced its own training scheme which aims to equip staff with ways of supporting families that eat out together. The idea is that it 'takes waiters on a journey to consider the hidden needs of a family from the moment they enter the restaurant to the moment they leave'.

The scheme offers practical guidelines – ranging from how to engage children in the restaurant experience to tackling children running a riot. Based on research that suggests that treating children in a more adult way encourages good behaviour, the scheme also gives staff the confidence to interact with children. Waiters are encouraged to speak directly to children, give them their own three-course menu (just like mum and dad's) and take their food order directly from them.

Waiters are also advised to seat children where they've got a good view of the restaurant and encourage engagement and interaction between children and others at the table. If the children look like they're getting restless, the staff are invited to lend a hand (we can imagine sensitive parents taking umbrage at this), or to take them to see their pizza being made. Conversely, kids should be praised by restaurant staff for their good behaviour.

Created in consultation with Rachel Holland – a high-profile 'super nanny' – the scheme is backed by renowned psychologist and father-of-four Dr Aric Sigman who opines that the programme is 'an excellent example of what has been lacking, not just in restaurants, but in public in Britain. Traditionally, British restaurants have viewed children as an annoyance to be coped with or tolerated, sidelining children to play areas and ignoring them during service and even conversation.'

The pizza chain's aim to include children in the process of eating out is a laudable one. We thoroughly approve of any initiative that will help children gain as much from eating out as their parents do, and may go some way to socialise the minor diners. After all, if children are given good reason to stay seated and engage with the rest of the table, they won't be running around upsetting busy waiters and upending their loaded trays.

Marine Ices

8 Haverstock Hill, NW3 2BL (7482 9003/ www.marineices.co.uk). Chalk Farm tube/ 31 bus. **Lunch served** noon-3pm, **dinner served** 6-11pm Tue-Fri. **Meals served** noon-11pm Sat; noon-10pm Sun. **Main courses** £7-£12.50. **Credit** MC, V.
This, always child-filled, gelateria/restaurant has been run by the same family since its inception. Marine occupies a soft spot in the heart of many locals of Chalk Farm and Camden, particularly families who bring successive generations to continue dearly held traditions. You'll want to join in with the uninhibited nippers screaming for ice-cream – the frozen treats here are so good they come with their own menu. The pizza and pasta main courses are immensely hearty, as our saucy linguine and lasagne attested. Its location is handy for the Roundhouse (over the road), Camden Market and Regent's Park.
Buggy access. Disabled access: ramp. High chairs. Takeaway service.

Story Deli

3 Dray Walk, Old Truman Brewery, 91 Brick Lane, E1 6QL (7247 3137). Liverpool Street tube/rail. **Meals served** noon-9.30pm daily. **Main courses** £9-£10. **Credit** AmEx, MC, V. **Map** p319 S5.
Just off bustling Brick Lane, this is a cosy little place for a chat and a chew, with rough-hewn tables, little pod stools, big wax church candles and ambient music, and a huge plate glass window through which to gaze out onto the hectic goings-on along Dray Walk. There's no menu. Everything is chalked on blackboards hanging on a wall, and 'everything' is pizzas – or more like Alsacienne tarte flambée: thin, crisp oven-baked dough – covered in delicious toppings (almost 20 of them) such as roast chicken with mushroom, prawn and green pepper, or more familiar five cheese. Pizzas are generously topped with well-sourced ingredients – ham and artichoke was coppa air-dried ham – served on a board with a pile of rocket. There are also plenty of coffees and

specialist teas, and ice-cream (butterscotch, honey and ginger) and biscuits to follow. *Buggy access. Tables outdoors (2, pavement). Takeaway service.*

JAPANESE

Abeno Too

17-18 Great Newport Street, WC2H 7JE (7379 1160/www.abeno.co.uk). Leicester Square tube. **Meals served** noon-11pm Mon-Sat; noon-10.30pm Sun. **Main courses** £7.80-£25.80. **Set lunch** £8.80-£19.80 2-5 courses. **Credit** AmEx, MC, V.
This is a neat little provider of okonomiyaki (like Spanish omelette), which is cooked on hot-plates set into the window tables and the main counter. It's fun for children to see their food being prepared, and the bill won't break the bank. Rice and noodle dishes are also on the menu. Bookings not accepted.
Booster seats. Buggy access. High chairs. Takeaway service.
Other locations Abeno, 47 Museum Street, WCIA 1LY (7405 3211); Abeno San, 66 Heath Street, NW3 1BN (7794 5252).

Benihana

100 Avenue Road, NW3 3HF (7586 9508/ www.benihana.co.uk). Swiss Cottage tube. **Lunch served** noon-3pm daily. **Dinner served** 5.30-10.30pm Mon-Sat; 5-10pm Sun. **Set lunch** £11.75-£37.50 4 courses. **Set dinner** £18-£57 6 courses. **Credit** AmEx, DC, MC, V.
Families come to Benihana for the showmanship – the chef assigned to you does cool tricks with eggs, salt cellars, onion rings, and bowls of rice. This ever-popular chain popularised 'Japanese-style' for Americans, where the teppan is used to cook steak and seafood, with side orders of beansprouts, fried rice and mushrooms. The food is tasty, if pricey, and the lunchtime bento boxes are pretty good. Benihana was a *Time Out* prizewinner in the past but on our two most recent visits, although the children loved the routine, we as adults were disappointed by the poor quality salad items and the increasingly corporate nature of the show. Perhaps the chain needs to motivate its staff better.
Booster seats. Buggy access. Children's menu (£10.50-£13.50; noon-3pm Sun). Entertainment: clown Sun lunch. High chairs. Takeaway service.
Other locations 37 Sackville Street, W1S 3DQ (7494 2525); 77 King's Road, SW3 4NX (7376 7799).

Yo! Sushi

Myhotel, 11-13 Bayley Street, WC1B 3HD (7636 0076/www.yosushi.com). Tottenham Court Road tube. **Meals served** noon-10pm Mon-Sat; 1-6pm Sun. **Dishes** £1.70-£5. **Credit** AmEx, DC, MC, V.
Purists may quibble at the food's authenticity, but children adore watching the Japanese delicacies gliding round on the conveyor belt. They grab 'em and you pay for 'em according to the price code. Happily, there's plenty for vegetarians, as well as raw fish fans.
Buggy access. Nappy-changing facilities. Takeaway service.
Other locations throughout town. Check website for details.

MODERN EUROPEAN

Ambassador

55 Exmouth Market, EC1R 4QL (7837 0009/ www.theambassadorcafe.co.uk). Angel tube/ Farringdon tube/rail/19, 38 bus. **Meals served** 9am-11pm Mon-Fri; 11am-11pm Sat; 11am-4pm Sun. **Main courses** £9.50-£17. **Set lunch** (noon-3pm Mon-Fri) £12.50 2 courses, £16 3 courses. **Credit** AmEx, MC, V.
A fine ambassador for a great family restaurant, this easy-going bistro does a fab weekend brunch. The children's brunch menu might be limited to bangers and mash, and banana and chocolate milkshake (£5.25 the pair), but there's also such temptations as waffles, muesli with yoghurt, pork-belly sandwich with caramelised onions, wild mushroom omelette, and warm chocolate pudding. Tables spread on to the street in summer. Service is so friendly that children can have a tour of the kitchen on request.
Buggy access. Children's menu (£1.50-£3.50 Sat, Sun brunch). Crayons. High chairs. Tables outdoors (10, pavement). Toys.

NORTH AMERICAN

Big Easy

332-334 King's Road, SW3 5UR (7352 4071/www.bigeasy.uk.com). Sloane Square tube, then 11, 19, 22 bus. **Meals served** noon-11.15pm Mon-Thur, Sun; noon-12.15am Fri, Sat. **Main courses** £8.85-£27.50. **Set lunch** (noon-5pm Mon-Fri) £7.95 2 courses. **Credit** AmEx, DC, MC, V. **Map** p313 E12.
This is a loud and jolly restaurant (avoid the evening with small children) with a menu that's made for gorging. The draw consists of huge steaks, enormous juicy burgers, vast seafood

platters and racks of ribs. The steaks are tender and well priced, Alaskan king crab and lobster are house specialities, side dishes are carefully done. The children's menu offers the likes of beefburgers, hot dogs and chicken dippers, all served with chips and a drink (ice-cream sodas, fresh fruit juices, milk).
Buggy access. Children's menu (£2.95-£6.95). Crayons. High chairs. Nappy-changing facilities. Tables outdoors (5, pavement). Takeaway service.

Bodean's

10 Poland Street, W1F 8PZ (7287 7575/www. bodeansbbq.com). Oxford Circus or Picccadilly Circus tube. **Lunch served** noon-3pm, **dinner served** 6-11pm Mon-Fri. **Meals served** noon-11pm Sat; noon-10.30pm Sun. **Main courses** £8-£16. **Credit** AmEx, MC, V.
Unless you're an ice hockey/baseball/US football fan (games are shown on the wide screens around the place) the main event here is barbecued meat, served in large portions, so vegetarians should look away now (the sweet baked beans and fries are good, though). Bodean's 'signature' trough is a mighty rack (or half rack for wussies) of baby back ribs. Then there are juicy steaks, burgers and fiery chicken wings. Children eat free (options include barbecue chicken breast or slices of smoked beef, turkey or ham with fries or mash, with ice-cream to follow) between noon and 5pm at the weekend when accompanied by an adult. At other times the children's menu costs £5. Kindly touches, such as jugs of iced tap water delivered without demur, and extra scoops of ice-cream for older siblings, make us love this place all the more.
Buggy access. Children's set meal (£5, free Sat, Sun). High chairs. Nappy-changing facilities. Takeaway service.
Other locations 4 Broadway Chambers, Fulham Broadway, SW6 1EP (7610 0440); 169 Clapham High Street, SW4 7SS (7622 4248); 57 Westbourne Grove, W2 4UA (7727 9503).

Dexter's Grill

20 Bellevue Road, SW17 7EB (8767 1858/ www.tootsiesrestaurants.co.uk). Wandsworth Common rail. **Meals served** 11am-10.30pm Mon-Fri; 10am-11pm Sat; 10am-10pm Sun. **Main courses** £7.50-£18. **Credit** AmEx, MC, V.
With attractive dark wood high chairs that match the floorboards, the key to this chain's success lies in giving kids the feeling that they're eating in a proper grown-up restaurant. The laid-back staff are happy to make a fuss of the nippers, who are treated to their own mini smoothies and shakes, individual fish pies, or ice-cream in sundae glasses. Despite the slight move upmarket (there are wine suggestions with every meal, and whole lobster among the specials), most families opt for the burgers here, which – with their own trays of relishes, mustards and sauces – are far superior to those served up by the 'gourmet' chains. Breakfasts and brunches are also popular and can be as healthy (fruit salad), or unhealthy (pancakes with maple syrup, full English), as you like. Arrive early, though: on our Good Friday visit, Dexter's was teeming by 12.30pm.
Buggy access. Children's menu (£3.75-£6.25). Crayons. Disabled access: toilet. High chairs. Nappy-changing facilities. Tables outdoors (8, terrace). Takeaway service.
Other locations throughout town. Check website for details.

Fine Burger Company

50 James Street, W1U 1HB (7224 1890/ www.fineburger.co.uk). Bond Street tube. **Meals served** noon-11pm Mon-Sat; noon-10pm Sun. **Main courses** £5.45-£7.75. **Set lunch** £5.95 Mon-Fri. **Credit** MC, V.
As well as gourmet burgers, this chain offers chicken breast six ways, falafel, minced lamb, even a splendid fish-finger sandwich. The children's menu includes a smaller burger (with or without cheese), a veggie burger, fish fingers with mayo, and chargrilled chicken breast, all served with fries. The medium-cooked beefburger is just right and the chips made from real potatoes are cooked just-so – and the tempura onion rings are champion.
Buggy access. Children's menu (£2.50-£4.95). Crayons. High chairs. Nappy-changing facilities.
Other locations throughout town. Check website for details.

Gourmet Burger Kitchen

44 Northcote Road, SW11 1NZ (7228 3309/ www.gbkinfo.co.uk). Clapham Junction rail. **Meals served** noon-11pm Mon-Fri; 11am-11pm Sat; 11am-10pm Sun. **Main courses** £5.45-£7.40. **Credit** MC, V.
GBK is a growing concern; there are now 19 branches across London. This was the first, and remains our favourite. The sesame-flecked buns have a firm texture, the tasty fillings are prime quality, and you'll find no finer Aberdeen Angus beef patties. Portions are huge, the fat chips are golden, and the extras are no-corners-cut. Among the many fabulous variations is the

Japanese fun at **Benihana**. *See p245.*

beetroot- and pineapple-layered kiwiburger: much better than it sounds, honest. Children have a couple of smaller options: the junior burger (the beef cooked well-done, with cheese and tomato sauce) and the junior chicken (breast meat with mayonnaise). Service is as friendly and welcoming as ever.
Buggy access. Children's set meal (£3.95). High chairs. Tables outdoors (4, pavement). Takeaway service.
Other locations throughout town. Check website for details.

Haché
24 Inverness Street, NW1 7HJ (7485 9100/ www.hacheburgers.com). Camden Town tube.
Meals served noon-10.30pm Mon-Sat; noon-10pm Sun. **Main courses** £5.95-£10.95.
Credit AmEx, DC, MC, V.
The good-quality Ayrshire steaks, chopped, grilled and served in ciabatta-style buns make great, posh burgers. Haché looks a cut above your average gourmet burger joint, with art on the walls and muted lighting, but it's nonetheless very welcoming to children. The burger toppings are excellent: bacon dry-cured in brine, proper cheese, huge mushrooms. Chips are frites-style, skinny or fat. Non-beef burgers include tuna steak, chicken, and three vegetarian variations. Crêpes have recently been added to the dessert options, but the brownies are the thing.
Buggy access. High chairs. Takeaway service.
Other locations 329-331 Fulham Road, SW10 9QL (7823 3515).

Hard Rock Café
150 Old Park Lane, W1K 1QR (7629 0382/ www.hardrock.com). Hyde Park Corner tube.
Meals served 11.30am-12.30am Mon-Thur, Sun; 11am-1am Fri, Sat. **Main courses** £8.45-£15.95. **Credit** AmEx, DC, MC, V.
Map p316 H8.
The hard-rocking, world-famous burger joint that tourists adore is also a powerful child attraction (older children and young teens are its happiest clientele). Rock memorabilia covers the walls, music blasts at impressive levels and hamburgers, nachos and salads are piled high on plates carried by waitresses in teeny-tiny uniforms. Fortunately, all this bluster does not mask the fact that the food is pretty darn good. Burgers are satisfyingly juicy, the nachos gooey, the salads main-coursey and the ice-cream sundaes are excellent. Further attractions include face-painting at certain times, a children's menu with pizza, pasta and burgers, and occasional themed activities.

Consumer

Buggy access. Children's set meal (£5.95). Crayons. Disabled access: toilet. Entertainment: face-painting Sat, Sun. High chairs. Nappy-changing facilities. Tables outdoors (10, pavement).

Jo Shmo's

33 High Street, SW19 5BY (8439 7766/ www.joshmos.com). Wimbledon tube/rail, then 93 bus. **Open** noon-11.30pm Mon-Sat, noon-11pm Sun. **Main courses** £6.95-13.95. **Credit** AmEx, DC, MC, V.

A lovely atmosphere, filling eat-with-fingers style food, cocktails and a back room like a crèche on Saturday lunchtimes make this diner dear to our hearts. Check out those strangely disorientating toilets too. There's a sensible children's menu, listing scaled-down, meaty burgers, decent hot dogs, pasta, chicken and ribs, and kids love the relish trays that come with the grub. Adults appreciate the well-cooked steaks and innovative seafood, such as popcorn crayfish.

Booster seats. Buggy access. Children's set meal (£4.95). Crayons. Disabled access: toilet. High chairs. Tables outdoors (12, pavement). Takeaway service.

Pacific Bar & Grill

320 Goldhawk Road, W6 0XF (8741 1994). Stamford Brook tube. **Meals served** noon-11pm Mon-Fri; 11am-11pm Sat, Sun. **Main courses** £9.95-£17.50. **Credit** AmEx, MC, V.

A sophisticated pan-American restaurant that's not just about burgers and hot dogs. There are cool, light salads (not dripping with cheesey nachos) that seem like a healthy choice, steaks and risottos. Yes, there are burgers too, made with lamb or chicken as well as beef. The children's menu includes fish cake, grilled chicken and penne pasta. Whatever you order, accompany it with a big side of crisp hand-cut fries. The apple pie is really good. At weekends the usual menu (for adults) gives way to brunch dishes such as buttermilk pancakes with bacon, eggs and maple syrup.

Buggy access. Children's set meal (£5). Crayons. Disabled access: ramp. Entertainment: magician 1-3pm Sun. High chairs. Tables outdoors (12, terrace).

Pick More Daisies

12 Crouch End Hill, N8 8AA (8340 2288/ www.pickmoredaisies.com). Finsbury Park tube/rail, then W7 bus/Crouch Hill rail. **Meals served** 9am-10pm Mon-Fri; 10am-10.30pm Sat, Sun. **Main courses** £8-£15. **Credit** MC, V.

PMD is a friendly Californian diner, whose laid-back philosophy is summed up in the delightfully fey name. Families make up much of the daytime clientele, they enjoy burgers, brunches, salads and excellent skin-on fries. The burgers are made from Kobe beef – very tender – and served between arctic flatbread, which is rather like quilted pitta. The free-range chicken used in dishes such as the house caesar salad is admirably moist. The children's menu is pleasingly all-American: peanut butter and jelly, macaroni and cheese, mini burger. An ice-cream sundae to share, with marshmallows and M&Ms on the side, is the star pudding. There are pictures to colour in, puzzles to solve, and even the bill comes in a little pot of M&Ms.

Buggy access. Children's menu (£3-£4.75). Crayons. Disabled access. High chairs. Nappy-changing facilities. Toys.

Planet Hollywood

13 Coventry Street, W1D 7DH (7287 1000/ www.planethollywoodlondon.com). Piccadilly Circus tube. **Meals served** 11.30am-1am daily. **Main courses** £10.45-£21.95. **Credit** AmEx, DC, MC, V. **Map** p317 K7.

Finger food for children and teens let loose on their first meal out together, is the main point of this tribute to La La Land. Movie memorabilia floor to ceiling, swinging klieg lights (just like in LA) and blasting film soundtracks might be overstimulating for the tinies but older children love it. The food is everything they like; burgers, rôtisserie chickens, fajitas and steaks all washed down with shakes and pop.

Booking advisable. Buggy access. Children's set meal (£7.95). Crayons. Disabled access: lift (Trocadero Centre). Entertainment: DJs Mon-Fri dinner; all day Sat, Sun. High chairs. Nappy-changing facilities.

Smollensky's on the Strand

105 Strand, WC2R 0AA (7497 2101/www. smollenskys.co.uk). Embankment tube/Charing Cross tube/rail. **Meals served** noon-11pm Mon-Wed; noon-11.30pm Thur-Sat; noon-4.30pm, 6.30-10pm Sun. **Main courses** £9.95-£23.95. **Credit** AmEx, MC, V. **Map** p317 L7.

A pleasant basement steakhouse with candles glittering everywhere and straightforward, foolproof ribstickers on the menu. The emphasis is still on steaks, which arrive with good chips and a choice of sauces. The children's menu is divided into two sections: one category for under-sevens (who are deemed only to want fried food – burgers, chicken, fish – apart from a vegetarian pasta dish) and one for 'mini adults' (who are treated to the likes of jambalaya or steak). Food

Playing with their food

Once upon a time parents considered a restaurant child-friendly if infants were permitted to join their parents for lunch without being summarily ejected. The offer of a balloon or a children's menu was enough to send them into paroxysms of gratitude. Times have changed, though, and so have parents' expectations.

Today, a restaurant manager who doesn't welcome children is considered a bit of a dinosaur. Indeed, in upmarket quarters like Chelsea's **Le Cercle** (*see p236*), children are treated as mini gourmands and given their own tasting menu, even if crayons and face-painting are conspicuous by their absence.

North London's **Brilliant** (*see p223*) keeps both sprogs and parents happy by offering decent cakes and cappuccinos, well-priced quality meals and workshops in the studio next door. Kensal Green's **Gracelands** (see *p226*) sees mums sip coffee and check their email, while the kids tuck into healthy food, get cracking in the home corner, read books on the sofas or attend a class or creative workshop.

West London's **Coffee & Crayons** (*see p225*) goes a step further, offering a staffed playroom with sofas where parents can take coffee while the children play and paint.

Few cafés make as much effort as Stoke Newington's **That Place on the Corner** (*see p231*). As the city's only children's café with a condition on its licence stating that you can only enter if accompanied by a child, TPOtC is more than just 'child-friendly'. This is a place where once the meal is over, the adults can relax while the kids dress up, listen to stories and play superheroes.

Sunday lunch at That Place gives families a roast with all the trimmings (veggie option too), Sunday papers, a glass of wine, and children's entertainment that changes weekly. Then there's the after-school teatime menu (3.30pm to 5.30pm, Monday to Friday, £4.95) offering a main meal, fruit juice and ice-cream or fruit. There are also 'Pizza nights', where kids are given the ingredients to build their own pizzas, have them baked, and then tuck in.

The most pleasing aspect is the service. Our visit coincided with a party at the playful end of the café, but we received unflustered attention and were struck by the proprietor's obvious fondness for children; a real plus, given Stokey's new role as north London's Nappy Uplands. For more classes and clubs at That Place, *see p192*.

Consumer

can be variable, but we've no complaints about the puddings: moreish chocolate mousse, and memorable Mississippi mud pie. Children's entertainment takes place every weekend lunchtime (noon-3pm), when there's also a TV and Playstation at their disposal.

Booking advisable. Children's menu (£3.95-£7.95). Crayons. Entertainment: clown, magician, noon-3pm Sat, Sun. High chairs. Nappy-changing facilities. **Other locations** 1 Reuters Plaza, Canary Wharf, E14 5AG (7719 0101).

TGI Friday's

6 Bedford Street, WC2E 9HZ (7379 0585/ www.tgifridays.co.uk). Covent Garden or Embankment tube/Charing Cross tube/rail. **Meals served** 11am-11.30pm Mon-Sat; noon-11pm Sun. **Main courses** £8-£17.99. **Credit** AmEx, MC, V. **Map** p317 L7.

The immensely cheery, overwhelmingly child-friendly (almost gloopily so) – staff here hand out balloons and crayons to children who are chatted to sweetly, even entertained on certain days (see the website for details). The restaurant

Pick More Daisies, or crayons, fruit, marshmallows… *See p248.*

is focused on a busy bar, but this only really gets noisy in the evenings. We'd recommend lunchtime visits. The food is varied, with an emphasis on sticky barbecues and tasty Tex-Mex dishes, as well as the inevitable burgers and fries. The children's menu has all the fried regulars too, but also a batch of pasta dishes, and fruity sundae for pudding – or dirt and worm pie, for chocolate and fudge fiends. Free Heinz baby food is provided for babes accompanying a dining adult.
Buggy access. Children's set meal (£2.99). Crayons. Disabled access: lift, toilet. Entertainment: face painting Sat lunch; occasional Sun. High chairs. Nappy-changing facilities.
Other locations throughout town. Check website for details.

Tootsies Grill
120 Holland Park Avenue, W11 4UA (7229 8567/www.tootsiesrestaurants.co.uk). Holland Park tube. **Meals served** 10am-11pm Mon-Thur; 10am-11.30pm Fri; 9am-11.30pm Sat, Sun. **Main courses** £6.95-£27.95. **Credit** AmEx, MC, V.
Families root for Tootsies if they love burgers and want to be made to feel a bit special. The waiters couldn't be friendlier. Every branch in town is light, bright and spacious, so it's a pleasant place to while away the hours. There are a dozen types of burgers – all good, including the veggie one: a beany, oniony taste sensation. Other more exotic numbers include Thai chicken burgers, pork and apple burgers, and lamb and rosemary burgers. Children, plied with wax crayons and colouring-in while they wait, have a choice of burgers, hot dogs, ribs or organic pasta meals, with drinks and a build-your-own sundae options for pudding. Junior heaven.
Buggy access. Children's menu (£3.75-£5.50). Crayons. High chairs. Tables outdoors (3, pavement). Takeaway service.
Other locations throughout town. Check website for details.

ORIENTAL

Wagamama
11 Jamestown Road, NW1 7BW (7428 0800/www.wagamama.com). **Meals served** noon-11pm Mon-Sat; noon-10pm Sun. **Main courses** £6.10-£10.35. **Credit** AmEx, DC, MC, V.
The Camden branch of this clever chain is light and spacious, so well suited to family groups bearing buggies and other baby paraphernalia.

The business still provides wholesome oriental fast food at a fair price. The menu is more extensive than in the beginning, when it focused on Japanese-style noodle dishes with South-east Asian flavours. You can now follow the filling main courses with desserts such as tamarind and chilli pavlova. For children, there's chicken katsu (chicken breast fried in breadcrumbs) with dipping sauce, rice and shredded cucumber, or vegetarian or chicken noodle dishes for just £3.50. The gyoza (steamed then grilled dumplings) are usually a hit with kids too. To drink there's saké, raw juices and free green tea.
Children's menu (£2.75-£4.25). High chairs. Takeaway service.
Other locations throughout town. Check website for details.

THAI

Blue Elephant
4-6 Fulham Broadway, SW6 1AA (7385 6595/www.blueelephant.com). Fulham Broadway tube. **Lunch served** noon-2.30pm Mon-Fri; noon-4pm Sun. **Dinner served** 7-11.30pm Mon-Thur; 6.30-11.30pm Fri, Sat; 7-10.30pm Sun. **Main courses** £11.90-£28. **Set buffet** (Sun lunch) £25; £12.50 4-11s. **Credit** AmEx, DC, MC, V.
An extravagant rainforest of palms and topiary, with waterfalls and ponds full of koi carp, this tantalising Thai is a feast for tiny eyes. Children like to be fussed over by the staff, and during Sunday brunch (when they eat for half price) are entertained by face-painters. The menu is well-thought-out, with some fiery dashes among the blander, comfort-food dishes. Flavours are well crafted; witness the orange prawn curry (a creamy, tamarind-flavoured concoction full of cherry tomatoes and jackfruit). The platter of classic starters (mostly deep-fried offerings such as spring rolls) is generally popular with children.
Buggy access. Crayons. Delivery service. Disabled access: toilet. Entertainment: face painting Sun lunch. High chairs. Nappy-changing facilities. Takeaway service.

TURKISH

Gallipoli Café Bistro
102 Upper Street, N1 1QN (7359 0630/ www.cafegallipoli.com). Angel tube/Essex Road rail. **Meals served** 11am-11pm Mon-Thur; 11am-midnight Fri; 9.30am-11pm Sat, Sun. **Main courses** £7-£10. **Credit** MC, V.

Children adore the Turkish bazaar decor here, with magic lamps all over the place (alas, no genies). They're also happy to tear off strips of chewy *pide* bread to dip in the mixed meze starters; a lovely selection is available. Follow this with filling moussaka, kebab, stuffed aubergine and spicy sausages. A great place to share dishes. *Buggy access. Children's menu (£5-£5.50). High chairs. Tables outdoors (6, pavement). Takeaway service.* **Other locations** Gallipoli Again, 120 Upper Street, N1 1QP (7226 8090); Gallipoli Bazaar, 107 Upper Street, N1 1QN (7226 5333).

Mangal II
4 Stoke Newington High Street, N16 8BH (7254 7888/www.mangal2.com). Dalston Kingsland rail/76, 149, 243 bus. **Meals served** noon-1am daily. **Main courses** £7-£12. **No credit cards**.
This is one of three connected Mangals in the area (but Mangals elsewhere aren't related, the name just refers to a type of grill). Fittingly, the grilled meats and fish are superb, which accounts for number II's huge popularity with families of all nationalities. Service here is friendly and efficient. For mains, the adana kebab (alternating patties of minced lamb and slices of aubergine grilled on a skewer) is excellent. Children love the grilled chicken and *pide* and *saç* bread.
Buggy access. High chairs. Takeaway service.

Tas/EV Restaurant Bar & Delicatessen
The Arches, 97-99 Isabella Street, SE1 8DA (7620 6191/www.tasrestaurant.com). Southwark tube/Waterloo tube/rail. Bar **Open** noon-midnight daily. **Meze** £3.55-£8.95. *Deli* **Open** 7.30am-10pm Mon-Fri; 9am-10pm Sat; 9am-8pm Sun. *Restaurant* **Meals served** noon-midnight daily. **Main courses** £6.95-£12.45. **Set lunch** Mon-Fri £5.95. **Set meal** £8.25 2 courses, £18.25 3 courses per person (minimum 2). **Set meze** £8.25-£15.95 per person (minimum 2). *All* **Credit** AmEx, MC, V.
There are several links in the successful Tas chain – called variously as Tas Café, Tas Pide and EV. This branch is set in three old railway arches, with a large bar next to an equally capacious restaurant, plus a bakery/deli. Though there are no obvious trappings of child-friendliness, there's ample space and family groups often eat here. Much of the menu will appeal to little ones: from meze favourites such as houmous and olives, and hot borek (little filo parcels stuffed with feta cheese) to pasta with tomato sauce. Adults might enjoy such innovative dishes as grilled chicken with orange and mustard sauce. Booking is advisable.
Buggy access. Disabled access: toilet. Entertainment: guitarist 7.30pm Mon-Sat. High chairs. Tables outdoors (50, pavement). Takeaway service.
Other locations throughout town. Check website for details.

VIETNAMESE

Namô
178 Victoria Park Road, E9 7HD (8533 0639/ www.namo.co.uk). Mile End tube, then 277 bus. **Lunch served** noon-3.30pm Fri-Sun. **Dinner served** 5.30-11pm Tue-Sun. **Main courses** £6.90-£8.90. **Credit** MC, V.
This modest little café, sister of the excellent Huong Viet in Dalston, has charming young waitresses pattering around attending to diners in mellow, slightly eccentric surroundings. The decor is striking, with smiling Buddhist statues, red flocked wallpaper and pale blue lanterns; there's also a tiny outdoor patio for warmer weather. The cha ca (fish cakes) and cha ca la vong (monkfish with turmeric and dill), are recommended. Our favourite, however, was the bun bo hue (spicy beef noodle soup) which was appropriately tongue-tingling. Children may prefer less sharp noodly and rice dishes or their own special menu.
Buggy access. Children's set meal (£4.50). Crayons. Disabled access. High chairs. Tables outdoors (4, patio). Takeaway service.

Sông Quê
134 Kingsland Road, E2 8DY (7613 3222). Bus 26, 48, 55, 67, 149, 242, 243. **Lunch served** noon-3pm, **dinner served** 5.30-11pm daily. **Main courses** £5.50-£9.80. **Credit** MC, V.
After all this time, Song Que still sets the benchmark for exceptional Vietnamese cooking in London. Commanding the corner of Kingsland Road and Pearson Street, this efficient, canteen-like operation attracts diners of all types (be prepared to share tables at busy times). It has a huge and complex menu, but children generally go for noodles in soup, delicate rice paper rolls with vegetables, or pancakes stuffed with chicken or prawns – a few of their favourite things wrapped up in a delightfully greasy treat. The beef phô is the best in this city – an unmatchable broth that's rich in spices and our muc rang ruoi (chilli salted squid) was perfectly battered and seasoned.
Buggy access. High chairs. Takeaway service.

Shopping

Bags of scope for spoiling the kids.

In a city of more than 40,000 shops and 80 markets, there's never a dull moment for families that enjoy a retail experience. This chapter brings together all our favourites. There are the showy, hands-on emporia like **Hamleys** (*see p280*), undoubtedly more delightful to children than their sceptical parents. The oldies might get more of a kick out of the eccentric, tucked-away specialists such as **Kristin Baybars** (*see p284*) – paradise for doll's house enthusiasts, not so great for bumptious babies. If you've toddlers to control and essential supplies to buy, it's best to stick to the spacious children's all-rounders, such as **John Lewis** (*see p254*), **Soup Dragon** (*see p257*) and **Born** (*see below*). Many have diversions for the young ones, leaving you in peace to purchase.

While you're out and about, it would be daft not to introduce the nippers to the glories of London's street markets. **Portobello** and **Northcote Road** markets (*see* **Rich pickings** *p282 and p258*) are great for children of all ages. **Camden Market** (*see p114* **Great Days Out**) is beloved by teens. **Greenwich Market** (*see p124* **Great Days Out**) is fabulous for sweets, crafts and children's clothes. And all the markets mentioned above are surrounded by excellent lunching spots, so you can plan a whole day out around them.

ALL-ROUNDERS

Born

168 Stoke Newington Church Street, N16 0JL (7249 5069/www.borndirect.com). Bus 73, 393, 476. **Open** 9.30am-5.30pm Tue-Sat; noon-5pm Sun. **Credit** MC, V.

A calm, nurturing space that specialises in pregnancy products, baby equipment, toys and clothes, Born has an organic and fair-trade ethos, right down to its cotton nappies. As well as friendly staff, attractions include organic baby clothes; toiletries and massage oils by Weleda and Green People, and Born's brand of pregnancy massage oils, Born Naked. Toys are made from renewable materials, products include the Keptin-Jr Organic Comforter and trendy baby transport systems such as the Stokke Xplory buggy, Phil and Ted's Explorer, Bugaboo and Bee, plus Cameleon and Gecko. The shop is a joy to visit with lively children: there's space to play, and a sofa for breastfeeding mothers. Born's network of support extends to a weekly mother's meeting on Mondays, plus parenting and breastfeeding groups, with visiting professionals in attendance. *Buggy access. Delivery service. Disabled access: ramp. Mail order. Nappy-changing facilities. Play area.*

Harrods

87-135 Brompton Road, SW1X 7XL (7730 1234/www.harrods.com). Knightsbridge tube. **Open** 10am-8pm Mon-Sat; noon-6pm Sun. **Credit** AmEx, DC, MC, V. **Map** p313 F9.

Service is friendly on the often horrendously busy fourth-floor children's universe. The brilliant Toy Kingdom (7225 6781), impresses us every year with its jolly demonstrators and wide range of toys and gifts. Clothes begin with baby-cool pieces from modish labels such as No Added Sugar and go through ultra-smart tweedy garb from the Harrods label (think proper winter coats with velvet collars and sports jackets for boys). School uniforms (22 London schools represented) are also stocked. Couture 'casualwear' with styles for newborns and upwards includes mini togs by Burberry, Christian Dior, Moschino and Armani. Bunny London also has a collection here. Footwear is by One Small Step One Giant Leap (*see p276*, who else? There's face-painting, haircutting and lots of interactive fun in the holidays and on selected weekends. The nursery department carries all the famous pram and buggy, cot, bed and high chair brands. *Buggy access. Café. Car park. Delivery service. Disabled access: lift, toilet. Hairdressing. Mail order. Nappy-changing facilities.*

Rich pickings East Dulwich

Consumer

This well-favoured adjunct to exclusive Dulwich Village is vying with Clapham as the nappiest valley of them all these days, as ever increasing numbers of well-off young couples choose to settle down here. They bring up their families in refurbished Victorian cottages that line the streets branching off from Lordship Lane. One such desirable street is North Cross Road, where the gentrification of East Dulwich really began back in the early '90s with the establishment of the **Blue Mountain Café** (*see chapter* **Eating**). These days Blue Mountain has as its neighbour the 'destination' sweet shop **Hope & Greenwood** (pictured; 20 North Coss Road, SE22 9EU, 8613 1777, www.hopeandgreenwood.co.uk), with its jars of confectionery favourites, such as bon bons, midget gems, pineapple chunks and cola cubes, as well as hand-made chocs and nostalgic gifts and toys. On North Cross, too, is the children's bookshop, **Never Ending Story** (*see p260*) and **Oranges & Lemons**, (*see p273*), a pregnancy/new baby shop. Lordship Lane is East Dulwich's high street, where chain retailers are limited to acceptably couth organisations, such as **JoJo Maman Bébé** (*see right*) and the **White Stuff** (28-30 Lordship Lane, SE22 8HJ 8693 9381, www.whitestuff.com). The East Dulwich branch of **Soup Dragon**

(*see p257*) shares premises with the **Family Natural Health Centre** (8693 5515), where frequent parent-and-baby music and movement classes provide a social hub for young families. The reliable shoe retailer, **John Barnett** (*see p275*) has been dealing with grumpy infants and their aversion to black leather sensible-shoes-for-school for many a long year.

Igloo

300 Upper Street, N1 2TU (7354 7300/ www.iglookids.co.uk). Angel tube/Highbury & Islington tube/rail. **Open** 10am-6.30pm Mon-Wed; 10am-7pm Thur; 9.30am-6.30pm Fri, Sat; 11am-5.30pm Sun. **Credit** AmEx, DC, MC, V. Igloo's highly original range of toys, clothes and accessories are sourced by two mothers with limitless savoir-faire. As the name suggests, it's a cosy, yet TARDIS-like interior with shelves of toys reaching to the ceiling. Indoor favourites include great educational ideas for bright sparks, such as ant and worm farms and telescopes. Make your way through these, plus bundles of lovely and wearable clothes for babies and children up to eight, to the back of the shop. Here there's a spacious Start-rite shoe corner with plenty of seating, and another area with more clothes from the likes of Petit Bateau and Miniature, as well as some fancy dress outfits. All bases are covered: there's a mirrored parlour area for children's haircuts, a table for reading and drawing, party essentials and even a gift-wrapping service.
Buggy access. Delivery service. Disabled access. Hairdressing. Mail order. Play area.
Other locations 80 St John's Wood High Street, NW8 7SH (7483 2332).

John Lewis

278-306 Oxford Street, W1A 1EX (7629 7711/www.johnlewis.co.uk). Bond Street or Oxford Circus tube. **Open** 9.30am-8pm Mon-Wed, Fri; 9.30am-9pm Thur; 9.30am-5pm Sat; noon-6pm Sun. **Credit** MC, V. **Map** p314 H6. Seven floors of consumer paradise, with a splendid restaurant on the fifth floor, Waitrose on the ground and a fourth floor dedicated to children. Parents agree this is one of the nicest shops for all their children's needs. Great for

school uniforms, John Lewis is also legendary for its range of well-designed childrenswear, sportswear, toys, nursery furniture and down-to-earth buying-for-baby advice. The toy department contains a pleasant balance of the latest toys and educational playthings, and many toys are left out for children to test. There's also a car-seat fitting advisory service. The kids' shoe department (Clarks, Start-rite, Kangaroo, Timberland) has a queue-resistant computerised ticketing system, computer games, CBBC on the telly and even free face-painting in those summer-holiday shoe-buying weeks.
Buggy access. Cafés. Delivery service. Disabled access: lift, toilet. Mail order. Nappy-changing facilities.

JoJo Maman Bébé

68 Northcote Road, SW11 6QL (7228 0322/ www.jojomamanbebe.co.uk). Clapham Junction rail. **Open** 9.30am-5.30pm Mon-Sat; 11am-5pm Sun. **Credit** MC, V.

Laura Tenison MBE's empire continues to grow. It's still a catalogue-based retailer (larger items are ordered from the book), but its small network of boutiques, which display some of its vast stock of clothing, accessories, equipment and furniture, sends tributaries out to areas of high child density. The distinctive pregnancy and children's wear is relaxed and affordable, with bright, stripey fleeces and sweatshirts, easy-wash cottons for comfort, a great range of maternity wear and any number of clever ideas for the nursery, home and people carrier. The company adheres to a strong code of ethical business practice in product manufacturing and buying – a spirit exemplified by the well-priced organic cotton babyclothes range and the Polartec fleeces, which are made from recycled plastic bottles. JoJo also supports Nema, a charity based in Mozambique.
Buggy access. Delivery service. Disabled access. Mail order. Nappy-changing facilities.
Other locations 3 Ashbourne Parade, 1259 Finchley Road, NW11 0AD (8731 8961); 80 Turnham Green Terrace, W4 1QN (8994 0379); 6 Lordship Lane, SE22 8HN (8693 2123); 30 Putney Exchange, Putney High Street, SW15 1TW (8780 5165).

Little White Company

90 Marylebone High Street, W1U 4QZ (7486 7550/www.thewhitecompany.com). Baker Street or Bond Street tube. **Open** 10am-7pm Mon-Sat; 11am-5pm Sun. **Credit** AmEx, MC, V. **Map** p314 G5.

Not just a little white, this place is blindingly white on a summer's day. Snowy cotton soft furnishings, achromatic nightwear and bedlinen and icy white-painted wooden nursery furniture provide a suitably pure background for classic striped towelling beach hoodies in fuchsia and navy, floral quilts and rainbow-coloured knitted toys. Christian Rucker, one of the founders of the White Company, started up this 'little' branch after she became a mother and it has proved to be one of the nicest lines for babies and children around. Prices are reasonable, with demure linen/cotton best summer dresses from £22.
Buggy access. Delivery service. Mail order.
Other locations 261 Pavillion Road, SW1X 0BP (7881 0783).

Mamas & Papas

256-258 Regent Street, W1B 3AF (0845 268 2000/www.mamasandpapas.co.uk). Oxford Circus tube. **Open** 10am-8pm Mon-Wed, Fri; 10am-9pm Thur; 9am-8pm Sat; noon-6pm Sun. **Credit** AmEx, MC, V. **Map** p314 J6.

For the overheated shopper with a bun in the oven, this flagship store is a spacious, air-conditioned oasis of calm. There are large changing rooms for bump and buggy manoevres, and fashion advisors float about ready to advise on whether your bump looks big in that. As well as the attractive range of maternity fashions and lingerie, there's a large range of baby transport options – the company's stock in trade – with strollers from £35 and complete systems from anything up to £399. On the first floor, a series of

Smile, it's **Honeyjam**. *See p281.*

'dream nursery' rooms display cots, changing tables, wardrobes and storage systems in all shapes and sizes. Babyclothes and christening robes are mostly tasteful and Dreampod baby sleeping bags cost from £20. When those varicose veins threaten, Cibo, the sophisticated café on the first floor, has a nutritious lunch menu for mothers-to-be and toddlers.
Buggy access. Café. Mail order.
Nappy-changing facilities.
Other locations Brent Cross Shopping Centre, Tilling Road, NW2 1LJ (0870 830 7700).

Mini Kin

22 Broadway Parade, N8 9DE (8341 6898).
Finsbury Park tube/rail then W7 bus. **Open**
9.30am-5.30pm Mon-Sat; 10.30am-5.10pm Sun.
Credit MC, V.
A trip to Mini Kin will see your child well groomed, well turned out and smelling gorgeous. It's a splendid one-stop shop for toiletries, clothes, accessories and hairdressing. The grooming takes place in the cheerfully decorated little salon at the back. Haircuts start at £10.95 – the special first haircut, with lots of fuss, certificate and samples, costs £15.95. Rails yield adorable clothes for infants by Mitty James, Imps & Elfs, Baby Organic and Their Nibs (*see p271*). There are salves, creams, oils and lotions by Aviva and Burt's Bees.
Buggy access. Disabled access. Hairdressing.
Nappy-changing facilities. Play area.

Soup Dragon

27 Topsfield Parade, Tottenham Lane, N8
8PT (8348 0224/www.soup-dragon.co.uk).
Finsbury Park tube/rail then W7 bus. **Open**
9.30am-6pm Mon-Sat; 11am-5pm Sun. **Credit**
AmEx, MC, V.
Like its Clangers namesake, Soup Dragon is a rewarding find. With its dinky mini-kitchen play area, range of traditional toys, unusual and affordable clothes and quirky baby equipment, it's a versatile beast. It's also proof that you can dress your child imaginatively without breaking the bank – Soup Dragon's trademark striped knits cost from £16 – designer stuff comes courtesy of Katvig, idaT.dk, Papo, Salty Dog and ej sikke lej. There's a wide range of party accessories and dressing-up gear. Then there are nursery products, high chairs, slings, pushchairs, traditional toys from LaMaze, Pintoy, Tomy and one-offs, such as rocking horses and doll's houses. Check the website for details of regular sales.
Buggy access. Disabled access. Mail order.
Play area.
Other locations 106 Lordship Lane, SE22 8HF (8693 5575).

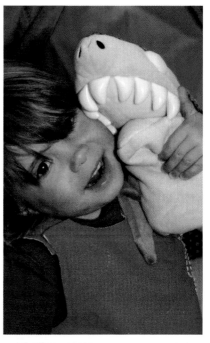

Lovely, cuddly **Igloo**. *See p254.*

Rich pickings Northcote Road

It comes as no surprise to discover that it was a typically enterprising Wandsworth mummy, Joanna Pearce, who won a National Sustainability Award for her brainchild, **www.nappyvalley.com**, an online baby equipment recycling centre. Family-friendly initiatives, particularly anything green or organic, have a natural home in this neck of the woods.

For a couple of decades now, Northcote Road, an exemplary shopping street located between Wandsworth and Clapham Commons, has been the backbone of the original Nappy Valley. Much of its appeal lies in the fact that however lauded the street is by the likes of us, it continues to remain true to its roots. Thus the street market is a refreshing mix of the workaday and the poncey, and old-established retailers, such as **QT Toys** (*see p282*), traditional butchers and bakers, and ungimmicky child-friendly cafés, such as **Boiled Egg & Soldiers** (the first of its kind; *see chapter* **Eating**), continue to flourish alongside upstarts such as **JoJo Maman Bébé**

(*see p255*) and **Fat Face Kids** (*see p274*). Of course, quality chains, such as the excellent shoe retailer **One Small Step One Giant Leap** (pictured; *see p276*) and **Jigsaw Junior** (*see p274*), both of which only open branches where moneyed young families cluster, are bound to be represented on Northcote Road, but the street makes room for the imaginative independent too. **Quackers** (*see p269*) is an established, helpful and friendly baby boutique and **Northcote Music** (*see p262*) has sounded the first notes of many a child's musical education.

The sweetest store in all of London, the **Hive Honey Shop** (No.93, SW11 6PL, 7924 6233, www.thehivehoneyshop.co.uk), with its live bees and honeys from Wandsworth, Wimbledon and Hampstead, is an old-timer. Relative newcomers **Tiny Impressions** (*see p264*), **Pretty Pregnant** (www.prettypregnant.co.uk) and the delicious **Crumpet** (*see chapter* **Eating**) have been clasped to the comforting bosom of Northcote Road and are now part of one big, happy, retailing family.

Others

Goody Gumdrops
128 Crouch Hill, N8 9DY (8340 3484/ www.goodygumdrops.co.uk). Finsbury Park tube/rail then W7 bus/Crouch Hill rail. **Open** 10am-5.30pm Tue-Sat. **Credit** MC, V.
Recently opened in Crouch End, GG bills itself as a 'children's lifestyle centre' for toys, clothes, nursery accessories, books and dressing-up gear. *Buggy access.*

Mothercare
526-528 Oxford Street, W1C 1LW (7629 6621/www.mothercare.com). Marble Arch tube. **Open** 10am-8pm Mon-Sat; noon-6pm Sun. **Credit** AmEx, MC, V. **Map** p314 G6.
A well-equipped two-floored parents' saviour that has everything for that first mad dash before baby arrives and most things you'll need later. Mothercare is great for bulk-buy basics, such as muslins and bath-time stuff, and the maternity wear isn't half bad these days.
Buggy access. Delivery service. Disabled access: lift, toilet. Mail order. Nappy-changing facilities. **Other locations** throughout town. Check website for details.

Pure Baby
208 Fulham Road, SW10 9PJ (7751 5544/ www.purebaby.co.uk). Fulham Broadway or South Kensington tube then 14, 414 bus. **Open** 10am-6.30pm Mon-Wed, Fri, Sat; 10am-7pm Thur; noon-6pm Sun. **Credit** AmEx, MC, V.
Cunningly positioned near Chelsea & Westminster Hospital's Maternity Unit, Pure Baby is a gleaming white shop with pink and blue trimmings, where pricey baby clothes, prams, nursery furniture, accessories, toys, gifts and linens are beautfully laid out.
Buggy access. Delivery service.

EDUCATIONAL

Books
Several toy shops (*see pp279-284*) also stock children's picture books.

Big Green Bookshop
Unit 1, Brampton Park Road, N22 6BG (8881 6767/www.biggreenbookshop.com). Turnpike Lane or Wood Green tube. **Open** 9.30am-6pm Mon-Sat; noon-5pm Sun. **Credit** AmEx, MC, V.

Consumer

tube. **Open** 9.30am-5.30pm Mon-Sat; 10am-1.30pm Sun. **Credit** MC, V.
This much-loved specialist children's bookshop has cosy spaces for reading. The stock is exemplary. Storytelling sessions for under-fives take place on Tuesdays and Thursdays (2pm) when badges and stickers are handed out.
Buggy access. Disabled access. Mail order.

Children's Bookshop
29 Fortis Green Road, N10 3HP (8444 5500). Highgate tube then 43, 134 bus. **Open** 9.15am-5.45pm Mon-Sat; 11am-4pm Sun.
Credit AmEx, MC, V.
Quiet, well-stocked and roomy, this is a good atmosphere in which to peruse neatly ordered shelves full of colour and interest. There's a children's corner with picture books at floor level. Book-related events, including regular author signings, are publicised in a quarterly newsletter.
Buggy access. Mail order.

Daunt Books
51 South End Road, NW3 2QB (7794 8206/ www.dauntbooks.co.uk). Belsize Park tube/ Hampstead Heath rail. **Open** 9am-6pm Mon-Sat; 11am-6pm Sun. **Credit** MC, V.
This branch of the well-loved independent has a cosy play area, with stacks of picture books and comics, and mini beanbags to lounge on.
Buggy access. Mail order.
Other locations 193 Haverstock Hill, NW3 4QG (7794 4006); 83 Marylebone High Street, W1U 4QW (7224 2295); 112-114 Holland Park Avenue, W11 4UA (7727 7022).

Golden Treasury
29 Replingham Road, SW18 5LT (8333 0167/ www.thegoldentreasury.co.uk). Southfields tube. **Open** 9.30am-6pm Mon-Fri; 9.30am-5.30pm Sat; 10.30am-4.30pm Sun. **Credit** MC, V.
Attractively laid out, with themed cabinets, this is a spacious treasury for local parents.
Buggy access. Play area.

Lion & Unicorn
19 King Street, Richmond, Surrey TW9 1ND (8940 0483/www.lionunicornbooks.co.uk). Richmond tube/rail. **Open** 9.30am-5.30pm Mon-Fri; 9.30am-6pm Sat; 11am-5pm Sun.
Credit MC, V.
'The Roar', this bookshop's quarterly newsletter, is invaluable for news about book signings, special events and reviews of books. Staff are happy to advise and the books crammed into the various rooms of this exciting shop are certainly diverse, and cater for all ages, including teens.
Buggy access. Mail order.

A new, friendly bookshop with an excellent children's section where young readers can relax with their favourite tome. During term time every Wednesday is a 'Big Green Wednesday', when local authors pop in to read and talk to the children.
Buggy access.

Bookseller Crow on the Hill
50 Westow Street, SE19 3AF (8771 8831/ www.booksellercrow.com). Gypsy Hill rail. **Open** 10am-7pm Mon-Fri; 9.30am-6.30pm Sat; 11am-5pm Sun. **Credit** AmEx, MC, V.
A local landmark that's been run by the Crow family for ages. Justine Crow, who runs the shop with Jonathan Main, writes amusingly about shop and home life in the local freesheet, *Families South East* magazine every month. The friendly shop has a wealth of baby, toddler, child, teen, parent and grandparent literature, alongside modern classics for youth – Rosen, Horowitz, Wilson and Rowling.
Buggy access. Mail order. Play area.

Bookworm
1177 Finchley Road, NW11 0AA (8201 9811/ www.thebookworm.uk.com). Golders Green

Consumer

Never Ending Story Bookshop

59 North Cross Road, SE22 9ET (8693 0123/ www.theneverendingstorybookshop.com). East Dulwich rail. **Open** 10am-5pm Tue-Fri; 10am-6pm Sat. **Credit** MC, V.

This neat bookshop is also headquarters for Future Matters, a family welfare consultancy that covers parenting programmes and play therapy. *Buggy access.*

Owl Bookshop

209 Kentish Town Road, NW5 2JU (7485 7793). Kentish Town tube. **Open** 9.30am-6pm Mon-Sat; noon-4.30pm Sun. **Credit** AmEx, MC, V.

Children's titles in this general bookshop are sorted by age and interest. It also hosts readings by local children's authors (join the mailing list). *Buggy access. Mail order.*

Tales on Moon Lane

25 Half Moon Lane, SE24 9JU (7274 5759/ www.talesonmoonlane.co.uk). Herne Hill rail/3, 37, 68 bus. **Open** 9am-5.30pm Mon-Fri; 9.30am-6pm Sat; 11am-4pm Sun. **Credit** MC, V.

The window displays in this delightful children's bookshop pull you right in. The range of reading matter is wide, and there are lovely picture books for pre-schoolers. Regular storytelling sessions are very popular (turn up early for a place on the sofa). *Buggy access. Mail order.*

Other locations 9 Princess Road, NW1 8JN (7722 1900).

Victoria Park Books

174 Victoria Park Road, E9 7HD (8986 1124/ www.victoriaparkbooks.co.uk). London Fields rail then 277 bus. **Open** 10am-5.30pm daily. **Credit** MC, V.

This friendly bookshop has a lovely community feel. One wall has book reviews from local school children, the space includes a central area with tables, chairs and toys, and there's a patio that's busy in summer. Books are categorised by look and feel as well as content – there's a section for interactive titles, and children can get their hands on cloth, bath and buggy books. Other stock is divided into user-friendly sections: history, art, dinosaurs, reference, a Ladybird corner and more. Teenagers and adults are also catered for. Staff are enthusiastic, authors visit regularly and there are reading events for pre-schoolers on Tuesdays and Fridays. *Buggy access. Mail order. Play area.*

Musical instruments

Chappell of Bond Street

152-160 Wardour Street, W1F 8YA (7432 4400/www.chappellofbondstreet.co.uk). Oxford Circus or Tottenham Court Road tube. **Open** 9.30am-6pm Mon-Fri; 10am-5.30pm Sat. **Credit** AmEx, MC, V. **Map** p314 J6.

The firm reckons to have the largest range of printed music in Europe. It's a Yamaha piano and keyboard specialist. Certain instruments (typically flutes, saxes, clarinets, trumpets) may be available on a rent-to-buy scheme, but quarter- and half-size instruments must be purchased. *Buggy access. Delivery service. Mail order.*

Dot's

132 St Pancras Way, NW1 9NB (7482 5424/ www.dotsonline.co.uk). Camden Town tube/ Camden Road rail. **Open** 9am-5.30pm Mon-Sat. **Credit** MC, V.

Run by an experienced music teacher, this is a wonderfully friendly community music shop. Dot's sells new instruments – mostly stringed and wind – from, say, £5 for a recorder, £40 for a guitar and £59 for a violin. There's a rent-to-buy scheme too. Check the website for tuition, second-hand instruments and Dot's recorder club. *Mail order. Repair service.*

Trotters. See p273.

Size 9
£14.99

Consumer

Dulwich Music Shop

9 Upland Road, SE22 9EE (8693 1477).
East Dulwich rail/40, 185, P13 bus. **Open**
2-5.30pm Mon; 9.30am-5.30pm Tue-Sat.
Credit AmEx, MC, V.
Guitar and string instrument specialist with hire
and buy-back options. Accessories are sold.
Buggy access. Mail order. Repair service.

Northcote Music

*155C Northcote Road, SW11 6QB (7228
0074). Clapham Junction rail then 319 bus.*
Open 10.30am-6pm Mon-Fri; 10am-5pm Sat.
Credit MC, V.
A tiny, friendly place to buy your child's first
recorder (from £4.99) and ask about purchasing
the big stuff. Northcote squeezes string,
percussion and wind instruments (which you can
rent or buy) into the space, as well as brass and
digital equipment. It's often a bit of a bunfight in
here at school chuck-out time, when parents
bring in their darlings for their latest cello book.
*Buggy access. Delivery service. Mail order.
Repair service.*

Robert Morley

*34 Engate Street, SE13 7HA (8318 5838/
www.morleypianos.com). Lewisham DLR/rail.*
Open 9.30am-5pm Mon-Sat. **Credit** MC, V.
To see if a child is serious about playing the
piano, Morley's will hire one out, charging £250
for delivery, then a monthly rental charge
starting from £30. If, after a year, the child is
still piano-friendly, you can buy it, and get half
the rental payments off the price, plus half the
delivery charge. Morley's also builds pianos,
clavichords, harpsichords and virginals.
Buggy access. Delivery service.

Educational toys & games

Education Interactive

*10 Staplehurst Road, SE13 5NB (8318 6380/
www.education-interactive.co.uk). Hither Green
rail.* **Open** 9.30am-5.30pm Mon-Wed, Fri, Sat;
9.30am-6.30pm Thur (phone to check times
before visiting). **Credit** MC, V.
High-quality educational resources are the big
deal in this Hither Green and online shop. The
idea is to provide games for children that
stimulate   thinking   through   intrigue,
involvement and engagement. EI also work with
teachers and parents to provide low-cost, high-
quality solutions to education. Games, puzzles
and activities, great for individuals, families and
schools, include electronic sudoku, Fraction
Action snap and the ever-popular Polydron.
Mail order.

Fun Learning

*Bentall's Centre, Clarence Street, Kingston-
upon-Thames, Surrey, KT1 1TP (8974 8900).
Kingston rail.* **Open** 9am-6pm Mon-Wed, Fri,
Sat; 9am-8pm Thur; 11am-5pm Sun. **Credit**
MC, V.
Fun Learning covers all types of play: creative,
thoughtful, raucous, and computer-based (the
computer games are mostly of an educational
bent). There are large sections devoted to
puzzles and number games, art and craft
activities, and science experiments. A wonderful
place to seek out an unusual Christmas present,
but there are affordable pocket money-priced
items, too (balloon-making gunk, bouncy balls,
puzzles, magnifying glasses).
Buggy access. Disabled access. Mail order.
Other locations Brent Cross Shopping
Centre, NW4 3FP (8203 1473).

EQUIPMENT & ACCESSORIES

Gifts

Blossom Mother & Child

*164 Walton Street, SW3 2JL (0845 262
7500/www.blossommotherandchild.com).
South Kensington tube.* **Open** 10am-6pm Mon-
Sat; noon-5pm Sun. **Credit** AmEx, MC, V.
Map p313 E10.
This softly-scented maternity wear specialist in
child-friendly Walton Street is a calming place
for hot and bothered pregnant mums. Designed
to flatter the temporarily full-frontal look,
clothes include own-label maternity wear and
sexy swimwear, plus lingerie joined by Michael
Stars, Cadeau, and 1 et 1 font 3. There are plenty
of things for the baby too – weeny new baby
clothes by Aztec and Tiny Te and Angel Baby
toiletries, lotions and potions for baby bathing
and baby massage.
Buggy access. Mail order.

Bob & Blossom

*140 Columbia Road, E2 7RG (7739 4737/
www.bobandblossom.com). Old Street tube/rail/
55 bus.* **Open** 9am-3pm Sun. **Credit** MC, V.
Danish wooden Noah's Ark sets, trademark
trendy T-shirts emblazoned with cheeky mottos,
Mexican jumping beans and spinning tops – the
selection at B&B is eclectic. The shop's doing a
roaring trade despite being open just six hours
a week to coincide with the hugely popular
Sunday flower market.

Rich pickings
Stoke Newington

Nestled between Islington and Hackney, 'Stokey' is home, it is claimed, to more buggies per square mile than anywhere else in London. Still pleasantly bohemian, the heart of the area is Church Street. Visit on a typical weekend and you'll find a heap of great little independent shops, an organic farmers' market, an antique yard and a few good second-hand bookshops.

One of the best toy shops around, **Route 73** (*see p283*) has the pocket money stuff and big boxed birthday specials to get excited about. A few doors away, lovely looking **Olive Loves Alfie** (*see p269*) has wonderfully decorative fashions for children. A newer addition to Stoke Newington's independent shops, **Frère Jacques** (*see p268*) offers distinctive children's clothes and shoes. One of the best children's shops in London, and the most typically Stokey – all green and caring – is all-rounder **Born** (pictured; *see p253*) on Church Street. There's also a branch of the bike shop **Two Wheels Good** (*see p265*).

Finnesse Lifestyle
453 Roman Road, E3 5LX (8983 9286/ www.finnesselifestyle.com). Bethnal Green tube then 8 bus. **Open** 9.30am-6pm Mon-Sat. **Credit** AmEx, MC, V.
Finnesse houses a dainty selection of organic and fairtrade children's clothes and toys from around the world alongside womenswear, home furnishing and tableware. Sri Lanka, South Africa, Bangladesh, Peru and Finland are the origins for interesting labels including Marimekko, Lanka, Leela, Kade, Noo Noo, and Turquaz, stocked alongside higher profile names like Nomads, People Tree and Hug. The sweet collection includes some especially pretty nightwear, baby bootees and girls' dresses.
Buggy access. Mail order.

Green Baby
345 Upper Street, N1 0PD (7359 7037/ www.greenbaby.co.uk). Angel tube/Highbury & Islington tube/rail. **Open** 10am-5pm Mon-Fri; 9.30am-5.30pm Sat; 11am-5pm Sun. **Credit** MC, V.
Adorable organic cotton basics for newborns, such as striped playsuits for summery babies and long, striped baby gowns for wintery ones. Green Baby also sells organic sheets, cotton washable nappy systems (and all the gear necessary for same), Tripp Trapp high chairs, pop-up baby beds, Huggababy slings and the ever-reliable Baby Björn Active Carrier. Nappy balms and baby lotions based on pure lanolin, sweet almond oil and cocoa butter take up the remaining space. Come here for the Skip-Hop changing bag (£49.99), fab cotton toys and bright, cosy beach wraps. Anything that won't fit in the shop can be ordered from the website or catalogue.
Buggy access. Delivery service. Mail order (0870 240 6894).
Other locations 5 Elgin Crescent, W11 2JA (7792 8140); 4 Duke Street, Richmond, Surrey TW9 1HP (8940 8255); 52 Greenwich Church Street, SE10 9BL (8858 6690).

Mini Kin
22 Broadway Parade, N8 9DE (8341 6898). Finsbury Park tube/rail then W7 bus. **Open** 9.30am-5.30pm Mon-Sat; 10.30am-5.10pm Sun. **Credit** MC, V.
All-rounder Mini Kin is not only splendid for children's haircuts and baby accessories, it's also one of the original purveyors of allergen and paraben-free toiletries for delicate young skins, especially those traumatised by eczema, as well as organic cotton clothes.
Buggy access. Disabled access. Hairdressing. Nappy-changing facilities. Play area.

Consumer

Rich pickings
Walton Street

Walton Street, a debonair thoroughfare leading to Knightsbridge from South Kensington, has long been something of a parent trap. These days, the old guard of unwaveringly traditional nursery shops have been joined by a clutch of cool chics. Where pregnant mammas once waddled purposefully toward **Nursery Window** (*see p267*) for moses baskets trimmed with Swiss lace, solid oak nursery furniture, and linen, accessories and gift sets, they're now distracted by a waft of **Blossom Mother & Child** (*see p262*) for all the unguents, calming candles, lotions, potions and pamperings a pregnant person could want, as well as new baby clothes.

On the traditional side of the street, lurks the impossibly winsome **Dragons of Walton Street** (*see p266*), the byword for smart nurseries. If all this seems a bit too English, cross over to the trendy side again for pink and blue expensive babywear from **Marie Chantal** (*see p273*), or take a deep breath and dive into the designer labels at **Guys & Dolls** (pictured; *see p268*), which is really rock 'n' roll. Genteel Walton Street doesn't know what's hit it.

Semmalina-Starbags
225 Ebury Street, SW1W 8UT (7730 9333/ www.starbags.info). Sloane Square tube. **Open** 9.30am-5.30pm Mon-Sat. **Credit** AmEx, MC, V.
Sisters Emma Forbes and Sarah Standing, who have five children between them, run this two-pronged business. They branched into the wonderful world of party bags after finding that many customers were coming into the children's shop for bespoke party bags, not only for littlies but but for grown up children (18-21) too. Semmalina's starbags are fantasy party bags wrapped in crackling cellophane and garlanded with bright ribbons. The stuff to fill them is arranged all about – from the neon-lit sweetie selection that catches the eye on entering to bubbles, potty putty, bouncy balls, hair trinkets, stationery and more. Out of party bag territory, there are gift boxes for new babies, Mamma Mio hospital pampering kits for women reaching the nine-month deadline, clothes for children and nostalgic toys.
Delivery service. Mail order.

Tiny Impressions
176 Northcote Road, SW11 6RE (7585 1115/ www.tinyimpressions.co.uk). Clapham Junction rail then 319 bus. **Open** 10am-6pm Mon-Sat; by appointment Sun. **Credit** MC, V.
Aspirational accessories for tinies include the CoCo babylounger, stylish bloom high chairs in leather and blonde wood, as well as out-and-about accessories by Babyjogger, Qype and Stork.
Buggy access. Delivery service. Mail order.

Bikes

Chamberlaine & Son
75-77 Kentish Town Road, NW1 8NY (7485 4488). Camden Town tube. **Open** 8.30am-6pm Mon-Sat. **Credit** AmEx, MC, V.
Hundreds of bikes and accessories, including reclinable baby seats, trailer bikes and kids' training bikes.
Buggy access. Delivery service. Disabled access. Mail order. Repair service.

Edwardes
221-225 Camberwell Road, SE5 0HG (7703 3676/5720). Elephant & Castle tube then 12, 68, 176, P3 bus. **Open** 8.30am-6pm Mon-Sat. **Credit** MC, V.
This good general bike shop has mounts for littleuns aged two to 12, in Pro Bike, Bronx and Giant ranges, and accessories such as bike seats, jolly helmets, trailers and tag-alongs.
Buggy access. Delivery service. Disabled access. Mail order. Repair service.

Two Wheels Good

143 Crouch Hill, N8 9QH (8340 4284/www.twowheelsgood.co.uk). Finsbury Park tube/rail then W7 bus. **Open** 9am-6pm Mon-Sat. **Credit** AmEx, MC, V.

TWG combines the cool side of adult biking with plenty of kids' equipment in its family-friendly shop.

Buggy access. Disabled access. Mail order. Repair service.

Other locations 165 Stoke Newington Church Street, N16 0UL (7249 2200).

Prams & accessories

Babyworld

239 Munster Road, SW6 6BT (7386 1904). Fulham Broadway tube then 211, 295 bus. **Open** 10am-6pm Mon-Wed, Fri; 10am-5.30pm Sat. **Credit** AmEx, MC, V.

Babyworld crams in as many baby transport systems, nursery equipment, toys and games for infants as the space allows and fills the gaps with Tomy, Lamaze and other toy brands. Transport systems (to buy or order) include the latest in Bugaboo convertible chic, as well as Jane stalwarts, mountain buggies and the last word in dual buggies.

Buggy access. Mail order.

Blue Daisy

13 South End Road, NW3 2PT (7681 4144/www.blue-daisy.com). Belsize Park tube/Hampstead Heath rail. **Open** 9.30am-5.30pm Mon-Fri; 10am-5.30pm Sat. **Credit** AmEx, MC, V.

Hampstead baby boutique, Blue Daisy has adorable clothes (Mokopuna, Blue Day, Swaddle Designs, Togz), toys and accessories. The stock – organic and fairtrade where applicable – is full of style and ingenuity. It's also well organised and presented: children make straight for the toys alcove where pretty traditional wooden cookers by Tiny Love are there for the playing with, and there's a changing area too. Home accessories include the new Kaboost chair booster, the best-selling Cuddledry towels, Mini-Micro Scooters, and groovy Splash About swimsuits. All can be ordered via the website.

Buggy access. Mail order. Nappy-changing facilities. Play area.

Pram Shop

57 Chepstow Road, W2 5BP (7313 9969/www.thepramshopnottinghill.co.uk). Notting Hill Gate tube then 28, 328 bus. **Open** 10.30am-6pm Mon-Sat; noon-4pm Sun. **Credit** AmEx, MC, V.

The latest in must-have transport systems fill the Pram Shop, the South East's main Emmaljunga stockist. Bugaboo and Phil and Teds – in up-to-the-minute colours are also present and correct. Accessories, such as foot muffs, rain covers and transport bags are also sold.

Buggy access. Delivery service.

Rub a Dub Dub

15 Park Road, N8 8TE (8342 9898). Finsbury Park tube/rail then W7 bus. **Open** 10am-5.30pm Mon-Fri; 9.30am-5.30pm Sat; 12.30am-5pm Sun. **Credit** MC, V.

The knowledgeable owner of RDD chooses stock with care and dispenses advice with alacrity – as do her staff. Top baby transport systems are still the ever-popular Bugaboo and the more rugged Mountain Buggy. The Phil and Ted double decker buggy costs from £299. Weather protection comes in the form of Outlook's Shade-a-babe, a pushchair cover offering UV protection. For indoors there's the posture-reforming Tripp Trapp high chair (£145), various travel cots, and fun things like wheely bugs in ladybird and bumblebee shapes for whizzing around the house. Every conceivable brand of eco-friendly nappy and bottom cream is stocked.

Buggy access. Delivery service. Disabled access. Mail order. Nappy-changing facilities. Play area.

The nursery

Aspace

140 Chiswick High Road, W4 1PU (8994 5814/www.aspaceuk.com). Turnham Green tube. **Open** 10am-6pm Mon-Sat; 11am-5pm Sun. **Credit** AmEx, MC, V.

This range of distinctive, co-ordinating furniture can be seen in all its glory in this Chiswick branch (there's also a concession in Heal's, www.heals.co.uk). Beds (first, brand, bunk, sleepover truckles), handsome wardrobes and chests of drawers, and tasteful soft furnishings – mattresses, quilts, throws, curtains, cushions and quilt covers – are all here.

Buggy access. Delivery service. Mail order (0845 872 2400).

Chic Shack

77 Lower Richmond Road, SW15 1ET (8785 7777/www.chicshack.net). Putney Bridge tube then 14, 22 bus. **Open** 9.30am-6pm Mon-Sat. **Credit** MC, V.

Chic Shack's romantic, refined and largely white-painted furniture and soft furnishings for children's rooms smack of clean living without being overly crisp or formal. Cots, chests, shelves

Consumer

Satisfy reading needs at **Tales on Moon Lane**. *See p260.*

and wardrobes are complemented by pink and pale blue floral or striped accessories and linens, but nothing is too sugary. Extras, like knitted bears and linen bags, quilted covers and cushions, pile on more charm.
Buggy access. Delivery service. Mail order.

Dragons of Walton Street

23 Walton Street, SW3 2HX (7589 3795/ www.dragonsofwaltonstreet.com).
Knightsbridge or South Kensington tube.
Open 9.30am-5.30pm Mon-Fri; 10am-5pm Sat. **Credit** AmEx, MC, V. **Map** p313 E10.
Dragons is a pleasant place to visit; staff are friendly, the mood relaxed, and personal service is guaranteed. Hand-painted nursery furniture comes with all sorts of child favourites: bunnies, boats, soldiers, fairies, pirate mice and vintage roses. Customers are also encouraged to come up with their own ideas for designs (£2,000 for a special artwork bed but personalised chairs and prettily finished quilts are more affordable). Curtains, cots, sofas, chaises longues and tiny chairs are made to order. Handsome, traditional toys are also sold.
Buggy access. Delivery service. Disabled access. Mail order.

Lilliput

255-259 Queenstown Road, SW8 3NP (7720 5554/0800 783 0886/www.lilliput.com).
Queenstown Road rail. **Open** 9.30am-5.30pm

Mon, Tue, Thur, Fri; 9.30am-7pm Wed; 9am-6pm Sat; 11am-4pm Sun. **Credit** MC, V.
An extensive one-stop baby shop underneath the railway arches, Lilliput has a vast range of stock. All the big names in pushchairs and prams are present and there's all sorts of baby bathing, changing, dressing, entertaining, feeding, listening and sleeping paraphernalia that nervous parents feel they have to have. In fact, Lilliput and baby guru Gina Ford have put together a helpful (if not exactly inexpensive) Baby Needs List for those last heady shopping days before the birth. And before all that kicks off there's the pregnancy (there's a Crave maternity wear concession).
Buggy access. Delivery service. Mail order. Nappy-changing facilities. Play area.

Natural Mat Company

99 Talbot Road, W11 2AT (7985 0474/ www.naturalmat.com). Ladbroke Grove tube.
Open 9.30am-6pm Mon-Fri; 10am-4pm Sat.
Credit MC, V. **Map** p310 A5.
Renowned for mattresses made of all natural materials, such as organic coir, latex straight from the rubber tree, mohair and unbleached cotton, Natural Mat makes for a toxin-free nursery environment. Infants may safely snooze under quilts, sheets and duck down pillows, lambswool and unbleached cotton, babies can forget about kicked-off sheet misery in sleeping bags of lightweight organic cotton or cotton fleece for

winter. Then there are lambskin fleeces, Welsh wool blankets and West Country willow cribs. *Buggy access. Delivery service. Mail order.*

Nursery Window

83 Walton Street, SW3 2HP (7581 3358/ www.nurserywindow.co.uk). Knightsbridge or South Kensington tube. **Open** 10am-6pm Mon-Sat. **Credit** AmEx, MC, V. **Map** p313 E10.

Soft, beautiful furnishings for the new arrival's room include cots, rocking chairs, Moses baskets and the linen sheets and pillowcases and cashmere blankets to set them off. The enchanting cashmere matinée jackets, little trousers, boottees and dresses hand knitted by Sue Hill make superior welcome presents. *Buggy access. Delivery service. Mail order.*

FASHION

Amaia

14 Cale Street, SW3 3QU (7590 0999/www. amaia-kids.com). Sloane Square or South Kensington tube. **Open** 10am-6pm Mon-Sat. **Credit** MC, V. **Map** p313 E11.

'Fresh, elegant, easy to wear' is the Amaia theme. Clothes for children up to eight are unmistakeably continental (French/Spanish in equal measure) and simplicity and classicism is key; there's no room for mini-me swank here. Hence you'll find shift dresses with four pretty buttons and piping, delicate cardies and skirts for the girls, and cotton shorts and button-down shirts for boys. Winter brings in woollen coats, soft jumpers and cords. Prices are middling to expensive. A cotton dress for a five-year-old costs between £40 and £60. *Buggy access.*

Aravore Babies

31 Park Road, N8 8TE (8347 5752/www. aravore-babies.com). Highgate tube/Crouch Hill rail/41, 91, W5,W7 bus. **Open** 10am-5.30pm Mon-Sat; noon-4.30pm Sun. **Credit** MC, V.

Aravore Babies is a luxury brand for babies and children up to five using only organic materials. A visit to the small shop reveals much to coo over: gorgeous handcrafted cream knits in merino wool (including tops and dresses) nestle alongside soft shawls and blankets. Aravore also stocks other organic ranges like Green Baby (*see p263*), Tatty Bumpkin and Bamboo Baby. There are also skincare and bath products on offer from Earth Mama Angel Baby, and a baby wish-list service too. *Buggy access. Mail order.*

Biff

41-43 Dulwich Village, SE21 7BN (8299 0911/www.biffkids.co.uk). North Dulwich rail/ P4 bus. **Open** 9.30am-5.30pm Mon-Fri; 10am-6pm Sat. **Credit** MC, V.

A wide-ranging stock and a family-friendly café next door makes this a village hub. It takes up two shops. At No. 41 there's a wide shoe selection for all ages from many brands, including Lelli Kelly, Ricosta, Crocs, Geox and Start-rite and clothes for boys and girls aged all the way from two to 16. Expect labels such as Pepe Jeans, Powell & Craft, Bench, Roxy, O'Neill, Quiksilver and French Connection. At No. 43 it's the babies: Grobags, socks, babysuits and swimwear (including confidence floats) and clothes for children aged up to two. *Buggy access. Disabled access. Mail order. Play area.*

Bonpoint

15 Sloane Street, SW1X 9NB (7235 1441/ www.bonpoint.com). Knightsbridge tube. **Open** 10am-6pm Mon-Sat. **Credit** AmEx, MC, V. **Map** p313 F9.

This shop looks gorgeous, like a French farmhouse, with distressed floorboards, faded woven rugs and vintage chairs and tables for children to crayon on. This, the original luxury clothing brand for children tends to echo this enchanting Gallic fantasy. It is, naturellement, far from cheap (tiny jumpers cost from about £60) but the knitwear, baby dresses with bloomers, sundresses, linen shorts, denims and floppy cotton print shirts have effortless charm. *Buggy access. Mail order.*

Other locations throughout town. Check website for details.

Caramel Baby & Child

77 Ledbury Road, W11 2AG (7727 0906/ www.caramel-shop.co.uk). Notting Hill Gate or Westbourne Park tube. **Open** 10am-6pm Mon-Sat; noon-5pm Sun. **Credit** AmEx, MC, V. **Map** p310 A6.

The bewitching Caramel brand was started by Eva Karayiannis, whose distaste for 'mass-produced clothing covered in logos' led to her own shop. Her togs for children aged 0-12 are relaxed and fun. This summer we have mostly fallen in love with the cotton print sundresses (from £66) and striped sweaters (from £54). We loved the Millie raincoat (£93) but could not justify the expense. Book ahead for haircuts on Tuesdays and alternate Wednesdays. *Buggy access. Hairdressing. Mail order.*

Other locations 259 Pavillion Road, SW1X 0BP (7730 2564); 291 Brompton Road, SW3 2DY (7589 7001).

Elias & Grace

158 Regent's Park Road, NW1 8XN (7449 0574/www.eliasandgrace.com). Chalk Farm tube. **Open** 10am-6pm Mon-Sat; noon-6pm Sun. **Credit** MC, V.

Modish, smart and effortless, Elias & Grace has a stylish mix of high fashion, luxury accessories, lush natural products, organic remedies and perfect gifts. As well as cool maternity wear, there's a great range of designer labels for children aged 0-10. Names from around the world include Chloe, Marni, Quincy, and Bonton, and quality toys and books are also sold. A relaxed atmosphere, with plenty of room for pushchairs, a mini play area and friendly assistants also make it a pleasure to visit.
Buggy access. Mail order. Play area.

Frère Jacques

121 Stoke Newington Church Street, N16 0UH (7249 5655). Finsbury Park tube/rail then 106 bus/73, 393, 476 bus. **Open** 11am-6pm Tue-Sat; noon-6pm Sun. **Credit** AmEx, MC, V.

The emphasis here is on stylish and durable design, rather than cute or delicate offerings, with equal weight given to boys' and girls' clothes. The stock includes Scandinavian labels Norlie, Minymo and Freoli, French names Petit Bateau, Trois Pommes and Confetti, and a newer collection from Deglingos. The colourful animal-themed mackintoshes and brightly patterned wellies from Kidorable are stand-out items while footwear from Italian labels Ecco and Primigi, US brand Pedi Ped, and Canada's Robeez forms a sturdy little shoe range.
Buggy access.

Guys & Dolls

172 Walton Street, SW3 2JL (7589 8990/ www.guysanddollsuk.com). Knightsbridge or South Kensington tube. **Open** 10am-6pm Mon-Fri; 11am-6pm Sat. **Credit** AmEx, MC, V.

It's much easier to find luxury baby and toddler wear than designer stuff for the 8-14 age group, which is why this eclectic boutique, with its Chloe, Missoni, Sonia Rykiel, Simonetta and Little Marc Jacobs designs goes down well with girls aged up to 14 and boys to about 12 (they can choose from Rare, Simple Kids and Joe Black). Nothing here is cheap. The shop is attractive, though, ewith its space age layout, with clothes attractively laid out on spiral rails, and little set pieces shown under shiny plastic pods. Children can lounge about on bean bags and in the ball pond while parents make with the credit card. There's also a garden out back.
Buggy access. Nappy-changing facilities. Play area (garden).

Humla

13 Flask Walk, NW3 1HJ (7794 8449). Hampstead tube. **Open** 10am-6pm Mon-Sat; noon-5.30pm Sun. **Credit** AmEx, MC, V.

A little rainbow of a shop, Humla's tiny interior is packed with stylish, jolly clothes in fun prints for babies and children up to 10. The shop is known for its own exclusive range of knitwear (a three-button jumper for a toddler costs about £29). Colourful separates by Moeller, Molo, Me Too, and French Connection jump off the rails – Molo's car print baby suit is simply adorable. Humla also specialises in wooden and educational toys for toddlers.
Buggy access.

Jakss

463 & 469 Roman Road, E3 5LX (8981 9454/www.jakss.co.uk). Bethnal Green tube then 8 bus. **Open** 10am-5.30pm Tue-Sat. **Credit** AmEx, MC, V.

A treat to visit, Jakss has been stocking designer fashion for newborns to teens since 1977. There are two stores: No. 463 is for babies to six year olds, with top labels such as Dolce and Gabbana Kids, Diesel Kids, Ralph Lauren Kids, DKNY Kids, Miss Sixty Kids, Stone Island Kids, and CP Company Kids. New additions include Missoni Kids, Juicy Couture Kids, and Chloe Kids. Oilily is a highlight with bold accessories including covetable (and washable) changing bags, plus travel bags you'll never miss on the carousel. The two to 14 age group is catered for at No. 469 with particularly beautiful coats, tops and dresses in the Chloe, Missoni and Miss Sixty ranges, plus Birkenstocks in both child and ladies' adult sizes.
Buggy access. Mail order.

Notsobig

31A Highgate High Street, N6 5JT (8340 4455). Archway or Highgate tube. **Open** 10am-6pm Mon-Sat; 11am-5pm Sun. **Credit** MC, V.

An adorable confection, Notsobig's current highlights include chic separates by Cacherel and cosy Woolrich arctic parkas, Pedi Ped baby shoes and trainers, and T-shirts and dresses by American Outfitters. The basement yields further favourites like pretty dresses by Antik Batik and funky printed pyjamas from Mini-a-Ture. New baby gifts include baby socks by Johnny Trumpette and No Added Sugar T-shirts. For parties the Pamela tutu with tulle and petals is a winner and the shop also offers costumes by Bandicoot Lapin, the French fancy dress specialists, which customers order ahead from the catalogue (prices from £40).
Buggy access. Delivery service. Mail order.

Web-wise
Jumbleworld.com

There's a new kid on the web. Developed in partnership with Kidscape, a children's charity established to prevent bullying and child sexual abuse, Jumbleworld is an eBay-style site set up especially for children in December 2007. The charity has a dedicated area within the site to advise children on how to protect against cyber-bullying and ten per cent of Jumbleworld.com fees are donated to Kidscape.

Jumbleworld.com provides a safe site for children to swap or sell items they no longer use and bid on and buy stuff they really, really want. It was founded by Henry Sparks, who saw how difficult and disappointing eBay trading was for his young grandson. All trading is monitored – parents or guardians are required to sign up to the site before children can become members – and the adults have to shoulder most of the responsibility, as they are committed to safety checks (electoral roll and postcode address checks, for example). They're also emailed first (no chatrooms or instant messaging) about their child's trading, which they must approve before any deals can be completed. All transactions are carried out via PayPal.

A £2.50 monthly membership fee is charged to the parent or guardian of the child member, but there is no charge for posting an unlimited number of items on the site. With help from the grown-ups, Jumbleworld trading is commission-free, safe and much more simple than the adult version and the site should help children improve their money management skills and learn about the value of their possessions.

Perhaps somewhat idealistically, children are encouraged to save for their heart's desire, rather than pestering their parents. We'll believe that when we see it.

Olive Loves Alfie

84 Stoke Newington Church Street, N16 0AP (7241 4212/www.olivelovesalfie.co.uk). Finsbury Park tube/rail then 106 bus/73, 393, 476 bus. **Open** 9am-5.30pm Mon-Fri; 10am-6pm Sat; noon-5pm Sun. **Credit** AmEx, MC, V.

A boutique with a strong aesthetic, Olive Loves Alfie houses design-led clothing for newborns, children and teens. There's no clichéd kids stuff in here and the gorgeous stock is wonderfully decorative and resonably priced – the walls are adorned with gorgeous outfits, including best-selling baby suits from hugely popular Scandinavian designers Katvig in stylish prints evoking Orla Kiely. These fly out of the shop along with the special limited collection of dresses from Danish label Ziestha. The Lucky Wang NYC and Rock-a-bye-Baby ranges continue to inspire shoppers, and the cool educational toy range includes puzzles, jigsaws and games by Djeco. The eye-catching monkey print pink lampshades that illuminate this handsome shop are also for sale. *Buggy access. Mail order.*

Quackers

155D Northcote Road, SW11 6QB (7978 4235). Clapham Junction rail then 319 bus. **Open** 9.30am-5.30pm Mon-Fri; 10am-5.30pm Sat. **Credit** MC, V.

A pleasing children's boutique, where rampaging toddlers are treated indulgently by owner Veronica McNaught. A wide range of clothes for babies and children aged up to ten includes smart labels such as German brand Kanz and Whoopi, cosy coats and cardies for winterwear and Blue Fish rainwear. Toys include floppy favourites by Moulin Roty and attractive wooden pull-alongs and trikes. *Buggy access.*

Rachel Riley

*82 Marylebone High Street, W1U 4QW
(7935 7007/www.rachelriley.com). Baker Street
or Bond Street tube.* **Open** 10am-6pm Mon-
Sat; 11am-5pm Sun. **Credit** AmEx, MC, V.
Map p314 G5.

Visiting this shop is like stepping into the more
picturesque aspects of the 1950s. The
floorboards creak as you creep about, and dark
wood, glass cabinets and a retro chandelier light
set off the quality clothes for babies, children
and women. The look, produced in the RR atelier
in the Loire Valley, is traditional, without being
too stuffy. Babies look delightful in their smocks
with matching bloomers, girls can wear
blossom-covered cotton shirts and ladybird
sundresses, and for the boys there are long
cotton shorts and collared shirts. We loved the
ruched swimsuits for bathing beauties (£45).
Buggy access. Delivery service. Mail order.
Other locations 14 Pont Street, SW1X 9EN
(7259 5969).

Ralph Lauren Children's Store

*143 New Bond Street, W1S 2TP (7535 4600/
www.polo.com). Bond Street tube.* **Open** 10am-
6pm Mon-Wed, Fri, Sat; 10am-7pm Thur;
noon-5pm Sun. **Credit** AmEx, MC, V.
Map p314 H6.

The classic shop interior – all dark wood, sepia
prints and strategically placed rocking horses, a
fish tank and antique toy cars – is so attractive
you stay wistfully turning price labels far longer
than you should. There are no bargains, the name
and the famous polo logo kicks those into touch,
but the clothes for babies and infants are all well
made, and the less formal separates are adorable.
Buggy access. Delivery service. Mail order.
Other locations 139-141 Fulham Road, SW3
6FD (7761 0310).

Roco

*6 Church Road, SW19 5DL (8946 5288/
www.rocochildrensboutique.com) Wimbledon
tube/rail.* **Open** 10am-6pm Mon-Sat; noon-
5pm Sun. **Credit** MC, V.

A smart boutique for newborns to 16-year olds,
this double-fronted store is bursting with bright
and colourful clothes and gifts. Split-level, the
ground floor is divided into two areas (noughts
to threes and four- to eight-year-olds). Parents
and children can browse at their leisure,
although the cartoons playing on the store's TV
will probably prove a distraction for tinier tots.
In the basement, the Roco Star teen boutique has
clothes for boys and girls aged 10 to 16. Brands
feature Guess, Polo, Ralph Lauren, French
Connection, O'Neill, Ted Baker and Miss Sixty,

as well as swimwear from Okay Brasil and Sea
Folly. A complete shopping experience for all,
especially flagging parents who can take a well-
earned break in the store's flowery back garden.
Buggy access. Play area (garden).
Other locations Coco, 27A Devonshire
Street, W1G 6PN (7935 3554).

Sasti

*8 Portobello Green Arcade, 281 Portobello
Road, W10 5TZ (8960 1125/www.sasti.co.uk).
Ladbroke Grove tube.* **Open** 10am-6pm Mon-
Sat; 11am-5pm Sun. **Credit** AmEx, MC, V.

Named after the Hindu goddess in charge of all
children and small creatures, Sasti is our fave,
affordable children's shop. This groovy little
shop was started in 1995 and is run by Julie
Brown, Ten Fingers Ten Toes and Rosie, R.Life.
All the clothes are made in the UK and are most
distinctive – there are quirky frilled print skirts,
dresses and shirts, striking Yetti coats in fluffy
pink and blue fun fur, blue star hoodies and
fleece trousers, or cute camouflage fleecey all-
in-ones for outdoorsy babies (all-in-ones cost
from a reasonable £28).
*Buggy access. Delivery service. Mail order.
Nappy-changing facilities. Play area.*

Bonpoint. *See p267.*

Selfridges

*400 Oxford Street, W1A 1AB (0800 123400/
www.selfridges.com). Bond Street tube.* **Open**
9.30am-8pm Mon-Wed, Fri, Sat; 9.30am-9pm
Thur; noon-6pm Sun. **Credit** AmEx, DC,
MC, V. **Map** p314 G6.

Children can gambol around in the spacious third
floor Kids' Universe while their parents go label
crazy. Phillip Lim's children's range includes
stylish separates in bright colours and blacks,
with hand embroidery and other quirky details.
Marc Jacobs' kids and teens range, Little Marc,
offers an arresting line of pretty sundresses,
denim and caption T-shirts. Another favourite is
the Miss Sixty look. Then there's D&G Junior,
Fransa and Ted Baker. For babies, there's
Absorba, Cacharel, Moschino and Catimini. The
atmosphere is teeny-bopperish, with pop on the
sound system and white, shiny pods to contain
the gear, but there's space to let a fractious toddler
run free. There are toys, sticker stations, sweetie
displays, partywear and fairy frocks and there's
a shoe shop with a range from Step 2wo.
*Buggy access. Cafés. Delivery service. Disabled
access: lift, toilet. Mail order. Nappy-changing
facilities.*

Their Nibs

*214 Kensington Park Road, W11 1NR (7221
4263/www.theirnibs.com). Ladbroke Grove or
Notting Hill Gate tube.* **Open** 10am-6pm Mon-
Sat; noon-5pm Sun. **Credit** AmEx, MC, V.

Their Nibs designs can now be found in many
good children's boutiques, but this shop is a big
treat to visit for all ages. There's a play corner
with blackboard, books and toys and a
hairdressing section (cuts available on Monday
after school; ring for details). Then there is the
gear. From quirky little dungarees for crawling
babes, to demure print summer frocks for
preening girls, they're all pretty special.
Distinctive signature prints include cowboys,
pirates and vintage cars, as well as the more
whimsical fairy and gardening girl. The party
wear, such as sticky-outy organza skirts and
trendy crocheted shift dresses cost from about
£45, but there's plenty that's a good deal cheaper,
not least the nostalgic items on the amusing
vintage rail. Covetable toys and stylish hair
accessories are also sold.
Buggy access. Hairdressing. Mail order. Play area.
Other locations 79 Chamberlayne Road,
NW10 3ND (8964 8444).

Web-wise
Toys and clothes

TOYS

www.alphabetcat.com
Well-made, quality toys for playing and learning include nostalgic items such as humming tops and skittles.

www.aspenandbrown.com
Quality baby and christening gifts.

www.brightminds.co.uk
Sparky ideas that make learning fun.

www.bumpto3.com
Grobag sleeping bags, dressing-up sets and traditional toys.

www.larkmade.com
Vintage toys, gifts and decorations for the home, including sweet knitted rattles and cuddly toys.

www.pedlars.co.uk
Eclectic mixture of toys, family games, music, books and more.

www.ptolemytoys.co.uk
A wide range of fabulous toys, baby products, dressing-up clothes and educational goodies.

www.punkrockbaby.com
CDs designed to get the offspring rocking; logo T-shirts also available.

www.talkingbooks.co.uk
An excellent selection of contemporary and classic children's books on tape, CD and MP3.

www.urchin.co.uk
Great kids' accessories.

CLOTHES

www.babywit.com
American site, with slogans including 'My Mama Drinks Because I Cry' as well as Ramones and Bob Marley T-shirts.

www.dribblefactory.com
Designs in flock, puff and glitter prints bearing legends such as 'Be Nice – Don't Forget Who Chooses Your Nursing Home'.

www.moretvicar.com
Online store selling work from a dozen contemporary designers. Lonely hearts ads ('You had a red balloon, I was on the swings') from Eat Yer Greens. Celebrity favourites Jakes and London fashion label Uniform are here too.

www.nappyhead.co.uk
Sells father-and-child sets ('Who's the Daddy?' and 'Who's the Babby?', £30), and 'Good Cop'/'Bad Cop' T-shirts (£24) for twins.

www.nippaz.com
Popular with urban-cool celebrity parents.

www.noaddedsugar.co.uk
Vendor of edgy kids' clothes and statement Ts; 'Lock Up Your Daughters!' and 'Future Supermodel' are faves (£15.50-£18.30).

www.planetboo.co.uk
Band T-shirts for cool rocker sprogs from £8 come with album-cover images from Blondie, Ramones and the Clash, for example. The classic 'Top of the Pops' logo is currently very popular.

www.snuglo.com
Lisa Quinn's range is typified by hip, grown-up colours and bold lettering: 'I Want Chips, Chocolate and Cake'.

www.susumama.co.uk
Ethically sourced tie-dyed and patchwork clothing; pentacle T-shirts for goths.

www.totsplanet.co.uk
Stockists of Snuglo's 'My Mummy Rocks' T-shirts, and funky baby socks.

www.vinmag.com
Cult movie posters as mini T-shirts.

www.woolshed.co.uk
Hand-knitted clothes in a rainbow of fab colours – and all machine-washable.

Consumer

Trotters

34 King's Road, SW3 4UD (7259 9620/ www.trotters.co.uk). Sloane Square tube. **Open** 9am-7pm Mon-Sat; 10.30am-6.30pm Sun. **Credit** AmEx, MC, V. **Map** p313 F11.
Aways a pleasure to trot round, this shop of many parts has clothes, toys, accessories, toiletries, shoes, books and a hairdressing station (from £13). The clothes are adorable, with print dresses from Chelsea Clothing Company and stripey tops and cotton shorts from Petit Breton. Toys include Jellycat soft toys and stationery, there are insulated lunch packs and wheelie suitcases, Nitty Gritty headcare treatments and organic suncreams, shoes from Start-rite and books that concentrate on picture varieties. There's a hairdressing station with a big fish tank to distract the littl'uns during their fringe trim. *Buggy access. Delivery service. Hairdressing. Mail order. Nappy-changing facilities.*
Other locations 127 Kensington High Street, W8 5SF (7937 9373); 86 Northcote Road, SW11 6QN (7585 0572).

Others

Catimini

52 South Molton Street, W1Y 1HF (7629 8099/www.catimini.com). Bond Street tube. **Open** 10am-6.30pm Mon-Wed, Fri, Sat; 10am-7pm Thur; 11am-5pm Sun. **Credit** AmEx, MC, V. **Map** p314 H6.
The Catimini look for children is vibrant, colourful and distinctive, with fine shift dresses, crocheted cardigans, cotton jackets, sweet baggy shorts and striped T-shirts. *Buggy access. Disabled access. Mail order. Play area.*
Other locations 33C King's Road, SW3 4LX (7824 8897).

Felix & Lilys

3 Camden Passage, N1 8EA (7424 5423/ www.felixandlilys.com). Angel tube. **Open** 10.30am-6pm Mon-Sat; 11am-5pm Sun. **Credit** AmEx, MC, V.
A luxury shop selling with bright designer togs for babies and children from ej sikke lef, IDAT and Katvig. Handsome toys include wooden food and pull along pals from Haba and zippy trainer bikes. *Buggy access. Mail order.*

Frogs & Fairies

69A Highbury Park, N5 1UA (7424 5159). Highbury & Islington tube/rail. **Open** 10am-5.30pm Mon-Sat; 10am-4pm Sun. **Credit** AmEx, MC, V.

A friendly children's clothes and toy shop with haircuts on Saturdays. Clothes for babies and tots include No Added Sugar and Start-rite shoes. *Buggy access. Hairdressing. Mail order.*

Jakes

79 Berwick Street, W1F 8TL (7734 0812/ www.jakesofsoho.co.uk). Oxford Circus tube. **Open** 11am-7pm Mon-Sat. **Credit** AmEx, MC, V. **Map** p314 J6.
Jake is a boy with cerebral palsy and part of the profits from the shop go towards his future. Kidswear consists of distinctive slogan T-shirts, ('Lucky 7'), sweatshirts and combat trousers. *Buggy access. Mail order.*

Litkey

2A Devonshire Road, W4 2HD (8994 4112). Turnham Green tube. **Open** 10am-5.30pm Mon-Fri; 10am-6pm Sat; 11am-4pm Sun. **Credit** MC, V.
Mostly Hungarian, with some Italian and French fashions for boys and girls. *Buggy access.*

Marie Chantal

148 Walton Street, SW3 2JJ (7838 1111/ www.mariechantal.com). Knightsbridge or South Kensington tube. **Open** 10am-6pm Mon-Sat. **Credit** AmEx, MC, V.
Softly styled, smart and exclusive clothes for babies and infants designed by mother-of-four Marie-Chantal, Crown Princess Pavlos of Greece. *Buggy access. Mail order.*
Other locations 61A Ledbury Road, W11 2AA (7243 0220).

Membery's

1 Church Road, SW13 9HE (8876 2910/ www.memberys.com). Barnes Bridge rail. **Open** 10am-5pm Mon-Sat. **Credit** AmEx, MC, V.
Special-occasion outfits for small boys and girls – particularly good for wedding wear. *Buggy access. Delivery service. Play area.*

Oranges & Lemons

61 North Cross Road, SE22 9ET (8693 9010). East Dulwich rail. **Open** 10am-5.30pm Mon-Fri; 10am-6pm Sat; 11am-5pm Sun. **Credit** MC, V.
This sister branch to the Pretty Pregnant maternity brand looks forward to dressing your bundle of joy in Ubang puppet trousers and tiny outfits by Lilliputian and Petit Bateau. *Buggy access. Mail order.*
Other locations Pretty Pregnant, 102 Northcote Road, SW11 6QW (7924 4850/ www.prettypregnant.co.uk).

Consumer

Tots Boutique

39 Turnham Green Terrace, W4 1RG (8995 0520). Turnham Green tube. **Open** 10am-6pm Mon-Sat; noon-5pm Sun. **Credit** AmEx, MC, V.
Turnham Green Terrace is turning into a bit of a shopping mecca for those with small children. Tots is one of the original players on the scene, and is often praised for the breadth of its designer stock for babies and children. Small and packed with labels, Tots has a frequently changing label cache, starring, for example, Jottum, Mini-pi, Roxy, Ralph Lauren and Catimini Atelier.
Buggy access. Mail order. Play area.

Chain stores

Adams

www.adams.co.uk
A good bet for affordable playwear, babywear and school uniforms.

Fat Face

www.fatface.com
This popular surfy label has sporty, relaxed wear in muted colours for girls and boys.

Gap Kids

www.gap.com
The superb babywear makes a perfect gift for new parents; the childrenswear is hardwearing and popular with all ages.

H&M

www.hm.com
Modish and gratifyingly cheap casualwear for babies, children and grown-ups.

Jigsaw Junior

www.jigsaw-online.com
The handsome branch at 190-192 Westbourne Grove, W11 2RH (7727 0322) has a silver slide instead of stairs down to the basement.

Monsoon

www.monsoon.co.uk
The pleasing smart/casual clothes for boys and girls are distinctive.

Petit Bateau

www.petit-bateau.com
Classic French cotton baby clothes, in floral, plain and trademark milleraies stripes.

Zara

www.zara.com
Unusual childrenswear and some bright and beautiful dresses for girls.

HAIRDRESSING

Many of the shops listed elsewhere in this chapter have a children's salon, with haircuts available on certain days of the week. See **Harrods** (*see p253*), **Caramel** (*see p267*), **Mini Kin** (*see p257*), **Trotters** (*see p273*); **Little Trading Company** (*see right*), **Their Nibs** (*see p271*) and **Igloo** (*see p254*). For the ultimate in children's barnet styling, however, have a **Tantrum** (*see below*). Those who had to tolerate parents bearing down on them with a pudding basin and the sewing scissors should look away now.

Tantrum

398 King's Road, SW10 0LJ (7376 3966/ www.yourtantrum.com). Sloane Square tube then 11, 19, 22, 319 bus. **Open** 10am-6pm Tue-Fri; 9am-6pm Sat; 11am-5pm Sun. **Credit** AmEx, MC, V.
The only dedicated children's hairdressers we know of in London, Tantrum likes to think of itself as 'a revolutionary new concept in children's hairdressing'. Basically it's all about spoiling them rotten with chill out rooms and Wii games (for eight-to-fourteen years olds) in the basement, and buzzing locomotives, starry skies and a play area (for the under-sevens) on the ground floor. Children having their hair cut sit in themed chairs equipped with flat screen TVs and DVDs. Tantrum also sells natural hair products and their own clothing range for girls. They can also arrange children's parties in this attractive venue (although presumably they hide the scissors).
Buggy access. Play area.

SECOND-HAND

Little Angel Exchange

249 Archway Road, N6 5BS (8340 8003). Highgate tube. **Open** 11am-5pm Mon-Fri; 10.30am-5.30pm Sat; 11am-4pm Sun. **Credit** MC, V.
A ready supply of nearly new or unused clothes, toys and equipment is sold here. Prices start from a couple of quid for a mid-range label T-shirt (such as H&M) to a few more for designerwear. You can also leave items of clothing here in the hope of obtaining half the price (if it goes for over £10), or a third (if it sells for less than £10) once the item is sold. After eight weeks, the goods are given to charity unless they're claimed back.
Buggy access.

Little Trading Company

7 Bedford Corner, The Avenue, W4 1LD (8742 3152). Turnham Green tube. **Open** 9am-5pm Mon-Fri; 9am-4.30pm Sat. **No credit cards**.

Local nannies (and there are plenty) bring in top-quality baby equipment, toys and clothes to be sold on a profit-share or sale-or-return basis. Prams and pushchairs sit outside and indoors hang some bargain treasures, such as Ralph Lauren shirts, outgrown ski suits, unwanted dressing-up costumes and DVDs and videos (which may be watched by children who come in for haircuts on Wed, Fri, Sat; ring for an appointment). New stuff is also sold, including leather first shoes by Starchild.
Buggy access. Hairdressing. Play area.

Merry-Go-Round

12 Clarence Road, E5 8HB (8985 6308). Hackney Central rail. **Open** 10am-5.30pm Mon-Sat; 11am-5pm Sun. **Credit** MC, V.

This ace environmentally friendly agency trades on behalf of its clients in second-hand clothing and baby equipment. The jungle of new and barely used car seats hanging from the ceiling, pushchairs, high chairs, baby-walkers and more, all allow budget- and eco-conscious families to be entirely kitted out in recycled goods. Go prepared for some serious browsing and buying; visitors generally leave with armfuls of stock.
Buggy access. Nappy-changing facilities. Play area.

Merry Go Round

21 Half Moon Lane, SE24 9JU (7737 6452). Herne Hill rail. **Open** 9.15-5pm Mon-Sat. **Credit** MC, V

No relation to MGR above, despite the name, but brilliant bargains can be expected all the same; there are also brand new lines in nightwear and essentials from Petit Bateau. There's a small maternity section too.
Buggy access.

SHOES

Brian's Shoes

2 Halleswelle Parade, Finchley Road, NW11 0DL (8455 7001/www.briansshoes.com). Finchley Central or Golders Green tube. **Open** 9.15am-5.30pm Mon-Sat; 10.30am-1.30pm Sun. **Credit** MC, V.

A centre of excellence for children's foot-measuring services. Diesel and Ricosta as well as sober Start-rite and Hush Puppies stocked.
Buggy access. Disabled access.

John Barnett

137-139 Lordship Lane, SE22 8HX (8693 5145). East Dulwich. **Open** 9.30am-5.30pm Mon-Sat. **Credit** MC, V.

This long-established Dulwich shoe shop has a great section for children.
Buggy access. Disabled access.

Petit Chou. Bless you. *See p284.*

Rich pickings Crouch End

This bohemian, middle-class, family-friendly neighbourhood was the unlikely location for the horror spoof *Shaun of the Dead*. But it's teething infants, not drooling zombies, that seem to make up most of the population round here. Their every need is catered for (the infants, not the zombies) by a huge range of independent, baby and child retailers. The orginal, happy, hippy infant all-rounder **Soup Dragon** (pictured; *see p257*), has been joined by a whole bunch of shops and boutiques that cater for every infant's need – top to tail. There's **Mini Kin** (*see p257*), for children's grooming, toiletries and babywear in organic cotton. Little feet can stamp along to the **Red Shoes** (*see right*) for expert fitting and a range of fancy footwear. If you can't choose between Phil & Teds or Maclaren, **Rub a Dub Dub** (*see p265*) has the gen on thoroughly modern kinder transport. When they get older, **Two Wheels Good** (*see p265*) will set the kids up with self-propelling vehicles. Indoor playtime is covered by **Word Play** (*see p283*).

Little Me
141 Hamilton Road, NW11 9EG (8209 0440). Brent Cross tube. **Open** 10.30am-6.15pm Mon-Thur; Fri phone to check; 11am-4pm Sun. **Credit** MC, V.
Wide range of continental children's shoes fitted with the precision Swiss shoe-measuring system. *Buggy access.*

Merlin Shoes
44 Westow Street, SE19 3AH (8771 5194/ www.merlinshoes.com). Crystal Palace rail. **Open** 9.30am-5.30pm Mon-Fri; 9.30am-6pm Sat. **Credit** MC, V.

Fab local shoe shop and top fitting centre. *Buggy access. Disabled access.*

One Small Step One Giant Leap
3 Blenheim Crescent, W11 2EE (7243 0535/ www.onesmallsteponegiantleap.com). Ladbroke Grove or Notting Hill Gate tube. **Open** 10am-6pm Mon-Fri; 9am-6pm Sat; 11am-5pm Sun. **Credit** MC, V.
Lucky you if there's a branch of this specialist children's shoe chain – consistent winner of the Shoe Retailer of the Year gong – nearby. It is a blissful place to take the children for all their footwear needs – summer sandals, gumboots, Crocs, ballet shoes, plimsolls trainers and, yes,

the dreaded school sensibles – all are present and correct. The best thing, though, is that there's space to spread out, the shoes are displayed with care and the highly regarded Bannock Device is used for fitting. Prices aren't all that much higher than in less attractive shoe shops and the service is smiley. Expect to pay about £12 for a jolly pair of One Small Step canvas sandals, £22.95 for children's Crocs and about £36 for Start-rite school shoes. Other labels include Geox, Puma, adidas, Timberland, Braqueez and some pretty shoes in hot colours by Lelli Kelly, .
Buggy access. Mail order.
Other locations throughout town. Check website for details.

Papillon
43 Elizabeth Street, SW1W 9PP (7730 6690/ www.papillon4children.com). Sloane Square tube/Victoria tube/rail. **Open** 10am-6pm Mon-Fri; 9.30am-4.30pm Sat. **Credit** MC, V.
Bright ballet-style pumps in a rainbow of colours and prints feature largely here but there are also school shoes and beach sandals for boys and girls, flip flops, moccasins and bridesmaids shoes. Hunter gumboots, socks and tights are also sold.
Buggy access. Mail order.

Red Shoes
30 Topsfield Parade, N8 8QB (8341 9555). Finsbury Park tube/rail then 41, W7 bus. **Open** 10am-5.30pm Mon-Sat; noon-4.30pm Sun. **Credit** MC, V.
There's plenty of floor space here for children to try out their new footwear and skedaddle around on the wheelie toys thoughtfully left out for their delectation. The children's shoe collection (there are adult shoes too) include Naturino, Start-rite, Brikenstock, Converse, the ubiquitous Crocs and Geox, the breathable choice. U/V resistant swimwear and baby clothes are also sold.
Buggy access.

Shoe Tree
1 Devonshire Road, W4 2EU (8987 0525). Turnham Green tube. **Open** 9.30am-5.30pm Mon-Sat; 11.30am-4.30pm Sun. **Credit** AmEx, MC, V.
One of the smartest independent shops we've seen, with decking and child-sized chairs and tables out front and plenty of goodies inside. Children can be measured up and coaxed into a wide range of Start-rite, Bopi, Angulus, Ricosta and Aster designs while they watch DVDs and CBeebies. Dancewear, including tap and jazz shoes, is also sold. There's a sofa, and plenty of toys, books, and crayons. Service is saintly.
Buggy access.

Shoe Station
3 Station Approach, Kew, Surrey TW9 3QB (8940 9905/www.theshoestation.co.uk). Kew Gardens tube. **Open** 9am-6pm Mon-Sat. **Credit** MC, V.
The sort of local shoe shop all parents need, the Station (right by Kew station) is run by two women with seven children between them. Children's shoes for every occasion are available, from child's size 2 to adult size 7. Brands include Start-rite (of course), Ricosta, Aster, Naturino, Babybotte, TTY, Giesswein, Mod8, Pom d'Api, Geox, Kenzo, Nike, Puma, Birkenstock, Primigi, Freed and Daisy Roots. Football boots, ballet shoes, slippers and gumboots are also covered. Staff are trained Start-rite fitters.
Buggy access.

Stepping Out
106 Pitshanger Lane, W5 1QX (8810 6141). Ealing Broadway tube then E2, E9 bus. **Open** 10am-5.30pm Mon-Fri; 9.30am-5.30pm Sat. **Credit** MC, V.
Start-rite, Ricosta, Mod8, Lelli Kelly and Geox are sold. Experienced assistants are trained fitters and specialise in advice on shoes for children with mobility problems.
Buggy access. Play area.

Vincent Shoe Store
19 Camden Passage, N1 8EA (7226 3141/ www.vincentshoestore.com). Angel tube. **Open** 11am-6pm Tue-Fri; 10am-6pm Sat; noon-4pm Sun. **Credit** MC, V.
A household name in Sweden, where it launched in 1999, Vincent's perky, affordable footwear includes appealing gumboots, show-stealing button-down leather daisy sandals and warm-feeling ski boots.
Buggy access. Mail order.

SPORT

Ace Sports & Leisure
341 Kentish Town Road, NW5 2TJ (7485 5367). Kentish Town tube. **Open** 9.30am-6pm Mon-Wed, Fri, Sat; 9.30am-7pm Thur. **Credit** AmEx, MC, V.
Ace has footwear for all sports, as well as junior rackets, bats and swimming equipment. Brands include Puma, adidas, Reebok and Nike. There are also small baseball mitts and footballs in all sizes, first cricket bats and balls, ping-pong balls and bats in all colours, tracksuits, swim nappies, goggles, earplugs and nose clips – everything, in fact, to get kids active.
Buggy access. Disabled access.

Consumer

David J Thomas

8 Croxted Road, SE21 8SW (8766 7400).
West Dulwich rail. **Open** 9.15am-5.15pm Mon-
Sat. **Credit** MC, V.
A school uniform and sports kit specialist with
a great line in cheap equipment in junior sizes.
Buggy access.

Decathlon

Canada Water Retail Park, Surrey Quays
Road, SE16 2XU (7394 2000/www.decathlon.
co.uk). Canada Water tube. **Open** 10am-8pm
Mon-Fri; 9am-7pm Sat; 11am-5pm Sun.
Credit MC, V.
In these two vast hangars by Surrey Quays
there's a huge range of gear for young sporty
types, including hard hats, jodhs, crops and
grooming kits for riders, brilliant snow wear in
all sizes for skiers, bikes, fishing rods, walking
boots, trainers any which way, footballs, golf
equipment, gym wear and more. Decathlon has
12 own brands, including Quechua (affordable
and hard wearing, for hiking, mountaineering
and snowboarding), and Domyos (for dancewear
and fitness equipment). You'll also find Nike,
Reebok and adidas. The young, often French
staff are bright and interested. Services include
racquet restringing, scuba tank refilling and ski
maintenance. More than 60 sports are covered.
Children enjoy coming on an expedition to
Decathlon, as there's always plenty of scope to
play – trying out gym equipment, bouncing balls
and testing bikes.
Buggy access. Disabled access. Mail order.
Repair services.

Lillywhites

24-36 Lower Regent Street, SW1Y 4QF (0870
333 9600/www.sports-soccer.co.uk). Piccadilly
Circus tube. **Open** 10am-9pm Mon-Sat; noon-
6pm Sun. **Credit** AmEx, MC, V. **Map** p317 K7.
Good for mainstream sports gear, concentrating
on urban activities, especially football.
Buggy access. Disabled access. Mail order.

Ocean Leisure

11-14 Northumberland Avenue, WC2N
5AQ (7930 5050/www.oceanleisure.co.uk).
Embankment tube. **Open** 9.30am-7pm
Mon-Fri; 9.30am-6pm Sat. **Credit** MC, V.
Map p399 L8.
A watersports emporium that takes up two
shops under the arches. One's all sailing and
scuba, the other mostly surfing. Some gear –
including wetsuits, Reef sandals and neoprene
Aquashoes – comes in very small sizes. There
are also baby life jackets, fins, masks and
snorkels, and even scuba equipment (from age

eight). Big names in stock include Padi,
Aqualung and Scubapro.
Buggy access. Disabled access. Mail order.

Slam City Skates

16 Neal's Yard, WC2H 9DP (7240 0928/
www.slamcity.com). Covent Garden tube.
Open 11am-7pm Mon-Sat; noon-5pm Sun.
Credit AmEx, MC, V. **Map** p315 L6.
Teen heaven for skateboards, sneakers of the
moment, rucksacks and accessories.
Mail order (0870 420 4146).

Soccerscene

56-57 Carnaby Street, W1F 9QF (7439 0778/
www.soccerscene.co.uk). Oxford Circus tube.
Open 10am-7pm Mon-Wed; 10am-8pm Thur-
Sat; noon-6pm Sun. **Credit** AmEx, MC, V.
Map p314 J6.
Scaled-down replica kits and footie and rugby
themed gifts and accessories.
Delivery service. Mail order.
Other locations 156 Oxford Street, W1D
1ND (7436 6499); 49-50 Long Acre, WC2E 9JR
(7240 4070).

Speedo

41-43 Neal Street, WC2H 9PJ (7497 0950/
www.speedo.com). Covent Garden tube. **Open**
10am-7pm Mon-Wed, Sat; 10am-8pm Thur,
Fri; noon-6pm Sun. **Credit** AmEx, MC, V.
Map p315 L6.
The junior range is cool for swimming lessons.
Children's accessories include swim nappies,
armbands, snorkels, goggles and caps that
match your swimsuit.
Buggy access. Disabled access. Mail order.

Wigmore Sports

79-83 Wigmore Street, W1U 1QQ (7486
7761/www.wigmoresports.co.uk). **Open** 10am-
6pm Mon-Wed, Fri, Sat; 10am-7pm Thur;
11am-5pm Sun. **Credit** AmEx, MC, V.
Map p314 G6.
London's premier racquet sports specialist
covers tennis, squash, badminton and more.
There's an extremely popular 'try before you
buy' practice wall, which children love when it's
not being used by some hard-bitten hitter. Junior
stock includes shoes by K-Swiss, adidas, and
Nike; shorter racquets (from 50cm/19in; £15-
£100) and softer balls are a speciality. Staff are
committed to the tennis cause and offer sensible
advice to young people while matching them up
to the right racquet. There's also a Wigmore
concession in Harrods.
Buggy access. Delivery service. Disabled access.
Mail order.

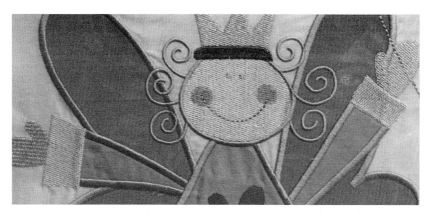

Mystical Fairies. *See p281.*

Consumer

TOYS & GIFTS

Art Stationers/ Green's Village Toy Shop

*31 Dulwich Village, SE21 7BN (8693 5938).
North Dulwich rail.* **Open** 9am-5.30pm Mon-Sat. **Credit** MC, V.

The shop at the front is fantastic for creative play. It has paints, pastels, pencils, paper, stationery, craft materials, isuch as clay and card, and all sorts of useful paperware for parties, including invitations and thank-you notelets. That's just half the story, though. There's a big sign bearing the legend TOYS, which has the children cantering down the passage for the booty: Brio, Sylvanian Families (it's an official collectors' shop), Playmobil, Crayola, Lego, Warhammer and other giants of playworld. Unusual companies such as Tantrix and Wow are also represented. The enormous pocket money-priced range goes from the 25p rubber goldfish to a £2.25 magnetic car racer. *Buggy access.*

Cheeky Monkeys

202 Kensington Park Road, W11 1NR (7792 9022/www.cheekymonkeys.com). Notting Hill Gate tube then 52 bus. **Open** 9.30am-5.30pm Mon-Fri; 10am-5.30pm Sat; 11am-5pm Sun. **Credit** MC, V. **Map** p310 A6.

An independent mini-chain that promotes good, durable, fun and educational toys for babies and children. Tempting, attractive and well made classic toys are set out in style. We're fans especially of their animal rockers, the always entertaining Wheeliebugs (ladybirds and bees are favourites) for toddlers and the colourful ride-on jungle wheelies. Then there are all sorts of puppets and theatres, handsome wooden kitchen toys, dressing-up costumes, pirate ships, Hama Beads and knitting sets. Pocket money trinkets cost from about £1.99 and include such delights as bath colour tablets, pavement chalks and farty goo.

Buggy access. Disabled access. Mail order.
Other locations 4 Croxted Road, SE21 8SW (8655 7168).

Disney Store
360-366 Oxford Street, W1N 9HA (7491 9136/www.disneystore.co.uk). Bond Street tube. **Open** 9am-9pm Mon-Sat; 11.30am-6pm Sun. **Credit** AmEx, MC, V. **Map** p314 J6.
The family film of the moment spawns figurines, stationery, toys and costumes at this most animated of toy shops. Enduring favourites are the character dolls, lunch-boxes, tableware costumes and classic DVDs.
Buggy access. Disabled access. Mail order.
Other locations 10 The Piazza, WC2E 8HD (7836 5037); 22A & 26 The Broadway Shopping Centre, W6 9YD (8748 8886).

Early Learning Centre
36 King's Road, SW3 4UD (7581 5764/ www.elc.co.uk). Sloane Square tube. **Open** 9.30am-7pm Mon-Fri; 9.30am-6pm Sat; 11am-6pm Sun. **Credit** AmEx, MC, V. **Map** p313 F11.
Dedicated to imaginative play for babies and young children, ELC is reliable. Everything is sturdy, brightly coloured and reasonably priced.
Buggy access. Delivery service. Mail order (08705 352352).

Other locations throughout town. Check website for details.

Fagin's Toys
84 Fortis Green Road, N10 3HN (8444 0282). East Finchley tube then 102, 234 bus. **Open** 9am-5.30pm Mon-Sat; 10am-3pm Sun. **Credit** MC, V.
Fagin's is a lovely long space, with favourites from Galt, Orchard, Brio, Lego, Playmobil and Sylvanian Families, outdoor toys and a central table of penny dreadfuls for the party bags. Have fun choosing between little rubber fish and stretching aliens, powerballs, pots of slime, magic screens, colouring sets and silk purses .
Buggy access. Disabled access. Play area.

Hamleys
188-196 Regent Street, W1B 5BT (0870 333 2455/www.hamleys.com). Oxford Circus tube. **Open** 10am-8pm Mon-Fri; 9am-8pm Sat; noon-6pm Sun. **Credit** AmEx, DC, MC, V. **Map** p314 J6.
As much a tourist attraction as a ginormous toy shop. Most must-have toys are here, and attractively displayed to boot, though prices

Rich pickings Hampstead

The Heath is this desirable area's biggest asset, especially where boisterous children are concerned. But the hilly high street, bristling with brasseries and replete with high-end retailers, holds some treasures for those with pocket money to spare. The pretty, exclusive side street Flask Walk, near the tube station, is, rather than the bottom of the garden, the first stop for fairy fans. The twinkly pink **Mystical Fairies** (pictured; *see right*) is all of a flutter with them. Just opposite this whimsical paradise is the excellent childrenswear outlet **Humla** (*see p268*), famed for its handknits. A toyshop with more universal appeal than the fairy one, **Happy Returns** (*see right*) is down Rosslyn Hill from here. Still further down, near the Royal Free Hospital, South End Green has a villagey set-up. That's where you'll find the pretty **Blue Daisy** (*see p265*) and its unusual range of toys, clothes and equipment, as well as **Daunt Books** (*see p259*), one of the most comfortable bookshops in London, with a gorgeous children's section.

seem to build in a margin for their guaranteed presence (well, almost: Hamleys isn't immune to that pre-Christmas panic when the number one gift toy becomes scarce). Arranged on five noisy floors, with perky demonstrators showing off certain wares, the ground floor is soft toys, floor one is games, two is for pre-schoolers, three is girls' stuff, four hobbies, and five is boys' toys and a nice little café. You can spend hours in here researching the Christmas wishlist. Children adore the festive atmosphere at any time of year. On top of all this daily excitement, there are large-scale family events held in the store thoughout the year. On the weekend of 19-20 July, for instance, Hamleys is hosting Paddington Weekend (check the website for the times of events, such as the grand marmalade sandwich treasure hunt) to commemorate that famous bear's 50th anniversary. Paddington will be visiting the shop and will also have his own exclusive window showcasing the last 50 years of the Paddington product.
Buggy access. Café. Delivery service. Disabled access. Mail order. Nappy-changing facilities. Play areas.

Happy Returns

36 Rosslyn Hill, NW3 1NH (7435 2431). Hampstead tube. **Open** 10am-5.30pm Mon-Fri; 10am-6pm Sat; noon-5.30pm Sun. **Credit** MC, V.
A pleasantly retro shop stocking toys old and new, with much of it geared towards parties. Stock up on the celebration essentials then go hunting for presents. There are products and prices to suit everyone: classics like glow-stars or Etch A Sketch, or more modern toys by Jellycat, a big Sylvanian Families collection, Schleich, Playmobil and Galt, plus doll's house accessories by Plan and jolly, chunky plastics by Wow Toys. The epic Gormiti game is a current best-seller.
Buggy access.

Honeyjam

267 Portobello Road, W11 1LR (7243 0449/www.honeyjam.co.uk). Ladbroke Grove tube. **Open** 9.30am-5.30pm Mon-Sat; 11am-4pm Sun. **Credit** AmEx, MC, V.
Run by Jasmine Guinness and Honey Bowdrey, this is a fashionable toy shop that's full of fun and has a strong line in traditional wooden toys from companies like Bigjigs and Le Toy Van, as well as a real eye-catcher in the form of a mini wooden Aga for the play kitchen. Made to order, with its lower oven full of painted glowing coals, it's a real hit with the locals. As well as the toys – both pocket money priced and credit card-

battering – there are baby and infant clothes with excellent pedigrees.
Buggy access. Disabled access.

Just Williams

18 Half Moon Lane, SE24 9HU (7733 9995). Herne Hill rail. **Open** 9.30am-6pm Mon-Sat. **Credit** MC, V.
A bright blue child's paradise, Williams has top names in toys, particularly Brio, Sylvanians, Schleich and Playmobil. There are traditonal wooden playthings from Bigjigs, Plan Toys, Pintoy and Santas. Games Workshop is there for all those prep school boys.
Buggy access.

Little Rascals

140 Merton Road, SW19 1EH (8542 9979). South Wimbledon tube. **Open** 9am-5.30pm Tue-Sat. **Credit** AmEx, MC, V.
A friendly, family-run local shop full of unusual wooden toys, clothes and gifts for babies.
Buggy access.

Mystical Fairies

12 Flask Walk, NW3 1HE (7431 1888/ www.mysticalfairies.co.uk). Hampstead tube. **Open** 10am-6pm Mon-Sat; 11am-6pm Sun. **Credit** MC, V.
An all-out pink and sparkly retail experience. The shop is a glittery grotto dedicated to dreams of princesses and ballerinas, where flower fairies, pixies and elfin toys hang from silver branches overhead. In fact, it's hard to see the wood for the fairies but there are around 2000 products including fairy bed-wear (canopies, bed covers, slippers, dressing gowns, pyjamas and duvet covers), fairy and princess books and stickers, and at the back of the shop costumes, including various types of wings, plus some token wizard and pirate outfits. Mystical Fairies run parties in the shop's Enchanted Garden (the basement).
Buggy access. Mail order.
Other locations Bluewater Shopping Centre, Greenhithe, Kent, DA9 9ST (01322 624997).

Play

89 Lauriston Road, E9 7HJ (8510 9960/ www.playtoyshops.com). Bethnal Green or Mile End tube then 277, 388 bus. **Open** 10am-6pm Mon-Sat; 11am-5pm Sun. **Credit** AmEx, MC, V.
A treasure trove in a pretty part of Hackney, Play lives up to its name. Currently a hit with little customers are the Miffy soft toys, the Sylvanian Families range, and the Brio Trains and Tobar bath toys. There's something for everyone, and every room, here including

Consumer

Rich pickings Notting Hill

The yummiest mummies of them all manoeuvre their Phil & Teds stylishly around the streets of Ladbroke Grove and Notting Hill. They're not just posing round trendy Portobello Market either. There are far too many brilliant children's stores around these fashionable streets to waste time on antiques and fresh veg.

Starting at the Ladbroke Grove end of Portobello Road, **Sasti** (see p270), tucked away in the Portobello Green shopping arcade, is a little independent boutique that has been keeping west London tots looking adorable on a budget since 1995. Another sweet thing at the business end of Notting Hill is **Honeyjam** (pictured; see p281), a toyshop run by a pair of women well known in the fashion world and having a lot of fun in the toy one. Honeyjam competes with the original branch of the well-known independent toy retailer down the road, **Cheeky Monkeys** (see p279).

For fashion, **Their Nibs** (see p271) has had praise heaped upon it since it launched its vintage-look styles for girls and boys a few years ago, and continues to enchant parents and children. Whoever had the bright idea of putting a slide in **Jigsaw Junior** (see p274) on Westbourne Grove should have a pat on the back.

musical instruments by New Classic Toys, natty fabric wall-hangers from Fiesta Crafts, mobiles by Flensted and even a sweet organic clothes range by Green-Eyed-Monster. There's also dressing-up stuff and messy play products (glitter, glue, dough, beads and paints), alongside trinkets by Jellycat, jewellery boxes from Roussellier and party paperware. *Buggy access. Mail order. Play areas.*

Nearly 60 years old and still game for anything, Patrick's is one of London's biggest toy and model shops, and the main service agent for Hornby and Scalextric. The model department specialises in rockets, planes, cars, military and sci-fi. The general toy department has traditional wooden toys, doll's houses and their accessories. *Buggy access. Delivery service (local). Disabled access. Mail order.*

Patrick's Toys & Models
107-111 Lillie Road, SW6 7SX (7385 9864/ www.patrickstoys.co.uk). Fulham Broadway tube. **Open** 9.30am-5.30pm Mon-Sat. **Credit** MC, V.

QT Toys
90 Northcote Road, SW11 6QN (7223 8637/ www.qttoys.co.uk). Clapham Junction rail. **Open** 9.30am-5.30pm Mon-Sat; 9.30am-5pm Sun. **Credit** MC, V.

Consumer

jigsaws, word games, craft packs, Jellycat soft toys, and Starchild's soft leather shoes for babies. *Buggy access. Disabled access.*

Little ones have fun in here while their more serious sisters browse the wares. More expensive, but undoubtedly cool and distinctive, the clothes at **Caramel Baby & Child** (*see p267*) are a big draw, as is the coffee shop in the basement.

For nursery equipment that's pure and natural, the allergy-free **Natural Mat Company** (*see p266*) ensures quiet nights. Finally, the best place to source those Phil & Teds, so you too can barge through the crowds on Portobello Road, is the **Pram Shop** (*see p265*), where aerodynamically tested perambulators of the highest quality await your approval.

All the big toy brands, as well as craft kits, modelling kits, stationery, and educational toys. *Buggy access. Disabled access. Mail order. Nappy-changing facilities.*

Route 73 Kids
92 Stoke Newington Church Street, N16 0AP (7923 7873). 73, 393, 476 bus. **Open** 10am-5.30pm Tue-Sun. **Credit** MC, V.
Guess which bus route this jolly toyshop is on? With a party-bag-tastic table full of pocket money toys, and a great selection of traditional names like Brio and Galt, Route 73 scores. Of the wide range of wooden toys, those by Plan are especially popular. Then there are books, puzzles,

Snap Dragon
56 Turnham Green Terrace, W4 1QP (8995 6618). Turnham Green tube. **Open** 9.30am-6pm Mon-Sat; 11am-5pm Sun. **Credit** MC, V.
A good general toy shop for big brands. *Buggy access. Delivery service (local).*

Sylvanian Families
68 Mountgrove Road, N5 2LT (7226 1329/ www.sylvanianfamilies.com). Finsbury Park tube/rail. **Open** 9.30am-5.30pm Mon-Fri; 9am-6pm Sat; 10am-4pm Sun. **Credit** MC, V.
This tiny outpost of Sylvania, where neatly dressed woodland folk have impeccable family values and desirable homes, has been hidden away on a quiet north London street for around 16 years. Here you can buy your fave dressed-up animals from the Babblebrook and Dappledawn dynasties, their homes, vehicles and accessories. *Buggy access. Mail order.*

Toy Station
6 Eton Street, Richmond, Surrey TW9 1EE (8940 4896). Richmond tube/rail. **Open** 10am-6pm Mon-Fri; 9.30am-6pm Sat; noon-5pm Sun. **Credit** (over £8) MC, V.
An old-fashioned, two-storey toy shop full of model animals, knights and soldiers, forts and castles, remote-control vehicles and traditional wooden toys. *Buggy access. Disabled access.*

Toys R Us
760 Old Kent Road, SE15 1NJ (7732 7322/ www.toysrus.co.uk). Elephant & Castle tube/ rail then 21, 56, 172 bus. **Open** 9am-8pm Mon-Fri; 9am-7pm Sat; 11am-5pm Sun. **Credit** AmEx, MC, V.
Industrial quantities of the toy of the moment, often hard to find an assistant. *Buggy access. Car park. Delivery service. Disabled access. Nappy-changing facilities.* **Other locations** throughout town. Check website for details.

Word Play
1 Broadway Parade, N8 9TN (8347 6700). Finsbury Park tube/rail then W7, 41 bus. **Open** 9am-5.30pm Mon-Sat; 11am-5pm Sun. **Credit** MC, V.
A great pocket money/party bag selection as well as a wide range of books, useful craft supplies and building toys. *Buggy access. Disabled access.*

Consumer

Traditional toys

Benjamin Pollock's Toyshop
44 The Market, WC2E 8RF (7379 7866/ www.pollocks-coventgarden.co.uk). Covent Garden tube. **Open** 10.30am-6pm Mon-Sat; 11am-4pm Sun. **Credit** AmEx, MC, V. **Map** p317 L7.
Superb for all sorts of unusual and traditional toys, Pollock's is best known for its toy theatres. These cost from £6.95 for the basic Pollock's Harlequinade, which is easy to put together and use, or you can blow about £70 on a serious one. They also stock charmers such as china tea sets, masks, glove puppets, spinning tops and those ever-fascinating 10p fortune-telling fish. *Mail order.*

Compendia Traditional Games
10 The Market, SE10 9HZ (8293 6616/ www.compendia.co.uk). Cutty Sark DLR/ Greenwich rail. **Open** 11am-5.30pm Mon-Fri; 10am-5.30pm Sat, Sun. **Credit** MC, V.
The ultimate shop for a rainy day, Compendia has all the traditionals – chess, backgammon, dominoes, Scrabble, Snakes & Ladders – as well as an appealing range of more obscure games from around the world to suit all ages. *Buggy access. Disabled access. Mail order.*

Enchanted Forest
6 Sheen Road, Richmond, Surrey TW9 1AS (0870 420 8632). Richmond tube/rail. **Open** 9.30am-5.30pm Mon-Sat; 11am-4pm Sun. **Credit** MC, V.
This shop holds a selection of the Tridias catalogue stock, including partyware. *Buggy access.*

Farmyard
63 Barnes High Street, SW13 9LF (8878 7338/www.thefarmyard.co.uk). Barnes or Barnes Bridge rail. **Open** 10am-5.30pm Mon-Fri; 9.30am-5.30pm Sat. **Credit** MC, V.
Personalised wooden toys and games for newborns to eight-year-olds, plus nursery gifts and dressing-up kit. *Buggy access. Delivery service.*

Kristin Baybars
7 Mansfield Road, NW3 2JD (7267 0934). Kentish Town tube/Gospel Oak rail/C2, C11 bus. **Open** 11am-6pm Tue-Sat. **No credit cards**.
This is too full a shop for rampagers or buggies, but older children with an interest in the miniature doll's house world will have a lovely time exploring the thousands of tiny treasures.

Although a good proportion of the items are cheap (tiny bottles of Coke are just 25p, for example), plenty of the doll's houses and their contents are valuable, and the items displayed in drawers and cabinets deeper inside the shop are for serious collectors only.

Never Never Land
3 Midhurst Parade, N10 3EJ (8883 3997/ www.never-never-land.co.uk). East Finchley tube. **Open** 10am-5pm Tue, Wed, Fri, Sat. **Credit** MC, V.
Old-world delights include doll's houses (from £99) and their accessories. Other attractions are Baby Safe Dollies with soft bodies, Heimess pram toys, tea sets, wooden firemen and their fire stations, soldiers with forts, cars with garages. There is pocket money potential here too. *Buggy access. Mail order.*

Petit Chou
15 St Christopher's Place, W1U 1NR (7486 3637/www.petitchou.co.uk). Bond Street tube. **Open** 10.30am-6.30pm Mon-Sat; noon-5pm Sun. **Credit** AmEx, MC, V.
A tasteful wooden toy enclave, where you can buy a gigantic tray of wooden blocks (£100) that will keep a toddler occupied until he starts thinking about his GCSEs, or buy aesthetically pleasing pull-alongs, skittles, soldiers, animals and ride-ons in warm painted wood. *Buggy access.*

Puppet Planet
787 Wandsworth Road, SW8 3JQ (7627 0111/07900 975276/www.puppetplanet.co.uk). Clapham Common tube. **Open** 9am-4pm Tue-Sat, phone to check; also by appointment. **Credit** AmEx, MC, V.
A specialist marionette shop run by Lesley Butler. There are classic Pelham characters, traditional Indian and African marionettes, Balinese shadow puppets, vintage carved puppets and felt hand puppets. You can even commission a lookalike puppet. *Buggy access. Delivery service. Disabled access. Mail order.*

Traditional Toys
53 Godfrey Street, SW3 3SX (7352 1718/ www.traditionaltoy.com). Sloane Square tube then 11, 19, 22 bus/49 bus. **Open** 10am-6pm Mon-Fri-Sat. **Credit** AmEx, MC, V. **Map** p313 E11.
It's the beautiful wooden toys that really grab you here, such as the tell-the-time clock face and rainbow-coloured clown stack, the wooden Noah's Arks and much more.

Directory

Time Out
Travel Guides

Worldwide

All our guides are written by a team of **local experts** with a unique and stylish insider perspective. We offer essential tips, trusted advice and honest reviews for everything you need to know in the city.

Over 50 destinations available at all good bookshops and at timeout.com/shop

Time Out Guides

Directory

GETTING AROUND

PUBLIC TRANSPORT

The prices listed for transport and services were correct at the time of going to press, but bear in mind that some prices (especially those of tube tickets) are subject to a hike each January.

Public transport information

Details can be found online at www.the tube.com and/or www.tfl.gov.uk, or by phoning 7222 1234.

Transport for London (TfL) also runs Travel Information Centres that provide maps and information about the tube, buses, Tramlink, riverboats, Docklands Light Railway (DLR) and national rail services within the London area. You can find them in Heathrow Airport, as well as in Liverpool Street and Victoria stations.

London TravelWatch
6 Middle Street, EC1A 7JA (7505 9000/www. londontravelwatch.org.uk). **Open** *Phone enquiries* 9am-5pm Mon-Fri.
This is the official, campaigning watchdog monitoring customer satisfaction with transport.

Fares, Oyster cards & Travelcards

Tube and DLR fares are based on a system of six zones stretching 12 miles (20 kilometres) out from the centre of London. A cash fare of £4 per journey applies across the tube for zones 1-4 (£4 for zones 1-5 or 1-6); customers save up to £2 with Oyster pay-as-you-go (*see below*). Beware of £20 on-the-spot fines for anyone caught without a ticket.

Children aged under 11 travel free on buses, DLR and all tubes. If you are using only the tube, DLR, buses and trams, Oyster pay-as-you-go will always be cheaper than a Day Travelcard (*see below*). If you are using National Rail services, however, the Day Travelcard may best meet your needs (children travelling with you can buy a Day Travelcard for £1). Under-16s get free travel on buses.

Travelcards, valid for tubes, buses, DLR and rail services, can be the cheapest way of getting around. Travelcards can be bought at stations, London Travel Information Centres or newsagents.

Day Travelcards

Peak Day Travelcards can be used all day Monday to Friday (except public holidays). They cost from £6.80 (£3.40 for under-16s) for zones 1-2, with prices rising to £13.80 (£6.90 for under-16s) for zones 1-6. Most people use the off-peak Day Travelcard, which allows you to travel from 9.30am Monday to Friday and all day Saturday, Sunday and public holidays. They cost from £5.30 for zones 1-2, rising to £7 for zones 1-6. Up to four children pay £1 each when accompanied by an adult with a Travelcard.

Oyster card

The Oyster card is a travel smart-card that can be charged with Pre-Pay and/or seven-day, monthly and longer-period (including annual) travelcards and bus passes. Oyster cards are currently available to adults and under-16 photocard holders when buying a ticket. Tickets can be bought from www.oystercard.com, by phone on 0870 849 9999 and at tube station ticket offices, London Travel Information Centres, some National Rail station ticket offices and newsagents. A single tube journey in zone 1 using Oyster to pay-as-you go costs £1.50 at all times (70p for under-16s, children under 11 go free).

Children

Under-16s can travel free on buses and trams; under-11s travel free on the tube at off-peak hours and at weekends with an adult with a valid ticket. Children aged 14 or 15 need a child – or 11-15 – photocard to travel at child rate on the tube, DLR and trams. Children who board National Rail services travelling with adult-rate 7-day, monthly or longer travelcard holders can buy a day travelcard for £1. An under-16 Oyster photocard is required by children aged 11-15 years to pay as they go on the Underground or DLR or to buy 7-day, monthly or longer period travelcards.

Three-day Travelcards

If you plan to spend a few days charging around town, you can buy a 3-Day Travelcard. The peak version can be used for any journey that starts between the ticket start date and 4.30am on the day following the expiry date, and is available for £17.40 (zones 1-2) or £40 (zones 1-6). The off-peak travelcard, which can be used from 9.30am, costs £20 (zones 1-6). Children aged 5-15 and New Deal Photocard holders pay £8.70 for zones 1-2 (peak and off-peak) and £6 (off-peak) or £20 (peak) for zones 1-6.

London Underground

The tube in rush hour (8-9.30am and 4.30-7pm Monday-Friday) is not pleasant, so it is best to travel outside these hours with children, if possible.

Using the system

Tube tickets can be purchased or Oyster cards topped up from a ticket office or self-service machine. Ticket offices in some stations close early (around 7.30pm), but it's best to keep an Oyster card charged with value. For buying Oyster cards, *see p287*.

To enter and exit the tube using an Oyster card, touch it to the yellow reader that will open the gates. Make sure you touch the card when you exit the tube otherwise you may be fined.

There are 12 Underground lines, colour-coded on the tube map for ease of use; we've provided a full map of the London Underground on the back page of this book. Note that the East London line is closed until 2010.

Timetable

Tube trains run daily from around 5.30am (except Sunday, when they start later). The only exception is Christmas Day, when there is no service. During peak times the service should run every two or three minutes.

Times of last trains vary, but they're usually around 11.30pm-1am daily, and 30 minutes to an hour earlier on Sunday. Debates continue as to whether to run the tube an hour later at weekends. The only all-night public transport is by night bus.

Fares

The single fare for adults within zone 1 is £4 (Oyster fare £1.50). For zones 1-2 it's £4 (Oyster fare £2 or £1.50). For zones 1-6 it's £4 (Oyster fare £3.50 or £2). The single fare for 5-15s in zone 1 is £1.50 (Oyster fare 50p with a valid Under 14, 14-15 or a Child Oyster photocard), £1.50 for zones 1-2 (Oyster fare £1 or 70p) or £2 for zones 1-6 (Oyster fare £1). Children under 11 travel free at all times.

Docklands Light Railway (DLR)

The DLR (7363 9700, www.dlr.co.uk) runs trains from Bank or Tower Gateway, close to Tower Hill tube (Circle and District lines), to Stratford, Beckton and the Isle of Dogs, then south of the river to Greenwich, Deptford and Lewisham. Trains run 5.30am to 12.30am Monday to Saturday and 7am to 11.30pm Sunday.

Fares

The single fare for adults within zone 1 is £4 (Oyster fare £1.50). For zones 1-2 it's £4 (Oyster fare £2 or £1.50). The zones 1-6 single fare is £4 (Oyster fare £3.50 or £2). Children under 11 travel free. Children aged 11-15 pay £1.50 (Oyster fare 70p) or £2 for zones 1-6 (Oyster fare £1). One-day 'Rail & River Rover' tickets combine unlimited DLR travel with hop-on, hop off boat travel on City

Cruises between Greenwich, Tower, Waterloo and Westminster piers, starting at Tower Gateway. Tickets cost £12 for adults, £6 for kids and £28 for a family pass; under-5s go free.

Buses

New buses, with low floors for wheelchair and buggy users, and bendy buses with multiple-door entry and the 'pay before you board' schemes now make up much of the fleet. Buses in central London also require you to have an Oyster card or buy a ticket before boarding from pavement ticket machines. Be sure to have a ticket or swiped Oyster card on you while travelling: inspectors can slap a £20 fine on fare-dodgers. Of the famous open-platform Routemaster fleet, only Heritage routes 9 and 15 remain in central London

Using an Oyster card (*see p287*) to pay as you go costs 90p at all times; the most you will pay a day is £3. Paying by cash at the time of travel costs £2 per trip. A one-day bus pass gives unlimited bus and tram travel at £3.50. Children under 16 and students up to age 18 and resident in London travel free on buses. New Deal and 16+ Oyster fare is half-price (45p) for those in education outside London.

Night buses

Many night buses run 24 hours a day, seven days a week, and some special night buses with an 'N' prefix to the route number operate from about 11pm to 6am. Most services run every 15 to 30 minutes, but many busier routes have a bus around every ten minutes. Travelcards and Bus Passes can be used on night buses until 4.30am on the day after they expire. Oyster Pre-Pay and bus Saver tickets are also valid on night buses.

Green Line buses

Green Line buses (0870 608 7261, www.greenline.co.uk) serve the suburbs and towns within a 40-mile (64km) radius of London. Their main departure point is Ecclestone Bridge, SW1 (Colonnades Coach Station, behind Victoria).

Coaches

National Express (0870 580 8080, www.nationalexpress.com) runs routes to most parts of the country; coaches depart from **Victoria Coach Station**, a five-minute walk from Victoria rail and tube stations.

Victoria Coach Station

164 Buckingham Palace Road, SW1W 9TP (08717818181/www.tfl.gov.uk/vcs). Victoria tube/ rail. **Map** p316 H1.
National Express, which travels to the Continent as Eurolines, is based at Victoria Coach Station.

Rail services

Independently run services leave from the main rail stations. Travelcards are valid on services within the right zones. The very useful London Overground line, run by TFL (0845 601 4867, www.tfl.gov.uk/rail) goes through north London from Richmond to North Woolwich, via Kew, Kensal Rise, Gospel Oak, Islington, Stratford and City Airport.

If you've lost property on an overground station or a train, call 0870 000 5151; an operator will connect you to the appropriate station.

Family Railcard

www.family-railcard.co.uk.
This is worth buying if you make even a couple of long rail journeys per year with the children, as the discounts it gives are substantial. The card costs £24 and lasts one year. Valid across Britain, it gives travellers with children one year of discounts from standard rail fares (a third off adult fares, 60 per cent off child fares, £1 minimum fare). Under-fives travel free. Up to two adults can be named as cardholders – they do not have to be related. The minimum group size is one cardholder and one child aged five to 15; maximum group size is two cardholders, two other adults and four children. To pick up a form for the Family Railcard, visit your local staffed station.

London's mainline stations

Charing Cross *Strand, WC2N 5LR*. **Map** p317 L7.
For trains to and from south-east England (including Dover, Folkestone and Ramsgate).
Euston *Euston Road, NW1 1BN*. **Map** p315 K3.
For trains to and from north and north-west England and Scotland, and a line north to Watford.
King's Cross *Euston Road, N1 9AP*. **Map** p315 L2.
For trains to and from north and north-west England and Scotland, and suburban lines to north London.
Liverpool Street *Liverpool Street, EC2M 7PD*. **Map** p319 R5.
For trains to and from the east coast, Stansted airport and East Anglia, and services to east and north-east London.
London Bridge *London Bridge Street, SE1 2SW*. **Map** p319 Q8.
For trains to Kent, Sussex, Surrey and south London suburbs.
Paddington *Praed Street, W2 1HB*. **Map** p311 D5.
For trains to and from west and south-west England, South Wales and the Midlands.
Victoria *115 Buckingham Palace Road, SW1W 9SJ*. **Map** p316 H10.
For fast trains to and from the channel ports (Folkestone, Dover, Newhaven); for trains to and from Gatwick Airport, and suburban services to south and south-east London.
Waterloo *York Road, SE1 7NZ*. **Map** p319 M9.
For fast trains to and from the south and south-west of England (Portsmouth, Southampton, Dorset, Devon), and suburban services to south London.

Tramlink

Trams run between Beckenham, Croydon, Addington and Wimbledon. Travelcards and bus passes taking in zones 3-6 can be used on trams; cash single fares cost from £2 (Oyster fare £1 or 50p for 16- to 17-year-old photocard holders). A one-day bus pass gives unlimited tram and bus travel at £3 for adults.

Water transport

The times of London's assortment of river services vary, but most operate every 20 minutes to one hour between 10.30am and 5pm, with more frequent services in summer. Call the operators for schedules, or see www.tfl.gov.uk. Travelcard holders can expect one-third off scheduled riverboat fares. Thames Clippers (0870 781 5049, www.thamesclippers.com) runs a commuter boat service. Clippers stop at all London piers, including: Savoy (near Embankment tube), Blackfriars, Bankside, London Bridge and St Katharine's.

The names in bold below are the names of piers.

Royal Arsenal Woolwich – **Greenwich** (15mins) – **Masthouse Terrace** (5mins) – **Greenland Dock** (4mins) – **Canary Wharf** (8mins) – **St Katharine's** (7mins) – **London Bridge City** (4mins) – **Bankside** (3mins) – **Blackfriars** (3mins) – **Savoy** (4mins); Thames Clippers 0870 781 5049.
Westminster – **Embankment** (5 mins) – **Festival** (5mins) – **London Bridge** (10mins) – **St Katharine's** (5mins); Crown River 7936 2033, www.crownriver.com.
Westminster – **Greenwich** (1hr); Thames River Services 7930 4097, www.westminsterpier.co.uk.
Westminster – **Kew** (1hr 30mins) – **Richmond** (30mins) – **Hampton Court** (1hr 30mins); Westminster Passenger Service Association 7930 2062, www.wpsa.co.uk.
Westminster – **Tower** (30mins); City Cruises 7740 0400, www.citycruises.com.

TAXIS

Black cabs

Licensed London taxis are known as black cabs – even though they now come in a variety of colours – and are a quintessential feature of London life. Drivers of black cabs must pass a test called the Knowledge to prove they know every street in central London and the shortest route to it. If a taxi's yellow 'For Hire' sign is switched on, it can be hailed.

If a taxi stops, the cabbie must take you to your destination, provided it's within seven miles. Expect to pay slightly higher rates after 8pm on weekdays and all weekend.

You can book black cabs in advance. Both Radio Taxis (7272 0272, credit cards only) and Dial-a-Cab (7253 5000) run 24-hour services for black cabs (there'll be a booking fee in addition to the regular fare). Enquiries or complaints about black cabs should be made to the Public Carriage Office (enquiries@pco.org.uk, www.tfl. gov.uk).

Minicabs

Be sure to use only licensed firms and avoid minicab drivers who tout for business on the street. There are plenty of trustworthy and licensed local minicab firms around, including Lady Cabs (7272 3300, www.ladyminicabs.co.uk), which employs only women drivers, and Addison Lee (7387 8888, www.addisonlee.com). Whoever you use, always ask the price when you book and confirm it with the driver when the car arrives.

DRIVING

Congestion charge

Everyone driving in central London – an area defined as within King's Cross (N), Old Street roundabout (NE), Aldgate (E), Old Kent Road (SE), Elephant & Castle (S), Vauxhall, Chelsea, South Kensington (SW), Kensington, Holland Park, North Kensington, Bayswater, Paddington (W), Marylebone and Euston (N) – between 7am and 6pm Monday to Friday, has to pay an £8 fee. Expect a fine of £60 if you fail to do so (rising up to £185 if you delay payment). Passes can be bought from newsagents, garages and NCP car parks; the scheme is enforced by CCTV cameras. You can pay by phone or online any time during the day of entry, even afterwards, but it's an extra £2 after midnight on the day following the day of travel. Payments are accepted until midnight on the next charging day after a vehicle has entered the zone.

For information, phone 0845 900 1234 or go to www.cclondon.com. The Congestion Charge zone is marked on the Central London by Area map on p308.

Parking

Central London is scattered with parking meters, but finding a vacant one can take ages and, when you do, it'll cost you up to £1 for every 15 minutes to park there, and you'll be limited to two hours on the meter. Parking on a single or double yellow line, a red line or in residents' parking areas during the day is illegal. In the evening (from 6pm or 7pm in much of central London) and at various times at weekends, parking on single yellow lines is legal and free. If you find a clear spot on a single yellow line during the evening, look for a sign giving the regulations. Meters are also free at certain times during evenings and weekends.

NCP 24-hour car parks (0845 050 7080, www.ncp.co.uk) in and around central London are numerous but expensive. Fees vary, but expect to pay £10-£55 per day. NCP car parks can be found at Drury Lane, Parker Street, Parker Mews,WC2; Upper St Martins Lane, WC2; and 2 Lexington Street, W1. Most NCPs in central London are underground, and a few are frequented by drug-users. Take care.

Driving out of town

Check out your route for possible delays and roadworks. Try the route-planner service available from the Royal Automobile Association (RAC, www. rac.co.uk) or the AA (www.theaa.com).

CYCLING

Parents who want to find out more about cycle training and commuting can visit www.bikeforall.net for info, or log on to the websites below. London Cycle Guide maps are available from some stations and bike shops, or the Travel Information Line (7222 1234).

London Cycle Network
7974 8747/www.londoncyclenetwork. org.uk.
A planned 560-mile (900km) network of routes for cyclists, which will be completed in 2009/10.

London Cycling Campaign
7234 9310/www.lcc.org.uk.
Looks after the city's pedallers.

WALKING

The least stressful way to see London is on foot. A selection of street maps covering central London is on pp308-319 but you'll need a separate map of the city: both the standard Geographers' *A–Z* and Collins's *London Street Atlas* versions are very easy to use.

The Guy Fox *London Children's Map* puts the power of planning fun excursions straight into the hands of young people. The comprehensive map is packed with colourful illustrations of city icons and landmarks; buy it at www.guyfox.co.uk at £2.95 or bookshops and tourist attractions.

RESOURCES

Councils

Barnet *8359 2000, www.barnet.gov.uk.*
Brent *8937 1200, www.brent.gov.uk.*
Camden *7278 4444, www.camden.gov.uk*
Corporation of London *7606 3030, www.cityoflondon.gov.uk.*
Ealing *8825 5000, www.ealing.gov.uk.*
Greenwich *8854 8888, www.greenwich.gov.uk.*
Hackney *8356 3000, www.hackney.gov.uk.*
Hammersmith & Fulham *8748 3020, www.lbhf.gov.uk.*
Haringey *8489 0000, www.haringey.gov.uk.*
Hounslow *8583 2000, www.hounslow.gov.uk.*
Islington *7527 2000, www.islington.gov.uk.*
Kensington & Chelsea *7361 3000, www.rbkc.gov.uk.*
Lambeth *7926 1000, www.lambeth.gov.uk.*
Lewisham *8314 6000, www.lewisham.gov.uk.*
Merton *8274 4901, www.merton.gov.uk.*
Newham *8430 2000, www.newham.gov.uk.*
Richmond upon Thames *8891 1411, www.richmond.gov.uk.*
Southwark *7525 5000, www.southwark.gov.uk.*
Tower Hamlets *7364 5020, www.towerhamlets.gov.uk.*
Waltham Forest *8496 3000, www.walthamforest.gov.uk.*
Wandsworth *8871 6000, www.wandsworth.gov.uk.*
Westminster *7641 6000, www.westminster.gov.uk.*

Education

Advisory Centre for Education (ACE) *0808 800 5793/exclusion advice line 7704 9822/www.ace-ed. org.uk.* **Open** 10am-5pm Mon-Fri.
Phone the centre for advice about your child's schooling; the advice line is for parents whose children have been excluded from school, or have been bullied, or have special educational needs. School admission appeals advice is also available.
British Association for Early Childhood Education *136 Cavell Street, E1 2JA (7539 5400/www.early-education.org.uk).* **Open** *Phone enquiries* 9am-5pm Mon-Fri.

A charitable organisation that provides information on infant education from birth to eight years.
Gabbitas Educational Consultants *Carrington House, 126-130 Regent Street, W1B 5EE (7734 0161/www.gabbitas.co.uk).* **Open** 9am-5.30pm Mon-Fri.
The consultants at Gabbitas give advice to parents and students on choosing an independent school.
Home Education Advisory Service *PO Box 98, Welwyn Garden City, Herts AL8 6AN (01707 371854/www.heas.org.uk).* **Open** *Phone enquiries* 9am-5pm Mon-Fri.
Call for information if you want to educate your child at home. An introductory pack costs £2.50, a year's subscription £15.
ISC Information Service London & South-east *0845 7246657/www.iscis.uk.net.* **Open** *Phone enquiries* 9am-5pm Mon-Fri.
The Independent Schools Council Information Service works to help parents find out about independent schools.
Kidsmart *www.kidsmart.org.uk.*
Kidsmart is an internet-safety-awareness programme run by Childnet International and is funded by the DFES and Cable & Wireless. Its guide is available to all primary schools.
National Association for Gifted Children *Suite 14, Challenge House, Sherwood Drive, Bletchley, Milton Keynes, Bucks MK3 6DP (0845 450 0295/www.nagcbritain.org.uk).* **Open** *Phone enquiries* 9am-4.30pm Mon-Fri.
Support and advice on education for parents of the gifted.
Parenting UK *Unit 431, Highgate Studios, 53-79 Highgate Road, NW5 1TL (7284 8389/www.parenting-forum.org.uk).* **Open** *Phone enquiries* 10am-4pm Mon-Fri.
Information about parenting classes and support for parents. It was set up for people who work with parents, but parents can call as well.
Pre-School Learning Alliance *The Fitzpatrick Building, 188 York Way, N7 9AD (7697 2500/www.pre-school.org.uk).* **Open** *Phone enquiries* 9am-5pm Mon-Fri.
A leading educational charity specialising in the early years. It runs courses and workshops in pre-schools around the country for parents of children under the age of five.

Fun & games

Activity camps

Barracudas Young World Leisure Group *Bridge House, Bridge Street, St Ives, Cambs PE27 5EH (0845 123 5299/www.barracudas.co.uk).*
School holiday camps based in country schools in outlying countryside. Children aged 5-16 welcome.
Cross Keys *48 Fitzalan Road, N3 3PE (8371 9686/www.xkeys.co.uk/www.miniminors.co.uk).*
Day camps in Finchley for kids aged 12 or under and rural week-long camps in Norfolk, for children aged up to 17.
eac Activity Camps *45 Frederick Street, Edinburgh, EH2 1EP (0131 477 7574/www.eacworld.com).*
Day and residential camps for children aged five to 16 in countryside sites.
PGL *Alton Court, Penyard Lane, Ross-on-Wye, Herefordshire HR9 5GL (0870 050 7507/www.pgl.co.uk).*

Directory

Sport and activity camps for children aged 7-16 in the UK and Europe.

Wickedly Wonderful *Russett Cottage, Itchenor, West Sussex PO20 7DD (0794 123 1168/ www.wickedlywonderful.com).*
A holiday company that runs weekly buses from London down to the beach in the summer holidays.

Indoor play

Crêchendo *www.crechendo.com.*
Active play classes for babies and pre-school kids.
Gymboree Play & Music *0800 092 0911/ www.gymboreeplayuk.com.*
A parent-and-child play organisation for children aged 16 months to four and a half years.
National Association of Toy & Leisure Libraries *(NATLL) 68 Churchway, NW1 1LT (7255 4600/ helpline 7255 4616/www.natll.org.uk).* **Open** *Helpline* 9am-5pm Mon-Fri.
For information on more than 1,000 toy libraries.
Toys Re-united *www.toys-reunited.co.uk.*
Check the website to see if a missing plaything might have been found.
TumbleTots *0121 585 7003/www.tumbletots.com.* **Open** *Phone enquiries* 9am-5.30pm Mon-Fri.
Phone to find out about TumbleTot play centres in your area.

Health

Asthma UK *0845 701 0203/www.asthma.org.uk.* **Open** 9am-5pm Mon-Fri.
Advice and help if you or your child has asthma.
Contact-A-Family *7608 8700/helpline 0808 808 3555/www.cafamily.org.uk.* **Open** *Helpline* 10am-4pm, 5.30-7.30pm Mon; 10am-4pm Tue-Fri.
Support for parents of children with disabilities. This organisation is a valuable resource for those who feel isolated while caring for their diabled children.
Euro Pair Agency *www.euro-pair.co.uk.*
An au pair agency that specialises in French candidates.
Family Natural Health Centre *106 Lordship Lane, SE22 8HF (8693 5515).* **Open** 9.30am-6pm Mon- Sat; 11am-5pm Sun.
A wide range of alternative therapies, from acupuncture to osteopathy, are practised here. French classes, sing and sign classes, children's yoga and art therapy are also offered.
Family & Parenting Institute *430 Highgate Studios, 53-79 Highgate Road, NW5 1TL (7424 3460/www.familyandparenting.org). Kentish Town tube/rail.* **Open** *Phone enquiries* 9.30am-5.30pm Mon-Fri; 24hr answerphone other times.
A resource centre that produces factsheets covering all aspects of parenting.
Food for the Brain Foundation *7498 8211/ www.foodforthebrain.org.*
The Food for the Brain schools project is designed to help parents throughout the UK make the right food choices to help improve their children's brain function, behaviour and intelligence. A downloadable leaflet called the 'Smart Food Smart Kids Shopping Guide' accompanies the scheme.
Greatcare *www.greatcare.co.uk.*
A useful resource for those looking for childcare. Greatcare has 20,000 registered users, including nannies, au pairs, babysitters, mothers' helps and maternity nurses.

NHS Direct Helpline *0845 4647/www.nhs direct.nhs.uk.* **Open** *Helpline* 24hrs daily.
Confidential information and health advice.
WellChild Helpline 0808 801 0330/email helpline@wellchild.org.uk is the only national advice line to connect people to the right information and support about children's health concerns.

Help & support

Bestbear *0870 720 1277/www.bestbear.co.uk.* **Open** 9am-6pm Mon-Fri; 24hr answerphone other times.
Information about childcare agencies.
Childcare Link *0800 234 6346/www.childcare link.gov.uk.* **Open** *Phone enquiries* 9am-5pm Mon-Fri.
Provides a list of childcare organisations in your area.
ChildLine *0800 1111/www.childline.org.uk.*
Confidental 24-hour helpline for young people in the UK. The counsellors are trained to listen and help. Sometimes they put callers in touch with someone who can help further.
Daycare Trust *21 St George's Road, SE1 6ES (7840 3350/www.daycaretrust.org.uk).* **Open** 9am-5pm Mon-Fri.
A national charity that works to promote high-quality, affordable childcare. If you are a parent or carer paying for childcare, the new website – www.payingforchildcare.org.uk – provides targeted information in a wide range of circumstances. It provides easy-to-read introductions to each of the main types of benefits, grants and subsidies that are available to help ease the financial burden of paying for childcare
4Children *7512 2112/information line 7512 2100/ www.4children.org.uk.* **Open** *Phone enquiries* 9am-5pm Mon-Fri.
4Children is the national children's charity for children and young people aged up to 19. It works with government, local authorities, primary care trusts, children's service providers, and children and parents to ensure joined-up support for all children and young people in their local community.
Kids *6 Aztec Row, Berners Road, N1 0PW (7359 3635/www.kids-online.org.uk).* **Open** *Phone enquiries* 9.30am-5.30pm Mon-Fri.
An organisation that seeks to enhance the lives of disabled children, through play, leisure, education, family support, information, advice and training, with a view to empowering them in society.
Kidscape *2 Grosvenor Gardens, SW1W 0DH (7730 3300/Helpline 08451 205204/ www.kidscape.org.uk).*
The first charity in the UK (established by the indomitable Dr Michele Elliott) set up specifically to prevent bullying and child abuse. The helpline is for the use of parents, guardians or concerned relatives and friends of bullied children.
London Mums *www.londonmums.org.uk.*
A group of new mums based in London who support each other, by sharing views and tips online and organising a number of activities for mums (and dads) and babies. They also get together for activities such as trips to view exhibitions at the National Gallery, movies at the local cinema and nature walks.

London Au Pair & Nanny Agency
www.londonnanny.co.uk.
Matches families with child carers.
Nannytax *PO Box 988, Brighton, East Sussex
BN1 3NT (0845 226 2203/www.nannytax.co.uk).*
Open *Phone enquiries* 9am-5pm Mon-Fri.
For £260 a year, Nannytax registers your nanny
with the Inland Revenue, organises National
Insurance payments and offers advice.
Night Nannies *7731 6168/www.nightnannies.com.*
Night Nannies provides a list of qualified carers who
may be able to offer respite from sleepless nights.
Parent Company *6 Jacob's Well Mews, W1U
3DY (7935 9635/www.theparentcompany.co.uk).*
Open *Bookings* 9am-3pm Mon-Fri.
The company runs first aid training courses for
parents and carers of babies and children. The
courses are delivered by paediatric nurses, either
in the home or workplace.
Parent Courses *Holy Trinity Brompton,
Brompton Road, SW7 1JA (7581 8255/
www.htb.org.uk). South Kensington tube.* **Open**
9.30am-5.30pm Mon, Wed-Fri; 10.30am-5.30pm Tue.
Runs the Parenting Course for parents with
children under the age of 12, and Parenting
Teenagers, for parents of children aged 13-18.
Each course costs £30 and takes place over five
weeks once a year.
Parentline Plus *Helpline 0808 800 2222/www.
parentlineplus.org.uk.* **Open** *Helpline* 24hrs daily.
Organises nationwide courses on how to cope with
being a parent. For more details, phone the free
helpline.
Parents for Inclusion *Helpline 0800 652 3145/
www.parentsforinclusion.org.* **Open** 10am-noon,
1-3pm Mon, Tue, Thur.
Organises workshops for parents of disabled
children as well as providing training for teachers
who want to develop inclusion in their schools.
The Parent Practice *Bookings 8673 3444/
www.theparentpractice.com.*
A support and training group that promises to
endow parents with the skills for transforming
family life. They also produce CDs (£18.50;
£33/pair) that provide harrassed mums and dads
with practical strategies to make family life calmer,
happier and more rewarding.
Parent Support Group *72 Blackheath Road, SE10
8DA (helpline 8469 0205/www.psg.org.uk).* **Open**
Helpline 10am-8pm Mon-Thur; 24hr answerphone
other times.
As well as the helpline, staff run one-to-one
support sessions and offer courses on parenting
skills to the parents and carers of adolescents who
are acting in an antisocial or criminal manner.
Post-Adoption Centre *5 Torriano Mews,
Torriano Avenue, NW5 2RZ (7284 0555/Advice
Line 7284 5879/www.postadoptioncentre.org.uk).*
Open *Advice Line* 10am-1pm Mon-Wed, Fri;
5.30pm-7.30pm Thur.
Registered charity providing advice, support
and information for anyone affected by adoption,
including adoptive/foster parents and their
children, adopted adults, birth relatives and the
professionals who work with them.
Simply Childcare *www.simplychildcare.com.*
If you're seeking a nanny, check this website.
Sitters *0800 389 0038/www.sitters.co.uk.* **Open**
Phone enquiries 8am-7pm Mon-Fri; 9am-4.30pm Sat.
A babysitting agency with locally based nurses,
teachers and nannies on its books.

FURTHER REFERENCE

Websites

11 Million *www.11million.org.uk.*
Led by the Children's Commissioner for England,
this website for children of all ages and abilities
aims to make life better for children and young
people, by letting them have their say.
BBC London *www.bbc.co.uk/london.*
London-focused news, weather, travel and sport.
Children First *www.childrenfirst.nhs.uk.*
Run by Great Ormond Street Hospital and
children's charity WellChild, this website has
information on all aspects of healthy living, with
special sections about going into hospital.
Department for Education and Skills
www.parentscentre.gov.uk.
The DfES website gives parents advice on schools
and other aspects of children's education.
Hidden London
www.hiddenlondon.com.
The city's undiscovered gems.
Learning Partnership
www.thelearningpartnership.com.
The Learning Partnership's online guide to
parenting, called Top Tips for Tiny Tots
(www.tt4tt.co.uk), provides new mums and dads
with all the information they need about pregnancy,
birth, and early development in one easy-to-use
downloadable course.
London Active Map *www.uktravel.com.*
Click on a tube station and find out which
attractions are nearby. A useful resource for
families who are unfamiliar with the city.
London Parks & Gardens Trust
www.parkexplorer.org.uk.
A website designed to help Key Stage 2 children
learn more about the parks, gardens and open
spaces of London.
London Town *www.londontown.com.*
The official tourist board website, full of
information and offers.
London Underground Online *www.thetube.com.*
Meteorological Office *www.met-office.gov.uk.*
The most accurate source of weather forecasts.
Parent Pages *www.parentpages.co.uk*
A useful listings site for families with children
and professionals working with children.
The River Thames Guide *www.riverthames.co.uk.*
Interesting places to stay, eat, drink and play, all
along the riverbank.
Shortwalk *www.shortwalk.blog.co.uk.*
A zone 1 underground map adapted by St Martins
School of Art students, showing how long it takes
to walk between stations on the underground. An
eye-opener for visitors.
Street Map *www.streetmap.co.uk.*
Grid references and postcodes.
Time Out *www.timeout.com.*
An essential resource, of course, with online city
guides and the best eating and drinking reviews.
Transport for London *www.tfl.gov.uk.*
The official website for travel information about
buses, DLR and river services, as well as travel
times and cycle routes.
Yellow Pages Online *www.yell.com.*
The best online resource for numbers and
addresses.

Directory

Advertisers' Index

Please refer to relevant sections for addresses/telephone numbers

A-Z Index

Note: page numbers in **bold** indicate section(s) giving key information on a topic; *italics* indicate illustrations.

Index

Index

Area Index

Index

Index

Maps

London Overview — 306

Central London by Area — 308

Street maps — 310

London Underground — 320

Place of interest and/or entertainment . . .
Hospital or college . . . .
Railway station . . . .
Park . . . .
River . . . .
Motorway . . . . =
Main road . . . .
Main road tunnel . . . .
Pedestrian road . . . .
Airport . . . . ✈
Church . . . . ✚
Synagogue . . . . ✡
Congestion charge zone . . . . ©
Underground station . . . . ⊖
Area name . . . . SOHO

A41 **Edgware Way** M1 A1
PALMERS GREEN
EDGWARE
STANMORE
Watford Way
Grt North Way
A1000
SOUTHGATE
NORTH CIRCULAR ROAD
FINCHLEY
WOOD GREEN
RAF Museum
Hendon
Edgware Road
A406
Lyttelton Road
HAMPSTEAD GARDEN SUBURB
Alexandra Palace
MUSWELL HILL
Highgate Wood
Archway Road
CROUCH END
Edgware Way
WEMBLEY
NORTH CIRCULAR ROAD
Shri Swaminarayan Mandir Temple
NEASDEN
Hendon Way
A41
GOLDERS GREEN
Kenwood House
Waterlow Park
Highgate Cemetery
Holloway
Wembley Stadium
A5
CRICKLEWOOD
WILLESDEN
Tricycle Theatre
KILBURN
Fenton House
Hampstead Heath
HAMPSTEAD
HIGHGATE
Jewish Museum
Freud Museum
KENTISH TOWN
HOLLOWAY
Kentish Town Road
Camden Road
Caledonian Way
Jewish Museum
A404
MAIDA VALE
Finchley Road
ST. JOHN'S WOOD
Lord's Cricket Ground & MCC Museum
London Central Mosque
Roundhouse
CAMDEN TOWN
p314
St Pancras International
King's Cross
A40
A406
Western
Hanger Lane
Gunnersbury Ave
Avenue
Grand Union Canal
Wormwood Scrubs
Regents Park
Marylebone
Marylebone Road
p310
p311
PADDINGTON
British Museum
To Southall
To Heathrow
EALING
ACTON
Uxbridge Road
A4020
Westway
A40(M)
M41
SHEPHERD'S BUSH
NOTTING HILL
Paddington
BAYSWATER
Bayswater Road
Hyde Park
Park Lane
MARYLEBONE
MAYFAIR
SOHO
COVENT GARDEN
Charing Cross
National Gallery
Gunnersbury Park
M4
Goldhawk Rd
Holland Road
Holland Park
Natural History, Science and V&A Museums
KENSINGTON
Buckingham Palace
Vauxhall Bridge
Houses of Parliament
Westminster Abbey
Olympia
Chiswick High Rd
West Road
Talgarth Rd
Cromwell Road
Victoria
Gt West Road
Kew Bridge Steam Museum
Great
HAMMERSMITH
Castelnau
Earl's Court
Chelsea FC
Fulham Palace Rd
Fulham Road
Chelsea
p316
AMP Oval
A4
CHISWICK
Chiswick House
p312
p313
FULHAM
New Kings Rd
Chelsea Embankment
Battersea Park
Battersea Power Station
VAUXHALL
BRENTFORD
Kew Gardens
BARNES
Fulham FC
River Thames
STOCKWELL
Syon House
Kew Road
KEW
MORTLAKE
A316
A205
Upper Richmond Road
A3220
BATTERSEA
Clapham Junction
Clapham Common
Balham High Rd
Clapham Road
CLAPHAM
Gt Chertsey Rd
A205
Battersea Rise
The Ave
Poynders Road
Twickenham & Rugby Union Football Museum
RICHMOND
PUTNEY
Roehampton Lane
WANDSWORTH
West
Wandsworth Common
Trinity Road
Marble Hill House
TWICKENHAM
Richmond Park
Kingston Road
All England Tennis Club & Museum
Tooting Bec Common
STREATHAM
Ham House
WIMBLEDON
Wimbledon Common
Polka Theatre
TOOTING
To Kingston & Hampton Court

A3
A24
To Gatwick
A23

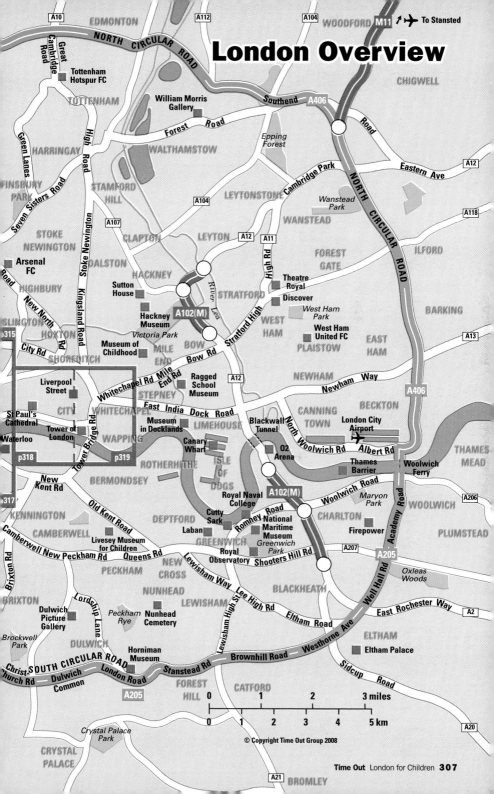

London Overview

© Copyright Time Out Group 2008

Central London
by Area

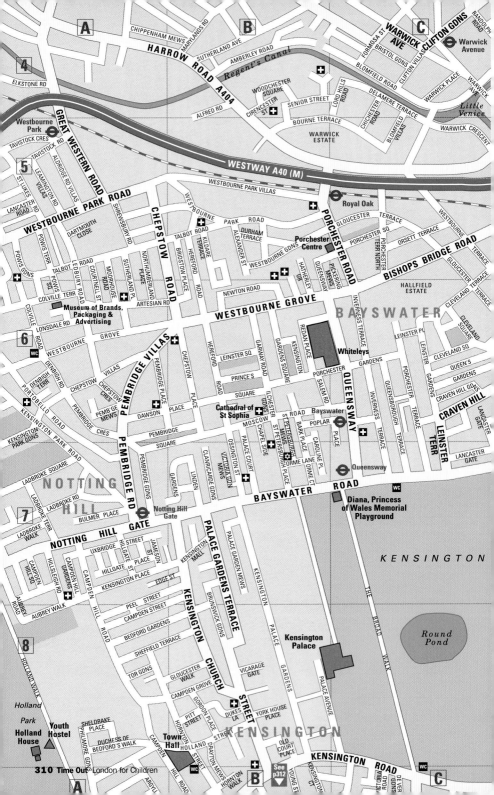

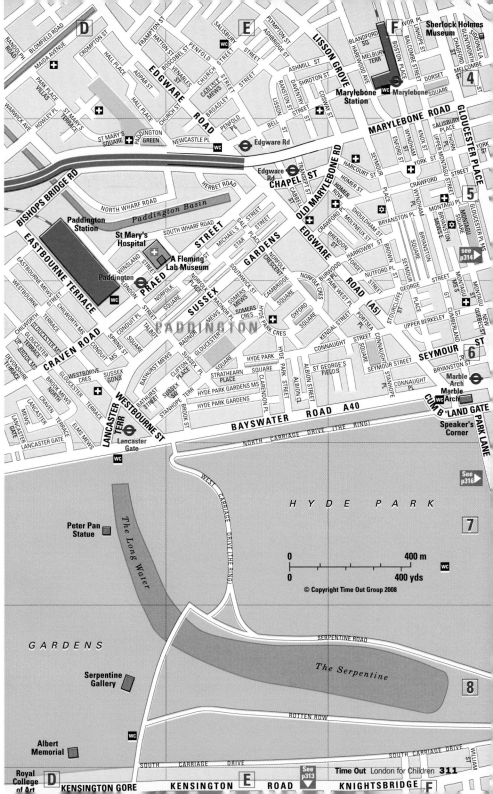

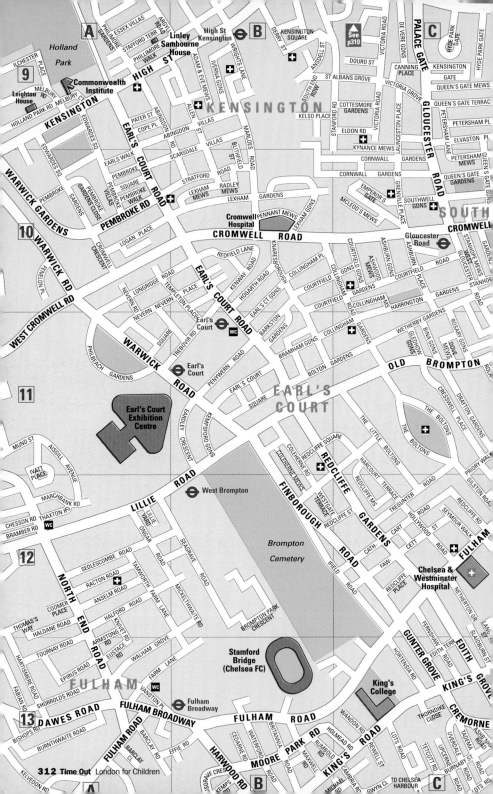

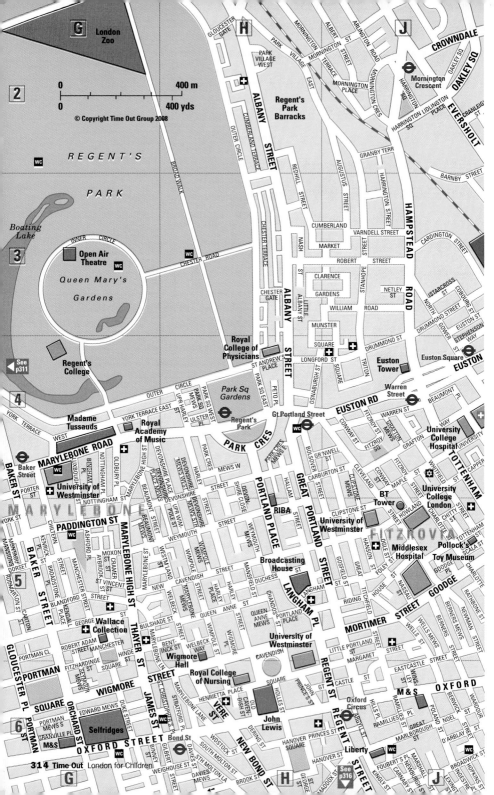

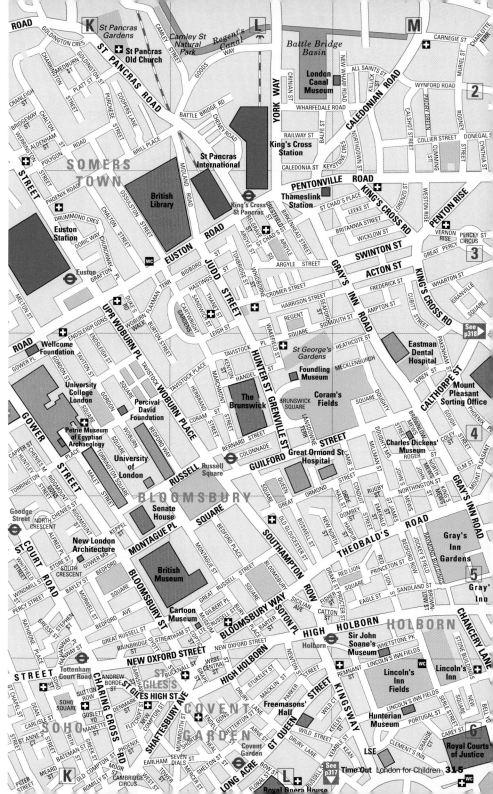

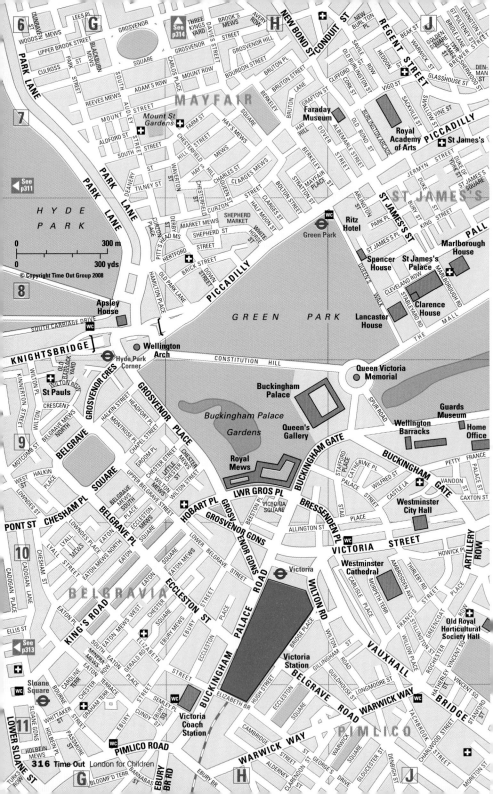

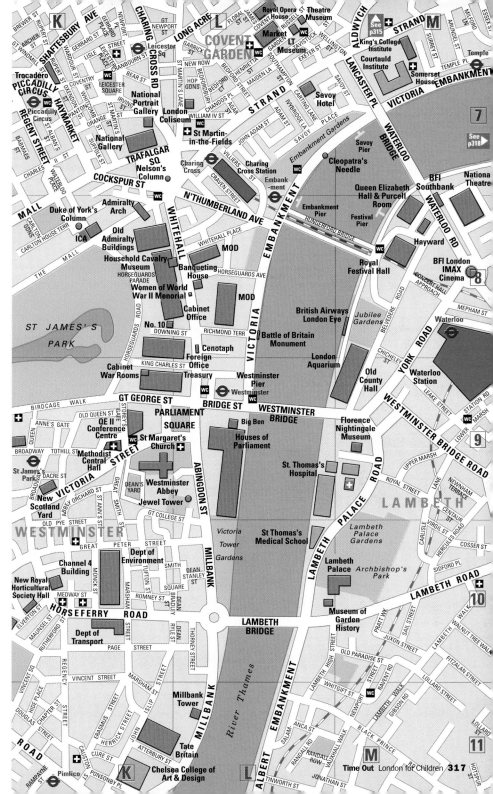

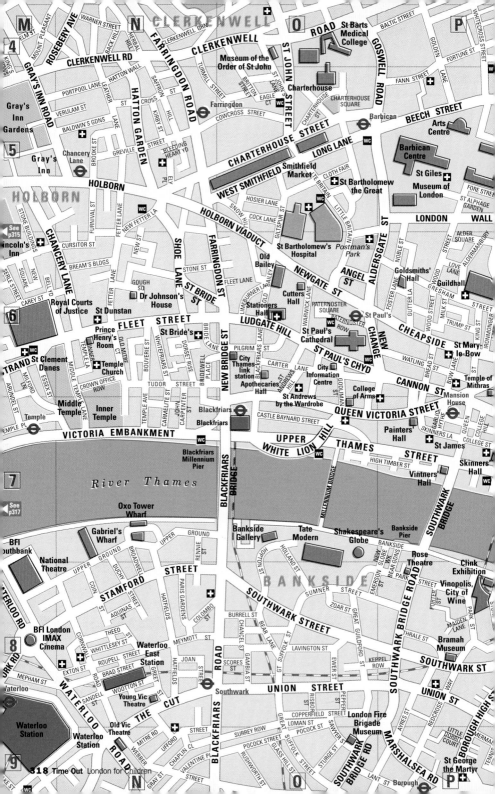

Transport for London

MAYOR OF LONDON